Web Information Systems

David Taniar
Monash University, Australia

Johanna Wenny Rahayu
La Trobe University, Australia

IDEA GROUP PUBLISHING
Hershey • London • Melbourne • Singapore

Acquisitions Editor:	Mehdi Khosrow-Pour
Senior Managing Editor:	Jan Travers
Managing Editor:	Amanda Appicello
Development Editor:	Michele Rossi
Copy Editor:	Jennifer Wade
Typesetter:	Jennifer Wetzel
Cover Design:	Lisa Tosheff
Printed at:	Yurchak Printing, Inc.

Published in the United States of America by
    Idea Group Publishing (an imprint of Idea Group Inc.)
    701 E. Chocolate Avenue, Suite 200
    Hershey PA 17033 USA
    Tel: 717-533-8845
    Fax: 717-533-8661
    E-mail: cust@idea-group.com
    Web site: http://www.idea-group.com

and in the United Kingdom by
    Idea Group Publishing (an imprint of Idea Group Inc.)
    3 Henrietta Street
    Covent Garden
    London WC2E 8LU
    Tel: 44 20 7240 0856
    Fax: 44 20 7379 3313
    Web site: http://www.eurospan.co.uk

Library of Congress Cataloging-in-Publication Data

Web information systems / David Taniar, editor ; Johanna Wenny Rahayu, editor.
    p. cm.
  ISBN 1-59140-208-5 (hardcover) -- ISBN 1-59140-283-2 (pbk.) -- ISBN 1-59140-209-3 (ebook)
  1. Information technology. 2. World Wide Web. I. Taniar, David. II. Rahayu, Johanna Wenny.
  T58.5.W37 2004
  004.67'8--dc22
2003022612

British Cataloguing in Publication Data
A Cataloguing in Publication record for this book is available from the British Library.

Web Information Systems

Table of Contents

Roland Kaschek, Massey University, New Zealand
Klaus-Dieter Schewe, Massey University, New Zealand
Catherine Wallace, Massey University, New Zealand
Claire Matthews, Massey University, New Zealand

Klaus-Dieter Schewe, Massey University, New Zealand
Bernhard Thalheim, Brandenburgian Technical University, Germany

Preface

The chapters of this book provide an excellent overview of current research and development activities in the area of web information systems. They supply an in-depth description of different issues in web information systems areas, including web-based information modeling, migration between different media types, web information mining, and web information extraction issues. Each chapter is accompanied by examples or case studies to show the applicability of the described techniques or methodologies.

The book is a reference for the state of the art in web information systems, including how information on the Web can be retrieved effectively and efficiently. Furthermore, this book will help the reader to gain an understanding of web-based information representation using XML, XML documents storage and access, and web views.

Following our call for chapters in 2002, we received 29 chapter proposals. Each proposed chapter was carefully reviewed and, eventually, 10 chapters were accepted for inclusion in this book. This book brought together academic and industrial researchers and practitioners from many different countries, including Singapore, Greece, Poland, Germany, New Zealand, the US and Australia. Their research and industrial experience, which are reflected in their work, will certainly allow readers to gain an in-depth knowledge of their areas of expertise.

INTENDED AUDIENCE

Web Information Systems is intended for individuals who want to enhance their knowledge of issues relating to modeling, representing, storing and mining information on the Web. Specifically, these individuals could include:

- **Computer Science and Information Systems researchers:** All of the topics in this book will give an insight to researchers about new development in web information system area. The topics on mining web usage data and mining data across geographically distributed environment will give researchers an understanding into the state of the art of web data mining. Information Systems researchers will also find this book useful, as it includes some topics in the area of information extraction and ontology, as well as techniques for modeling information on the Web.
- **Computer Science and Information Systems students and teachers:** The chapters in this book are grouped into four categories to cover important issues in the area. This will allow students and teachers in web information system field to effectively use the appropriate materials as a reference or reading resources. These categories are: (i) information modeling; (ii) information representation, storage and access; (iii) information extraction; and (iv) information mining.

The chapters also provide examples to guide students and lecturers in using the methods or implementing the techniques.

- **Web-based Application Developers:** The chapters in this book can be used by web application developers as a reference to use the correct techniques for modeling and design, migrating from other media devices, as well as efficiently handling huge amount of web information. For example, the practical techniques for materialized ontology view, as well as the techniques for deriving customized web views, can be used to manage large web-based application development more effectively.
- **General community who is interested in current issues of web information systems:** The general computer (IT) community will benefit from this book through its technical, as well as practical, overview of the area.

PREREQUISITES

The book as a whole is meant for anyone professionally interested in the development of web information systems and who, in some way, wants to gain an understanding of how the issues in modeling and implementation of a web-based information system differ from the traditional development techniques. Each chapter may be studied separately or in conjunction with other chapters. As each chapter may cover topics different from other chapters, the prerequisites for each may vary. However, we assume the readers have at least a basic knowledge of:

- Web representation techniques, including HTML, XML, XML Schema, and DTD.
- Web information repository, including XML databases, Relational databases, and Object-Relational databases.

OVERVIEW OF
WEB INFORMATION SYSTEMS

The era of web technology has enabled information and application sharing through the Internet. The large amount of information on the Internet, the large number of users, and the complexity of the application and information types have introduced new areas whereby these issues are explored and addressed. Many of the existing information systems techniques and methods for data sharing, modeling, and system implementation are no longer effective and, therefore, need major adjustment. This has stimulated the emergence of web information systems.

First, the way we model web information system requires different techniques from the existing information system modeling. The fact that a web-based system is accessed by numerous (often unpredictable) user characteristics, different end-user devices, and different internet connectivity, has introduced high complexity in defining a suitable modeling technique that will be capable and flexible enough to facilitate the above aspects. Another issue related to designing a web information system is how to migrate existing information between different media types, in particular from another media type to a web-based system.

The second important issue in web information system is how information can be represented in a uniform way to allow communication and interchange between different information sites. XML has been widely used as a standard for representing semi-structured information on the Web. Currently, one of the major issues in XML-based information systems includes how to efficiently store and access the XML documents. The fact that relational databases have been widely used and tested has encouraged many practitioners in this area to use it as XML data repository. On the other hand, native XML database systems are currently being developed and tested for a different alternative in storing XML documents.

The third issue relates to the way we can efficiently retrieve and use the large amount of information on the Web. Moreover, very often users have interest in a specific aspect of the information only, and, therefore, downloading or accessing the whole information repository will be inefficient. In this book, techniques for deriving a materialized ontology view and for generating a personalized web view are presented.

Another issue, which is also closely related to data retrieval, is data or information mining. Data mining is discovering new information or patterns which were previously unknown in the collection of information. With web accesses, mining over web data becomes important. Web mining is basically a means for discovering patterns in user accesses and behaviour on the Web. This information will be particularly useful in building a web portal which is tailored for each user. New techniques for mining distributed information on the Web are needed.

All of these issues need to be addressed, particularly in order to understand the benefits and features that web information systems bring, and this book is written for this purpose.

ORGANIZATION OF THIS BOOK

The book is divided into four major sections:
I.   Web information modeling
II. Web information representation, storage, and access
III. Web information extraction
IV. Web information mining

Each section, in turn, is divided into several chapters:

Section I focuses on the topic of modeling web information. This section includes chapters on general web information system modeling and data intensive web system modeling techniques. This section also incorporates a chapter which describes a model to allow information migration and preservation between different media types.

Section I consists of three chapters. Chapter 1, contributed by *Roland Kaschek, Klaus-Dieter Schewe, Catherine Wallace*, and *Claire Matthews*, proposes a holistic usage centered approach for analyzing requirements and conceptual modeling of web information systems (WIS) using a technique called *story boarding*. In this approach, WIS is conceptualized as an open information system whereby the linguistic, communicational and methodological aspects are described. The WIS is viewed from a business perspective, and this perspective is used to distinguish WIS from IS in general.

Chapter 2, presented by *Klaus-Dieter Schewe* and *Bernhard Thalheim*, discusses a conceptual modeling approach for the design of data intensive WIS. In this chapter, the notion of *media type*, which is a view on an underlying database schema that allows transformation of database contents into a collection of media objects representing the data at the web interface, is utilized. The view is extended by operations and an adaptivity mechanism, which permits the splitting of media objects into several smaller units in order to adapt the WIS to different user preferences, technical environments and communication channels. The information entering the design of media types is extracted from the story boarding phase described in Chapter 1.

Chapter 3, presented by *Richard Hall*, introduces a model for the migration of communication between media devices based on ideas from information theory and media modeling. The huge amount of information generated across the years has been supported by the ability to invent devices that record, store, retrieve, and communicate this information in a variety of media, presented by a variety of devices. Since new media devices are continually emerging, and each device has different utility, it is possible that a great deal of information will need to be migrated between media devices in order to take advantage of their utility. This is especially true with the era of WIS, where many existing information currently available on different media types need to be migrated to the Web. The model offers an approach where a number of interacting components, including the dimensions and utility of the media device, the media of and structure of communication, and conversion functions between media devices are considered.

Section II concentrates on the topic of web information representation, storage, and access. This section focuses on the major issues of using XML as a representation for information on the Web. These issues include storage and access control.

Section II consists of two chapters: Chapters 4 and 5. Chapter 4, presented by *George Pallis*, *Konstantina Stoupa*, and *Athena Vakali*, describes a comprehensive classification for different methods of storing and accessing XML documents. The differences between various approaches for storing XML, including DBMS, file systems, and native XML databases are presented. This chapter also discusses recent access control models which guarantee the security of XML-based data which are located in a variety of storage topologies.

Chapter 5, presented by *Nathalia Devina Widjaya*, *David Taniar*, and *Johanna Wenny Rahayu*, discusses a practical methodology for storing XML schemas into Object-Relational Databases (ORDB). The chapter describes the modeling of XML and why the transformation is needed. A number of transformation steps from the XML schema to the Object-Relational Logical model and XML to ORDB are presented. The transformation focuses on the three conceptual representations of relationships in a XML schema, namely aggregation, association and inheritance.

While the first two sections deal with conceptual modeling and information storage techniques, **Section III** focuses on improving the efficiency of information extraction through the use of views. There are two different mechanisms that can be used to increase the efficiency of retrieving such a large data repository available on the Web. One method is to create optimized views from an underlying base ontology to cater for specific web application domain. Another method is to create views from the web interface level, so that only relevant parts of the interface are made available to the user. Each of these mechanisms is discussed in Chapters 6 and 7, respectively.

Chapter 6, presented by *Carlo Wouters, Tharam Dillon, Johanna Wenny Rahayu, Elizabeth Chang*, and *Robert Meersman*, discusses the issue of materialised ontology views derivation. As web ontology grows bigger, user application may need to concentrate on certain aspects of the base ontology only. Therefore, there is a need to be able to efficiently derive optimized sub-ontology from an underlying base ontology. The chapter describes the formalisms for such a derivation process and its applicability to a practical example, emphasizing the possibility for automation. Furthermore, the issue of optimizing the derived ontology views in order to develop a high quality derived ontology is also discussed. It is shown that the benefits of a derivation process like this are immense, as they not only enable non-experts to derive a high quality materialized ontology view to use for their own system, but also to do this with only minimal human intervention.

Chapter 7, presented by *Wee Keong Ng, Zehua Liu, Zhao Li*, and *Ee Peng Lim*, discusses the issue of web information extraction that aims to automatically extract information from target web pages and convert them into structured formats for further processing. In this chapter, the main issues that have to be considered in the extraction process are presented. Furthermore, a software framework, called the WICCAP system, has been implemented that enables ordinary users to create personalized views of websites in a simple and flexible manner, using the defined extraction process. In the WICCAP system, one can follow some steps whereby one or more global logical views of a target website is first constructed; and then, based on these global views, different users create their own views; and finally, users specify how and when their views should be visually shown to them. With these steps and the help of the tools provided by the WICCAP system, users are able to easily and quickly design their preferred views of websites.

Finally, **Section IV** presents interesting techniques for mining information on the Web. This section consists of three chapters: Chapters 8, 9, and 10. These chapters deal with the issue of integrating classifiers from databases that are geographically distributed across the Web, and the issues of mining and indexing web usage data.

Chapter 8, written by *Grigorios Tsoumakas, Nick Bassiliades*, and *Ioannis Vlahavas*, presents the design and development of a knowledge-based web information system for the fusion of classifiers from geographically distributed databases. The system, called *WebDisC*, has an architecture based on the web services paradigm that utilizes the open and scalable standards of XML and SOAP. It has also been developed to take into consideration syntactically heterogeneous distributed classifiers, semantic heterogeneity of distributed classifiers.

Chapter 9, presented by *Yannis Manolopoulos, Mikolaj Morzy, Tadeusz Morzy, Alexandros Nanopoulos, Marek Wojciechowski*, and *Maciej Zakrzewicz*, describes indexing techniques that support efficient processing and mining of web access logs. Web access logs contain access histories of users who have visited a particular web server. Pattern queries are normally used to analyze web log data which includes its navigation schemes. In this chapter, it is shown that, using the proposed indexing method, pattern queries can be performed more efficiently.

Finally, Chapter 10, written by *Yongqiao Xiao* and *Jenq-Foung Yao*, presents different types of web usage traversal patterns and the related techniques to analyze them, including Association Rules, Sequential Patterns, Frequent Episodes, Maximal Frequent Forward Sequences, and Maximal Frequent Sequences. As a necessary step for pattern discovery, the preprocessing of the web logs is also described. Some important issues such as privacy and sessionization are raised, and the possible solutions are also discussed in this chapter.

HOW TO READ THIS BOOK

Each chapter in this book has a different flavor from any other due to the nature of an edited book, although chapters within each section have a broad topic in common. A suggested plan for a first reading would be to choose a particular part of interest and read the chapters in that section. For more specific seeking of information, readers interested in conceptual modeling of web information systems and how to migrate existing information in a different media type to the Web may read Chapters 1, 2, and 3. Readers interested in looking at XML and the recent development for efficiently storing and accessing XML documents may study the chapters in the second section. Readers who are interested in web-based information extraction in order to support more efficient query and retrieval may go directly to the third section. Finally, those interested in mining data across geographically distributed databases, mining web access logs, and creating index for pattern query of the user access logs may go directly to Section IV.

Each chapter opens with an abstract that gives the summary of the chapter, an introduction, and closes with a conclusion. Following the introduction, the background and related work are often presented in order to give readers adequate background and knowledge to enable them to understand the subject matter. Most chapters also include an extensive list of references. This structure allows a reader to understand the subject matter more thoroughly by not only studying the topic in-depth, but also by referring to other works related to each topic.

WHAT MAKES THIS BOOK DIFFERENT?

A dedicated book on important issues in web information systems is still difficult to find. Most books are about either web technology focusing on developing websites, HTML, and possibly XML, or covering very specific areas only, such as information retrieval and semantic web. This book is, therefore, different in that it covers an extensive range of topics, including web information conceptual modeling, XML related issues, web information extraction, and web mining.

This book gives a good overview of important aspects in the development of web information systems. The four major aspects covering web information modeling, storage, extraction and mining, described in four sections of this book respectively, form the fundamental flow of web information system development cycle.

The uniqueness of this book is also due to the solid mixture of both theoretical aspects as well as practical aspects of web information system development. The chapters on web conceptual modeling demonstrate techniques for capturing the complex requirements of web information systems in general, and then followed by more specific techniques for the development of data intensive web information systems. These chapters are more specialized than the topics on traditional information system modeling normally found in information systems publications. Web information extraction is described using the concept of views, both at the interface level using web views as well as at the underlying ontology level using ontology views. Both concepts are described in a practical manner, with case studies and examples throughout the chapters. The chapters on information mining are solely focused on mining web information, ranging from mining web usage data to mining distributed web information. Hence, it is more specific than the topics available in general data mining books.

A CLOSING REMARK

We would like to conclude this preface by saying that this book has been compiled from extensive work done by the contributing authors, who are researchers and industry practitioners in this area and who, particularly, have expertise in the topic area addressed in their respective chapters. We hope that readers benefit from the works presented in this book.

David Taniar, PhD
Johanna Wenny Rahayu, PhD
Melbourne, Australia
July 2003

Acknowledgments

The editors would like to acknowledge the help of all involved in the collation and review process of the book, without whose support the project could not have been satisfactorily completed. A further special note of thanks goes to all the staff at Idea Group Publishing, whose contributions throughout the whole process, from inception of the initial idea to final publication, have been invaluable. In particular, our thanks go to Michele Rossi, who kept the project on schedule by continuously prodding us via email, and to Mehdi Khosrow-Pour, whose enthusiasm initially motivated us to accept his invitation to take on this project.

We are also grateful to our employers, Monash University and La Trobe University, for supporting this project. We acknowledge the support of the School of Business Systems at Monash and the Department of Computer Science and Computer Engineering at La Trobe in giving us archival server space in the completely virtual online review process.

In closing, we wish to thank all of the authors for their insights and excellent contributions to this book, in addition to all those who assisted us in the review process.

David Taniar, PhD
Johanna Wenny Rahayu, PhD
Melbourne, Australia
July 2003

SECTION I

WEB INFORMATION MODELING

Chapter I

Story Boarding for Web-Based Information Systems

Roland Kaschek, Massey University, New Zealand

Klaus-Dieter Schewe, Massey University, New Zealand

Catherine Wallace, Massey University, New Zealand

Claire Matthews, Massey University, New Zealand

ABSTRACT

The present chapter is about story boarding for web information systems (WIS). It is a holistic usage-centered approach for analyzing requirements and conceptual modeling of WIS. We conceptualize web information systems as open information systems and discuss them from a business point of view, including their linguistic, communicational and methodological foundations. To illustrate story boarding, we discuss a simple application example.

INTRODUCTION

Information technology impacts economy. It additionally has started changing the modern way of life, e.g., look at work on the so-called semantic web (Berners-Lee et al., 2001), or a web of ideas (Cherry, 2002), or on new business models due to the impact of information technology (see Kaner, 2002; Kaschek et al., 2003a). Since long information systems (IS) are an important area of active research, lots of competing IS development approaches are available. The problem of somehow developing a right IS is connected to the problem of developing the IS right.

In the present chapter, we focus on the so-called high level phases of IS development. In particular, we deal with analyzing WIS requirements and modeling. Our approach is called story boarding. It is a holistic, usage-centered and agile approach to WIS development. We comment on WISs from a business perspective, and use this perspective to distinguish WISs from ISs in general. We further discuss the linguistic, communicational and methodological foundations of IS development. Story boarding is introduced and explained in terms of these.

Technological achievements such as the World Wide Web (in short, WWW or Web) allow new kinds of ISs, namely WISs, to evolve. Dealing with WISs implies challenges, opportunities and threats. We believe that WISs soon will be the dominant kind of IS, and that development methodology for WISs is of prime importance. To contribute to this field, we adapt and enhance available methodology where this is reasonable, and use new methods, techniques and concepts elsewhere.

Chapter Outline

We continue the chapter with a discussion of how ISs and, in particular, WISs appear from a business point of view. We use the abstraction layer model (ALM) to relate the most important phenomena in WIS development to each other and discuss related work. We continue discussing linguistic, communicational and methodological foundations of IS development. We proceed with a discussion of story boarding, customer types and customer profiles, and the language SiteLang, followed by a relatively detailed example. Finally, we summarize the chapter and outline future work.

A BUSINESS VIEW ON WIS

We here deal with WISs that conform to the type business to customer (B2C). We consider WISs as sets of services offered to customers. They shall be business enablers and simplifiers. We look at WISs from the angles: **conceptual definition**, i.e., what functionality do they offer to customers; **usage**, i.e., the way customers interact with the WIS; **beneficiaries**, i.e. the individuals or organizations benefiting from them, and **construction**, i.e., the measures and activities which make the WIS effective. Clearly, for a more complete understanding of ISs, their maintenance, i.e., the measures and activities required for keeping them efficient, as well as deployment, i.e., actually making them effective, and retirement, i.e., the measures to make them stop being effective, would need to be discussed.

Information Systems

Hirschheim et al. (1995, p. 11) say:

"Traditionally, an information system has been defined in terms of two perspectives: one relating to its function; the other relating to its structure. From a structural perspective ... an information system consists of a collection of people, processes, data, models, technology and partly formalized language, forming a cohesive structure which serves some organizational purpose or function. From a functional perspective ..., an information system is a technologically implemented medium for the purpose of recording, storing, and disseminating linguistic expressions as well as for the supporting of inference making."

The functional definition has its merits in focusing on what actual users, from a conceptual point of view, do with the information system while using it: They communicate with experts to solve a particular problem. The structural definition makes clear that IS are socio-technical systems, i.e., systems consisting of humans, behavior rules, and conceptual and technical artifacts. Similar definitions are collected by Bernus and Schmidt (1998).

ISs nowadays are used according to a linguistic model, i.e., humans enter linguistic expressions into the system, the IS then processes them and, if no fatal error occurs, outputs a linguistic expression. Humans, for problem solving in a universe of discourse (UoD), may then use an IS. Identifying solution plans and solutions for each of these problems might be stated as not knowing the answer to a particular question. Humans, perhaps applying a particular encoding, turn the respective question into a machine processable form and enter it into the IS. The reply to this inquiry is then used to determine or carry out further action. One such action might be issuing a further inquiry. However, finally, action might be taken that is not related to an IS.

Information Spaces

Inspired by Mayr et al. (1985), we use the metaphor that an IS creates an information space (InS). An InS consists of locations at which information objects are located and the connections between these. Customers may enter or leave an InS. After entering it, customers can allocate a location in an InS to them. They can navigate through an InS, locate linguistic expressions and operations in it, and launch operations against data. Invoking an operation often requires customers to identify and locate it, position themselves on the identified location, and then trigger the operation. The linguistic expressions inside an InS are called data.

To illustrate the various kinds of operations, let a data collection represent the customers of a company. This collection will contain several items of equal structure, and each item will describe a particular customer. A customer's characteristics, such as name, given name, address, gender, customer number, open orders and similar, will be represented by components of the list item.

- A **filter operation** chooses data items that match a selection criterion out of the collection. Choosing those customers that have an address in Palmerston North is a filter operation.

- A **projection operation** chooses parts of composite data items. Choosing the name, but not the given name, for each customer is a projection operation.

- An **ordering operation** defines the sequence of appearance of data. Arranging the data items according to the customer number is an ordering operation.

- A **shaping operation** defines the structure of the data. Combining customer name and given name into a new component is a shaping operation.

- A **processing operation** invokes a business function, i.e., a function being relevant only for particular universes of discourse (UoDs). Identifying the customer with the highest number of unpaid bills and determining his creditworthiness is a processing operation.

- A **retrieval operation** inserts data in, copies, or deletes data from a collection.

- A **disseminating operation** imports data from or exports data to an InS.

Web Information Systems as Open Information Systems

ISs traditionally were **closed systems** in three respects. Exchange of data with other than the foreseen systems was not easy to establish, if possible at all. Only staff of the organization running the IS were given access to it. Only one access channel was available. Systematically using 'links' turns an IS into WIS, i.e., an IS implementing an open InS. Data exchange with other WISs becomes easy; exposing an IS to the links of other ISs enables virtually everyone to

Figure 1: Traditional IS as Opposed to WIS

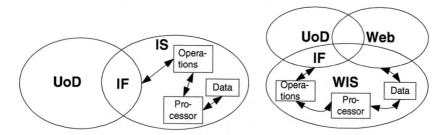

The left diagram shows traditional IS as overlapping the UoD in the interface (IF). For WIS, the right diagram shows that the interface is still the intersection of UoD and system but now contains a part of the Web.

access it. It is relatively easy to introduce new access channels. Figure 1 illustrates the relationship between an IS and a WIS. Note that the diagram sketching a traditional IS, i.e., non-WIS somewhat modified, is taken from Jackson (1995). Due to their openness, the use of WISs creates more challenges for their designers than traditional ISs create for theirs. These challenges, in part, are a consequence of the competition between WISs, introduced by individuals being allowed to freely traverse links and, thus, enter and leave a WIS.

The WIS-based competition for customers makes responsible designers wish to come up with and run a WIS. At the same time, however, organizations need to protect their investments in hardware, software and data. They further need to guarantee the availability of the functionality offered, e.g., prevent 'denial of service attacks' being successful. Thus, organizations need to run protecting means, such as 'log-in-mechanisms,' 'firewalls' and the like. WIS **interaction roles**, or user roles, are an important means to design secure systems. They typically are defined as sets of access privileges to the WIS's resources. Typical interaction roles are 'customer,' 'administrator,' 'data typist' and 'maintenance staff.'

Usage

Using ISs generally fits what we call the linguistic **usage model**. Customers choose and ship linguistic expressions (then considered as input) to the IS for processing. The IS processes the input in three steps: input analysis, response generation and response presentation. At least the last two steps, if intended to aid the customer, optimally require the incorporation of a customer model in the IS. In case the differences between the various customers are not discussed at all, considered as unimportant, or the customer's assessment of the IS is not considered as important, then the customer model might only be implicitly present and not be customer specific.

Human-WIS interaction is a mediated customer-expert communication. Communication takes place because customers want to benefit from experts' knowledge, which we here assume to be a true belief that can be justified by the believer. To obtain this knowledge might have required experts to undertake long-lasting studies and investigations or simply keeping records of certain events or facts. Customers do not care about this. They need some information and expect to get it by querying the IS. We do not distinguish between knowledge and ability since ability roughly can be understood as a 'knowing how,' and knowing means having obtained knowledge. The so-called Zachmann framework, according to (Morgan, 2002, pp. 19-21), identifies the following kinds of knowing: Knowing **what**, addressing facts; knowing **how**, addressing abilities; knowing **why**, addressing causality; knowing **what for**, addressing purpose; knowing **who**, addressing the subject of activities; and knowing **when**, addressing the temporal circumstances of action. We add knowing **with what**, addressing tools or resources used for action. For a recent discussion on what knowledge is, see, e.g., Sutton (2001).

Beneficiaries

Customers and vendors of WISs benefit from these. The customers benefit in so far as they are freed from the limitations of experts, e.g., with respect to availability, inabilities, knowledge of the business, or prejudices against certain customer types. These are only benefits for certain types of customers. Customers of other types might suffer from WISs.

The vendor might benefit in several ways from making the WIS effective. The throughput of business cases (per unit of time) might increase due to various customers concurrently accessing the system. The response time to customer inquiries might be reduced, resulting in more business cases performed and the infrastructure used more efficiently. Availability of services might be increased and, thus, the volume of business might increase. Furthermore, the cost of business cases on average might be reduced, since they need less staff time allocated to them. Staff satisfaction due to work and, thus, staff productivity might increase because they can focus more on the more interesting non-standard cases; and, in the standard cases, monotonous and error-prone tasks might be carried out by equipment. Finally, due to integration into the Web, visibility of the vendor for customers and partners is increased. This increases competition, which is an advantage for competition fit enterprises.

Information System Construction Concepts

We use Thalheim's so-called **Abstraction Layer Model** (ALM) for information systems, which, slightly modified, is depicted in Figure 2 as the base of our analysis of ISs. The ALM classifies IS development-relevant phenomena according to the five layers it introduces. These layers are referred to as layers of abstraction. The ALM's top layer is the **strategic layer**. It corresponds to the purpose of the WIS and the expected customers. The second highest ALM layer is the **business layer**, corresponding to the usage. The **conceptual layer** is the middle layer. It corresponds to data and operations maintained by the WIS. The **presentation layer** is the second-lowest layer. It is corresponds to allocating access channels to system resources. Finally, the lowest, i.e., the **implementation layer**, allows for the addressing of all sorts of implementation issues. This includes setting up the logical and physical database schemata, implementation of functionality, and dialogue control. As far as possible, decisions on the implementation layer should not impose restrictions on phenomena dealt with at higher layers. Classifying phenomena occurring in IS development according to these layers relates these phenomena by a cause-effect relationship. The ALM is represented as a pyramid, rather than as a couple of lines signifying the layers, to address the increased and more specific knowledge about the WIS on lower layers compared to higher ones.

On each layer except the strategic layer, ALM identifies two dimensions for the description of the linguistic expressions affecting the IS: **focus** and **modus**. The focus enables distinguishing between customers referring to the UoD in its totality (global) or only to a part of it (local). The modus enables distinguishing between customers referring to a particular UoD-state (static) or a transition between such states (dynamic). Using these dimensions, ALM characterizes the system resources **data** as global and static, **operation** as global and dynamic, **view** as local and static, and **dialogue** as local and dynamic. Following Kaschek and Zlatkin (2003), one can introduce a further dimension **kind**, allowing distinguishing between customers referencing to something because of their interest in it (self contained) or because of its relation to something else (referential). The above-mentioned resources can easily be characterized in the space with dimensions focus, modus and kind. This space allows us to characterize links as global, dynamic and referential, or as local, dynamic and referential resources, depending on whether the link leaves the InS.

Each ALM layer is connected to the layer immediately below it by a specific activity. Case modeling and customer profiling connect the strategic and business layers. Conceptual modeling, i.e., systems analysis, connects business and conceptual layers. Presentation and business layers are connected by the definition of presentation styles. Finally, implementation connects the presentation and implementation layers. No temporal order of the respective development activities is imposed by ALM. Thalheim's co-design methodology (CDM) recommends, for all but the top-most layer, consideration of all the resources determined by the dimensions focus and modus. See Thalheim (2000) for more detail on ALM and CDM.

RELATED WORK

Wallace (2002) reports on a pilot study on the ways organizations were using the Internet, i.e., web pages, intranets and email. The analysis showed that those **critical success factors** having the greatest impact on an organization's successful Internet use are more strongly related to human factors than to technical ones. A closer examination revealed that they were more specifically concerned with communication and customer service. The strongest factors, in descending order of importance, were: having a plan for dealing with site-related communication, meeting customer demand, regarding the web site as part of the overall communication strategy, considering marketing aspects of the site, and updating and refocusing of the web site.

The result of the pilot study implies that communication aspects of design, development and implementation of the web presence of organizations are key to successfully using web technology. We refer to Schulz von Thun (2000) for dimensions of messages that we can use here, since the general literature on business communication (e.g., see Dwyer, 1993; Francis, 1987; Guffey, 1997; McLaren & Locker, 1995), seems not to focus as much as needed on disturbances in technically mediated communication with customers.

Atzeni et al. (1998) emphasize **content**, **navigation** and **presentation** design, respectively leading to databases, hypertext, and page layout. Other authors (e.g., Baresi et al., 2000; Bonifati et al., 2000; Gädke & Turowski, 1999; Rossi et al., 1999) follow the same lines of thought. Garzotto et al. (1993) and Schwabe and Rossi (1998) concentrate on the 'add-on' to database design, emphasizing mainly the hypertext design targeting navigation structures. Feyer et al. (1998) caused Schewe and Thalheim (2001) to investigate **media types**. These provide a theoretically sound way to integrate

Figure 2: Abstraction Layers Concerning IS

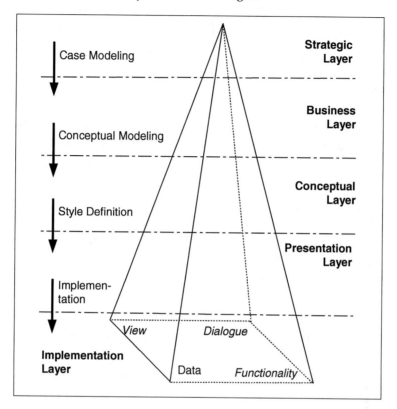

databases, external views, navigation structures, operations, and even support adaptivity to different users, environments and channels. The **adaptivity** feature distinguishes them from the **dialogue types** that are used to integrate database systems with their user interfaces (see Schewe & Schewe, 2000).

Schewe and Thalheim (2001) emphasize that conceptual abstraction from content, functionality and presentation of an intended site is insufficient for conceptual modeling of web-based systems. Atzeni et al. (1998), Baresi et al. (2000), and Bonifati et al. (2000) do not deal with story boarding, nor do Gädke and Turowski (1999), Rossi et al. (1999), Garzotto et al. (1993) or Schwabe and Rossi (1998). Neglecting story boarding is likely to cause difficulties in capturing the business content of the system under development.

Kaschek et al. (2003c) and Kaschek et al. (2003b) started a more thorough investigation of story boarding that focuses on user intentionality, i.e., context modeling. Conceptual modeling traditionally considered more onto-logical aspects than epistemological ones. The latter now need to be taken more seriously: Openness implies WIS adaptation to customers and, thus, conclusions that need to be drawn. See Wallace and Matthews (2002) for a respective discussion concerning the representation of the information space to customers.

Schewe and Thalheim (2001) suggest that the story boarding concepts comprise directed graphs, called scenarios. This extends the proposal of Feyer et al. (1998), who instead used partially ordered sets. In addition, user profiling is approached with the help of user dimensions, capturing various aspects of users. This has been extended in Srinivasa (2001) to a formal description of interactive systems.

Düsterhöft and Thalheim (2001) describe the language **SiteLang** to support the specification of story boards. The work also indicates ideas on how to exploit word fields for designing dialogue steps in story boards. Schewe et al. (1995) and Schewe (1996) have discussed refinement primitives for dialogues. Due to the connection between dialogues and scenarios, this approach to refinement is also useful for story boarding. The work in Schewe et al. (2002) applies story boarding and user profiling to the area of online loan systems.

Thalheim and Düsterhöft (2000) suggested using metaphorical structures in the application domain to support story boarding. Using word fields in web-based systems was suggested by Düsterhöft et al. (2002), based on computational linguistics (see Hausser, 2001). Preliminary results on the subject of this paper were presented in Schewe et al. (2002) and Wallace and Matthews (2002). Matthews (1998) and Kaschek et al. (2003a) study New Zealand bank web sites.

FOUNDATIONS

We do not cover all the foundations of information systems in the present chapter. We focus on the linguistic, the communicational, and the methodological foundations. For the philosophical foundations of information system development, we refer to Hirschheim et al. (1995). More specifically, we refer to Sowa (2000) for logical, philosophical and computational foundations of knowledge representation, which we roughly equate with conceptual modeling. For the cognitive basis of model-based reasoning (in science), we mention Nersessian (2002). For the mathematical foundations, we refer to Wechler (1992) and Barr and Wells (1990).

Linguistic Foundations

ISs have to support organizations in recording, storing, processing and disseminating linguistic expressions. We briefly follow (Linke et al., 2001, pp. 17-24) in our discussion of elementary linguistic concepts. A **sign** is something with which one can refer to something else. There are no restrictions for this something else besides that it must be possible to refer to it. E.g., we respectively can refer to a unicorn, dragon, Donald Duck by means of the string 'unicorn,' 'dragon,' 'Donald Duck,' though in physical reality, none of them exists. What one refers to by means of a sign is called the sign's **referent**. Nouns like 'head,' 'tree,' and 'sun' are signs. Road signs are signs. Following Peirce (1998), linguistics distinguishes three kinds of signs: icon, index, and symbol. An **icon** is a sign that is related to its reference by means of a mapping relationship, i.e., a similarity. An **index** is a sign that is related to its reference in a temporal or causal relationship. Finally, a **symbol** is a sign that is neither an icon nor an index.

Linguistics does not restrict its sign concept to printed, drawn or written signs, as we do here. It takes into account representations in all kinds of media that enable perception with our senses. Smoke may be considered as an index for fire, as is the case with lurching for being drunk. Due to the restricted coverage of signs in the present paper, the mapping relationship between an icon and its reference is a similarity in terms of shape, graphical structure and color.

According to O'Grady et al. (2001, pp. 632-633), linguistics signs are considered to be either graded or discrete:

"Graded signs convey their meaning by changes in degree. ... There are no steps or jumps from one level to the next that can be associated with a specific change in meaning. ... Discrete signs are distinguished from each other by categorical (stepwise) differences. There is no gradual transition from one sign to the next."

Instances of semiosis, i.e., processes of sign usage (following Morris, see, e.g., Morris, 1955), are often, e.g., in Falkenberg et al. (1998), understood according to the dimensions:

- **Syntax**, addressing sign composition out of elementary, i.e., non-composite signs.
- **Semantics**, addressing the reference of signs.
- **Pragmatics**, i.e., '... the origin, uses, and the effects of signs' (see Morris, 1955, p. 352).

According to our linguistic usage model, ISs are used by means of uttering, perceiving and processing **linguistic expressions**, i.e., composite signs. Using ISs, thus, is an instance of semiosis that requires a transition from the sign to its reference and vice versa. Using ISs, thus, involves **abstraction**, i.e., omitting characteristics ascribed to the sign or the reference that are not relevant for the actual use of the IS. Sign usage and, in particular, abstraction involve understanding. According to the Longman Dictionary of Contemporary English (1995), understanding mainly is an understanding of something. One can identify two approaches to the understanding of something:

- **Understanding** something **in terms of itself**. This is often aimed at by methods or techniques of requirements engineering, such as conducting interviews, issuing and evaluating questionnaires, document analysis, field studies, brainstorming, role playing and the like.
- **Understanding** something **in terms of something else**. This is what the application of signs, metaphors and models attempts to achieve.

For more detail on the techniques for understanding something in terms of itself, see, e.g., Henderson-Sellers (1998) and Quade (1985). Concerning models, we mention the important work in Stachowiak (1992), Stachowiak (1983) and Stachowiak (1973). Concerning modeling, see also Minsky (1968), Oberquelle (1984), and, in particular, Quade (1985), as well as newer work, such as Rothenberg (1989) and Wieringa (1990). Of the most recent work, we mention Falkenberg et al. (1998b).

The relationship between models and metaphors was investigated in Black (1966). Metaphorical structures have been used for WIS design by Thalheim and Düsterhöft (2000). They define (p. 168) **metaphorical structure** as "… the unusual usage of a language expression, i.e., using a language expression in a meaning which is not expected in the application context. The language expression is used as a language pictorial which works on the basis of a similarity of two objects/words." They mention that four kinds of metaphorical structures are usually identified: **Metaphor**, a language expression in which two semantic fields are claimed to be similar. Supplementary information concerning metaphors and, in particular, theories on how they work can be found in Gregory (1998). **Allegory** is 'an extended metaphor' representing a complex idea. **Metonymy** is a language expression containing a term replacing a related term. **Synecdoche** is a metonymy, the term relation of which is a meronymy, i.e., a part whole relationship.

Communicational Foundations

Cragan and Shields (1998, pp. 1-64) discuss the information systems theory of communication that was originated by Shannon. Following it, we understand communication as an exchange of messages between at least two **actors** by means of signal transfer. Message exchange may be called **dialogue**. The individual action in a dialogue, i.e., either uttering or perceiving a statement, can be denoted as **dialogue step**. A message first is chosen and encoded, such that it can be represented in a media or channel the intended receivers of the message have access to. Elementary, i.e., non-composite parts of this representation, are called a **signal**. This media may be a natural one, like the air. It may also be an artificial one, such as a book, journal or some kind of wires. Representing the encoded message might require using sophisticated technology, such as telephone, radio, TV, or the Web. Some media may allow encoded message representations to persist in them, while others do not. Those that allow it are called storage media.

Once a message is selected, the respective actor might want to represent it in a particular (natural or artificial) language, i.e., to encode it. The processes of encoding a message, representing it in a media, in particular, recording it, are error prone. Disturbing attacks on each of these processes might occur. Received signal sequences, thus, after rule conform decoding, might not translate to the message sent. Not only errors and disturbances make communication difficult. Received messages need to be interpreted for information construction. Often the receiver is required to find out what the sender wanted to achieve with his utterance. If the sender's background or context differs too much from those of the receiver, successful communication might be very hard to achieve. Ensuring successful communication requires a dialogue, i.e., a turn taking of the roles of sender and receiver.

We abstract from differences between human-computer interaction and oral human communication, i.e., talking with each other. From Schulz von Thun (2000), we borrow the dimensions of messages:

- **Content**, addressing what the message is about, i.e., its reference, if considered as a sign.
- **Revelation**, addressing what the sender reveals about himself with the message and the way it is uttered.
- **Relationship**, addressing the way sender and receiver are related as understood by the sender.
- **Appeal**, addressing what the sender wants the receiver to do.

IS usage above was characterized as computer mediated customer-expert communication. Neglecting some of these message dimensions in the dialogue design (or the dialogue design at all) is likely to impose communication barriers and, thus, reduce the effectiveness and efficiency with which customers use IS. Quality aware IS developers aim at reasonably few and low communication barriers. They further aim at customers being capable of efficiently doing their job and only dealing with tool issues if necessary.

Methodological Foundations

Before discussing understanding IS, we consider understanding arbitrary systems. We presuppose a strong meaning of understanding, including the ability to construct a respective system.

Systems Analysis and Design

Systems may be very complex. Humans have only a limited capacity for dealing with complexity. Understanding systems, thus, may require a separation of concern, such that only parts of complex systems need to be considered at once. According to Van Gigh (1991), a system is a unit of interacting system parts, the system components. System components can be considered as systems. System interaction takes place as an exchange of energy, matter, data or similar. The respective input-output (or stimulus-response) relation systems implement can classify these.

A subset of the set of components of a system S, together with their interaction (in S), is called a subsystem of S. Two subsystems of a system S are often distinguished: its interface and its kernel. The interface is the subset of the components of S directly interacting with systems not contained in S. The kernel of S is the complement of the interface of S in S. It may be reasonable to distinguish subsystems of the interface of S according to the class of systems they interact with.

A well-known method for analysis and synthesis, according to Polya (1988, pp. 141-143), already obtained by Euclid, Apollonius of Perga, and Aristaeus the elder, was reported by Pappus. Polya (p. 142) paraphrases Pappus: "In analysis we start from what is required, we take it for granted, and we draw consequences from it, and consequences from the consequences, till we reach a point that we can use as a starting point in synthesis. ... This procedure we call analysis ... But in synthesis, reversing the process, we start from the point which we reached last of all in our analysis, from the thing already known or admittedly true. We derive from it what preceded it in the analysis, and go on making derivations until, retracing our steps, we finally succeed in arriving at what is required. This procedure we call synthesis ...."

IS Analysis and Design

Applying the method for analysis and synthesis to information systems development by Sølvberg and Kung (1993) is ascribed to Langefors. Analysis is presupposed to be a process of nested system decomposition into interacting system components, such that each decomposition step results in a specification of the system input-output relation in terms of input-output specifications of the very system's components and their interaction. The starting point of synthesis is reached as soon as all components can be implemented. The process of synthesis, then, is presupposed to be a process of repeatedly aggregating interacting systems into a higher-level system. This process stops when a system is synthesized that meets the initial input-output specification or when such a system appears not to be obtainable. If the required input-output specification cannot be obtained by synthesis, then analysis can be carried out again, followed by a further synthesis step. Proceeding that way, either the input-output relation can be implemented or indicated as not implementable as a system.

This generic procedure for analysis and synthesis employs separation of concern in systems development and, thus, has the merit of complexity control. It, however, does not explicitly address several phenomena occurring in or relevant for IS development:

- **IS are socio-technical systems**, i.e., humans are part or stake holders of these systems and, thus, legal restrictions may apply to the system's working style, the referent of the data stored in the system, the way the data is stored, accessed, linked to other data, or processed.
- **IS are artificial systems**, i.e., they exist to serve for a certain purpose. Operating and maintaining them must be possible while meeting certain cost and time restrictions.
- **IKIWISI**, i.e., customers often cannot verbally express a specification of an IS that would satisfy their needs. They, however, believe that they can recognize such a system once they have access to it, compare, e.g., Boehm (2000).
- **Low requirements quality**, i.e., customers often specify their needs incompletely, inconsistently, open to interpretation, or even falsely. Further quality defects of requirements statements might apply as well.

- **Wicked problems**, i.e., attempting to specify and implement a system meeting the customers' needs changes these needs. Certain systems, thus, cannot be specified prior to their development.

These phenomena are related to the requirements of an anticipated system. We believe that they only can be better dealt with when the system requirements can be understood better. Therefore, we believe that analysis and synthesis, to be applicable to IS development, need to more specifically address the system requirements. Once these are reasonably fixed, Langefors' method can be applied. Below, we discuss story boarding as a means to better understand the system requirements.

Personalization

Personalization is the customer specific tailoring of the IS interface. It aims at modeling customers, their context and behavior. The effect of attempts to develop high quality IS will be limited if customers cannot use them well. Personalization becomes important when awareness evolves of the different needs of customers of different types. Using IS for problem solving requires: identifying of the business problems, the solution of which can be reasonably supported by the IS; identification of suitable business solution procedures for already identified problems; and realizing the business solution procedures based on the IS. Customers sometimes experience difficulties in solving these problems. A flawed IS design or implementation might be the cause. One such flaw is an insufficient domain analysis; another one is a too complex customer interface. Customer specific interfaces may be significantly less complex than customer independent ones.

Customers require aid concerning **identifying** data and operations to be used best, **locating** operations and data in the information space, **navigating** the information space, and in **handling** the IS efficiently. According to an idealizing refinement of the linguistic usage model, customers firstly identify the resources they want to access, i.e., respectively, the data or the operation they want to use. Secondly, they locate the resources they need. Thirdly, they navigate themselves onto locations from which the required resources are accessible. Finally, customers deal with how to actually handle the accessible resources. Presupposing this refined linguistic usage model of WIS, customers need aid in the above mentioned cognition intensive task. Metaphorical structures may help reusing knowledge. They seem to offer potential for aiding customers to master the tasks mentioned above. Furthermore, ALM supports developers in providing customer aid concerning identifying data and operations and locating these. Localization abstraction dealt with by Wallace and Matthews (2002), and context modeling discussed in Kaschek et al. (2003b) and Kaschek et al. (2003c), may help provide aid for search.

Consider, as an example, the (hypothetical) Biggest Bank of Switzerland (BBS). Swiss banking laws relatively strictly regulate how to run the business. BBS operates internationally and must be capable of running country specific operations for specific tasks. E.g., in Switzerland, it is forbidden to test the new module CheckCreditWorthiness (CCW) in the risk information system (RIS) with real data, which might not be the case in other countries. Furthermore, concerning balance sheets to US based parts of BBS, rules apply that are different from the ones applying to Switzerland based parts of BBS.

Staff at ultimo dealing with CCW need to know what customer data to use and which modules to apply to it. Not only the data must be made anonymous. It must also be the data to which the booking preparation, as well as day-end-processing, has already been applied. BBS branches operating in regions of the world in which the business follows similar rules and legislation are being served from centralized computing infrastructure. Thus, not only country specific data might be worked with, but also country specific software might apply. RIS should point out to the user what rules and legislation apply to identify the data to be processed for his purpose and functionality to actually do the job. Clearly, knowing which data to use does not imply knowing the name of the database to be used, on which disk it is located, and on which machine it is managed. Similar conditions apply for the operations.

The example illustrates that users who have a relatively clear understanding of what to do to perform a business transaction can be aided by measures targeting the task areas mentioned above. Handling aid aims at helping to efficiently use RIS. This concerns how to actually invoke operations, i.e., the functions implemented by CCW. Furthermore, pre- or post-processing steps might be required, such as ordering the data in a particular way to increase performance of some CCW-functions. Similarly, it might be required to print results on a specific, particularly fast printer, or on one that can print on A3- or endless paper. Clearly, information concerning these prescriptions should be available via CCW's customer interface.

It, however, might be the case that a business transaction has to be performed that was unforeseen, and for which there is not optimum automatized support. A work around might be used. Missing the respective functionality actually might be the reason for CCW being developed. RIS should offer means for customers to navigate its information space to allow for the work around until CCW is deployed and has passed acceptance test.

STORY BOARDING

Prior to explaining what story boarding is and how to actually use it, we discuss customer profiles and then introduce the language SiteLang.

Customer Profiles

Introducing customer types can target personalization. A list of **customer dimensions**, or attributes, may be ascribed to customer types. Respective examples are gender, education, ethnicity, computer literacy, age group, objective, data required, experience with the business (e.g., something like novice, average and expert might do), the accessible operations, and the like. To a customer dimension δ a scale $Sc(\delta)$ is associated. The scale is assumed to be a finite, totally ordered set. For a customer type 'novice,' the dimension 'experience with the business' could have associated the scale $\{1,\dots,12\}$, the elements of which could signify the number of months active in the business. Given a set Δ of customer dimensions, the **customer profile** $Cp(\Delta)$ of Δ is the set $\times_{\delta\Delta} Sc(\delta)$. A **customer type**, then, is defined as a convex subset of the $Cp(\Delta)$. Given a 'customer type' T and, within it, a pair (x,y) of customer models, i.e., type instances, then all such models on the line between x and y belong to T.

A customer type T can be specified by means of a set $Spec(T)=\{(m_\delta, M_\delta)|$ $m_\delta, M_\delta \in Sc(\delta),\ \delta \in \Delta\}$, where for each $\delta \in \Delta$, the values m_δ, M_δ respectively are the minimum and maximum values $v(u,\ \delta)$ for customers u of type T in dimension δ. If, once, caused by assessment of the behavior of a customer u, it is found that, for one of the dimension δ, the value $v(u,\ \delta)$ no more fits in the interval $[m_\delta, M_\delta]$, then this can be taken as an index to re-allocate the type to customer u. A type re-allocation, however, should only take place with customer permission.

Customer types, in practice, can be used to validate the design of a story board (see below for a definition). A New Zealand bank, e.g., for each customer type, creates a hypothetical instance as a typical representative of it. For this hypothetical person, then, a quite complete biography is invented. Even photographs are used to make this individual appear more real. The main cases for each customer type are then walked through, simulating the behavior of the representative. All its anticipated actions can then be discussed, referring to whatever biographic detail appears to be required. Clearly, the respective discussion is an interdisciplinary one: Marketing, IT and management should be involved. Occasionally, redesign of a story space might be necessary due to the findings of this role game.

SiteLang

Starting WIS development with an analysis of the actual process of using the WIS by a customer focuses the analysis on the business transactions or cases carried out by this customer. It supports in introducing helpful dialogues, and in anticipating and designing appropriate representation functionality. A **case** here is understood as a goal-striking course of action, intentionally leading to the invocation of a major business operation. A case, thus, is a process of successively using operations accessible in the information space and occasionally positioning to a new location. A case, therefore, can be represented as a path in the information space, such that to each of its vertices, i.e., locations in information space, a customer-WIS interaction takes place. Paths are not always sufficient to describe usage processes. Including branches, joins and loops, however, allows to specify all interaction scenarios that can take place in information space.

The diagram in Figure 3 shows a directed labeled graph on the five vertices 'Fill travel application form,' 'Pass filled application form to chief,' 'Boss deals with application,' 'Book flight & accommodation, etc.,' and ''Travel.' Such a vertex, i.e., a location in information space in the sequel, will be called a **scene**. Each arrow is called a **transition**. The scene pointed at by a transition is called target scene. The scene a transition starts at is called a source scene. Transitions may be labeled with conditions. The label 'KO' does not mean 'OK.' Such a graph in the sequel will be called a **scenario**. The integration of all scenarios relevant for a given WIS in the sequel is called the **story board**.

The customer-WIS interaction in the scene 'Fill travel application form' could consist of the customer first identifying the form applicable to both his position in the company and the type of intended trip. S/he then locates and retrieves the respective form. But filling it might make him/her feel the need to look up explanations and company rules concerning traveling. Ideally, all the respective information would be available via the WIS. The diagram does not show the discussed interaction at scene 'Fill travel application form.'

Figure 3: Example Scenario: Business Trip Application

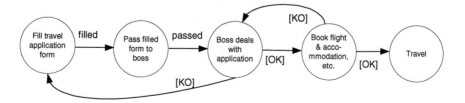

Having filled in the form, the applicant needs to pass the form to the boss. Specific rules might apply because the travel is expensive or needs to be started immediately. Thus, it might be necessary to provide the form for the immediate boss as well as the head of the group and the head of the department. Furthermore, it might be necessary to identify the deputy of the boss, since the boss is not available or has signaled not being able to deal with the case. This indicates that the neglected interaction in scenes, if considered, might significantly increase the complexity of a real scenario compared to the one shown in the diagram.

The scene 'Boss deals with application' introduces branching and looping to the scenario. The boss might have been asked to accept a new, very urgent project and, therefore, the applicant cannot go on the trip, i.e., the application is rejected. The applicant can decide not to accept the rejection and redo the form, e.g., he could improve the rationale to indicate the importance of doing the respective trip. Then the scenes already discussed could be approached again, with the respective cycle even repeated several times. Clearly, the boss, while working on the application, might feel the need to look for instructions concerning it, e.g., in cases of doubt or latitude. S/he should be aided in all the required activity by the WIS. Note that the scenario implicitly involves three roles: applicant, boss and clerk. The clerk would book flight and accommodation. If the required bookings could not be made, it might be necessary for the boss to deal again with the application. To keep the model simple, it was decided not to include reimbursement issues in the diagram. Reimbursement either could be introduced or another scenario dealing with it could be given. Precondition to start the process described by this reimbursement scenario would be eligibility to do so.

Starting from story boarding, the transition to system design can be carried out easily: Customer-WIS interaction at a particular scene causes data being retrieved from or shipped to an underlying database. The respective data, for the convenience of the user, is held in a **media object**. A description of media objects at a high level in the sense of classification is said to be its **media type**. See Schewe and Thalheim (2003) in the present book for more information on media types and their theory.

The activity that takes place in a scene is understood as a dialogue between customer and media object. The dialogue can be modeled with an interaction diagram or similar. This, then, gives us, at a still vague level, syntax and semantics of the language **SiteLang**. Summing up, the modeling notions of SiteLang are:

- **Story space**, i.e., the smallest subspace of the information space sufficient for creation of the story board.
- **Story board**, i.e., a net of locations in information space. It is represented as a directed graph. Its vertices, the locations, are called scenes. Its arrows, called transitions, are labeled with both the action triggering their traversal and the data being available at the target scene due to this action. A scene is labeled with the type of customers being granted access to it.
- **Scenario**, i.e., a subgraph of the story board.
- **Story**, i.e., a path in the story board.
- **Scene**, i.e., a vertex in the story board. According to (Longman Dictionary of Contemporary English, 1995) a scene is "… a single piece of action that happens at one place."
- **Actor**, i.e., user, dialogue object, or media object.
- **Media object**, i.e., a unit of business- and representation functionality, mediating between customer and database of the WIS.
- **Content**, i.e., data, information.

Stories are particular scenarios. They do not add to the expressiveness of SiteLang. They merely are justified by methodological consideration. They represent a simple case. A number of alternatives is left out (branch scenes), each of which adds to the case. Stories enable a separation of concern introduced to further reduce the complexity to be dealt with at once. One doesn't get rid of the complexity in this manner. It reappears as relationships between processes and the conditions and constraints characterizing these. Assessment of the overall design requires the various scenarios integrated into the story board.

In the story board, usage processes can be defined by means of the modeling notions introduced by SiteLang. This is the starting activity of story boarding. Each such process involves actors that exchange messages with each other. The processes focused on throughout story boarding need to be chosen such that customers are interested in them. This can be done based on a good forecast of the customer's purpose in running the very process. One can expect that processes represent methods for solving a particular business problem. Such a process is considered a scenario if it contains branch or fork scenes or loops. Otherwise, it is a story. The modeled processes can be used to identify the data and operations accessed by the customer driving the process. Story boarding goes, then, on and, for each modeled process, obtains database schemas describing the data accessed in a process. These schemas are then integrated, and the integrated schema is used to derive, for each process, a view specifying the data accessed throughout this process.

From a methodological point of view, story boarding, thus, is a particular variant of analysis and synthesis. The system of customer-WIS interaction is discussed, as well as particular subsystems of it: the scenarios or stories. The complexity reduction resulting from the respective separation of concern is used to derive database schemas enabling to record, store and maintain the data required in the very subsystem. The analysis, however, goes one step further: It generates an integrated database schema that allows handling all the data required. This integrated schema, then, is the starting point of the synthesis. View definitions are obtained to produce data descriptions suitable for the individual customer-WIS interactions. These, then, have to be implemented by means of dialogues. Customers, then, will assess these descriptions, and either will accept or reject them. At best, prototype systems are offered to the customers for this purpose. In case of rejection, the analysis-synthesis cycle has to be started again to come up with an improved artifact.

EXAMPLE

The example does not cover the whole development process. We rather focus on aspects of story boarding and do not intend to show the completed story board. Rather than discussing how modern interfaces are operated, we assume familiarity of readers with them. We further assume that the used terminology, as far as the interface is concerned, is reasonably self-explaining. We use terminology and, where possible, notation introduced above.

Enjoyment WIS

Assume that a consortium of local companies, in a collective attempt headed by the chamber of commerce, pays for and coordinates the development of an enjoyment WIS (EWIS). All legal organizations targeting at the high price segment of the enjoyment market may join the consortium. The mission statement of EWIS is for the consortium members to extend the business volume. Using EWIS is free of charge.

Gourmets and Connoisseurs

'Gourmet' and 'Connoisseur' are natural candidates for customer types in the businesses of dining and beverages. The stories 'Wine Tasting' (see Figure 4) and 'Fine Dining' (see Figure 5) are respectively assumed to be descriptions

Figure 4: A Story for Wine Tasting

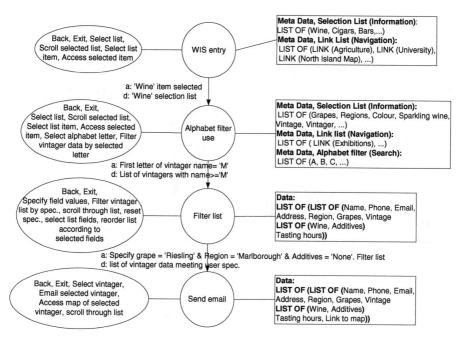

of typical cases of customers of type 'Gourmet' and 'Connoisseur.' The operations available at a scene are listed within the ellipse that is connected with a line to the very scene. Similarly, the data (including the links) available at a scene is listed within the rectangle connected to the scene by a line. We do not distinguish here between data and view, and do not explicitly model the dialogues, since these consist in successively invoking operations. The arrow labels prefixed by 'a:' denote the action causing the transition from the source scene to the target scene of the arrow. The arrow label prefixed with 'd:' indicates the data accessible at the target scene of such a transition.

Two Customer Types

The dimensions d for 'food quality,' and e for 'wine quality,' respectively measuring the average score of accessed food and wine places, are used. The food and wine quality scale, respectively, is the set of Roman and Arab numbers from one to 10. High scale values indicate high quality. 'Connoisseur' and 'Gourmet' are defined such that the former are a subset of the latter, but not vice versa. 'Gourmet' is defined as $[m_\delta, M_\delta] = [VII, X]$ and $[m_\varepsilon, M_\varepsilon] = [3, 7]$. 'Connoisseur' is defined as $[m_\delta, M_\delta] = [VIII, X]$ and $[m_\varepsilon, M_\varepsilon] = [5, 7]$.

Figure 5: A Story for Fine Dining

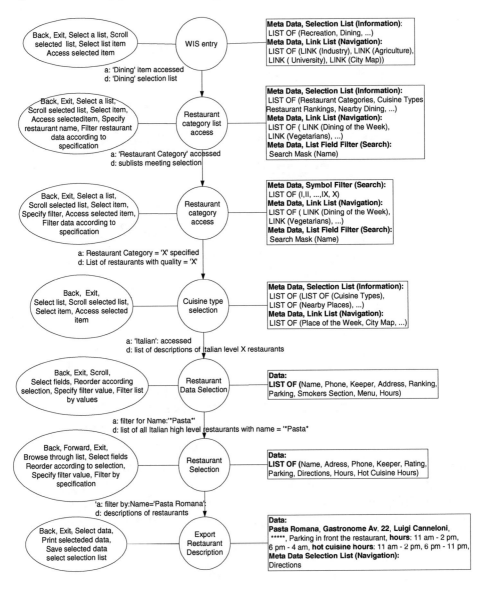

The Stories Integrated

A part of the story space of EWIS is specified with help of the adjacency matrix in Figure 6. It was generated from the top three scenes of each of the stories presented. Adjacency matrixes may be easier to understand than scenarios with lots of crossing edges. Diagonal elements of the matrix represent

Figure 6: Parts of 'Fine Dining' and 'Wine Tasting' Integrated

M1	M2	M3	M4	M5	
WIS entry	'Dining' item selected		'Wine' item selected		All
	Restaurant category list access	'Restaurant Category' accessed			Gourmet
		Restaurant category access			Gourmet
			Alphabet filter use	1st. letter of name = 'M'	Connoisseur
				Filter list	Connoisseur

scenes and are labeled with the scene's name. Beginning with *1*, they are numbered from top left to bottom right. An entry *A* in the *i-th* row and *j-th* column of the matrix means that action *A* leads to a transition from scene *i* to *j*. Transitions from a scene into itself are indicated by an asterisk. Customer type *T* may access scene *s* if *T* is listed right from the table in an additional column in the row of *s*. Association of media types to scenes, similarly, is specified by an additional row below the table. If roles are included in scenarios, they can be treated as if they were scenes.

Integrated Database Schema and View Derivation
Connoisseur Database Schema

The top left corner diagram of Figure 7 is a database schema suitable to describe the connoisseur data, as far as it occurs in the wine tasting story. This story at the scene 'WIS entry' shows the offers relevant for connoisseurs. The only one of them for which data is then specified in the examples is the offer 'Wine.' Selecting it leads to a transition into scene 'Alphabet filter use.' This scene describes wine. Thus, it appears reasonable to have an entity type 'Wine description.' It would have multi-valued attributes: 'grape' and 'region,' and would, additionally, have the attributes 'color' and 'sparkling wine.'

Further, the data offered at the scene 'Filter list' indicates an entity type 'Vintager' should exist, with attributes 'Name,' 'Phone,' 'Email,' 'Address,'

Figure 7: Conceptual Schemata for the Scenarios Discussed

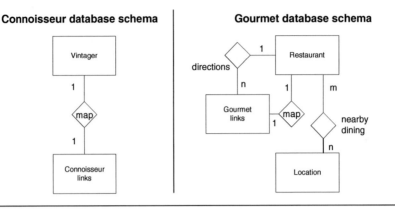

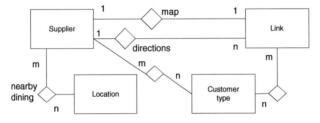

'Region' and 'Vintage.' This entity type would further have a multi-valued attribute 'Grape,' and a multi-valued composite attribute without name. The components of this attribute would be 'Wine' and the multi-valued attribute 'Additive.' Finally 'Vintager' would have an attribute 'Tasting hours.' As the scene 'Send mail' indicates, there should be a 'map' available for this entity type. It appears, thus, reasonable to have an entity type 'Connoisseur link' that stores the URLs required. The map for an entity of type 'Vintager' could, thus, be associated to this entity by a relationship 'map.'

Entity type 'Connoisseur link' can also store the links occurring at the scenes 'WIS entry,' and 'Alphabet filter use.' To permit the links offered to the user that are specified by the scenes just mentioned, it is sufficient that 'Connoisseur link' has attributes 'Exhibition' and 'Type.' Looking back to the somewhat artificial entity type 'Wine description,' it seems better to include its attributes in the list of attributes of 'Vintager.'

Gourmet Database Schema

Similarly, we can analyze the story 'Fine Dining.' We see, firstly, that there are several offers to the gourmet at 'WIS entry.' However, only for 'Dining' are further characteristics given. Arguing similarly as before, we can conclude that an entity type 'Gourmet links' is required.

To group together the characteristics given in scene 'Restaurant category list access,' we chose an entity type 'Restaurant.' As the analysis of the further sequences shows, this entity type would have attributes: 'Name,' 'Phone,' 'Keeper,' 'Address,' 'Ranking,' 'Parking,' 'Smokers Section,' 'Menu,' 'Hours,' and 'Hot Cuisine Hours.' There also would be attributes 'Category' and 'Cuisine.' which could be multi-valued. We omit respective detail. To allow for the presentation of the dining of the week and of the vegetarian restaurants, attributes 'DOW' and 'Veg' are available for entity type 'Restaurant.' Maps with directions and the restaurant location would be associated to a restaurant by means of associations 'directions' and 'map.'

Figure 8: Derivation of the Connoisseur and the Gourmet View

```
-- The database for the integrated database schema is called IDS.
-- The solution presented here only is to show how one could work in principle.
CREATE      SCHEMA      Connoisseur;
CREATE      VIEW        Vintager AS
            SELECT      * FROM IDS.Supplier AS S, IDS.Supplier_to_Cusromer_type AS
S2U,
            WHERE       S.ID = S2U.SuppID,
            AND         S2U.UserType = 'Connoisseur';
-- All attributes from IDS.Supplier that apply to vintagers, might be a proper subset of all
-- attributes of IDS.Supplier.
CREATE      VIEW        Connoisseur_links AS
            SELECT      * FROM IDS.Link AS L, Supplier AS S,
            WHERE       S.LinkID = L.Supp.ID;
GRANT       ...

CREATE      SCHEMA      Gourmet;
CREATE      VIEW        Restaurant AS
            SELECT      * FROM IDS.Supplier AS S, IDS.Supplier_to_User_type AS S2U,
            WHERE       S.ID = S2U.Suppld,
            AND         S2U.UserType = 'Gourmet';
-- All attributes from IDS.Supplier that apply to restaurants, might be a proper subset of all
-- attributes of IDS.Supplier.
CREATE      VIEW        Gourmet_links AS
            SELECT      * FROM IDS.Link AS L, IDS.Supplier_to_Link AS S2L,
            WHERE       L.ID = S2L.LinkID,
            AND         S2L.UserType = 'Gourmet';
CREATE      VIEW        nearby_dining AS
            SELECT      * FROM IDS.nearby_dining;
CREATE      VIEW        Location AS
            SELECT      * FROM IDS.Location;
GRANT       ...
```

In Figure 8, the user originating types are introduced by means of the 'CREATE SCHEMA' statements. These also provide the type name. A sequel of 'CREATE VIEW' commands specifies, for the create schema command that they are immediately following, the components the user originated type consists of, i.e., the views. These have a customer-controlled extent and inherit this property to the schema.

RESUME AND FUTURE WORK

In this chapter, we have introduced story boarding, a method for elicitation and analysis of requirements concerning WIS. We have shown that story boarding is a particular version of analysis and design applied to the system of customer-WIS interaction. We have discussed the foundations of story boarding in linguistics, communication and methodology. Core aspects of our discussion of story boarding have been customer profiling and the language SiteLang. We showed that both of them introduce a separation of concern, significantly simplifying the development activity: customer profiling enables, in usage, modeling to have a local focus, i.e. not considering all the data and operations but only the ones relevant for the particular customer type. We, finally, presented an example for the application of story boarding, and showed how it can be complemented with database design to obtain the base of an operative WIS.

There should be developed a CASE tool set, based on the language SiteLang, that allows to define a story space and, within it, a number of scenarios, in particular, stories. The tool set, then, should be capable of generating proposals for the schema of the database of each of these scenarios. Furthermore, the tool set should integrate available tools for schema integration. Finally, also, view derivation should be supported. The tool set could then be used to conduct empirical studies of the application of story boarding. This, then, would provide the empirical base of comparing story boarding to other approaches. It further would simplify learning the concepts and method. We expect that such studies give evidence for the strengths of our approach to WIS design discussed here.

ACKNOWLEDGMENTS

The work presented here was supported by the Massey University Academy of Business Research Fund (Project: 'Story boarding for web-based services,' 2002/03). We thank Inga Hunter and Alexei Tretiakov from the

Department of Information Systems, Massey University, Palmerston North, New Zealand, for their comments on earlier versions of this chapter.

REFERENCES

Atzeni, P., Gupta, A., & Sarawagi, S. (1998). Design and maintenance of data-intensive web-sites. In *Proceedings of the EDBT'98* (Vol. 1377 of LNCS, pp. 436-450). Berlin: Springer-Verlag.

Baresi, L., Garzotto, F., & Paolini, P. (2000). From web sites to web applications: New issues for conceptual modeling. In *ER workshops 2000* (Vol. 1921 of LNCS, pp. 89-100). Berlin: Springer-Verlag.

Barr, M. & Wells, C. (1990). *Category Theory for Computing Science.* New York: Prentice Hall.

Berners-Lee, T., Hendler, J., & Lassila, O. (2001). The semantic web. *Scientific American.*

Bernus, P. & Schmidt, G. (1998). Architecture of information systems. In P. Bernus, K. Mertins & G. Schmidt (Eds.), *Handbook on Architectures and Information Systems* (pp. 1-9). Berlin: Springer-Verlag.

Black, M. (1966). *Models and Metaphors: Studies in Language and Philosophy* (3rd ed.). Ithaca, NY: Cornell University Press.

Boehm, B. (2000). Requirements that handle IKIWISI, COTS and rapid change. *IEEE Computer*, 33(7), 99-102.

Bonifati, A., Ceri, S., Fraternali, P., & Maurino, A. (2000). Building multi-device, content-centric applications using WebML and the W3I3 tool suite. In *ER workshops 2000* (Vol. 1921 of LNCS, pp. 64-75). Berlin: Springer-Verlag.

Cherry, S. M. (2002). Weaving a web of ideas. *IEEE Spectrum*, 39(9), 65-69.

Cragan, J. F. & Shields, D. C. (1998). *Understanding Communication Theory: The Communicative Forces of Human Action.* Needham Heights, MA: Allyn & Bacon.

Düsterhöft, A. & Thalheim, B. (2001). SiteLang: Conceptual modeling of Internet sites. In H. S.~K. et al. (Eds.), *Conceptual Modeling - ER 2001* (Vol. 2224 of LNCS, pp. 179-192). Berlin: Springer-Verlag.

Düsterhöft, A., Schewe, K.-D., Thalheim, B., & Tschiedel, B. (2002). *XML-based website development through media types and word fields.* Submitted for publication.

Dwyer, J. (1993). *The Business Communication Handbook*. Australia: Prentice Hall.

Falkenberg, E. D., et al. (1998). A framework of information system concepts. *The FRISCO Report* (Web Edition). IFIP.

Feyer, T., Schewe, K.-D., & Thalheim, B. (1998). Conceptual modeling and development of information services. In T. Ling & S. Ram (Eds.), *Conceptual Modeling - ER'98* (Vol. 1507 of LNCS, pp. 7-20). Berlin: Springer-Verlag.

Francis, D. (1987). *Unblocking Organizational Communication*. Cambridge, UK: Cambridge University Press.

Gädke, M. & Turowski, K. (1999). Generic web-based federation of business application systems for e-commerce applications. In *EFIS 1999* (pp. 25-42).

Garzotto, F., Paolini, P., & Schwabe, D. (1993). HDM — A model-based approach to hypertext application design. *ACM ToIS*, 11(1), 1-26.

Gigh, J. P. Van (1991). *System Design, Modeling and Metamodeling*. New York: Plenum Press.

Gregory, R. L. (ed.). (1998). *The Oxford Companion to the Mind*. Oxford, UK: Oxford University Press.

Guffey, M. (1997). *Business Communication: Process and Product*. USA: South Western College Publishing.

Hausser, R. (2001). *Foundations of Computational Linguistics*. Berlin: Springer-Verlag.

Henderson-Sellers, B., Simons, A., & Younessi, H. (1998). *The OPEN Toolbox of Techniques*. New York: ACM Press, Addison-Wesley.

Hirschheim, R., Klein, H. K., & Lyytinen, K. (1995). *Information Systems Development and Data Modeling, Conceptual and Philosophical Foundations*. Cambridge, UK: Cambridge University Press.

Jackson, M. (1995). *Software Requirements & Specifications*. Wokingham, UK: ACM Press, Addison-Wesley.

Kaner, C. (2002). UCITA: A disaster in progress. *IEEE Spectrum*, 39(8), 13-15.

Kaschek, R. & Zlatkin, S. (2003). Where ontology affects information systems. In H. Mayr, M. Godlevsky, & S. C. Liddle (Eds.), *ISTA 2003 Proceedings*. Bonn, Germany: GI.

Kaschek, R., Matthews, C., & Wallace, C. (2003a). e-Mortgages: NZ state of the art and perspectives. In *Proceedings of the SCI 2003*.

Kaschek, R., Schewe, K.-D., & Thalheim, B. (2003b). *Modeling context in web information systems*. In short paper of CAiSE'03.

Kaschek, R., Schewe, K.-D., Thalheim, B., & Zhang, L. (2003c). Integrating context in conceptual modeling for web information systems. *WES'03 Proceedings*.

Linke, A., Nussbaumer, M., & Portmann, P. R. (2001). Studienbuch Linguistik. *Reihe Germanistische Linguistik* (4th ed.). Tübingen, Germany: Max Niemeyer Verlag GmbH.

Longman Dictionary of Contemporary English. (1995). Munich: Langenscheidt-Longman GmbH.

Matthews, C. (1998, March). Internet banking in New Zealand — A critique. *New Zealand Banker* (pp. 26-28).

Mayr, H. C., Lockemann, P. C., & Bever, M. (1985). A framework for application systems engineering. *Information Systems*, 10(1), 97-111.

McLaren, M. & Locker, K. (1995). *Business and Administrative Communication*. Irwin, Australia.

Melton, J. & Simon, A. R. (1993). *Understanding the New SQL: A Complete Guide*. San Francisco, CA: Morgan Kaufmann.

Minsky, M. (1968). Matter, mind and models. In M. Minsky (Ed.), *Semantic Information Processing* (pp. 425-432). Cambridge, MA: MIT Press.

Morgan, T. (2002). *Business Rules and Information Systems: Aligning IT with Business Goals*. Boston, MA.

Morris, C. W. (1955). *Signs, Language and Behavior*. New York: George Braziller. (Original work published 1946 by Prentice Hall).

Nersessian, N. J. (2002). The cognitive basis of model-based reasoning in science. In P. Carruthers, S. Stich, & M. Siegal (Eds.), *The Cognitive Basis of Science* (pp. 133-153). Cambridge, UK: Cambridge University Press.

O'Grady, W., Archibald, J., Aronoff, M., & Rees-Miller, J. (2001). *Contemporary Linguistics* (4th ed.). Boston, MA: Bedford/St. Martin's.

Oberquelle, H. (1984). On models and modeling in human-computer co-operation. In G. C. Van der Meer, M. J. Tauber, T. R. G. Green, & P. Gorny (Eds.), *Readings on Cognitive Ergonomics — Mind and Computers: Proceedings of the 2nd European Conference* (pp. 26-43). Berlin: Springer-Verlag.

Peirce, C. S. (1998). What is a sign? In Project Peirce edition (Ed.), *The Essential Peirce: Selected Philosophical Writings* (Vol. 2, pp. 4-10). Bloomington, IN: Indiana University Press.

Polya, G. (1988). *How to Solve It*. Princeton, NJ: Princeton University Press.

Quade, E. S. (1985). Predicting the consequences: Models and modeling. In H. Miser & E. S. Quade (Eds.), *Handbook of Systems Analysis:*

Overview of Uses, Procedures, Applications and Practice (pp. 191-218). New York: Elsevier Science Publishing.

Rossi, G., Schwabe, D., & Lyardet, F. (1999). Web application models are more than conceptual models. In *Advances in Conceptual Modeling* (Vol. 1727 of LNCS, pp. 239–252). Berlin: Springer-Verlag.

Rothenberg, J. (1989). The nature of modeling. In L. E. Widman, K. A. Loparo, & N. R. Nielson (Eds.), *Artificial Intelligence, Simulation, and Modeling* (pp. 75-92). New York: John Wiley & Sons.

Schewe, B. (1996). *Kooperative Softwareentwicklung*. Wiesbaden, Germany: Deutscher Universitätsverlag.

Schewe, B., Schewe, K.-D., & Thalheim, B. (1995). Objektorientierter Datenbankentwurf in der Entwicklung betrieblicher Informationssysteme. *Informatik — Forschung und Entwicklung*, 10, 115-127.

Schewe, K.-D. & Schewe, B. (2000). Integrating database and dialogue design. *Knowledge and Information Systems*, 2(1), 1-32.

Schewe, K.-D. & Thalheim, B. (2001). Modeling interaction and media objects. In E. Métais (Ed.), *Advances in Conceptual Modeling* (Vol. 1959 of LNCS, pp. 313-324). Berlin: Springer-Verlag.

Schewe, K.-D. & Thalheim, B. (2003). *Structural media types in the development of data-intensive web information systems*.

Schewe, K.-D., Kaschek, R., Matthews, C., & Wallace, C. (2002). Modeling web-based banking systems: Story boarding and user profiling. In H. Mayr & W.-J. Van den Heuvel (Eds.), *Proceedings of the Workshop on Conceptual Modeling Approaches to E-commerce*. Berlin: Springer-Verlag.

Schulz von Thun, F. (2000). *Miteinander reden: Störungen und Klärungen* (Vol. 1). Hamburg, Germany: Rowohlt Taschenbuch Verlag GmbH.

Schwabe, D. & Rossi, G. (1998). An object oriented approach to web-based application design. *TAPOS*, 4(4), 207-225.

Sowa, J. F. (2000). *Knowledge Representation*. Pacific Grove, CA: Brooks/Cole, a division of Thomson Learning.

Sølvberg, A. & Kung, D. (1993). *Information Systems Engineering*. Berlin: Springer-Verlag.

Srinivasa, S. (2001). *A calculus of fixed-points for characterizing interactive behavior of information systems*. PhD thesis. Cottbus, Germany: BTU Cottbus, Fachbereich Informatik.

Stachowiak, H. (1973). *Allgemeine Modelltheorie*. Vienna: Springer-Verlag.

Stachowiak, H. (1983). Erkenntnisstufen zum Systematischen Neopragmatismus und zur Allgemeinen Modelltheorie. In H. Stachowiak (Ed.), *Modelle-*

Konstruktionen der Wirklichkeit (pp. 87-146). Munich: Wilhelm Fink Verlag.

Stachowiak, H. (1992). Erkenntnistheorie, neopragmatische. In H. Seiffert & G. Radnitzky (Eds.), *Handlexikon zur Wissenschaftstheorie* (pp. 64-68). Munich: Deutscher Taschenbuch Verlag GmbH.

Sutton, D. C. (2001). What is knowledge and can it be managed? *European Journal of Information Systems*, 10, 80-88.

Thalheim, B. (2000). *Entity-relationship Modeling*. Berlin: Springer-Verlag.

Thalheim, B. & Düsterhöft, A. (2000). The use of metaphorical structures for internet sites. *Data & Knowledge Engineering*, 35, 61-180.

Wallace, C. (2002). *The impact of the internet on business*. PhD thesis. Palmerston North, NZ: Massey University.

Wallace, C. & Matthews, C. (2002). Communication: Key to success on the web. In H. C. Mayr & W.-J. Van den Heuvel (Eds.), *Proceedings of eCoMo 2002*. Berlin: Springer-Verlag.

Wechler, W. (1992). *Universal Algebra for Computer Scientists*. Berlin: Springer-Verlag.

Wieringa, R. (1990). *Algebraic foundations for dynamic conceptual models*. PhD thesis. Amsterdam: Free University of Amsterdam.

Chapter II

Structural Media Types in the Development of Data-Intensive Web Information Systems

Klaus-Dieter Schewe, Massey University, New Zealand

Bernhard Thalheim, Brandenburgian Technical University, Germany

ABSTRACT

In this chapter, a conceptual modeling approach to the design of web information systems (WIS) will be outlined. The notion of media type is central to this approach. Basically, a media type is defined by a view on an underlying database schema, which allows us to transform the data content of a database into a collection of media objects that represent the data content presented at the web interface. The view is extended by operations and an adaptivity mechanism, which permits the splitting of media objects into several smaller units in order to adapt the WIS to different user preferences, technical environments and communication channels. The information entering the design of media types is extracted from a previous story boarding phase. In consecutive phases, media types have to be extended by style patterns as the next step toward implementation.

INTRODUCTION

In this chapter, we address the conceptual modeling of web information systems following the *abstraction layer model* that was already presented in another chapter of this book (Kaschek et al., 2003). We concentrate only on the structural aspects, i.e., operations will not be discussed. Thus, the central task will be the specification of the data content that is to be made available on the Web. The goal is to provide conceptual means for describing the content in a way that it can be tailored to different users, different end-devices and different communication channels without designing multiple systems.

The chapter will guide the reader through a three-layer model of describing such data. Describing the structure of the data as it is presented on the Web will lead to defining the structure of *media types*. However, these structures will be full of redundancies and, thus, hard to maintain as such. Therefore, the data has to be restructured in order to define a suitable database schema, which defines the second layer. As database design follows different objectives, the content specification should lead to *views*, i.e., transformations, which turn the content of a database into the content of a media type. The third layer is made up by data types, i.e., immutable sets of values that can be used in the description of the other two layers.

Thus, a media type will basically be defined by a view on an underlying database schema, which allows us to transform the data content of a database into a collection of media objects that represents the data content presented at the web interface. Then, we extend media types in a way that they become adaptive to users, devices and channels. The *adaptivity* of a media type permits the automatic splitting of media objects into several smaller units, allowing a user to retrieve information, in a step-by-step fashion, with the most important information presented first. The reader will see two different ways to specify which data should preferably be kept together, and how this will impact on the splitting of media objects.

The result of conceptual modeling will be a *media schema*, i.e., a collection of media types, which adequately represents the data content of the story board. In this chapter, we will formalise this idea of conceptual modeling of web information systems by the use of media types. In the remainder of this chapter, we will first look at related work on conceptual modeling of web information systems. This will provide the reader with the necessary framework of the theory of media types. In a second step, we will illustrate in detail, but quite informally, the central ideas underlying media types. This is to convince the reader about the naturalness of the approach. The third and fourth steps are devoted to introducing, formally, data types, database schemata, and media types on top of such schemata. The adaptivity extension will be introduced last, before we summarise the chapter, put again the media types into the context of the abstraction layer model and discuss follow-on activities, and draw some conclusions. Throughout the chapter, we will use a simple bottleshop example.

RELATED WORK

There are a few major groups working on conceptual modeling of web information systems. One of them is the group around Paolo Atzeni (University of Rome), who defined the ARANEUS framework (Atzeni et al., 1998). This work emphasises that conceptual modeling of web information systems should approach a problem triplet consisting of content, navigation and presentation. This leads to modeling databases, hypertext structures and page layout.

However, the ARANEUS framework does not explicitly separate between the content at the database layer and the web information system layer, i.e., the aspect of dealing with views. The navigation is not treated as an integrated part of such views, but more as an "add-on" to the content specification. Besides navigation, no further operations that could cover the functionality of the system are handled. There is quite a fast drop from conceptual modeling to the presentation, instead, of a more sophisticated work on the presentation and implementation aspects. The conceptual modeling approach is not integrated in an overall methodology, e.g., the aspect of story boarding is completely neglected. Adaptivity, with respect to users, used technology, and channels is not incorporated into the conceptual model.

Of course, the work in the group continues and addresses most of these issues. Also, other authors refer to the ARANEUS framework. The work in Baresi et al. (2000) addresses the integrated design of hypermedia and operations, thus, picking up the functionality aspect but remaining on a very informal level. Similarly, the work in Bonifati et al. (2000) presents a web modeling language WebML and starts to discuss personalisation of web information systems and adaptivity, but, again, is very informal.

Another group working on integrated conceptual modeling approaches is the one around Gustavo Rossi (Argentina) and Daniel Schwabe (Brazil), who developed the OOHDM framework (Schwabe et al., 1996), which is quite similar to the ARANEUS approach. A major difference is that the Roman group has its origins in the area of databases, whereas the Latin American group originally worked in the area of hypertext (Schwabe & Rossi, 1998).

The OOHDM framework (see also Rossi et al., 2000) emphasises an object layer, hypermedia components, i.e., links (discussed in more detail in Rossi et al., 1999) and an interface layer. This is, more or less, the same idea as in the work of the Roman group, except that Rossi and Schwabe explicitly refer to an object oriented approach.

A third group working on integrated conceptual modeling approaches to web information systems is the group around Stefano Ceri and Piero Fraternali (Polytecnico di Milano) (see Ceri et al., 2002 and Fraternali, 1999). The work emphasises a multi-level architecture for the data-driven generation of web sites, thus, taking the view aspect into account. The work addresses the personalisation of web sites by providing user-dependent site views, thus, being aware of the problem of adaptivity. The work emphasises structures, derivation and composition, i.e., views, navigation and presentation, thus, addressing the same problem triplet as the ARANEUS framework. Remaining differences to our work on media types are the fast drop from the conceptual level to the presentation, the treatment of navigation as an "add-on" and not an integrated part of the views, and the missing emphasis on higher-level methods such as story boarding. Besides that, the theory of media types is formally more elaborate.

Our own work started with the Cottbus*net* project, addressing the design and development of a regional information service (see Thalheim, 1997) for a detailed description of the project, its approach, and the achieved results). As a large project arising from practice, all problems had to be addressed at the same time. This even included the demand for adaptivity to different end-devices. The research challenge was to formalise the concepts and to bring them into the form of an integrated design and development methodology for web information systems.

This resulted in a methodology oriented at abstraction layers and the co-design of structure, operations and interfaces (see Schewe & Thalheim 2000). Central to the methodology is the *story boarding* (Feyer et al., 1998; Feyer & Thalheim, 1999). The work in Düsterhöft and Thalheim (2001) contains an explicit language SiteLang for the purpose of story boarding. The work in Schewe et al. (2002) applies story boarding to electronic banking. For the conceptual level, the methodology provides the theory of media types (Feyer et al., 1998; Feyer et al., 2000) — more elaborate work on this subject is contained in Schewe and Thalheim (2000). The theory of media types addresses the objectives described in the previous subsection. It will be described in detail in the remainder of this chapter.

Finally, there is uncountable work on the *eXtensible Markup Language* (XML). The Roman group has investigated how ARANEUS could be supported by XML (Mecca et al., 1999), and we did the same with the theory of media types (Kirchberg et al., 2003). However, as Lobin emphasises in Lobin (2000), XML should be considered as a "bridge" between the areas of databases and the Web; and, as such, is neither completely part of databases nor of web documents. Therefore, it is debatable whether XML should be treated as a new data model or just kept for modeling views.

CONCEPTUAL MODELING OF CONTENT AND ADAPTIVITY

The content aspect concerns the question: Which information should be provided? This is tightly coupled with the problem of designing an adequate database. However, the organisation of data that is presented to the user via the pages in a web information system differs significantly from the organisation of data in the database. We conclude that modeling the content of a web information system has to be addressed on at least two levels: a logical level leading to databases, and a conceptual level leading to the content of pages. Both levels have to be linked together.

Consider an arbitrary web page. Ignore all the fancy graphics, colours, etc., and concentrate on the data content. For instance, consider a page used in a bottleshop site, showing the label on a wine bottle together with a description of the wine. You can describe the content saying that it consists of the picture of the label, the name of the wine, its year, the description of the winery, the used grapes, information about colour, bouquet, acidity level, residue sugar, and many other details. You can write down this description in a formalised way, e.g.:

(name : "Chateau-Lafitte Grand Crus", picture : "pic4711.gif", year : 1998, winery : (name : "Chateau Lafitte", region : "Hérault", country : "France", address : "..."), composition : { (grape : "Merlot", percentage : 65), ...}, ...)

The components of this complex value need not only be strings, tuples, numbers, etc. They can be also complex values, such as tuples, sets, or URLs representing links to other pages.

The URL associated with the arbitrary web page can be considered as an abstract identifier associated with this complex value. Thus, an adequate abstract description would be a pair (u, v), where u is a URL and v is a complex value, as shown above. We decide to call such a pair a *media object*. The term 'object' is used because pairs constructed out of an abstract identifier and a complex value are called 'objects' in the context of object oriented databases. Here, they refer to 'media,' as their collection describes the content of the whole web information system as some kind of electronic media.

Content Types of Media Types

The example suggests that several raw media objects share the same structure. Continuing the bottleshop example, there may be lots of different wines but, in all cases, the structure of the complex value would almost look the same. *Classification abstraction* means to describe the common structure of these values. Formally, we can introduce data types, such as *STRING* for character strings, *NAT* for natural numbers, *DATE* for dates, etc. We may even have composed types, such as *ADDRESS*. In general, we may think of a data type as providing us with a set of values. Thus, the wines in the bottleshop examples could be described by the following expression:

> (name : *STRING*, picture : *PIC*, year : *NAT*, winery : (name : *STRING*, region : *STRING*, country : *STRING*, address : *ADDRESS*), composition : { (grape : *STRING*, percentage : *NAT*) }, …)

We have taken the freedom to assume that we may use a data type *PIC* for pictures. We may also assume to be given a type *URL* for all the possible URLs. This data type also uses the notation (…) for tuple types, i.e., all possible values are tuples, and { … } for set types, i.e., all possible values are sets.

We call an expression as the one above a *content type*. Content types are a relevant part of *media types*. In our example, we would define a media type with the name WINE and specify that the expression above is its content type. In general, every data type can become the *content type of a media type*. Thus, if M denotes a media type, the *media objects of type M* are pairs (u, v), consisting of a value u of type *URL* and a value v of the content type of M. We call u the *URL of the media object* and v its *content value*.

For example, if we define the content type of a media type WINE as above, a media object of type WINE could be:

("www.bottleshop.co.nz/wine/wine_tmp234",(name: "Chateau-Lafitte Grand Crus", picture: "pic4711.gif", year: 1998, winery: (name: "Chateau Lafitte", region: "Hérault", country: "France", address: "..."), composition : { (grape: "Merlot", percentage: 65), ... }, ...))

taking a "virtual" URL and the complex value that we started with.

A little subtlety comes in here, which makes the definition still a bit more complicated. When a value of type *URL* appears inside the content value *v*, this may be a URL somewhere outside the Web Information System that we want to develop. However, in the case where the URL is an internal one, it will be the URL of a media object, say of type *M′*. For instance, for a wine, i.e., a media object of type WINE, the description of the winery may involve a history component. As this history can be a long structured text on its own, we may separate it from the wine and place it on a separate page that is reachable by a navigation link. However, we would always get a link to (the URL of) a media object of type WINERY_HISTORY.

Therefore, we extend content types in such a way that, instead of the type *URL*, we may also use *links* $\ell: M′$, with a unique link name ℓ and a name of a media type *M′*. In our WINE example, the content type would change to

(name : *STRING*, picture : *PIC*, year : *NAT*, winery : (name : *STRING*, region : *STRING*, country : *STRING*, address : *ADDRESS*, history : WINERY_HISTORY), composition: { (grape: *STRING*, percentage: *NAT*) }, ...)

We used a bit of meta-level syntax here: small capitals are used for the names of media types, italic letters for data types, and normal letters for link names and other labels.

In order to obtain a media object, we would have to replace the links $\ell: M′$ by the data type *URL* first. However, the link $\ell: M′$ would force us to use only values of type URL that are URLs of the media type *M′*.

In summary, the content of a web page may be described as a complex value. Combining a complex value with the URL for the web page forms a media object. Several media objects may share the same structure; in other words, the complex values share the same structure. A content type is the generic expression capturing the structure of these complex values.

Database Types

Media objects support an individual user and only provide a section of the data of the system. The question arises how the data can be described globally. In fact, we would need to combine all the content types. For instance, in the bottleshop example we will not only have the content types of media types WINE and WINERY_HISTORY. There may also be a PRICE_LIST or an OFFER. Some of the data that we use in media objects of type WINE may also appear in media objects of type OFFER, e.g., the information about the winery or the grapes. Similarly, we could have added the price of a wine (for a bottle or a case) to the media object of type WINE.

This indicates that it is not the best idea to directly use the content types of the media types for global data storage because this may lead to redundancy. Instead, we reorganise the global data content and set up a *database*. Designing the schema for such a database underlies completely different quality criteria. For instance, for databases we would like to avoid redundancies as much as possible. We would also have to pay much attention to providing fast and concurrent access to the data.

Therefore, we use a separate layer defined by *database types*. Thus, we obtain a description of the static components on at least two layers: the global or database layer, and the local or media type layer. More than that, we even use a three layer approach consisting of a layer of data types, a layer of database types, and a layer of raw media types.

The Data Type Layer

The first layer is defined by *data types*, which define sets of possible values for using them in content types and database types. We have already seen examples of such data types, which are either base types such as *STRING*, *NAT*, *URL*, etc., or complex types, composed of base types and other complex types such as tuple or set types. The example content type that we have seen already used such tuple and set types. Tuple types (also called record types) can be written using the notation $(a_1 : t_1, ..., a_n : t_n)$ with arbitrarily chosen labels $a_1 ..., a_n$ and data type names, $t_1, ..., t_n$. Set types can be written using the notation $\{t\}$. In the cases of tuple and set types, we call $t_1, ..., t_n$ (or t, respectively) the component types of the complex type.

To repeat, the content type of raw media type WINE was a tuple type

(name : *STRING*, picture : *PIC*, year : *NAT*, winery : (name : *STRING*, region : *STRING*, country : *STRING*, address : *ADDRESS*, history

:WINERY_HISTORY), composition : { (grape : *STRING*, percentage : *NAT*), ... }, ...)

with the labels a_1 = name, a_2 = picture, a_3 = year, a_4 = winery, a_5 = composition, etc., and the component types $t_1 = STRING$, $t_2 = PIC$, $t_3 = NAT$, t_4 = (name: ...), $t_5 = \{(...)\}$, etc. The component type t_4 is, again, a tuple type; the component type t_5 is a set type, which has a tuple type as its component type, etc. We see that, with composed data types, we can have any depth of nesting.

We call the collection of all possible data types a *type system*. There are lots of choices for type systems. Which one is used in a particular application depends on the needs of the application and on the systems that are available. For our purposes here, the theory of media types, we may take the viewpoint that any type system will work as long as one of its base types is the data type *URL*.

The Database Type Layer

The second layer is defined by *database types* over the type system. These database types are, more or less, defined in the same way as the content types. For instance, we may define a database type as:

(name : *STRING*, year : *CARD*, composition : { (grape : *STRING*, percentage : *CARD*) }, colour : *STRING*, bouquet : *STRING*, acidity : *STRING*, sugar : *DECIMAL*)

In particular, they may already include links. However, relational database systems would not be able to support such links. In general, the format of database types depends on the *data model* that has been chosen for the application.

The Media Type Layer

The third layer is defined by the *media types* which we have already discussed above. Remaining questions are: how these media types differ from the database types and how they are connected to the database types.

We already stated that, when we look at the content types of media types only, there is no formal difference between such content types and database types. The major difference concerns their purpose and usage. The database types are used to represent the global data content of the WIS. The collection of all the database types — this is what we call a *database schema* — is organised in such a way that the desirable quality criteria for databases, such as fast access, redundancy freeness, etc., can be met, whereas the content types of media types are organised in a way that the information needs of the users who navigate through the WIS are met. Redundancy among content types is not only unavoidable, it is even intended.

Furthermore, links may already exist between database types, but this need not be the case. For the media types, however, the links are an important means to represent the navigation structure of the WIS. Thus, links between media types are unavoidable and intended.

Finally, media types are not independent from the database types. The information represented by the content types is already present in the database schema. Therefore, we need transformations from the database schema to the content types of the raw media types. Such transformations are called *views*.

Therefore, we have to add a description of the transformation from the database schema to the content type. Such a transformation is called a *query*. In fact, a view is given by an input database schema, an output database schema — in our case the content type — and a query, which transforms a database over the input schema into a database over the output schema. In general, a query could be any such (computable) transformation. In most cases, however, the query languages that come with the used data model determine which queries can be used. In doing so, they limit the expressiveness of the queries.

Adaptivity

Adaptivity, in general, deals with the ability of a system to adapt itself to external needs. We distinguish between three different lines of adaptivity.

- Adaptivity to the user deals with needs arising from different users. Users may prefer to receive information in a dense or sparse form. In the former case, a larger portion of information would be transmitted to the user, whereas, in the latter case, the information would be delivered step by step. Furthermore, it should be possible to provide different levels of detail and let the user switch between these levels.

  For instance, taking up again the example of wines, a user may prefer to see the information about a wine together with detailed information about the grapes or the winery. Another user may prefer to see a list of several wines at a time, each coupled with only rough information about name, year, grapes.

- Adaptivity to the technical environment copes with technical restrictions of end-devices. For instance, if mobile end-devices with small screens or TV-based end-devices are to be supported, it would, nevertheless, be desirable to have only one conceptual description, and to tailor the media objects to the specific needs of the technical environment only when these needs arise.

- Adaptivity to the communication channel deals with adaptation to needs arising from various communication channels. As users do not want to wait too long for the information to be transferred, a restricted channel capacity should imply a step-by-step delivery of the information.

Structural media types deal with adaptivity by extending the definition of media types by cohesion, which allows a controlled form of information loss. On the level of content types, we determine which data should preferably be kept together. In all cases where user preferences or technical constraints force the information to be split, the split will be made in such a way that data that is to be kept together will be kept together. The lost information will become available in a follow-on step.

DATABASE TYPES AND DATA TYPES

In this section, we start describing media types in a more formal way. We concentrate first on the data type and the database layer, that are used to define media types. Recall that the data type layer introduces data types, i.e., sets of possible values, whereas the database layer introduces database types, which define the structure of the possible databases.

This section can be treated as a short introduction to conceptual data modeling. In particular, if the central notions of this section, such as database schema, are known, it is possible to skip this section and proceed directly with the introduction of media types in the next section.

Our presentation in this section will introduce a data model that is quite close to the Entity-Relationship model. It lies somewhere between the basic Entity-Relationship model and the Higher-order Entity-Relationship model (Thalheim, 2000). Recall from the introduction above that structural media types could take any other data model. The choice of data model for this section is mainly due to the fact that its structural units leave only a small gap between the data model and the media types.

Data Types

Data types are used to classify values. In general, types are used for classification. Thus, the name "data type" suggests that we classify data. However, in our context, the term "data" is used for several quite different purposes. We should distinguish between the data treated by data types, the data treated by database types, and the data treated by media types. Therefore, in the context of data types, we talk of *values*; in the context of databases, we will talk of *objects*; and in the context of media types, we will talk about *media objects*.

Thus, a data type gives some notation for a set of values. To be precise, data types should also provide the operations that can be applied to these values. For the moment, these operations are not important for us, so we will ignore them. A collection of data types that is defined by some syntax is called a *type system*. If we use abstract syntax, we can define a type system by writing:

$$t = b \mid (a_1 : t_1, \ldots, a_n : t_n) \mid \{t\} \mid [t] \mid (a_1 : t_1) \uplus \cdots \uplus (a_n : t_n)$$

This description of syntax needs some further explanation. We use the symbol b to represent an arbitrary collection of *base types*, such as the following types:

- *CARD* for non-negative integers, *INT* for integers,
- *CHAR* for characters, *STRING* for character strings,
- *DATE* for date values, *BOOL* for truth values,
- *URL* for URL-addresses, *MAIL* for e-mail-addresses, *OK* for a single value *ok*, etc.

Thus, the definition of the type system above states that a type t is either a base type or has one of the following four forms:

- We can have $t = (a_1: t_1, \ldots, a_n : t_n)$ with arbitrary, pairwise different labels $a_1, \ldots, a_n$ and types $t_1, \ldots, t_n$. Such a type is called a *tuple type*. The types $t_1, \ldots, t_n$ used to define the tuple type are called the *component types* of the tuple type. The intention of a tuple type is to provide a set of tuple values, each of which has the form $(a_1: v_1, \ldots, a_n :v_n)$, using the labels $a_1, \ldots, a_n$ and values v_1 of type t_1, v_2 of type t_2, etc.
- We can have $t = \{t'\}$ with another type t'. Such a type is called a *set type*. The intention of a set type is to provide a set of values, each of which is itself a finite set $\{v_1, \ldots, v_n\}$, with values $v_1, \ldots, v_n$ of type t'.
- Similarly, we can have $t = [t']$ with another type t'. Such a type is called a *list type*. The intention of a list type is to provide a set of values, each of which is a finite, ordered list $[v_1, \ldots, v_n]$, with values $v_1, \ldots, v_n$ of type t'.
- Finally, we can have $t = (a_1: t_1) \uplus \cdots \uplus (a_n : t_n)$ with arbitrary, pairwise different labels $a_1, \ldots, a_n$ and types $t_1, \ldots, t_n$. Such a type is called a *union*

type. The types $t_1, \ldots, t_n$ used to define the union type are called the *component types* of the union type. The intention of a union type is to provide a set of values, each of which has the form $(a_i : v_i)$, using one of the labels $a_1, \ldots, a_n$ and values v_1 of type t_1, v_2 of type t_2, etc.

We say that $(\cdots)$, $\{\cdot\}$ and $[\cdot]$ and $\cdots \uplus \ldots$ are *constructors* for records, sets, lists and unions.

Example 1. Define a data type *NAME* by:

$NAME = (\text{first\_names} : [STRING], \text{middle\_initial} : (y : CHAR) \uplus (n : OK),$
$\qquad\qquad \text{titles} : \{STRING\}, \text{family\_name} : STRING).$

This is a tuple type with four components according to the following intention:
- The first component gives a list of character strings for the first names.
- The second component is either a single character for a middle initial or *ok*, which indicates that there is no middle initial.
- The third component gives a set of character strings for titles.
- The last component is a single character string for the family name.

Thus, possible values of type *NAME* would be:

(first_names : ["George", "Francis", "Leopold"], middle_initial : (n : *ok*),
titles : { "Professor", "Sir"}, family_name : "Stocker")

and

(first_names : ["Harry"], middle_initial : (y : 'F'), titles : { },
family_name : "Rugger").

Let us now define the semantics of data types, i.e. we will associate with each data type t a set $dom(t)$ of values, called *values of type t*. In the definition of data types, and in Example 1, we already gave a glimpse of what the definition of semantics will look like.

We follow the inductive definition of data types to define the set $dom(t)$ of values of type t as follows:

- For a base type t, we obtain
  - $dom(CARD) = \mathbb{N} = \{0, 1, 2, \ldots\}$ is the set of natural numbers.
  - $dom(INT) = \mathbb{Z} = \{0, 1, -1, 2, -2 \ldots\}$ is the set of integers.
  - $dom(CHAR) = \{A, a, B, b, \ldots\}$ is a fixed set of characters.
  - $dom(BOOL) = \{\mathbf{T}, \mathbf{F}\}$ is the set of Boolean truth values.
  - $dom(OK) = \{ok\}$.
  - $dom(DATE) = \{dd\text{-}mm\text{-}yyyy \mid d, m, y \in \{0, 1, \ldots, 9\}\}$ is the set of all date values.
  - $dom(STRING) = dom(CHAR)^* = \{a_1 \ldots a_n \mid n \in \mathbb{N}, a_i \in dom(CHAR)\}$ is the set of all character strings over $\{A, a, B, b, \ldots\}$.
  - $dom(MAIL)$ is the set of all syntactically valid mail addresses.
  - $dom(URL)$ is the set of all syntactically valid URLs.
  - If further base types are defined, we associate with them a fixed set of values in the same way.
- $dom((a_1 : t_1, \ldots, a_n : t_n)) = \{(a_1 : v_1, \ldots, a_n : v_n) \mid v_i \in dom(t_i)$ for all $i = 1, \ldots, n\}$ is the set of n-tuples with component values in $dom(t_i)$ for $i = 1, \ldots, n$.
- $dom(\{t\}) = \{A \in P(dom(t)) \mid |A| < \infty\}$ is the set of all finite subsets of $(dom(t)$. Thus, we have $dom(t) = \{\{v_1, \ldots, v_k\} \mid k \in \mathbb{N}$ and $v_i \in dom(t)$ for all $i = 1, \ldots, k\}$
- Similarly, $dom([t]) = \{[v_1, \ldots, v_k] \mid k \in \mathbb{N}$ and $v_i \in dom(t)$ for all $i = 1, \ldots, k\}$ is the set of all finite lists with elements in $dom(t)$.
- $dom((a_1 : t_1) \uplus \cdots \uplus (a_n : t_n)) = \{(a_1 : v_1) \mid v_1 \in dom(t_1)\} \cup \cdots \cup \{(a_n : v_n) \mid v_n \in dom(t_n)\}$ is the *disjoint union* of the sets $dom(t_i)$ $(i = 1, \ldots, n)$, i.e. elements in $dom(t_i)$ are labeled with a_i before the union is built.

Example 2. Let us continue Example 1 and consider again the data type:

$NAME = (\text{first\_names} : [STRING], \text{middle\_initial} : (y : CHAR) \uplus (n : OK),$
$\qquad \text{titles} : \{STRING\}, \text{family\_name} : STRING).$

As the outermost constructor is the tuple type constructor, each value in $dom(NAME)$ is a tuple of the form:

$(\text{first\_names} : v_1, \text{middle\_initial} : v_2, \text{titles} : v_3, \text{family\_name} : v_4).$

Here, v_1 must be a value of type $[STRING]$, i.e. is a finite list of strings: $v_1 = [v_{11}, v_{12}, \ldots, v_{1k}]$ with all $v_{1i} \in dom(STRING)$. v_2 must be a value of type $(y$

: $CHAR$) $\uplus$ (n : OK), so it is either (y : v_2) with a value $v_2 \in dom(CHAR)$ or (n : ok). v_3 is a value of type {$STRING$}, i.e., it is a finite set of strings: $v_3 = \{\, v_{31}, v_{32}, \ldots, v_{3\ell}\,\}$ with all $v_{3i} \in dom(STRING)$. Finally, v_4 is a character string.

Database Types

We now proceed with the second layer, which deals with database types and database schemata. Look again at the bottleshop example that we used so far. A basic unit of information in this example is given by the wines. So, we may describe a wine by its name, its year, the used grapes, information about colour, bouquet, acidity level, and residue sugar. Assume that we do not have to provide further details. We may want to keep the description of the winery separate, but it is not intended to provide any details about grapes. So, we create *attribute names* such as name, year, composition, colour, bouquet, acidity and sugar. These attributes are sufficient to describe wines, provided that, for each of these attributes, we declare a data type, which will describe the possible values for this attribute.

Thus, a first definition would be the following:

*A **database type of level** 0 has a name* E *and is described by a finite set* attr (E)={ a_1, ..., a_m } *of attributes. Each attribute* a_i *is associated with a data type* type(a_i).

We will extend this definition below by adding key attributes.

Example 3. Taking the example of wines from above, we define a database type with the name WINE and the attribute set

attr(WINE)={name, year, composition, colour, bouquet, acidity, sugar}.

Associated data types could be *type*(name) = *STRING*, *type*(year) = *CARD*, *type*(colour) = *STRING*, *type*(bouquet) = *STRING*, *type*(acidity) = *STRING*, *type*(sugar) = *DECIMAL*, and *type*(composition) = {(grape : *STRING*, percentage : *CARD*)}. Thus, we would describe an *object* of type WINE by a combination of values for all these types or, equivalently, by a single value of the following tuple type:

(name : *STRING*, year : *CARD*, composition : { (grape : *STRING*, percentage : *CARD*) }, colour : *STRING*, bouquet : *STRING*, acidity : *STRING*, sugar : *DECIMAL*)

using the attribute names of the database type as labels.

Similarly, we can define a database type WINERY with attributes name, founded, owners, address, and maybe more. We omit the details of such a type.

Besides database types of level 0, we may also define database types on higher levels. For instance, in the bottleshop example, we may relate wines with wineries that produce them. In this case, the entity types WINE and WINERY would become components of a new type PRODUCER. Such a type is a *database type of level k*, with $k-1$ being the maximum of the levels of the component types. Of course, we may extend the higher-level database type by adding attributes such as start_date, end_date, and maybe others.

A *database type of level k* has a name E and consists of:

- a set $comp(E) = \{ r_1 : E_1 ,..., r_n : E_n \}$ of components with pairwise different role names r_i and names E_i of database types,
- a set $attr(E) = \{a_1,..., a_m\}$ of attributes, each associated with a data type $type(a_i)$, and
- a key $id(E) \subseteq comp(E) \cup attr(E)$,

such that the database types $E_i \in S$ are all on levels lower than k, with at least one database type of level exactly $k-1$.

Note that the role names are only needed to allow the same database type to appear more than once as a component of another database type. Obviously, in this case, the occurrences have to be distinguished by using different role names.

Example 4. Let us complete the description of a relationship type PRODUCER. We define this type by the set of components $comp(\text{PRODUCER}) = \{\text{of} : \text{WINE}, \text{by} : \text{WINERY}\}$ and the set of attributes $attr(\text{PRODUCER}) = \{\text{start\_date}, \text{end\_date}\}$. The associated types can be $type(\text{start\_date}) = DATE$ and $type(\text{end\_date}) = (\text{f} : DATE) \uplus (\text{nf} : OK)$.

In Example 3, we have seen that we can associate a single data type with a database type of level 0 by turning the attribute names into labels of a tuple type. The question is how this can be generalised to database types on higher levels. The easiest solution would be to treat the attributes in the same way as database types of level 0, and to use the role names also as labels, using the data types associated with the lower level database types as components. For instance, for the database type PRODUCER in Example 4, we would obtain the data type:

(of : t_{WINE}, by : t_{WINERY}, start_date : *DATE*, end_date : (f : *DATE*) ⊎ (nf : *OK*)),

with the component type t_{WINE} defined in Example 3, and a component type t_{WINERY} defined elsewhere. Values of this type would be called *objects* of type PRODUCER.

Though this approach is formally correct, it has certain disadvantages, as the resulting data types will be quite big and, in each value, we would have to repeat values that have been described on lower levels. Instead of this, we will exploit the keys, i.e., combinations of components and attributes that uniquely identify objects.

In the following, we often write $E = (\{ r_1 : E_1, \ldots, r_n : E_n \}, \{ a_1, \ldots, a_m \}, id(E))$ to denote a database type. The first component in this triple is the component set *comp(E)*. The second component is the attribute set *attr(E)*. The third component is the key *id(E)*.

We use this notation to associate two data types with each database type *E*. These data types are called the *associated data type* of *E* and the *associated key type* of *E*. These types are defined as follows:

*   The *associated data type* of *E*, denoted as type(*E*), is
    $(r_1:$ key-type(E_1), …, $r_n :$ key-type(E_n), $a_1: type(a_1)$, …, $a_m : type(a_m))$.
*   The *associated key type* of *E*, denoted as key-type(*E*), is defined analogously with the difference that only those r_i and a_j are considered that occur in *id(E)*.

In particular, if we have a database type *E* of level 0, then *comp(E)* is the empty set. This implies that there will be no labels r_i in type(*E*) nor in key-type(*E*).

Example 5. In Example 3, we have seen a database type of level 0. The following definition extends this database type by a key:

WINE = ({ }, {name, year, composition, colour, bouquet, acidity, sugar}, {name, year}).

We keep the associated data types:

type(name)	=	*STRING*,
type(year)	=	*CARD*,
type(composition)	=	{(grape : *STRING*, percentage : *CARD*)},
type(colour)	=	*STRING*,
type(bouquet)	=	*STRING*,
type(acidity)	=	*STRING*,
type(sugar)	=	*DECIMAL*.

So, as we have already seen in Example 3, the associated data type type(WINE) would be the data type:

(name : *STRING*, year : *CARD*, composition : { (grape : *STRING*, percentage : *CARD*) }, colour : *STRING*, bouquet : *STRING*, acidity : *STRING*, sugar : *DECIMAL*).

The associated key type key-type(WINE) would be the data type:

(name : *STRING*, year : *CARD*).

In Example 4, we discussed a database type PRODUCER of level 1. We extend this definition by a key, which leads to:

PRODUCER = ({of : WINE, by : WINERY}, {start_date, end_date}, {of : WINE, by : WINERY, start_date}.

We keep the same associated data types:

type(start_date)	=	*DATE*,
type(end_date)	=	(f : *DATE*) ⊎ (nf : *OK*).

Then, the associated data type and the associated key type of the database type PRODUCER are:

(of : (name : *STRING*, year : *CARD*), by : ..., start_date : *DATE*, end_date : (f : *DATE*) ⊎ (nf : *OK*)), and

$$(of: (name: STRING, year: CARD), by: \ldots, start\_date: DATE),$$

respectively. In both data types, the dots have to be replaced by the associated key type key-type(WINERY). As we omitted the definition of the database type WINERY, we have to omit the replacement of these dots by a real data type, too.

Cluster Types

Before we introduce database schemata and databases, we still have to discuss one further extension. This will be the introduction of so-called cluster types. In order to get started, look again at Example 5, in which we presented a database type PRODUCER of level 1. The component database types of PRODUCER were the types WINE and WINERY. Now, assume that our bottleshop also offers beers, and these beers are produced by breweries. So, we would add two other database types of level 0: BEER and BREWERY. We can now extend the of-component in PRODUCER in such a way that it refers to WINE or BEER. In the same way, we could change the by-component so that it refers to WINERY or BREWERY. In order to do so, replace the of-component in PRODUCER by a new type BEVERAGE, and the by-component by a new type COMPANY, while defining BEVERAGE by the "disjoint union" of WINE and BEER, and COMPANY by the "disjoint union" of WINERY and BREWERY. Such disjoint unions are defined by cluster types.

A *cluster type of level k*, written $E = (id_1 : E_1) \oplus \cdots \oplus (id_n : E_n)$, has a name E and consists of a non-empty sequence of components $E_1, \ldots, E_n$, which can be database types or cluster types, with pairwise different component identifiers id_i, such that the level k is the maximum of the levels of the E_i.

Example 6. Formalising our motivating example from above we define the two cluster types BEVERAGE $= (w : WINE) \oplus (b : BEER)$ and COMPANY $= (w : WINERY) \oplus (b : BREWERY)$ of level 0.

Now we can extend the definition of associated data types and associated key types to cluster types. According to the motivation above, it should not be surprising to see that we now use union types. Therefore, let $E = (id_1 : E_1) \oplus \cdots \oplus$

$(id_n : E_n)$ be a cluster type. The associated data type type(E) and the associated key type key-type(E) are defined as follows:

$$\text{type}(E) = \text{key-type}(E) = (id_1 : \text{key-type}(E_1)) \; \square \; \cdots \; \square \; (id_n : \text{key-type}(E_n)).$$

Database Schemata and Databases

Let us now conclude the presentation of the global database layer by defining database schemata. A database schema is simply a collection of database and cluster types. Of course, if E_i is a component of a database or cluster type E, and E is defined in the schema, then E_i must also be defined in the schema. Formally, we can define a database schema as follows:

A *database schema* **S** is a set of database types and cluster types satisfying the following two conditions:

*   If $E \in$ **S** is a database type, then, for all components $r_i : E_i \in comp(E)$, we must also have $E_i \in$ **S**.
*   If $E = E_1 \oplus \cdots \oplus E_k$ is a cluster type in **S**, then, for all components $E_i (i=1,\ldots,k)$, we must also have $E_i \in$ **S**.

We define the semantics of database schemata by the collection of possible *databases* by the database schema. Thus, let **S** be a database schema. For each database or cluster type $E \in$ **S**, we have defined an associated data type type(E) and an associated key type key-type(E). As these two are indeed data types, they define fixed sets of values, which we call the set of *objects of type E* and the set of *keys of type E*, respectively:

$$\text{Obj}(E) = dom(\text{type}(E)) \quad \text{and} \quad \text{Key}(E) = dom(\text{key-type}(E))$$

As the key $id(E)$ in a database type E is a subset of $comp(E) \cup attr(E)$, each object of type E can be projected to a key of type E. Let $O_{[\text{key-type}(E)]} \in \text{Key}(E)$ denote the projection of the object $O \in \text{Obj}(E)$ to the value of its key. For a cluster type E each object O of type E, we have $O_{[\text{key-type}(E)]} = O$. We use the sets of objects and keys for the database and cluster types $E \in$ **S** to define a *database over* **S** as follows:

A *database db over* **S** assigns to each database or cluster type $E \in$ **S** a finite set $db(E) \subseteq \text{Obj}(E)$ of objects of type E such that the following conditions are satisfied:

1. Key values are unique, i.e., there cannot be two different $O_1, O_2 \in db(E)$ with $O_{1[\text{key-type}(E)]} \neq O_{2[\text{key-type}(E)]}$.

2. Component values exist in the database, i.e., for each $O \in db(E)$ and each $r:E' \in comp(E)$, there must exist some $O' \in db(E')$, such that $r:O'_{[\text{key-type}(E')]}$ is part of O.

3. Clusters are disjoint unions, i.e., for a cluster $E = (id_1 : E_1) \oplus \cdots \oplus (id_n : E_n)$, we obtain $db(E) = \{ (id_i : O_{i[\text{key-type}(E_i)]}) \mid O_i \in db(E_i) \text{ and } i \in \{1, \ldots, n\} \}$.

Finally, let us briefly introduce a graphical representation for database schemata, which we call a *(database) schema diagram*:

- We use rectangles to represent database types on level 0 — in this case, we always have $comp(E) = \{\}$ — and place the name of the type inside the rectangle.
- We use diamonds to represent database types on higher levels — in this case, we always have $comp(E) \neq \{\}$ — and place the name of the type inside the diamond.
- We use arrows from a type to all its component types, and attach the role names to these arrows.
- We use $\oplus$ to represent cluster types, and arrows to the components of the cluster type.
- We attach attributes directly to the rectangles or diamonds.
- We underline the attributes in the key, and mark the arrows corresponding to components in the key with a dot.

If schema diagrams tend to become large, we usually omit the attribute names. Sometimes we even drop the names of the cluster types.

Example 7. Let us consider an example database schema for a bottleshop application illustrated in Figure 1. A bottleshop is to deliver wines, beers, juices and other soft drinks, and hard alcoholics drinks such as Cognac, Grappa, Scotch and Irish Whiskey. The sales are to be supported by a web information system. The Web Information System shall provide a catalogue containing the offered products, as well as occasional special offers. Additional information about wines, grapes, vineyards (also for Cognac, Grappa, Calvados and Whiskey) shall be provided, as well. The system must offer information about the shop itself, historical and actual information about certain grapes, wine producers, etc. The system should

Figure 1: Schema Diagram of the Example Database Schema

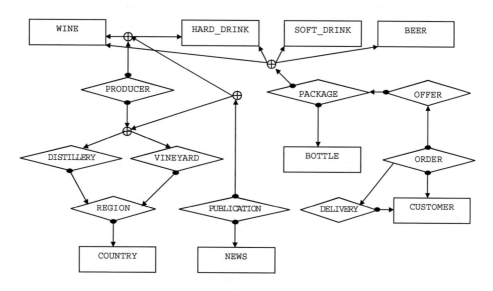

also provide special information about best sellers, new products, etc. Comments from (hopefully pleased) clients shall be made available on the Web.

QUERIES AND STRUCTURAL MEDIA TYPES

In this section, we address the layer of media types. The intention behind the media types is to provide a local view on the data that are stored in the underlying database. The emphasis of this layer is to specify data as they are to appear on web pages, however, without any consideration of how the data should be presented. Thus, the media types are used to structure data according to a usage perspective rather than a storage perspective.

Formally, a structural media type is defined by a *content type* and a *defining query*. There is no big, formal difference between content types of structural media types and database types, except that content types should support links, whereas the existence of links in database types depends on the data model. The major difference is given by the fact that structural media types need a defining query which links the media type with an underlying database schema. If Q is the defining query of a structural media type M, it may be executed on databases *db* over the underlying database schema S. The query will result in the set of media objects of type M. Of course, if databases are updated, the database *db* and consequently also the set of media objects changes.

In the following, we will first briefly discuss queries. It is beyond the scope of this chapter to go into details of query languages, but we will emphasise the need and difficulty of creating links (Schewe, 2001). In fact, each data model requires its own query languages, and the theory of media types can be based on any data model. In a second step, we will then give a formal definition of structural media types and media objects.

Queries

Let us consider queries. In general, a *query* is a transformation from one database schema into another one. In most cases, the target schema of such a transformation is significantly simpler than the source schema.

For instance, consider the database schema from the bottleshop example which we developed in the previous section. Suppose we are given a database *db* over this schema, i.e. we have information about wines, producers, vineyards, etc. Suppose we want to have a list of New Zealand wines from 1998 on, with at least 30% Cabernet Sauvignon, together with some information about the vineyard and the region. In this case, we define a target database schema with exactly one database type NZ_WINE. This database type — which is, of course, a database type of level 0 — can be defined as follows:

NZ_WINE   = ({ }, {name, year, composition, vineyard, owners, since,
                   history, region, climate}, {name, year}).

The data types of the attributes can be defined as follows:

type(name)	=	*STRING*
type(year)	=	*CARD*
type(composition)	=	$\{(\text{grape} : STRING, \text{percentage} : CARD)\}$
type(vineyard)	=	*STRING*
type(owners)	=	$\{STRING\}$
type(since)	=	*DATE*
type(history)	=	*STRING*
type(region)	=	*STRING*
type(climate)	=	*STRING*

Formally, a query can be defined as follows:

*A **query** Q consists of a source database schema* src(Q), *a target database schema* trgt(Q), *and a map* q(Q), *which takes as its input all databases over* src(Q) *and produces databases over* trgt(Q).

How would we process such a query? Of course, we can only sketch an idea of query processing. Actually, techniques used in query processing differ significantly from this simple outline here, but we are only interested in getting an idea of the database transformation, not of its technical realisation. In our example query looking for New Zealand wines, we could take a database *db* over the source schema, i.e., the database schema from the previous section. The set *db*(WINE) contains finitely many values of type *type*(WINE), which is a tuple type with labels name, year, composition, colour, bouquet, acidity and sugar. First, we use a *projection*, i.e., we simply "forget" the last four components. Each tuple will be reduced to a tuple of a tuple type containing only the labels name, year and composition.

Looking into the details of the component labeled by 'composition,' we know that we must have a set of pairs, the first component of which is labeled by grape, the second one by percentage. We only keep those tuples, where this set contains a pair ("Cabernet Sauvignon", x) with a value $x \geq 30$. This is called a *selection*. Similarly, we only keep tuples where the value y of the year component satisfies $y \geq 1998$. In doing this, we would already obtain the wines from 1998 on with at least 30% Cabernet Sauvignon.

However, we want to have New Zealand wines only, and for these we demand information about the vineyard and the region. Therefore, we have to look at the cluster BEVERAGE_H and the database type PRODUCER. We only keep those tuples where the values for name and wine appear as a pair labeled by *b* in the component labeled by *of* in objects in *db*(PRODUCER). However, as we want to get vineyards and not distilleries, we only consider those objects in *db*(PRODUCER) with a *by*-component labeled by *v*. Using this component, we obtain objects of type VINEYARD. We rename the label name in these objects to vineyard, in order to avoid mixing up the name of wines with vineyard names, and we forget the size and grapes components. Adding the remaining components to the tuples gives new tuples with components name, year, composition, vineyard, owners, since, history, and *in*.

The latter one can be used for another join with *db*(REGION). Again, in this way we obtain the name component of the region, which we rename to region, the climate component, the wines component, which we forget, and the specialities component, which we forget, as well. The *in*-component finally leads to *db*(COUNTRY). We only keep tuples where the join gives a value "NZ" for the code component.

This rough sketch of query processing shows how a database over the source schema can be transformed into a database over the target schema. The query may have produced a tuple such as the following:

> (name : "Otago Red", year : 2000, composition : { (grape : "Cabernet Sauvignon", percentage : 65), (grape : "Malbec", percentage : 35) }, vineyard : "Martha's Vineyard", owners : { "Rudi Müller", "Martha Thurgau" }, since : 1967, history : "Once upon a time …'', region : "Otago", climate : "The climate in Otago …").

Now, recall that a media object is not only a complex value, but it is a pair (u, v), with a value u of type *URL* and a complex value v. Queries, as we discussed them above, would only result in a set of objects of the database types in the target database schema. Thus, instead of obtaining the value above, we would also like to obtain a URL, or at least a unique identifier, which could later be replaced by an actual URL. As such URLs are not stored in the database, they have to be created by processing the query.

This implies requiring that the query language should allow the creation of URLs and links. We call this property *create facility* (see, e.g., Abiteboul et al., 2000, Chapter 6). In terms of our sketch of query processing, this simply means that, at any stage, we may introduce URLs by transforming a set $\{v_1, …, v_m\}$ or list $[v_1, …, v_m]$ of values into a set $\{(u_1, v_1), …, (u_m, v_m)\}$ or list $[(u_1, v_1), …, (u_m, v_m)]$ of pairs, with new values u_i of type *URL*, respectively, or simply by transforming a value v of any type into a pair (u, v) with a value u of type *URL*.

Note that once we process a query on a database *db*, we may add the result to the database. Processing further queries may then also include the newly created URLs into their results. In this way, navigation structures can be set up.

Structural Media Types

We are now ready to formally round up this section and define structural media types. We first need an exact definition of a content type. Recall that a content type is an extended data type, in which the place of a base type may be occupied by a pair $\ell : M'$, with some label ℓ and a name M' of a media type

— in fact, this means to choose any name.

Thus, using abstract syntax again (as we did for data types **on page 45**), we can define the *system of content types* by writing:

$$ct = b \mid (a_1 : ct_1, \ldots, a_n : ct_n) \mid \{\, ct \,\} \mid [\, ct \,] \mid (a_1 : ct_1) \uplus \cdots (a_n : ct_n) \mid \ell : N$$

The explanation we gave on data types is still valid. However, the extension by pairs $\ell : M'$ is of pure syntactical nature. We cannot associate a set of values with a content type. Instead, for a content type $cont(M)$, we define a *representing datatype* t_M, which results from $cont(M)$ by replacing all $\ell : M'$ by the base type *URL*. Of course, t_M is a real data type, and this means that $dom(t_M)$ is defined.

Let S be a database schema. A *structural media type* over S has a name M and consists of:

- a *content data type* $cont(M)$, in which the place of a base type may be occupied by a pair $\ell : M'$, and
- a *defining query* q_M with source schema S and target schema $\{ (url : URL, value : t_M) \}$, where t_M is the representing datatype of M.

Example 8. Let us define some structural media types over the database schema from the previous section. We will concentrate on the content type and the representing data type. However, we will only sketch the defining query, as we have not yet introduced a concrete query language.

Of course, the type *type*(NZ_WINE) that we used in the target schema in the previous subsection is a content type defined as follows:

(name : *STRING*, year : *CARD*, composition : { (grape : *STRING*, percentage : *CARD*) }, vineyard : *STRING*, owners : { *STRING* }, since : *CARD*, history : *STRING*, region : *STRING*, climate : *STRING*).

However, it does not contain any links $\ell : M'$, which implies that it is identical with its representing data type t_{NZ_WINE}. Adding a formal description of a defining query q_{NZ_WINE} as sketched in the previous subsection turns NZ_WINE into a structural media type.

Now assume that we want to represent information about New Zealand wines by a slightly changed structural media type NZ_WINE* with the following content type:

(name : *STRING*, year : *CARD*, composition : { (grape : *STRING*,
percentage : *CARD*) }, vineyard : *STRING*, owners : { *STRING* },
since : *CARD*, history : *STRING*, region : REGION*).

In this case, the content type contains the link region : REGION*.
Consequently, the representing data type t_{NZ_WINE*} is the following:

(name : *STRING*, year : *CARD*, composition : { (grape : *STRING*,
percentage : *CARD*) }, vineyard : *STRING*, owners : { STRING },
since : *CARD*, history : *STRING*, region : *URL*).

Of course, we also would have to define a structural media type with the
name REGION* with a content type chosen to be (name : *STRING*, climate :
STRING), which, again, is identical to the representing data type $t_{REGION*}$. The
defining query $q_{REGION*}$ for REGION* would select all regions in New Zealand,
reduce them to their name and climate components, and create URLs for all the
resulting objects.

Then the defining query q_{NZ_WINE*} for the structural media type NZ_WINE*
would be processed in the same way as sketched in the previous subsection.
However, components region and climate would be replaced by the URL that
has been created while processing the query $q_{REGION*}$. Furthermore, the
operation create_urls would be applied to the result. We omit formal details
on how to write the queries $q_{REGION*}$ and q_{NZ_WINE*}.

Note that, with the introduction of links between structural media types,
the defining queries are no longer independent from each other. In Example 8,
the processing of the query q_{NZ_WINE*} depends on the result of the query
$q_{REGION*}$. As long as there are no cyclic dependencies, the query processing
can be done in a particular order. However, in the case of cycles, the process
requires calculating a fixed point. Queries that demand fixed point calculation
are one of the most advanced topics in the field of databases.

Content Schemata

Finally, let us look at the analog of a database schema on the level of
structural media types. For this, assume that we have fixed a database schema S.
As structural media types abstract from content, a collection of structural media
types over S will be called a *content schema*. Analogously to the definition of
database schemata, where we had to ensure that components of database

types are defined in the database schema, we now have to ensure that the structural media types that occur in links are defined in the content schema. Therefore, we define a content schema as follows:

A **content schema** C *over a database schema* S*is a finite set of structural media types over* S, *such that for each* M $\in$ C *and each link* ℓ*:* M′ *occurring in the content type* cont(M), *we also have* M′ $\in$ C.

Finally, assume that we are given a database schema S and a content schema C over S. We may now define a *site s* over C analogously to a database over S.

For this, let *db* be a database over S. We may evaluate the defining query q_M for each structural media type M $\in$ C. These result in sets s(M) of pairs (u,v), such that u is a value of type *URL* and v is a value of the representing data type t_M of M. We call s(M) the set of *media objects of type M* in the site s. Of course, we must ensure that for each URL u′ that appears inside the complex value v at a place occupied by ℓ: M′ in the content type *cont*(M) of M, we have a media object (u′, v′) $\in$ s(M′).

The family of all the sets s(M) with M $\in$ C defines the *site s* over C determined by the database *db* over S.

ADAPTIVITY

In this section, we extend media types by adding *adaptivity* to users, technical environment, and channels. In all three cases, the idea is to split the information provided by a structural media object in such a way that parts that are preferred to be kept together — we use the term *cohesion* for this — will be kept together, if this is possible. This can be seen as a controlled form of information loss.

The Idea of Adaptivity

As indicated above, cohesion intends to declare "parts" of a content type *cont*(M) to belong closer together than others. We will approach this in two different, but similar, ways. In both cases, we consider all possible content types that result from *cont*(M) by losing information. If *ct* is such a content type with reduced information, we write *cont*(M) $\leq$ *ct*. Thus, we first have to define this relation $\leq$, which, in fact, is a partial order.

The idea of using the partial order is by choosing one such possible content type *ct*, which is as close to the original *cont*(M) as possible. Instead of creating a media object of type M using the content type $cont(M)$, we reduce the content to the one described by the content type ct, and present this to the user. If further information is needed, the user may request it by following a link added to ct. There should be a complementary content type ct' covering the lost information. This complementary content type can then be treated again in the same way.

For instance, take again the example of a structural media type NZ_WINE. Its content type was defined as follows:

(name : *STRING*, year : *CARD*, composition : { (grape : *STRING*, percentage : *CARD*) }, vineyard : *STRING*, owners : { *STRING* }, since : *CARD*, history : *STRING*, region : *STRING*, climate : *STRING*).

Losing information would mean to drop the year, or the composition, or the percentages of the grapes, or the history, etc. Assume that we want to keep the information on name, year and composition together with the highest priority, followed by the information on the vineyard, its owners and history, and leaving the lowest priority for the information on the region and its climate. Then we could first choose the following content type ct_1:

(name : *STRING*, year : *CARD*, composition : { (grape : *STRING*, percentage : *CARD*) }, further : NZ_WINE$_2$).

Here, the link further : NZ_WINE$_2$ provides a link to a dynamically constructed structural media type named NZ_WINE$_2$. The content type of this new structural media type should contain the lost information. Thus, it could be the following content type ct_2:

(name : *STRING*, year : *CARD*, vineyard : *STRING*, owners : { *STRING* }, since : *CARD*, history : *STRING*, further : NZ_WINE$_3$).

Here, we find the information about the vineyard, its owners, and its history. We also repeat the name and year of the wine. Furthermore, the link further : NZ_WINE$_3$ provides a link to another dynamically constructed structural media type named NZ_WINE$_3$. The content type of this new structural media type should contain further information, because the information on the region is still lost. Thus, it could be the following content type ct_3:

(name : *STRING*, year : *CARD*, region : *STRING*, climate : *STRING*).

The alternative is to provide a priori such a split of the content type. In our example, we would define the split by the three content types ct_1, ct_2 and ct_3. These three content types define an *antichain* with respect to the partial order $\leq$, i.e., each two of them are incomparable in the sense that $ct_i \not\leq ct_j$ holds for all $i \neq j$.

For both ideas, we first have to define the partial order $\leq$ on content types. This is done as follows:

- For any content type ct, we have $ct \leq ct$.
- For any content type ct, we have $ct \leq OK$.
- For content types of the form $(a_1 : ct_1, ..., a_m : ct_m)$, we have:

$$(a_1 : ct_1, ..., a_m : ct_m) \leq (a_{\sigma(1)} : ct'_{\sigma(1)}, ..., a_{\sigma(1)} : ct'_{\sigma(n)}),$$

with injective $\sigma : \{1, ..., n\} \to \{1, ..., m\}$ and $ct_{\sigma(i)} \leq ct'_{\sigma(i)}$.

- For content types of the form $[ct]$, we have $[ct] \leq [ct']$ iff $ct \leq ct'$ holds.
- For content types of the form $(a_1 : ct_1) \uplus \cdots \uplus (a_m : ct_m)$, we have $(a_1 : ct_1) \uplus \cdots \uplus (a_m : ct_m) \leq (a_1 : ct'_1) \uplus \cdots \uplus (a_m : ct'_m)$ iff $ct_i \leq ct'_i$ holds for all $i = 1, ..., m$.
- For content types of the form $\{ct\}$, we have $\{ct\} \leq \{ct'\}$ iff $ct \leq ct'$ holds.

We use the notation $sup(cont(M))$ to denote the set of all content types ct with $cont(M) \leq ct$. If, in the example above, we remove the links 'further : NZ_WINE$_2$' and 'further : NZ_WINE$_3$' in ct_1 and ct_2, respectively — these were added only as a link to follow-on information — then we obtain $cont(M) \leq ct_i$ for all $i = 1, ..., 3$.

Cohesion Preorder

Let us now go into details of our first idea (Feyer et al., 2000). The partial order $\leq$ also defines a partial order on $sup(cont(M))$. However, the order is not total, i.e., there can be content types $ct_1, ct_2 \in sup(cont(M))$ with neither $ct_1 \leq ct_2$ nor $ct_2 \leq ct_1$. Thus, in case of making a choice among the elements in $sup(cont(M))$, both ct_1 and ct_2 have equal rights. Making a choice in favour of one of them, say ct_1, means to state that the information represented by ct_1 is more important than the one represented by ct_2.

Therefore, the first idea can be realised by extending $\leq$ to a total order. Nevertheless, we may state explicitly that we do not want to prefer ct_1 over ct_2 nor vice versa, even in case they were comparable with respect to $\leq$. Therefore, we only require to obtain an extension by a pre-order as defined now:

A *cohesion pre-order* on a structural media type M is a total pre-order $\trianglelefteq_M$ on $sup(cont(M))$ extending the order $\leq$, i.e., whenever $ct_1 \leq ct_2$ holds, we also have $ct_1 \trianglelefteq_M ct_2$.

The major idea behind the cohesion pre-order is that, in order to adapt to different users, channels or environments, smaller content types with respect to $\trianglelefteq$ are preferred over larger content types. In all three cases, we assume that the amount of data to be transmitted at a time and presented to the user is limited by some bound. If the presentation of a structural media object of type M exceeds this bound, the content type will be split according to the following procedure:

- First, we determine the maximum amount of data that should be transmitted.
- Then, we determine the least element ct_1 with respect to $\trianglelefteq_M$ that requires not more than the available capacity. As $\trianglelefteq_M$ is only a preorder, there may be more than one such t_1, in which case, one of these content types is chosen randomly.
- Taking t_1 instead of $cont(M)$ means that some information is lost. Therefore, we include a link to a possible successor. The link name and the name of the successor structural media type will be randomly chosen.
- In order to determine such a successor, all content types $ct' \in sup(cont(M))$ with $ct_1 \ntrianglelefteq_M ct'$ are considered. We choose a least content type ct_2 among these ct' with respect to $\trianglelefteq_M$, such that ct_2 does not require more than the available capacity.

Continuing this way the whole communication using the structural media type M is broken down into a sequence of suitable units $ct_1, ct_2, \ldots, ct_n$ that, together, contain the information provided by the structural media type.

Example 9. Let us consider again the content type of the structural media type NZ_WINE used earlier. However, as $sup(cont(\text{NZ\_WINE}))$ will be large, we reorganise the content type and outline the splitting procedure without looking into details of the content type. Thus, assume that we have the following content type:

(wine-info : (name : *STRING*, year : *CARD*, composition : { (grape : *STRING*, percentage : *CARD*) }), vineyard : (name : *STRING*,

owners : { *STRING* }, since : *CARD*, history : *STRING*), region :
(name : *STRING*, climate : *STRING*)).

In order to shorten our presentation, we consider only

(wine-info : ..., vineyard : ..., region : ...)

and ignore the inner structure, which is indicated by the dots. Ignoring the inner structure, we could define a cohesion pre-order by:

$$(\text{wine-info} : ..., \text{vineyard} : ..., \text{region} : ...)$$
$$\trianglelefteq (\text{wine-info} : ..., \text{vineyard} : ...)$$
$$\trianglelefteq (\text{wine-info} : ..., \text{region} : ...)$$
$$\trianglelefteq (\text{vineyard} : ..., \text{region} : ...)$$
$$\trianglelefteq (\text{wine-info} : ...)$$
$$\trianglelefteq (\text{vineyard} : ...)$$
$$\trianglelefteq (\text{region} : ...)$$

Assume that only the complete content type exceeds the computed maximum capacity. Then, the first content type to be chosen would be:

(wine-info : ..., vineyard : ...),

which will be extended to:

$$(\text{wine-info} : ..., \text{vineyard} : ..., \text{next} : \text{NZ\_WINE}_2).$$

This leaves the following content types:
$$(\text{wine-info} : ..., \text{vineyard} : ..., \text{region} : ...)$$
$$\trianglelefteq (\text{wine-info} : ..., \text{region} : ...)$$
$$\trianglelefteq (\text{vineyard} : ..., \text{region} : ...)$$
$$\trianglelefteq (\text{region} : ...).$$

Thus, the second content type to be chosen will be:

(wine-info : ..., region : ...).

This will become the content type of the dynamically generated structural media type NZ_WINE$_2$. The splitting process stops here, as further processing would not lead to more information.

Proximity Values

Finally, let us consider the alternative approach (Feyer et al., 1998). In this approach, the content types that will be chosen instead of *cont(M)* are determined a priori. We only determine whether they will be transmitted one by one, or whether some of them will be recombined. Thus, we choose a maximal antichain $ct_1, ..., ct_n$ in $sup(cont(M))$ with respect to $\leq$. This antichain already represents a possible split of information. In addition, we define a symmetric $(n \times n)$-matrix $\{p_{ij}\}_{1 \leq i,j \leq n}$ of *proximity values* with $0 \leq p_{ij} \leq 1$. The intention is that the higher the proximity value, the more do we wish to keep the components together.

Splitting is processed analogously to the case a using a cohesion pre-order:
- For each $X \subseteq \{1, ..., n\}$, we determine its *weight*, i.e., $w(X) = \sum_{i,j \in X, i<j} p_{ij}$.
- For each $X \subseteq \{1, ..., n\}$, we determine its *greatest common subtype* $gcs(X)$, i.e., the greatest element $ct_1 \in sup(cont(M))$ with $t_1 \leq ct_i$ for all $i \in X$.
- Then, we choose the X with largest weight, such that the $gcs(X)$ does not require more than the available capacity.

Example 10. We take the same media type as in Example 9 and the antichain

$$ct_1 = (\text{wine-info} : ...) \qquad ct_2 = (\text{vineyard} : ...) \qquad ct_3 = (\text{region} : ...).$$

Let the proximity values be chosen as $p_{1,2} = 0.8$, $p_{1,3} = 0.5$ and $p_{2,3} = 0.1$.

X	w(X)	gcs(X)
{ 1 }	0	(wine-info : ...)
{ 2 }	0	(vineyard : ...)
{ 3 }	0	(region : ...)
{ 1, 2 }	0.8	(wine-info : ..., vineyard : ...)
{ 1, 3 }	0.5	(wine-info : ..., region : ...)
{ 2, 3 }	0.1	(vineyard : ..., region: ...)
{ 1, 2, 3 }	1.4	(wine-info : ..., vineyard : ..., region: ...)

Then, we obtain the following weights and greatest common subtypes:

The result will be the same sequence of content types as in Example 9.

We discussed adaptivity to users, environment and channels. This was done in the form of allowing structural media types to be extended by a controlled form of information loss, coupled with the notion of cohesion.

A *cohesion extension* of structural media type M is given either by a cohesion pre-order $\trianglelefteq$ on *sup(cont(M))* or by a pair consisting of maximal antichain $ct_1,...,ct_n$ in *sup(cont(M))* with respect to $\leq$ and a symmetric $(n \times n)$-matrix $\{p_{ij}\}_{1 \leq i,j \leq n}$ of proximity values with $0 \leq p_{ij} \leq 1$.

A *media type* is a structural media type M together with a cohesion extension. A *media schema* is a content schema, in which all structural media types are media types.

Given a media schema, then, it is basically a content schema over an underlying database schema. Thus, any database determines sets of media objects. The cohesion extension further determines variants of the media objects that are dynamically constructed when the need arises. It leads to a step-by-step delivery of a media object.

CONCLUSION

We presented a conceptual model for data-intensive web information systems, which is centered around the central notion of *media type*. Roughly speaking, a media type is defined as an extended view on an underlying database schema, and includes operations and adaptivity features.

Conceptual modeling with structural media types is embedded in an integrated methodology based on an abstraction layer model for web information systems. Prior to this activity, we have an activity of story boarding, which models the WIS from a usage perspective (Kaschek et al., 2003). The scenes in the story board are used as the data source for the media types. Further on, the media types do not yet specify anything on their web presentation. For this, media types have to be associated with style options. Using these style options and suites of XML representations leads to the implementation. The complete methodology has been applied in more than 30 large projects. The report (Thalheim, 1997) describes the first of these projects; for others, the work and publication rights have been transferred to professional companies.

We have seen that several other groups have also developed conceptual modeling approaches for web information systems. The theory of media types is one of these approaches. As work progresses, the ideas produced by the different groups are now converging, though the theory of media types is still the most advanced model with respect to formal foundations. Furthermore, it is still more elaborate with respect to adaptivity, the scope of the overall methodology, in particular, with respect to an integration with story boarding, the work on implementation and presentation issues, and applications in practical projects.

Taking the convergence of ideas, the currently existing advantages of the theory of media types in comparison to other approaches will disappear. For instance, other approaches will take up the work on adaptivity. Conversely, the theory of media types will benefit from the work of others and become even more elaborate. However, the convergence trend concerns the concepts, not concrete languages. In particular, the theory of media types will be likely to preserve its connections to theory.

The role of XML will become even more important. On one side, XML may pick up ideas that will enable a better support for media types or similar conceptual modeling approaches. On the other side, XML will always remain a concrete language and may distract from the important issue of conceptual modeling. If XML is treated as a data model, most of the hardest database problems still have to be solved in this context. Therefore, we think it is better not to fix the attention only on XML. Using XML for representing the views is uncritical, but it is unlikely that it will be able to replace completely the theory of media types. As this theory can be based on any data model, it is much more generic than any concrete language.

REFERENCES

Abiteboul, S., Buneman, P., & Suciu, D. (2000). *Data on the Web: From Relations to Semistructured Data and XML*. San Francisco, CA: Morgan Kaufmann.

Atzeni, P., Gupta, A., & Sarawagi, S. (1998). Design and maintenance of data-intensive web-sites. In *Proceedings of the EDBT'98* (Vol. 1377 of LNCS, pp. 436-450). Berlin: Springer-Verlag.

Baresi, L., Garzotto, F., & Paolini, P. (2000). From web sites to web applications: New issues for conceptual modeling. In *ER workshops*

2000 (Vol. 1921 of LNCS, pp. 89-100). Berlin: Springer-Verlag.

Bonifati, A., Ceri, S., Fraternali, P., & Maurino, A. (2000). Building multi-device, content-centric applications using WebML and the W3I3 tool suite. In *ER workshops 2000* (Vol. 1921 of LNCS, pp. 64-75). Berlin: Springer-Verlag.

Ceri, S., Fraternali, P., & Matera, M. (2002). Conceptual modeling of data-intensive web applications. *IEEE Internet Computing*, 6(4), 20-30.

Düsterhöft, A. & Thalheim, B. (2001). SiteLang: Conceptual modeling of internet sites. In H. S. Kunii, S. Jajodia, & A. Sølvberg (Eds.), *Conceptual modeling – ER 2001* (Vol. 2224 of LNCS, pp. 179-192). Berlin: Springer-Verlag.

Feyer, T. & Thalheim, B. (1999). E/R based scenario modeling for rapid prototyping of web information services. In P. P.-S. Chen (Ed.), *Advances in Conceptual Modeling* (Vol. 1727 of LNCS, pp. 253-263). Berlin: Springer-Verlag.

Feyer, T., Kao, O., Schewe, K.-D., & Thalheim, B. (2000). Design of data-intensive web-based information services. In Q. Li, Z. M. Ozsuyoglu, R. Wagner, Y. Kambayashi, & Y. Zhang (Eds.), *Proceedings of the 1st International Conference on Web Information Systems Engineering (WISE 2000)* (pp. 462-467). IEEE Computer Society.

Feyer, T., Schewe, K.-D., & Thalheim, B. (1998). Conceptual modelling and development of information services. In T. Ling & S. Ram (Eds.), *Conceptual Modeling – ER'98* (Vol. 1507 of LNCS, pp. 7-20). Berlin: Springer-Verlag.

Fraternali, P. (1999). Tools and approaches for developing data-intensive web applications: A survey. *ACM Computing Surveys*, 31(3), 227-263.

Kaschek, R., Schewe, K.-D., Wallace, C., & Matthews, C. (2003). Story boarding for web-based information systems. In W. Rahayu & D. Taniar (Eds.), *Web Information Systems*. Hershey, PA: Idea Group.

Kirchberg, M., Schewe, K.-D., & Tretiakov, A. (2003). *Using XML to support media types*. Submitted for publication.

Lobin, H. (2000). *Informationsmodellierung in XML und SGML*. Berlin: Springer-Verlag.

Mecca, G., Merialdo, P., & Atzeni, P. (1999). ARANEUS in the era of XML. *IEEE Data Engineering Bulletin*.

Rossi, G., Garrido, A., & Schwabe, D. (2000). Navigating between objects: Lessons from an object-oriented framework perspective. *ACM Computing Surveys*, 32(1).

Rossi, G., Schwabe, D., & Lyardet, F. (1999). Web application models are more than conceptual models. In P. C. et al. (Eds.), *Advances in Conceptual Modeling* (Vol. 1727 of LNCS, pp. 239-252). Berlin: Springer-Verlag.

Schewe, K.-D. (2001). Querying web information systems. In H. S. Kunii, S. Jajodia, & A. Sølvberg (Eds.), *Conceptual Modeling – ER 2001* (Vol. 2224 of LNCS, pp. 571-584). Berlin: Springer-Verlag.

Schewe, K.-D. & Thalheim, B. (2000). *Conceptual modelling of internet sites.* Tutorial notes. 19th International Conference on Conceptual Modelling (ER 2000). Available at: http://infosys.massey.ac.nz/~kdschewe/pub/slides/ER00tuti.ps with $i = 0, \ldots, 6$.

Schewe, K.-D., Kaschek, R., Matthews, C., & Wallace, C. (2002). Modelling web-based banking systems: Story boarding and user profiling. In H. Mayr & W.-J. Van den Heuvel (Eds.), *Proceedings of the Workshop on Conceptual Modelling Approaches to E-commerce.* Berlin: Springer-Verlag.

Schwabe, D. & Rossi, G. (1998). An object oriented approach to web-based application design. *TAPOS*, 4(4), 207-225.

Schwabe, D., Rossi, G., & Barbosa, S. (1996). Systematic hypermedia design with OOHDM. In *Proceedings of Hypertext '96* (pp. 116-128). New York: ACM Press.

Thalheim, B. (1997). *Development of Database-backed Information Services for CottbusNet.* Cottbus, Germany: BTU Cottbus. (Technical Report No. CS-20-97).

Thalheim, B. (2000). *Entity-relationship Modeling: Foundations of Database Technology.* Berlin: Springer-Verlag.

Chapter III

Toward a Model of the Migration of Communication Between Media Devices

Richard Hall, La Trobe University, Australia

ABSTRACT

The ever-increasing volume of information generated by humanity has been supported by our ability to invent devices that record, store, retrieve and communicate this information in a variety of media, presented by a variety of devices. Since new media devices are continually emerging, and each device has different utility, it is possible that a great deal of information will need to be migrated between media devices in order to take advantage of their utility. While computer programs that perform migration automatically would help to process the potential volume of information being migrated, such programs will require a model of the migration of communication between media devices. In this chapter, we propose such a model that is based on ideas from information theory and media modeling. The model represents a number of interacting components including: the dimensions and utility of the media device; the media of and structure of communication; and conversion functions between media devices. We evaluate it by applying it theoretically to one of the important tasks in digital libraries: the digitisation (migration) of a set of highly structured textbooks to hypertext. We argue that emerging web-technologies could assist the automatic migration of communication between media devices as long as specific components of the migration model are present in the information. Applications of this model lie in the preservation of digital libraries, which must be able to migrate between media devices in order to be immune to degradation and technological obsolescence.

INTRODUCTION

There is a lot of information in the world. In 1997, it was estimated that there were a few thousand peta-bytes of information, based on aggregated estimations of the information volumes stored in major vessels such as the Library of Congress, the Internet, and various collections of cinema and broadcasting (Lesk, 1997). For people to gain access to this information, they require the ability to retrieve and engage with it, using some media device for interaction and presentation.

Like information, the number and types of media devices continue to grow. While books originally became the ubiquitous media device, the onset of the electronic age has seen a great increase in the number of media devices. There are enough devices now such that they are typically classified by the type of sensory input they provide to a user (visible, audible, or haptic), and include such devices as microfiche, personal computer monitors, headphones, and force-feedback devices (M. Bordegoni, 1997). It is predicted that new electronic devices will continue to emerge in the foreseeable future, thus, flexibility in the way information is represented is critical (Nunberg, 1996).

The emphasis of migration in the computing world has largely been focused on moving legacy information systems software from its original environment to modern architectures, tools and databases, running on a new hardware platform (J. Bisbal, 1999). The effort expended on this type of migration is, and will continue to be, significant: It is estimated that legacy information systems maintenance consumes 90% to 95% of information systems resources (M. Brodie, 1993). Typically, such migration occurs without change in either the media or the media devices; rather, the underlying representation of the information is modified so that the information can be better used with new applications that work with the same media device. The simple order of magnitude of the task of conversion in legacy information systems leaves little room for consideration of other media devices.

In digital libraries, where communities of users engage with shared sources of communication, the issue of media device independence is important because information that cannot be accessed on any device becomes obsolete (A. Paepcke, 1998; Sornil, 1999). Without automated assistance, obsolescence may be inevitable simply because the volume of information may make migration by hand infeasible. Also, where such migration needs to be performed by expensive content experts for any reason, these large volumes will quickly make the process prohibitive. Consequently, for information to be communicated to a user using any preferred media device in a timely and cost-effective manner, automatic migration techniques must be investigated.

There are three types of people for whom this chapter is written. Firstly, those who are involved with the migration of information, such as the digitization of books for digital library projects or information redesign for electronic publishing. Secondly, those people who are interested in an exploration of the limitations of hypertext media and electronic publishing tools from the viewpoint of electronic publishers. Finally, those people who are interested in exploring the type of problems inherent in information delivery via the Internet that emerging technologies will inevitably address.

This chapter is divided into four sections. Firstly, the requirements of the migration model are specified in terms of existing models of communication, information and media. Secondly, a representation of the model is constructed that satisfies these requirements. Thirdly, it is evaluated by comparison to its requirements and application in the task of digitization. Finally, the applications of emerging web technologies to realizing this model are discussed.

REQUIREMENTS OF THE MIGRATION MODEL

Before creating a representation of any model, it is necessary to specify its requirements. Such specification allows the scope of the representation to be constrained and provides a benchmark against which the representation can be compared. It is not claimed that these requirements for a model of the migration of communication between media devices are complete, but, as such models evolve over time, their requirements do become more complete.

We propose that such a migration model should integrate models from four domains: communication, information, media, and expert systems. Where the first three domains are directly related to representing the *object* of migration, the latter is related toward representing the *process* of migration. The reasons for choosing each of these particular domains are now discussed.

A model of the migration of *communication* must contain a representation of the system by which communication occurs. Although the media device will change when migration occurs, concepts of communication remain static. The migration itself must not retard the ability of the information to represent communication. Instead, it must further the ability of information to be communicated, thus be preserved. The *information* itself must also be modeled, since all communication occurs using information. This distinction between communication and information is made because the focus of this chapter is on the information that is communicated to the user of a media device, not on the information (software) that controls the media device, because such software is outside the scope of this discussion.

The *media* that represents the information must be modeled because some media devices only present and allow interactions with specific media types, and the media largely determines the way that a user interacts with a media device in order to access the information (Munson, 1996). In addition, if specific parts of communication are unable to move between different media types, these parts will be limited to specific devices. The media model should distinguish between structural and non-structural content, since structure is important in retrieval and making documents smart (Chestnutt, 1997; Macleod, 1990).

Finally, *expert systems* must be modeled because, without automated assistance, an expert in migration must perform the conversion functions between two media devices manually, a potentially impossible task given the ratio of information to experts. An expert system (that simulates this particular expertise) would represent the knowledge of migration with one of the various types of knowledge representations, such as rules or frames (Riley, 1998). For example, an electronic publisher is an expert in the migration of books to hypertext—an expert system for electronic publishing would contain all of the conversion functions used by an electronic publisher.

Now that the components of the migration model have been identified, and reasons for their inclusion have been discussed, it is appropriate to begin constructing a representation of the migration model using these components.

REPRESENTATION OF THE MIGRATION MODEL

In the previous section, it was argued that models from four domains should be incorporated: communication, information, media and expert systems. While a number of models have been proposed in these different domains, it is necessary to make a selection of a single representative model — the models believed to be the simplest and most general were chosen. The following four subsections present a summary of each of these models, and reasons why each of these models is incomplete of itself are mentioned. Subsequently, they are integrated to produce the model of migration of communication between media devices.

The *Communication* Component of the Migration Model

Shannon's information theoretic measures are well known in both computer science and engineering. Shannon is known as the father of information theory. Consequently, we adopt his model of a communication system, shown in Figure 1 (Shannon, 1948). His discussion of the components of the model follows.

An *information source* produces a message or sequence of messages to be communicated to the receiving terminal. The message may be of various types:

(a) A sequence of letters, as in a telegraph of teletype system;
(b) A single function of time $f(t)$, as in radio or telephony;
(c) A function of time and other variables, as in black and white television — here the message may be thought of as a function $f(x;y; t)$ of two space coordinates and time, the light intensity at point $(x;y)$ and time t on a pickup tube plate;
(d) Two or more functions of time, say $f(t), g(t), h(t)$ — this is the case in "three dimensional" sound transmission or, if the system is intended to service several individual channels, in multiplex;
(e) Several functions of several variables — in color television, the message consists of three functions $f(x;y;t), g(x;y;t)$, and $h(x;y;t)$ defined in a three-dimensional continuum — we may also think of these three functions as components of a vector field defined in the region — similarly, several black and white television sources would produce "messages" consisting of a number of functions of three variables.

Figure 1: Schematic Diagram of a General Communication System

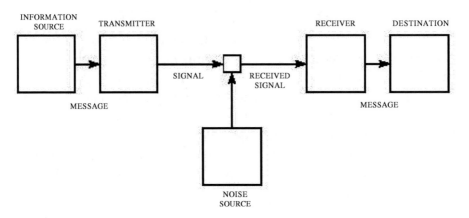

Various combinations also occur, for example, in television with an associated audio channel.

- A *transmitter* operates on the message in some way to produce a signal suitable for transmission over the channel. In telephony, this operation consists merely of changing sound pressure into a proportional electrical current. In telegraphy, we have an encoding operation which produces a sequence of dots, dashes and spaces on the channel corresponding to the message. In a multiplex PCM system, the different speech functions must be sampled, compressed, quantized and encoded, and finally, interleaved properly to construct the signal. Vocoder systems, television, and frequency modulation are other examples of complex operations applied to the message to obtain the signal.

- The *channel* is merely the medium used to transmit the signal from transmitter to receiver. It may be a pair of wires, a coaxial cable, a band of radio frequencies, a beam of light, etc.

- The *receiver* ordinarily performs the inverse operation of that done by the transmitter, reconstructing the message from the signal.

- The *destination* is the person (or thing) for whom the message is intended. We wish to consider certain general problems involving communication systems. To do this, it is first necessary to represent the various elements involved as mathematical entities, suitably idealized from their physical counterparts. We may roughly classify communication systems into three main categories: discrete, continuous and mixed. By a discrete system, we will mean one in which both the message and the signal are a sequence of discrete symbols. A typical case is telegraphy, where the message is a sequence of letters, and the signal a sequence of dots, dashes and spaces. A continuous system is one in which the message and signal are both treated as continuous functions, e.g., radio or television. A mixed system is one in which both discrete and continuous variables appear, e.g., PCM transmission of speech.

Shannon's communication system lacks a number of features required by a model of migration of communication between media devices. While Shannon's system represents the physical environment of communication, it does not distinguish between symbols which have semantic content and those with none, nor does it represent the purpose of the communication (Horvath, 2001). Also, while the physical environment represents the *medium* of communication, the *media* represented by the information, and the way in which the destination interacts with this media via a media device, is not considered. Finally, this is an isolated system—while internal relationships are represented, the relationship between this system and others is not considered.

Since the scope of this paper focuses on communication between people, it assumes the communication has semantic content, such as all the information stored in a digital library. Consequently, a model for information is required.

The *Information* Component of the Migration Model

A number of information theories have been proposed that could fill the void of semantic content left out by Shannon's model of a communication system. We adopt Gitt's information theory (Gitt, 1989) because this theory is supposedly the most complete (Horvath, 2001). Gitt's levels of information are now summarized.

- *Statistical level:* Shannon's information theory is well suited to an understanding of the statistical aspect of information. This theory makes it possible to give a quantitative description of those characteristics of languages that are based intrinsically on frequencies.
- *Syntactical level:* The code system that represents the information.
- *Semantic level:* The decisive aspect of the transmitted information. It shows the message that the information contains.
- *Pragmatic level:* To achieve the intended result, the transmitter considers how the receiver can be made to satisfy his planned objective; what kinds of actions should be accomplished. He differentiates between modes of actions (a) without any, (b) with a limited, and (c) with the maximum degree of freedom.

- *Apobetic level:* The purpose of the information. The result of the communicated information at the receiving end is based at the transmitting end on the purpose, the objective, the plan, or the design.

While information theory provides a more complete representation of the information and of the relationship between the author at the information source and the audience at the destination than Shannon's communication system, it also lacks a number of features required by a model of migration of communication between media devices. Without a representation of the communication system, there can be no consideration given to the relationship between the message type and the structure of information. And, without a representation of the media in which information is contained, the migration between different media devices cannot be considered.

The *Media* Component of the Migration Model

In Shannon's model, a distinction is made between the message — the information communicated, and the signal - the physical representation of the message. Since a message can be represented by a number of media types, it is necessary to represent media itself. While a number of media models exist, we adopt Munson's operational model because it characterizes interaction with media as dependent on its type, independent of media combinations or context-dependent usage (Munson, 1996; Pfeiffer, 1997).

A medium is a four-tuple, $M = (T; D; A; O)$:

- A type, $t_i \in T$, is a set of values. Each t_i may be finite (e.g., Booleans) or infinite (e.g., ASCII strings), atomic (e.g., integers) or composite (e.g., two-dimensional splines). The set of types, T, is formed by the union of three subsets: T_P, the primitive media data types; T_O, the types of data produced by the formatting operations; and T_A, the types of the attributes in A.
- D is a set of dimensions in which layout is performed. The set of dimensions for a medium, D, has k members, whose Cartesian product is the coordinate space in which material is laid out.

$$d_1 * d_2 * \ldots * d_k$$

Each dimension, d_i, may be continuous or discrete, bounded or unbounded.

- A is a set of attributes. The elements of the set of attributes, $a_i \in A$, represent the style parameters that control the medium's formatting process. Each attribute has a type, $t \in T_A$, which specifies the set of values that the attribute may hold. Examples of possible attributes include stroke width (for 2D graphics), font size (for any medium supporting text), and transition style (used with video and having values like "cut," "fade" and "dissolve").
- O is a set of formatting operations. Each medium has k operations, where $k \geq 1$. Each operation $o_i \in O$ is a tuple $o_i = (t^{in}_i ; t^{out}_i ; A_i ; f_i)$, where:
  - t^{in}_i is the input data type;
  - t^{out}_i is the output data type;
  - $A_i \subset A$ is the set of m attributes relevant to the operation, where $A_i = \{a_{i1} ... a_{im}\}$;
  - f_i is the function performed by the operation, where

$$f_i : t^{in}_i * a_{i1} * .. * a_{im} \rightarrow t^{out}_i$$

Munson's model of media represents what an audience will perceive via a media device and the attributes of a media that an author can manipulate. In conjunction with a model of communication and information, it will form the basis of our model of communication. As it stands, though, none of these models can represent conversion rules between media devices; such capability is incorporated using expert systems.

The *Expert Systems* Component of the Migration Model

An expert system is an intelligent computer program that uses knowledge and inference procedures to solve problems that are difficult enough to require significant human expertise for their solutions (Feigenbaum, 1982). The basic model of an expert system (shown in Figure 2) was originally proposed for the expert system MYCIN, and is now the de-facto standard (Riley, 1998). His brief discussion of the components of the model follows. Note that his discussion uses rules as the knowledge representation, although there are many types of knowledge representation.

- *Working memory:* Contains a global database of facts used by the rules.
- *Inference engine:* Makes inferences by deciding which rules are satisfied by facts or objects, prioritizes the satisfied rules, and executes the rule with the highest priority.
- *Knowledge base:* Stores all rules in the system.
- *Explanation facility:* A facility that can explain the reasoning of the system to a user.

Figure 2: Expert Systems Model

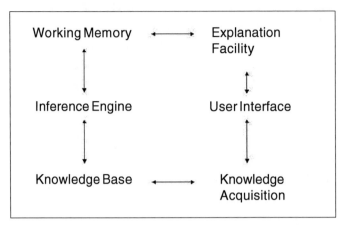

- *User interface:* The mechanism by which the user and the expert system communicate.
- *Knowledge acquisition:* An automatic way for a user to enter knowledge in the system, as opposed to a knowledge engineer explicitly coding knowledge.

In this chapter, the scope is limited to the left-hand side of the diagram, since we are interested in representing a model of the migration of communication between media devices, as opposed to knowledge acquisition/explanation of conversion, although we believe that there is much scope for future work in these areas. Now that all the individual models have been introduced, they can now be integrated in order to satisfy the requirements of this migration model for communication between media devices. The integration occurs in two stages: combining communication oriented models, then extending this model of communication with an expert systems model for conversion.

Combining Model Components into a Model of Communication

The models of communication, information and media mentioned above immediately appear to be complementary, and appear to overlap in various ways. In this section, we reconcile these three models into a unified model for communication before extending this model to consider migration between media devices.

Figure 3: Unified Model of Communication

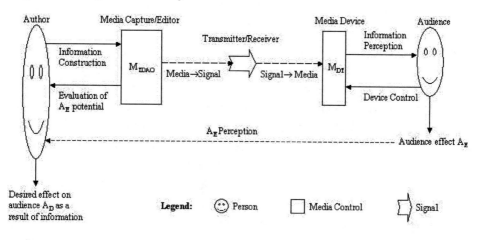

The proposed unified model is shown in Figure 3. An explanation of its components with respect to the other three models follows.

- *Author:* The author(s) are the producers of the information using the media capture/editing devices. They evaluate the potential of the information they are constructing in terms of the desired effect it will have on the mind of the audience A_D (pragmatic level of information), and they have a purpose for having such an effect on an audience (apobetic level of information). While this effect occurs in the mental state of the audience, like all mental states, it can lead to action. Constructing the author in this way is in agreement with Searle's speech-act theory (Searle, 1969). In relation to Shannon's model, the author, in cooperation with the media capture/editor, is equivalent to the information source.

- *Media Capture/Editor:* This is a device that records the author's manipulation of all aspects of one or more media types. Thus, any physical object that is manipulated by an author for the purpose of having a desired effect on an audience acts as media. Such devices, thus, include paper, canvas, tape recorders, and video cameras. Note that, according to Munson's model of media, each might support multiple primitive data types. For example, the text medium provided by the typesetting program L^AT_EX supports text, mathematical symbol, rule, line, circle, rectangle, and glue data types (Munson, 1996).

We extend Munson's model of media in the following way. Primitive media data types T_0 are merged with the information level of syntax to such that they are labeled with one of three types: reference-source, reference-target and content-only. *Reference-source* means that the data refers the audience to another piece of data in the media. *Reference-target* means that the data either can be referred to by a reference source, or is necessary to support other reference targets. For example, consider the reference-target of page numbers in a book. Although the table of contents or index might not refer to all page numbers, it is necessary for each page to have a number so that subsequent pages that are referenced can be found easily. *Content-only* refers to all other data that is not the previous two types. The purpose of this extension is to represent structure, one of the requirements of this model.

Having constructed these three components, we then construct a higher-level syntax element that we call an information unit (*iunit*). An *iunit* consists of any media that begins with a reference-target and stands as a unit that is complete in terms of the information contains. Complete means that the information represented by the media has a discernible semantic whole in terms of an identifiable beginning, middle and end. Examples of *iunits* include a scene in a movie or a chapter or subsection in a book. *Iunits* can be nested. For example, a book subsection is generally part of a chapter; a scene in a play may be part of an act.

A difference between this component and Shannon's information source is that Shannon considers the purpose of the information source to only be the construction of a message, as opposed to representing the message (information) within media and recognizing that it is the media that is communicated, and the message, potentially.

- *Transmitter/Receiver*: This component subsumes Shannon's transmitter, receiver and noise source components. Shannon's model, however, only considers communication in the frequency domain. However, it could be argued that the situation whereby a book is sent to a publisher and made into many copies is analogous. Thus, this stage can be extended to all media where the audience does not perceive the object manipulated directly by the author. The reason for the dotted lines in Figure 3 is that the media type determines the necessity of transmission. Given that any object can be media, it is possible that the media perceived by the audience is the exact same physical object manipulated by the author, e.g., a painted canvas.
- *Media Device:* This component is the device perceived by the audience. Note that in Figure 3 it shows M_{DT} only (the dimension and type aspects

of media). The audience needs no awareness of the underlying attributes and operations involved in the construction process; they are simply exposed to the media and, consequently, extract information from it. It must be noted that the device itself has a dimension component D_D that interacts with M_D.

- *Audience:* The audience is the people who perceive and control the media device. Their use of the device is deliberate, and they attempt to minimize the amount of effort required to find the information they desire. Structure becomes increasingly important as information volume grows, as the task of the audience in matching what they desire to perceive with what can possibly be perceived becomes increasingly difficult. The information perceived by an audience will affect their mental state A_E. The dotted line linking this state with the author means that there may exist a feedback path to the author, such that the author can measure the similarity between A_D and A_E. An exact match means that the author will have achieved their purpose in communicating, and no change to the media is necessary to accomplish the desired effect. On the other hand, an inexact match may inspire the author to re-edit the media in an attempt to increase similarity.

Now that the communication component of the migration model has been constructed, the component allowing conversion between media devices can be added.

Extending the Communication Model for Migration

The integrated communication component is now extended to represent migration between media devices using concepts from expert systems. The model shown in Figure 4 takes particular components from the model in Figure 3, instead of adding directly to the model in Figure 3 for reasons of space. Note that the author is now on the right hand side of the diagram, simply to show that their perception of the media devices is important. The most important components in migration, as opposed to communication, are shown in this view, while all other relationships are maintained.

- *Author:* In addition to authors producing the information and evaluating the potential of the information they are constructing in terms of the desired effect it will have on the mind of the audience A_D, authors attempt to evaluate the effect of different media devices upon A_E. This relationship defines the *utility* of a media device; authors will desire their media to migrate between different devices because of the different utilities of different devices. Given the importance of structure in information selec-

Figure 4: A Model of Communication Migration Using an Expert System

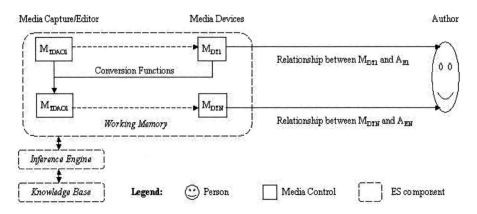

tion for large information volumes, it is assumed that migration will often move in the direction of media devices with increasingly powerful representations of structure.

- *Media Capture/Editor/Devices:* All three media controls may be involved in migration. Firstly, the media capture control may be used to produce alternative representations of the information. Secondly, the media editor control may have a representation of the information that can be directly converted without resorting to converting from the media device itself. Finally, the media device by which the information is presented may need to be accessed directly in order to attempt conversion. For example, in the process of digitization, books are scanned, then converted to text using optical character recognition software.

- *Working Memory:* This expert system (ES) component requires a representation of the media types, both within the media editor and media devices that can be processed by the inference engine in order to determine which conversion functions to apply. In an ideal case, the working memory will contain a digital representation of the media that the inference engine can automatically modify by translating the information into different media file types using media editor functions.

Note that migration between M_1 and M_N does not necessarily mean that M_{D1} is the same as $M_{DN;}$ nor does it mean that exactly the same structural information must be maintained. For example, while page numbers are useful reference-targets in the context of the book due to its sequential layout, page numbers on pages in a web site might be meaningless since web pages can contain multiple reference-sources and reference-targets that are attached to multiple media types.

- *Inference Engine:* This software process matches all present media components to function parameters in the knowledge base. Where a match occurs, the function is applied. The quality of conversion, thus, depends to a large degree on the accuracy of the knowledge base in representing the way that an expert in conversion would manually migrate communication between media devices.
- *Knowledge Base:* This expert system component stores all of the conversion functions that will be applied to the media represented within working memory. Having constructed our theoretical model for the migration of communication between media devices, the knowledge-base content can be developed.

Toward the Migration Model Knowledge Base

In order to construct a knowledge base for migration, we consider two types of interactions in media: dimension and structure, and the ways in which utility can be maximized with respect to these interactions. By exploring the characteristics of these interactions, it allows an appropriate knowledge representation to be selected. The following two subsections consider these two interaction types, and subsequently, interactions between dimension and structure are considered.

Dimension Interactions

Dimension interactions are considered in terms of two elements: the relationship between the media and the media device; and in terms of the relationship between different media devices. The *dimension relationship between the media* M_D *and media device* D_D is explored using the example of the display of a web page M on a standard portable computer monitor as the media device D. For maximum utility, the screen (currently displayed) must contain all of the information desired by the audience. However, monitor real estate does not necessarily coincide with the real estate used by the program displaying the media. For example, consider the utilization of the two different screen-shots for the same web page shown in Figure 5. Also, with maximum utilization $M_D \cong D_D$, but these changes in the media device dimension affect utilization. A pocket-sized monitor will never achieve the same utilization at a glance as a standard monitor.

Figure 5: Media/Device Utilization

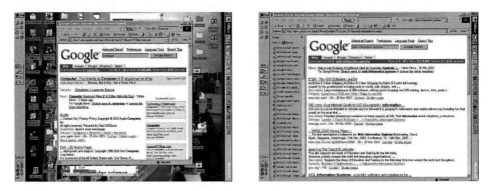

The *relationship between the dimensions of different media devices* M_{D1} *and* D_{D2} is also considered. Since M_{D1} is generally laid out specifically to fit D_{D1} in a manner which achieves maximum utilization of available space, where $D_{D2} < D_{D1}$ it may mean that $D_{D2} < MD_1$, or $D_{D2} > MD_1$ when $D_{D2} > D_{D1}$. For example, consider these implications in terms of web pages shown in Figure 6.

To maximize utility, it is desirable to avoid cases where there is a great mismatch between media dimensions and device dimensions. We define cases where $M_D << D_D$ as *underutilization*, and cases where $M_D >> D_D$ as *overflow*. We assume that there are acceptable lower and upper bounds $D_D^{min} < M_D < D_D^{max}$ that an author would regard as acceptable, that an automatic knowledge acquisition component of an expert system could obtain in the process of observing manual migration, or that an author could define.

Having considered the interaction between media dimensions and media devices, we now consider the various types of interactions between structural elements of the media.

Figure 6: Media Dimensions and Device Dimensions Mismatch

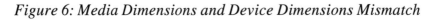
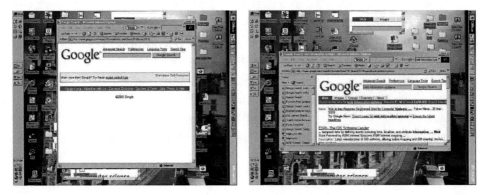

Structure Interactions

Structure interactions are considered in terms of three elements: reference-source/target completeness, reference-source/target co-existence, and the relationship between media structures and the media device. *Reference-source/target completeness* (RCO) means that every type of reference-target has a reference-source that exists within a set of reference-sources for similar target types. For example, every *iunit* could have a link within a table of contents, since every *iunit* begins with a reference target, by definition. However, there may be reasons why RCO, while possible to achieve, is not achieved for certain media types. Book authors may choose to only include subsections down to a particular depth in a table of contents for aesthetic reasons or size limitations. Thus, migrating between media may mean that RCO needs to be considered, with respect to the utility of complete representation.

Reference-source/target co-existence (RCX) means the structure of the media (a set of reference-sources) is presented simultaneously to the presentation of the elements referred to by the structure (content and reference-target media types). The utility of information is increased, in theory, because a user has access to the big picture at all times, in addition to access to the small picture (specific content), so that users can more rapidly find the information they desire to perceive.

There appear to be two types of situations where RCX is not completely achievable. Firstly, there is nothing to stop an author from replicating the same information anywhere within a body of work, such that a single reference-target has multiple reference-sources. For example, a large table in a book appendix might be referenced multiple times in the one book, and this same table, if general enough, might exist in a set of books that are all to be migrated into a digital library. Consequently, a piece of information might exist in multiple places in the structure, and if the structure representation overflows D_D, then it is possible that some of the reference-sources may not coexist. Secondly, the set of headings in a representation of information structure might use particular grammar that indicates their relationships, but this relationship may not necessarily be maintained in the content representation of the *iunit*, thus, the headings of the content differ from the headings in the structure of the content.

There are two areas in which the relationship between media structures and the media device is considered: external references and internal cross-media references. *External references* mean reference-targets that lie outside the media, although they are of the same media type. Given the volume of information, some of these reference-targets may be outside the control of the author, thus, the content referred to may change, or the actual reference-target may disappear without the author's knowledge. *Cross-media references* mean that the communication exists within two media forms, and there are references between the two forms. It is assumed that, in the usual migration case, cross-media references do not exist- such that all reference sources now target the new media.

Having considered the interaction between media dimensions and structures separately, we now consider the various types of interactions between these two interaction types.

Dimension-Structure Interactions

We now consider interactions between two dimension issues with structure: underutilization and overflow. We also consider two structure interactions with dimension: reference-source/target completeness and reference-source/target co-existence. The third structure interaction (the relationship between media structures and devices) does not interact with the dimension component as the reference-targets are external to the media, thus, they have no effect on the internal dimension.

The situation of *underutilization* may be addressed in migration by merging one *iunit* with another, such that the sum of the dimensions of the two *iunits* together approximates D_D. However, the relationship between the merged contents must be considered. If one *iunit* is supposed to be perceived before another, and their order is important, then it needs to be maintained during migration. Also, if one *iunit* exists at a higher level of generality than a set of *iunits*, it cannot be merged with an individual member of this set without destroying the relationship between this merged *iunit* with other members of the set.

The situation of *overflow* may be addressed by subdividing an *iunit* so that each element approximates D_D. However, during migration, the relationship of generality between *iunits* needs to be maintained. If one *iunit* exists at a higher level of generality than a set of *iunits*, it can be separated in two ways, but each is problematic. If it is subdivided to create a new member of the set, the relationship between the other set members and the new member will be incorrect. On the other hand, if it is subdivided into a new *iunit*, and the set is attached to the new *iunit*, the relationship between the set and the old *iunit* will be incorrect.

The *completeness of reference-source/target* (RCO) has a dimension impact because the more reference-sources, the more space they require for their representation. Each collection of reference sources requires a way to reach each collection, and each way has a dimension impact. For example,

Figure 7: Reference Source Completeness Dimensional Requirement

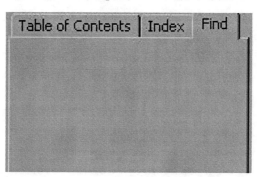

consider Figure 7, where there are three tabs for three collections of reference-sources. With three tabs only, the tabs all fit nicely across the display pane. However, if another tab were added, it would reduce the amount of space to display the contents of each tab (the blank area of the tab). In addition, the more reference-sources that are members of each individual reference-source collection, the more overflow that occurs in the presentation of structure.

The *reference-source/target co-existence* aim has a dimension impact simply because D_D is finite, and presenting the structure of the media at the same time as presenting the content means that there is less space available for display of the content. In Figure 8, a web page has been subdivided such that the structure is presented in the left-hand frame, while the content is presented in the right-hand frame, a common practice in web site design.

In this section, we considered a number of interactions between media and the media devices that impact migration in terms of dimension and structure. We now develop a knowledge representation for migration that attempts to maximize utility with respect to these interactions.

Figure 8: Reference-Source/Target Coexistence Dimension Requirement

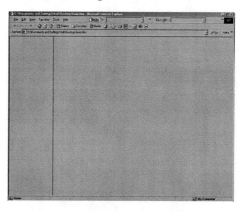

The Migration Knowledge Representation

There are possibly a number of different knowledge representations that would be suitable to represent expertise in migrating from one media to another. We chose to use rules as the knowledge representation scheme because rules have the following four characteristics: independence, ease of understanding, ease of modification, and our belief that migration knowledge can be specified with certainty (Riley, 1998). The migration rules we constructed by analyzing the interactions are represented below, with Boolean expressions capitalized. Note that each iunit begins a reference-target that is referred to by a reference source. This source exists either in a collection of reference sources or as an individual reference. Also note that each iunit is considered separately, even though a single iunit can consist of a number of sub-iunits.

Overflow rule:

IF $M_{D1} >> D_D$ AND
     $M_{D2} \cong D_D$ AND
     Iunit$_1$ is not a higher-level *iunit* for a number of lower-level *iunits*   AND
     Adding *iunit$_3$* reference-source to collection does not cause overflow AND
     The *iunit$_3$* reference-target makes sense

THEN

Iunit$_1$ is subdivided into *iunit$_2$* and *iunit$_3$*;
Iunit$_2$ replaces *iunit$_1$*;
Iunit$_3$ follows *iunit$_2$* at the same level in the structure hierarchy so that the order of perception is maintained.

Note, when very large MD1 is subdivided, only the dimension of *iunit$_2$* is considered with respect to D_D because *iunit$_3$* can now be considered as a separate entity to which the overflow or underutilization rules can be applied if necessary.

Underutilization rule:

IF $M_{D1} << D_D$ AND $M_{D2} << D_D$ AND
     $M_{D2} + M_{D1} = M_{D3} \cong D_D$
     AND
     Iunit$_1$ is not a higher-level *iunit* for a number of lower-level *iunits*   AND
     Iunit$_2$ is not a higher-level *iunit* for a number of lower-level *iunits*   AND
     Iunit$_2$ is to be perceived AFTER *iunit$_1$* is perceived   AND

Adding *iunit₃* reference-source to collection does not cause overflow AND
The *iunit₃* reference-target makes sense   AND
All other possible merger combinations are considered to maximize the
number of mergers
THEN
Merge *iunit₂* with and following *iunit₁* into *iunit₃*.

Collection construction rule:

IF   The reference-target type of *iunit₁* belongs to a useful collection   AND
No collection exists   AND
A new collection does not cause overflow
THEN
Construct a new collection;
Add *iunit₁* to the new collection.

Collection addition rule:

IF   Adding *iunit₁* to the collection does not cause overflow   AND
A reference-source for *iunit₁* does not already exist in the collection   AND
The grammar of the reference-source is appropriate to others in the
collection
THEN
Add *iunit₁* to the collection.

Note that grammatical modifications that are made for this second rule may
mean that the reference-sources in the collection are not identical to reference-
target, but the changes can only be cosmetic, as the meaning must be the same
in order for the audience to understand what information is described by the
content without having to perceive the content.

Collection replication rule:

IF   Adding *iunit₁* to the collection does not cause overflow   AND
A reference-source for *iunit₁* exists in the collection   AND
THEN
Add *iunit₁* to the collection;
Represent this multiplicity within *iunit₁* so that the audience can perceive it.

This rule allows the problem of information replication to be sidestepped
by making the audience completely aware of its incidences within the content
itself, thus, assisting the aim of reference-source/target co-existence.

Collection positioning rule:

IF   *Iunit$_1$* is referred to by multiple non-collection reference-sources   AND

These sources exist within *iunits* that are close together in a collection AND

Moving *iunit$_1$* does not interrupt the audience perceiving the content.

THEN

Move *iunit$_1$* to follow the last *iunit* in this group at the same level as the last *iunit*.

This rule reduces the distance between information that has strong links in terms of internal references. For example, a book appendix (positioned at the end of the book) might be referred to by one chapter only. In migration, this appendix can be moved so that it is closer to the chapter.

Reference-target stripping rule:

IF   reference-source/target$_1$ that is NOT connected with an *iunit*

THEN

Delete reference- source/target$_1$.

This rule means that references that are constructed to point to specific parts of the media are stripped out during migration. Thus, page numbers and references to page numbers would be stripped out of a book that was migrated to another device.

Reference-target indirect indexing rule:

IF   *iunit$_1$* is associated with an index by which the audience navigates the material

THEN

Look up the index to find the position of *iunit$_1$*;

Associate the reference-source in the collection with the index for *iunit$_1$*.

This rule allows indirect indexing of an *iunit*. For example, if hypertext is migrated to book form, then the migrated table of contents would need to refer to page numbers.

Having specified all rules for the knowledge base in the migration model, the development phase of this migration model is complete. We now begin to evaluate this model in terms of the requirements of the model and by applying it, theoretically, to a migration task.

EVALUATION OF THE PROPOSED MIGRATION MODEL

In the requirements of the evaluation model, it was proposed that we integrate models from four domains: communication, information, media and expert systems. The reasons why we needed these models were also described. The extent to which our integration addresses these reasons must be considered. Subsequently, a case study is explored to assess the accuracy of the model.

Firstly, a *communication* model was incorporated with minor changes, based on Shannon's communication system. Minor changes included focusing on information-content messages that are represented within a media form. The noise contribution to the signal was also removed, as perfect signal transmission of media was assumed. The basic concepts of communication remained the same.

Secondly, an *information* model was incorporated which remained completely intact, although its incorporation caused changes in other models. Gitt's information theory was positioned entirely within the context of a communication system, so that only the information that is perceived by the audience is considered. Although electronic devices are information processors, the information required to control the device was not considered. The device is simply seen as a platform for media delivery.

Thirdly, a *media* model was included. Munson's operation model of media provided a generic way to describe the delivery of information to the audience that was independent of a particular media type or group of media types. This media model was extended to represent syntactical elements of information, such that structural and non-structural content could be distinguished. Without the construction of these distinctions, it would have been impossible to construct a knowledge representation for migration.

Finally, Feigenbaum's *expert system* model was included in order to represent the knowledge of migration. The interactions between the other models were investigated in terms of utility, with respect to dimension and structure. These interactions were then codified into an initial set of conversion rules that attempted to maximize utility in migration of communication between media devices.

All of the requirements of the model have been satisfactorily met. Consequently, we now assess the accuracy of the model by its theoretical application.

Theoretical Application of the Model

The accuracy of any model can be evaluated by comparing its components, behavior and interactions with the real world. However, it is necessary to select that part of the real world that is useful for comparison. In this case, selection is important because it would be possible to compare this model of the migration of communication between media devices with a huge number of cases. Since the digitization task is important in digital libraries, we compare the model to the task of migrating information from a set of technical books to hypertext. This comparison occurs at two levels: matching components of the model to this migration; and matching conversion rules to this migration. We do not consider the interaction between dimensions as these are codified into the conversion rules.

Component Comparison

- *Author:* Authors produce technical textbooks these days using word-processing software, and typesetting may be performed using a typesetting program. Technical textbooks are often used for teaching purposes or as a quick reference, thus, these books are often highly structured, containing extensive various handcrafted indexes. The utility of migration may focus on the speed of reference. Migration will tend toward media devices that present faster, more accurate, and more convenient ways of quickly accessing the information and allowing authors to keep this information up-to-date. Migrating a set of textbooks to hypertext and delivering them over the Internet allows access from anywhere in the world and allows the process of information updates to be centralized. Other potential advantages in this migration could include the ability to easily reference the huge body of growing information online, and also for this electronic content to potentially be used in conjunction with computer-assisted workflow software.

- *Media Capture/Editor/Devices:* The media that was originally captured using word-processing software is migrated into electronic publishing software (note that, while these functions may be bundled together into the one software package, there are a number of specialized electronic publishing software products available). Since the basic representation of the textbook exists in digital form, we assume that the electronic representation is transformed in this migration task, as opposed to scanning in pages and pages of a textbook in order to (re)create this electronic representation. The practical advantage of manipulating the electronic representation of the media is that an expert system can only manipulate electronic representations. With respect to our modification of the model of media, the set of textbooks becomes an *iunit*. Also, each individual book becomes an *iunit*, as does every unique section at any depth. The reference-target required to start an *iunit* is the heading for every section.

- *Transmitter/Receiver:* A web server becomes the centralized transmitter, and the internet service provider becomes the receiver. The signal component becomes discrete data packets that are routed through the Internet. Noise source components are not considered, as internet communications have built in error-checking and recovery procedures that make noise invisible to a user.

- *Media device:* The media device is the monitor on which an internet browsing program displays the reconstituted data packets. Unfortunately, both the dimensions of this device and the presentation program are inconsistent, and it is difficult for authors to assess how their information will work with different sized displays. Consequently, authors often assume that the user will have a window-optimized program running on the most popularly sized monitor. For this migration example, we assume that $D_{D1} < D_{D2}$, that is, a web page can display the text of a number of book pages, thus, for small sub-sub-sections (*iunits*), underutilization occurs regularly with direct migration.

- *Audience:* The audience is the person controlling the Internet browsing program that contains the migrated hypertext version of the textbook. In order to find the information they seek as quickly as possible, the audience uses the multiple structures and electronic find capabilities that are presented along with the hypertext content. The feedback path to the author can also be increased via hypertext delivery of information, as convenient contact using electronic mail can be linked to the information, or electronic surveys can actually be embedded in the content itself.

- *Expert systems components:* The three parts of an expert system we included — working memory, inference engine, and knowledge base — could all be used for such a migration. The *working memory* would have direct access to both the word-processing software and electronic publishing software, using built in control procedures to automatically format the information. The *inference engine* would match the information in the word-processing software to the conversion rules in the *knowledge representation* component, and apply the consequents of these rules in the electronic publishing package to produce the migrated hypertext. We now assess the applicability of the conversion rules for migrating a textbook to hypertext.

Conversion Rule Comparison

The eight conversion rules proposed are now considered with respect to the migration of a set of textbooks to hypertext: overflow, underutilization, collection construction, collection addition, collection replication, collection positioning, reference-target stripping, and reference-target indirect indexing rule.

In order to properly consider the potential application of these rules, we need to give an example book structure that is migrated. As previously mentioned, the structure of body-text can be discussed in terms of headings that delineate the beginning of subdivided pieces of text (each piece being an *iunit*). Any set of contiguous pieces can form larger pieces, thus, headings can exist at different levels reflected by common level names. For example, a textbook is often subdivided into chapters, chapters into sections, sections into subsections, and so on. The precise level of each heading can be indicated using a numbering scheme with which most people who have seen textbooks would be familiar. For example, consider the book structure below BS_1 with a single chapter having two sections, and the latter section having two subsections.

> 1.
> > 1.1.
> > 1.2.
> > > 1.2.1.
> > > 1.2.2.

This simple structure BS_1 will be used in examples describing structure issues, in addition to the following terms describing the relationship between headings in BS_1:

- A *sibling* is a heading at the same level, e.g., 1.1 is a sibling of 1.2
- A *child* is the heading of a subsection, e.g., 1.1 is a child of 1
- A *parent* is a heading which has a child, e.g., 1 is the parent of 1.1
- An asterisk (*) means a new heading is introduced for a particular conversion operation

With respect to the *overflow* rule, there might be a number of book sections (*iunits*) that need to be subdivided across a number of web pages in migration to hypertext. Consider the two examples below using *BS* where 1 and 1.2 are subdivided respectively.

Heading 1 subdivided:	Heading 1.2 subdivided
1.	1.
1.1. *	1.1.
1.2.	1.2.
1.3.	1.2.1. *
1.3.1.	1.2.2.
1.3.2.	1.2.3.

Note that neither of these cases of subdivision would be permitted by the migration rules, and rightly so; in each case, the generality relationship between sections is broken. In the first case, it would be inferred from the structure that section 1.2 would be at the same level as section 1.1, but, in fact, the content does not reflect the structure. In the second case, it would be inferred from the structure that 1.2.2 and 1.2.3 were at the same level as 1.2.1, but this would not be true.

With respect to the *underutilization* rule, there might be a great deal more book sections (*iunits*) that need to be joined in a number of web pages in migration to hypertext because of the previous assumption that $D_{D1} < D_{D2}$. Consider the two examples below using *BS* where 1.1 and 1.2 are merged and 1.2.1 and 1.2.2 are merged respectively.

Headings 1.1 & 1.2 merged	Headings 1.2.1 & 1.2.2 merged
1.	1.
1.1.*	1.1.
1.1.1.	1.2.
1.1.2.	1.2.1. *

Note that the merger between 1.1 and 1.2 would not be permitted as 1.2 has children, and such a merger would confuse the generality relationships between the children and heading 1.1. On the other hand, a merger between 1.2.1 and 1.2.2 causes no issues with generality relationships and could be completely permissible under the underutilization rules.

With respect to the *collection construction* rule, *BS* is a useful collection, and, since we are only discussing one collection type (a table of contents), the small number means that it probably will not cause overflow on most electronic media devices, such that reference-source/target coexistence is possible. With respect to the *collection-addition* rule, the size of *BS* is very small, and, although the headings do not actually have text content (thus, no grammatical modifications need to be considered), a representation of *BS* on most size electronic media devices would be possible. It is also assumed that, with this small size, any appendix is already close to other content, thus, it is unnecessary to consider the *collection positioning* rule for this example of a small collection.

With respect to the *collection replication* rule, it is practically unlikely that a section would be replicated in such a small structure as *BS*, but consider the example below where this is the case, since this might occur where a particularly useful section could be replicated in a set of textbooks.

1.
   1.1. → *1.2.2*
   1.2.
      1.2.1.
      1.2.2. →   *1.1*

It is useful to consider this example because some electronic publishing software packages come with plug-ins that provide dynamic tracking of table of contents. For example, if a user clicks on links within a web page, without using the table of contents hyperlinks, the position of the new web page presented is reflected by an automatic update of the presentation of the table of contents. However, a problem occurs with content replication, in that each web page can only point to one position in the table of contents. Consequently, a user can navigate to a web page using a structure in one section, but, to their surprise, the table of contents jumps to another section that is different from where they were looking. It might take a novice user a frustrating amount of time to find where in the structure they were originally looking, depending on the size and overflow of the table of contents. The *collection-replication* rule, on the other hand, which insists on copying the multiplicity of references within the web page itself, would assist the user finding finding the original location.

The *reference-target* stripping rule would remove all page numbers from the content if they were represented within it, assuming the author has no use for page numbers on the web pages. With a reference text book, for example, the book is subdivided into many discrete pieces, and it is faster for the user to be able to directly reach a piece without physically bypassing other pieces. The *reference-target indirect indexing* rule would be applied in the construction of hyperlinks, such that the physical location of the web page and target within it is known.

Having considered all components, and conversion rules, it appears that the proposed model does theoretically describe the migration of a set of textbooks to hypertext reasonably well. We now consider how emerging technologies could support the implementation of our model.

APPLICATIONS OF EMERGING TECHNOLOGIES

While this migration model identified a number of interactions between dimension and structure that needed to be considered in migration, and proposed conversion rules that take these interactions into account in migration, the practical implementation of these rules has yet to occur. In this section, we identify the technology requirements for these rules to be implemented and suggest ways in which emerging technologies could be applied, particularly with respect to the semantic web.

Ideally, an author would not need to consider overflow or underutilization. The media device being perceived by the audience would inform the transmitter about its dimensions, and the transmitter would automatically convert the media appropriately for any specific device. Such flexibility would undoubtedly be appreciated by web programmers, who can spend many hours attempting to make the same site interoperable for multiple size browsers (among many other things).

Both the *overflow* and *underutilization* rules have three technical requirements:

- The ability to recognize the relationship between media and device dimensions.
- The ability to recognize the generality relationship and between *iunits* and the order in which *iunits* are supposed to be perceived, where important to the author.
- The ability to recognize whether a reference-target 'makes sense' in a linguistic sense.

The order of these three requirements goes from easy to more complex. Dimensions can be represented as numbers that can easily be compared. Generality relationships between *iunits* could be described and stored using emerging meta-data approaches. In a book example, if one *iunit* contains two others, and each has its own heading, then presumably each heading will make sense in isolation. However, creating a computer program that can automatically summarize a section of text (independent of its complexity) and construct a heading that makes sense 'on-the-fly' is a non-trivial problem.

The *collection construction* rule requires knowledge about what is deemed a 'useful' collection, such that it knows whether or not to construct a collection. Given the utility definition, something that is useful assists the audience to find what they are looking for, so a feedback path from users is necessary to store this information. There may be some value in finding out user profiles for a number of types of information, but it is also possible that, in some situations, the type of collection is entirely dependent on the context of the information, such that pooling this knowledge is less useful in some cases.

The *collection addition* rule requires that the grammar of the reference-source is appropriate relative to others in the collection. Technical requirements may be storing a large number of grammatical cases that are wrong, and matching the reference-source to these cases then causes a hard-wired grammatical change. This requirement assumes that grammar of any language is almost static, such that it can be defined and does not change so fast that it is difficult to update.

The *collection replication* rule requires the replication of multiplicity within the *iunit*. Dynamic tracking should allow for context-sensitivity, such that the reference-source collection does not jump to a fixed place, but the audience should still be made aware that multiplicity exists.

The *collection positioning* rule adds three implementation requirements:

- The ability to identify where an *iunit* is being referred to by a number of non-collection reference-sources.
- The ability to judge how close reference-sources are together in a structure (collection).
- The ability to identify whether moving discrete *iunits* around would disrupt reading order, where it is important.

The final requirement relates to external hyperlinks, an identified structure interaction that does not contribute a conversion rule; however, it is important in the context of digital libraries. If the content of an external web page changes in any significant way, or its file name changes, it should inform the reference-source, such that an author can reconsider this link. With the current state of the internet, web pages can just suddenly disappear, such that hyperlinks lead nowhere. It is infeasible to expect an author to manually and continually check the thousands of hyperlinks that might branch out from their hypertext. It requires that hyperlinks become more bi-directional than present; that an author can define the type of change they consider to be significant. For example, if only the directory name of the file changed but the web page content and context remained identical, the author might not care, and their web site could automatically update the link.

In this section, we found that emerging technologies could make an implementation of a migration model of communication between media devices possible to some degree, perhaps in the relatively near future. In particular, meta-data and the semantic web could be used to assist the application of the conversion rules.

CONCLUSION

In this chapter, a model of the migration of communication between media devices was proposed, combining models of communication, information, media and expert systems. The model was evaluated by applying it theoretically to one of the important tasks in digital libraries: the migration of a set of highly structured textbooks to hypertext. It was argued that emerging technologies could assist migration by representing and using the relationships that exist within information in a conversion process. The dawn of automatic migration techniques may allow content experts to focus on the authoring of information within one media device, freeing them from involvement in the migration process. Such techniques may also allow the vast and growing volume of information to avoid obsolescence as new media devices continue to emerge.

REFERENCES

A Paepcke, C.-C. C., Garcia-Molina, H., & Winograd, T. (1998). Interoperability for digital libraries worldwide. *Communications of the ACM*, 41(4), 33-43.

Bisbal, J., Wu, D. L., & Grimson, J. (1999). Legacy information systems: Issues and directions. *IEEE Software*, 16(5), 103-111.

Bordegoni, M. et al. (1997). A standard reference model for intelligent multimedia presentation systems. *Computer Standards and Interfaces*, 18, 477- 496.

Brodie, M. (1993). *DARWIN: On the incremental migration of legacy information systems*. GTE Labs. (Technical Report No. TR-022-10-92-165).

Chestnutt, D. (1997, July). The model editions partnership: "Smart text" and beyond. *D-Lib Magazine*.

Feigenbaum, E. (1982). *Knowledge Engineering in the 1980s*. Stanford, CA: Stanford University, Department of Computer Science.

Gitt, W. (1989). Information: The third fundamental quantity. *Siemens Review, 6*, 36-41.

Horvath, G. K. et al. (2001, September). *Communication model for the user interface of a shape conceptualisation system*. Paper presented at the Proceedings of the ASME International Design Engineering Technical Conference, Pittsburgh, Pennsylvania.

Lesk, M. (1997). *How much information is there in the world?* Available at: http://www.lesk.com/mlesk/ksg97/ksg.html.

Macleod, I. (1990). Storage and retrieval of structured documents. *Information Processing and Management*, 26(2), 197-208.

Munson, E. (1996, September). *Towards an operational theory of media*. Paper presented at the 3rd International Workshop on Principles of Document Processing, Palo Alto, California.

Nunberg, G. (1996). *The Future of the Book*. Berkeley CA: University of California Press.

Pfeiffer, E. M. a. M. (1997). *A representation of media for multimedia authoring and browsing systems*. Available at: http://citeseer.nj.nec.com/9760.html.

Riley, J. G. G. (1998). *EXPERT SYSTEMS: Principles and Programming* (3rd ed.). Boston, MA: PWS Publishing.

Searle, J. (1969). *Speech Acts: An Essay in the Philosophy of Language*. Cambridge: Cambridge University Press.

Shannon, C. (1948). A mathematical theory of communication. *The Bell System Technical Journal*, 27, 379-423.

Sornil, E. F. a. O. (1999). Digital Libraries. In R. B.-Y. & B. Ribeiro-Neto (Eds.), *Modern Information Retrieval* (chap. 11). UK: AWI.

SECTION II

WEB INFORMATION REPRESENTATIONS, STORAGE, AND ACCESS

Chapter IV

Storage and Access Control Issues for XML Documents

George Pallis, Aristotle University of Thessaloniki, Greece

Konstantina Stoupa, Aristotle University of Thessaloniki, Greece

Athena Vakali, Aristotle University of Thessaloniki, Greece

ABSTRACT

XML documents management is becoming an area of great research value and interest since XML has become a popular standard for data communication and knowledge exchange over the Internet. Therefore, new issues have emerged in terms of storage and access control policies for XML documents. Concerning the storage issues, the majority of proposals rely on the usage of typical database management systems (DBMSs), whereas XML documents can also be stored in other storage environments (such as file systems and LDAP directories). It is important to consider storage and access control together since these issues are essential in implementations for XML documents management. Moreover, the chapter focuses on the recent access control models which guarantee the security of the XML-based data, which are located in a variety of storage topologies. This chapter's goal is to survey and classify existing approaches for XML documents storage and access control, and, at the same time, highlight the main differences between them. The most popular XML database software tools are outlined in terms of their storage and access control policies.

INTRODUCTION

Internet is currently the core media for data and knowledge exchange. XML (eXtensible Markup Language)[1], a subset of SGML (Standard Generalized Markup Language), is introduced by the World Wide Web Consortium (W3C) to complement and enhance HTML (Hypertext Markup Language) in electronic data representation and exchange on the Web. XML is becoming wide spread and is a text-based markup language (like HTML), but it supports a richer set of features. The main advantage of using XML is that an XML document (differently from an HTML document) can be written once and visualized in a variety of ways. Therefore, XML is currently the most popular standardization effort in web documents representation, and is rapidly becoming a standard for data representation and exchange over the Internet. As a result, large amounts of XML documents are being generated, and their efficient management has become a major necessity. Researchers in both industry and academia have focused on efficiently storing, manipulating and retrieving XML documents.

The main XML-related research issues refer to the XML data accessing, storing, querying and exchanging. Indeed, even if XML lends its power to its ease-of use and extensibility, it is this structure of XML that results in a controversial fact. From one point of view, this structure characterizes XML as an ideal building block on high-speed applications, whereas, from another point of view, it is this structure that makes XML unsuitable for usage under pre-existing data management environments. Most implementations rely on the usage of typical database management systems (DBMSs), whereas others are based on specific systems (providing ad-hoc functionalities). Moreover, since XML can be used over various application platforms, different management approaches have to be devised, depending on the type of the considered XML documents (structured vs. unstructured), the platform type (DBMS vs. file-based systems), and their main usage. Whatever is the chosen solution, a crucial point in efficiently managing XML documents is devising efficient storage and accessing control techniques. Among data management issues, storage and

Figure 1: Architecture of the Considered Topology

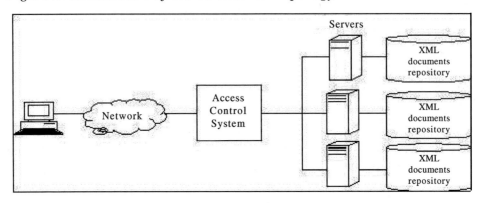

securing techniques have a particular importance, since the performance of the overall XML-based web information system relies heavily on them.

Several solutions for storing XML have been proposed, both in the scientific literature and in commercial products, such as flat files, relational database management systems, object-oriented database management systems, native XML database systems, and LDAP directories. In this framework, the majority of storage and retrieval approaches are based on the usage of existing DBMSs or on specialized system implementations. Furthermore, these approaches can be classified with respect to the type of the system on which they rely and on the used XML document representation model.

Access control is essential in guaranteeing the security of such storage approaches. Several types of access control models have been introduced so far, ranging from the conventional ones (appropriate for centralized systems with low workload) to the most recent and flexible ones (such as the role-based). The implementation of models controlling storage and access to such documents has become a major research issue since hypertext documents are the most common form of information exchanged through the Internet.

This chapter presents a survey for XML documents storage and access control issues, and aims at contributing to identifying the most important policies for storage and accessing in web-based information systems (which use the XML as their data representation format). Therefore, the goal of this chapter is to survey and classify such approaches and, at the same time, highlight the main differences between them. Moreover, the aim of this chapter is to provide a survey of the currently proposed storage and accessing approaches for XML documents, categorized with respect to qualitative parameters, and focusing on the applicability and the efficiency of their structures. The architecture of the system discussed in this chapter is depicted in Figure 1, where a group of servers (supporting XML document repositories) is protected against unautho-rized access (through an access control mechanism). More specifically, XML is used both for XML documents storage in repositories and XML-structured access control.

Moreover, the chapter discusses the storage and access control policies applied in the most popular XML-based software tools, which primarily consider assuring authorized access and protecting documents (located in web-accessible databases). Finally, we will focus on the recent role-based control models since most XML-based storage systems use roles to manage the requested accesses to the protected resources.

This chapter covers the storage and access control issues concerning XML documents. The whole discussion is based on a common case study. The whole chapter is organized into two parts: in the first part, XML documents storage issues are overviewed; and in the second one, a description of the main functions of XML-based access control and authorization models is given and emphasized by the use of various examples. Moreover, the most well-known software tools for XML documents storage and access control are presented, and their approach to storage and access control is highlighted and identified. Finally, an outline of the current research trends concludes the chapter.

XML DATA REPRESENTATION

Each XML document may be based on a structural description of its content, which is specified either by Document Type Definitions (DTDs) or XML Schemas. More specifically, the DTD defines the document structure with a list of legal elements (which describe the rules for associating tags with their content). The main purpose of the DTD is to provide a definition of the proper structure of an XML document. A DTD can be declared as an embedded object in the XML document, or as an external reference. An alternative to DTDs is the definition of scheme by a more sophisticated language, the *XML Schema* (which is more extensible and flexible than conventional DTDs). More specifically, the XML schema provides a means for defining the structure, content and semantics of XML documents. On the other hand, the DTD (or the XML schema) structure contributes in facilitating (for one application) the use of an XML document (created by any application) and improves the data communication over the Internet. Unfortunately, the syntax of XML Schemas has not yet been standardized and, currently, the W3C organization works on version 1.1 of XML Schemas.

For reasons of uniformity, we will use a case study which will be extended and referenced in the following sections. We refer to a library containing book catalogs in digital form. These catalogs include books whose authors are authorized to modify them. Subscribers to this digital library are able to read such catalogs. An example of such an XML document, which describes a fragment of a book catalog, is depicted in Figure 2. In addition, Figure 3 shows the XML Schema that conforms to the previous XML document, while Figure 4 presents the DTD of the XML document. As shown in Figure 3, XML Schema is a superset of DTDs, and it is specified by XML syntax. In particular, the benefits that an XML Schema offers over DTDs can be summarized as follows:

- User-defined types are created.
- The text that appears in elements is constrained to specific types (such as numeric types in specific format).
- Types are restricted in order to create specialized types (e.g., specifying minimum and maximum values).
- Complex types are extended by using a form of inheritance.

However, the cost that is paid for these features is that XML Schema is significantly more complicated than DTDs.

Figure 2: An Example of an XML Document for a Book Catalog

```
<?xml version="1.0"?> <!DOCTYPE BOOKS SYSTEM "books.dtd">
<catalog>
   <book bookID="bk101">
   <authors>
      <person perID="P101">
         <fname>Angappa</fname>
         <lname>Gunasekaran</lname>
      </person>
      <person perID="P102">
         <fname>Omar</fname>
         <lname>Khalil</lname>
      </person>
      <person perID="P103">
         <fname>Syed Mahbubur </fname>
         <lname>Rahman</lname>
      </person>
   </authors>
   <title>Knowledge and Information Technology Management</title>
   <category>Computer</category>
   <price>84.95</price>
   <publish_year>2003</publish_year>
   <publisher>Idea Group Publishing</publisher>
   </book>
   <book bookID="bk102">
      ...
   </book>
</catalog>
```

Figure 3: The XML Schema Definition for the Document in Figure 2

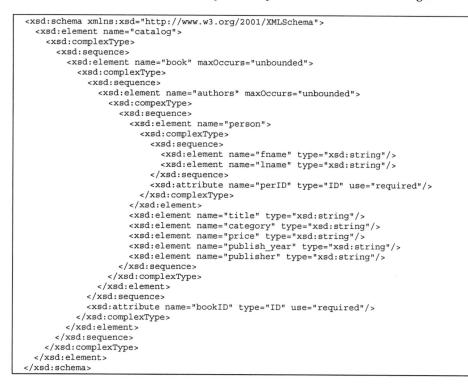

```
<xsd:schema xmlns:xsd="http://www.w3.org/2001/XMLSchema">
  <xsd:element name="catalog">
    <xsd:complexType>
      <xsd:sequence>
        <xsd:element name="book" maxOccurs="unbounded">
          <xsd:complexType>
            <xsd:sequence>
              <xsd:element name="authors" maxOccurs="unbounded">
                <xsd:compexType>
                  <xsd:sequence>
                    <xsd:element name="person">
                      <xsd:complexType>
                        <xsd:sequence>
                          <xsd:element name="fname" type="xsd:string"/>
                          <xsd:element name="lname" type="xsd:string"/>
                        </xsd:sequence>
                        <xsd:attribute name="perID" type="ID" use="required"/>
                      </xsd:complexType>
                    </xsd:element>
                    <xsd:element name="title" type="xsd:string"/>
                    <xsd:element name="category" type="xsd:string"/>
                    <xsd:element name="price" type="xsd:string"/>
                    <xsd:element name="publish_year" type="xsd:string"/>
                    <xsd:element name="publisher" type="xsd:string"/>
                  </xsd:sequence>
                </xsd:complexType>
              </xsd:element>
            </xsd:sequence>
            <xsd:attribute name="bookID" type="ID" use="required"/>
          </xsd:complexType>
        </xsd:element>
      </xsd:sequence>
    </xsd:complexType>
  </xsd:element>
</xsd:schema>
```

The most common abstract data representation model for XML documents is a tree-like structure. Here, we will use a simplified tree form, where the nodes represent only elements, attributes and data. The tree for the document presented in Figure 2 is depicted in Figure 5, where the rectangles represent the elements of the XML document, the ellipses the attributes, and the edges the relationship(s) between an element and its sub-elements (or its attributes).

There are three typical processing steps in manipulating XML documents. Firstly, the XML document is parsed by using an XML parser. Secondly, the document is processed (this step depends on the chosen XML parser). And finally, the data are interpreted and a report is produced.

In order to process the XML documents effectively, two application program interfaces (APIs) have been proposed: SAX (Simple API for XML)

Figure 4: The DTD for the Book Catalog Example: books.dtd

```
<!ELEMENT catalog(Book)>
  <!ELEMENT book (authors,title,category,price,publish_year,publisher)>
  <!ATTLIST book bookID ID default >
  <!ELEMENT authors (person+)>
  <!ELEMENT person(fname,lname)>
  <!ATTLIST person perID ID default >
  <!ELEMENT fname (#PCDATA)>
  <!ELEMENT lname(#PCDATA)>
  <!ELEMENT title (#PCDATA)>
  <!ELEMENT category (#PCDATA)>
  <!ELEMENT price (#PCDATA)>
  <!ELEMENT publish_year (#PCDATA)>
  <!ELEMENT publisher (#PCDATA)>
```

and DOM (Document Object Model). The first is based on the textual processing of XML documents. The second is based on the tree representation of XML documents. These APIs are the de-facto standards for processing XML documents.

- **SAX**[2]: An event-based API for XML. SAX is based on a parser where the users provide event handlers for parsing various events. More specifically, the SAX parser sends events (as it parses the whole document), supporting a (LIFO) stack-oriented access for handling these events. SAX processes the XML documents as a stream. Experiments have shown that SAX is suitable in two cases: when the system's memory is limited, or when only parts of documents are required.

- **DOM**[3]: The DOM API (developed by W3C) follows a tree-like structure, and XML documents are parsed into a tree representation. More specifically, the elements have parent-child relations with other elements. The parser builds an internal structure such that an application can navigate it (in a tree-like fashion). DOM allows an application to have random access to the tree-structured document (at the cost of increased memory usage). In this context, a variety of functions for traversing the DOM tree have appeared. Compared to SAX, DOM is suitable when processing XML documents for multiple times, whereas its disadvantage is that loading and parsing are needed in every step.

XML DOCUMENTS STORAGE POLICIES

XML data storage policies are related with locating XML documents in an effective manner, on persistent memory. Several approaches have been developed for high performance storage and retrieval of XML documents.

Figure 5: A Tree-Like Structure of the XML Document

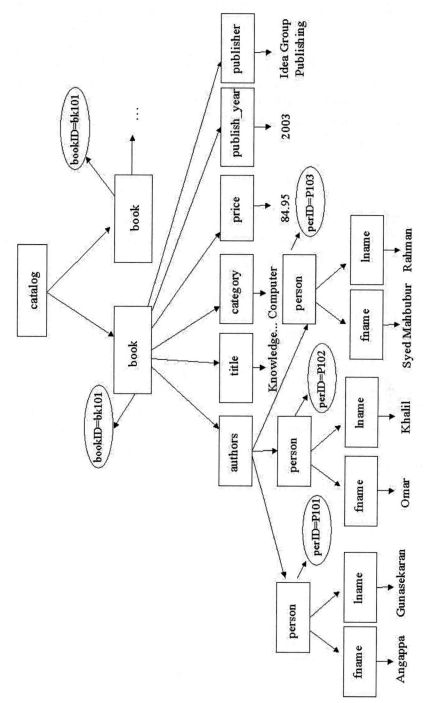

Here, we categorize placement approaches with respect to the corresponding underlying storage environments. In particular, a typical approach is to store the XML documents in a relational DBMS (flat files are converted to relational representation), inheriting both the benefits and drawbacks of the relational databases. In a second approach, XML documents are stored in non-relational databases, whereas a number of Object-Oriented, Object-Relational and Native DBMSs have been proposed. Finally, in a third approach, XML documents can be stored in other XML storage environments such as file systems and LDAP directories.

XML Storage Under Relational DBMSs

A relational DBMS uses a collection of tables to represent both data and relationships among these data. More specifically, in order to represent XML data by using tables, it is necessary to break down the XML documents into rows and columns. The tree-like structure of XML facilitates both their decomposition and storing in relational tables. However, this process is expected to cause some performance overhead mainly due to the continuous translation of trees to tables (and vice versa). In this context, an XML document (depicted in Figure 2) can be represented easily by relation tables (as illustrated in Figure 6).

Due to its popularity, several models have been proposed to store XML documents in Relational DBMSs (e.g., Shimura et al., 1999; Silberschatz et al., 2002; Tian et al., 2000; Zhu & Lu, 2001). In this framework, mapping relation is one of the most popular ways of storing XML documents in Relational databases. Existing XML to relational mapping techniques can be classified into the following two categories (Amer-Yahia & Fernandez, 2002):

- **Schema-driven Techniques:** These techniques require the existence of a DTD or XML schema (Florescu & Kossmann, 1999; Khan & Rao, 2001). In particular, XML elements (whose DTD or XML Schema is known) are mapped effectively to relations and attributes. This is done by using either a fixed or a flexible set of rules. More specifically, fixed

Table 1: XML DTD and Relational Database Schema Relationship

XML DTD	RELATIONAL DATABASE SCHEMA
Element	Table
ID Attribute	Primary key
#REQUIRED	NULL
#IMPLIED	NOT NULL

mappings (using basic, shared and hybrid inlining techniques) are defined from DTDs to tables. When converting an XML DTD to relations, it is tempting to map each element in the DTD to a relation, and to map the attributes of the element to attributes of the relation. Table 1 summarizes the simulating between an XML DTD and a relational database schema. On the other hand, flexible mappings can be supported by using an XML Schema. In this case, more information might be captured than the previous one (in which a DTD is given). In general, XML schema have specific features which are useful for storage. One can specify precise data types (e.g., strings, integers) instead of just text. For example, in the XML schema, the type information should be associated to attributes. The mapping approach described by Bohannon et al. (2002) is based on the principle of mapping groups in XML schema into tables in the relational schema. However, there are some common principles which are applied in both mappings (fixed and flexible). Therefore, sub-elements that can occur multiple times are mapped into separate tables. Non-repeated sub-elements may become attributes. The optionality is another principle which is handled using nullable fields. Finally, the choice is represented by

Figure 6: Relations for XML Data Representation

Catalog relation

bookID	title	category	price	publish_year	publisher
bk101	Knowledge and Information Technology Management	Computer	84.95	2003	Idea Group Publishing
...	.....	.....	.....	.....	.....

Author relation

perID	bookId	fname	lname
P101	bk101	Angappa	Gunasekaran
P102	bk101	Omar	Khalil
P103	bk101	Syed Mahbubur	Rahman
...	...	...	.....

using multiple tables or a universal table with nullable fields. Experiments have shown that the schema-driven techniques provide efficient QoS (Quality of Service). Furthermore, XML queries can be translated into SQL and executed efficiently. However, this approach cannot store all the XML documents. In particular, XML documents whose DTD (or XML Schema) is unknown cannot be mapped to relations. In such a case, these documents can be stored as a tree representation or as strings. Another approach proposed by Yoshikawa et al. (2001) (called *XRel*) is based on such a mapping, by which a fixed database schema is used to store the structure of all XML documents (based on path expressions).

- **User-defined Techniques:** These techniques have been proposed by commercial databases (such as IBM DB2, Oracle 8i and 9i, Microsoft SQL Server 2000). In this case, the user gives the underlying relational schema. Therefore, the mapping is provided either by using a declarative interface or programmatically, through special purpose queries.

Moreover, a technique for automatic mapping of XML documents to relations under a relational DBMS is presented by Khan and Rao (2001), whereas a study on how XML data can be stored and queried under a standard relational database system is presented by Florescu and Kossmann (1999). Furthermore, a data model and an execution process for efficient storage and retrieval of XML documents under a relational DBMS are presented by Schmidt et al. (2000). Overall, all existing storage methodologies in Relational DBMSs are categorized in a more general perspective, and all the above models can be categorized in:

1. **XML Data as a Tree:** the XML documents can be easily represented as a tree, and node types in the tree are: element, attribute and text (Kanne & Moerkotte, 2000). Therefore, XML data can be stored by using a pair of relations: *nodes* and *child*. In particular, each element and attribute in the XML data is given a unique identifier (primary key). This representation has the advantage that all XML information can be represented directly in relational form, and many XML queries can be translated into relational queries and executed inside the database system. The key issue for this approach is the mapping from the tree structure of an XML document to tuples in relational tables. In this context, several approaches have been proposed which model the XML documents as trees and store them by using various relations (Florescu & Kossmann, 1999; Kanne & Moerkotte, 2000; Khan & Rao, 2001; Silberschatz et al., 2002). More specifically, the existing relations are the following:

- **Nodes and edges:** XML documents, in this relation, can be stored using the following pair: nodes(id, type, label, value) and edges(parent-id, child-id, order). More specifically, each element/attribute is given a unique identifier. The type is either "element" or "attribute," and the label specifies the tag name of the element or the name of the attribute, respectively. The value is the text value of the element. On the other hand, the relation "edges" indicates the parent-child relationships in the tree. The attribute order (which is optional) records the ordering of children. The main drawback of this relation is that each element gets broken up into many pieces, and a large number of joins is required to reassemble elements.

- **Nodes and values:** In this case, the pair of relations is the following: nodes(tag, docId, startPos, endPos, level) and values(word, docId, position). This relationship is based on partitions. The position indicates the word displacement within the XML document. The interval [startPos, endPos] determines the relationship between parent-child and ancestor-descendant. The drawback of this approach is that special types of joins are needed to evaluate path queries. Even simple queries require a large number of joins.

- **Nodes and paths:** XML documents can also be stored by using the following pair of relations: nodes(docId, pathId, tag, order, position, type, value) and paths(pathId, path). In this relation, each node has a unique path from the root of the document. For supporting this kind of relation, it is required to have implemented index structures on path expressions. Finally, the positions are used to find sub-trees.

  Therefore, the tree structure is decomposed into relations (we can easily access and reuse) by the unit of logical structure, and index structures can be used (such as B+ trees, R trees, etc.). These index structures are also provided in relational database systems in order to support the tree data model. The decomposition of XML documents is executed when they are parsed by using an application program interface (DOM or SAX). However, it has the disadvantage that each element is broken up into many pieces, and a large number of joins is required to reassemble elements.

2. **XML Data as a String:** A common way to store XML data in a relational DBMS is to store each child element as a string in a separate tuple in the database (Kanne & Moerkotte, 2000). For example, the XML document (Figure 2) can be stored as a set of tuples in a relation *elements(data)*, with the attribute *data* of each tuple storing one XML element (e.g., Title, Category, Price) in string form. An advantage of this

approach is that, as long as there are several top-level elements in a document, strings are small compared to full document, allowing faster access to individual elements. Furthermore, XML documents can be stored without DTD (or XML schema). A disadvantage of this approach is that we cannot query the data directly (since the database system does not have knowledge about the stored elements schema). A solution to this problem is to store various types of elements in different relations, and store the values of some critical elements as attributes of the relations to enable indexing. It is important to indicate that indexing techniques play a crucial role in improving the performance of storage systems. In fact, several database systems (such as Oracle 8i, 9i) support function indices, which can help avoid replication of attributes between the XML string and relation attributes.

XML Storage Under Object-Relational DBMSs

As web applications manipulate an increasing amount of XML, there is a growing interest in storing XML documents in Object-Relational (O-R) DBMSs. In particular, several Relational DBMS vendors (such as Microsoft (MS) SQL Server 2000, Oracle 8i and 9i, IBM DB2, Informix, etc.) include Object-Oriented (O-O) features in their products in order to offer more powerful modeling capabilities for storing XML documents. These products are discussed in detail in the next sections.

In general, the XML documents in O-R databases are stored in a nested table, in which each tag name in DTD (or XML schema) corresponds to an attribute name in the nested table. In O-R DBMSs, the procedure for storing XML data to relation mapping is modeled by an O-R model. More specifically, each nested XML element is mapped into an object reference of the appropriate type. Then, several mapping rules are indirectly embedded in the underlying model. For the construction of XML document, the DBMS translates all the object references into a hierarchical structure of XML elements. For example, in an XML document (Figure 1), the elements *authors* and *person* are nested, and the latter one is the child element of the former one. Therefore, two objects are defined, namely *authors-obj* and *person-obj*, and the second one will make an object reference to the first one.

For mapping of an XML document into an O-R DBMS, it is required to traverse the XML document. For this reason, an XML DOM is usually used to facilitate the construction of a tree structure in the main memory. In particular, this tree structure will contain the document's elements, attributes, text, etc. It is important to recall that a DOM-based parser exposes the data, along with a programming library — called the DOM Application Programming Interface (API) — which will allow data in an XML document to be accessed and manipulated. This API is available for many different programming languages (Java, C++, etc.).

XML Storage Under Object-Oriented DBMS

Another option is to use O-O databases for storing the XML documents. In particular, XML documents are stored as collections of object instances, using relationships based on the O-O idea (Vakali & Terzi, 2000) since O-O DBMSs have been designed to work well with object programming languages (such as C++, C# and Java). Inheritance and object-identity are their basic characteristics. In particular, O-O DBMSs tend to store XML in a way approximate to the DOM, (which has already been presented). However, O-O DBMSs cannot easily handle data with a dynamic structure since a new class definition for a new XML document is needed and the use of O-O DBMSs for XML document storage is not as efficient and flexible.

For such reasons, the use of O-O DBMSs has shown very limited commercial success (especially when compared to their relational counterparts). The most indicative O-O are:

- **Lore** (McHugh et al., 1997): It is one such example that has been built to manage XML documents. The data model used for semi-structured data representation in Lore is the *Object Exchange Model* (OEM). This model can be thought of as a labeled directed graph. The vertices in the graph are *objects*, and each object has a unique object identifier. This model is flexible enough to encompass all types of information, including semantic information about objects.

- **Extensible Information Server (XIS)**[4]: An O-O system which stores XML documents under eXcelon's ObjectStore O-O database as DOM trees, stored in a proprietary, B-tree-like structure (for performance reasons), and which can be indexed by using both value and structural indexes. In particular, XIS stores XML documents in a preparsed format in order to reduce the overhead associated with parsing on demand. Furthermore, XIS supports queries through XPath with extension functions and a proprietary update language. It also supports server-side functions (written in Java), and can directly manipulate data in the database (through a server-side DOM implementation). Moreover, XIS provides a distributed caching mechanism for improving concurrent access and overall application performance.

- **SHORE (Semantic Hypertext Object REpository)** (Hess et al., 2000): This system stores information extracted from XML documents, whereas an object-based XML data representation model is used for effective XML data placement. In particular, it stores information extracted from XML documents using a variant of R-trees and B-trees structure.

XML Storage Under Native XML DBMSs

Most recent advances in XML technology have presented another approach — created specifically for XML — known as the "Native" XML database. Native XML databases satisfy the need for a more robust XML approach by offering a solution that is specifically designed to handle and optimize XML's unique structure. Using a relational database management system to store XML documents can create serious performance problems for large-scale applications since data hierarchy, context and semantics are often lost (when XML documents are retrieved and processed with SQL). As an alternative, storing and indexing XML documents in their native form preserves the document structure, content and meaning, and increases the performance of the underlying applications.

In this context, native XML DBMSs use XML as their basic data model. More specifically, a native XML database defines a (logical) model for an XML document, and stores and retrieves documents according to that model. In order to store the XML documents on a native XML database, two basic steps are involved:

1. Describe the data via its structure (DTD or XML schema); and
2. Define a native database XML schema (or a data map) to use for storage and retrieval.

In this case, the XML document is the fundamental unit of (logical) storage, such as a relational database has a row in a table as its fundamental unit of (logical) storage. Therefore, it is not required to support any particular underlying physical storage model in native XML databases. For example, it can be built on a relational, hierarchical, or O-O database, or it can use a proprietary storage format such as indexed, compressed file. XML schemas are implemented in native XML databases to record rules for storing and indexing data, and to provide data retrieval and storage information to the underlying database engines.

Furthermore, native XML databases can be categorized into two policies: text-based storage and model-based storage. The first one stores the entire document in text form (such as a binary large object-BLOB — in a relational database). The second one stores a binary model of the document in an existing or custom database. They are particularly suited to store, retrieve and update XML documents. Typical examples include Natix (Kanne & Moerkotte, 2000), Tamino (Schoning, 2001), SODA, Ipedo, Xyleme, etc. In fact, native XML DBMSs satisfy the need for a more robust XML storage approach by offering a solution that is specifically designed to handle and optimize XML's unique structure.

Several commercial native XML DBMSs have also been developed, but, until now, they have not become very popular. The main reason is that these systems (including physical distribution of data, the index mechanism, etc.) must be built from scratch. In general, native DBMSs differentiate based on their purpose (research or commercial implementations), and their storage structure is employed accordingly. More specifically, the research-oriented implementations support trees and/or sub-trees for the structural unit, whereas the commercial-oriented tools use collections (like directories) as their main structural unit. The most indicative of them are given in Appendix A.

Other Environments for XML Storage

Alternatively, XML documents can also be stored in other storage environments such as file systems and LDAP directories.

- **File System Storage:** Since an XML document is a file, a typical storage approach is to store it simply as a flat file. In particular, this approach uses a typical file-processing system supported by a conventional operating system (as a basis for database applications). The wide availability of XML tools for data files results in a relatively easy accessing and querying of XML data (which are stored in files). By using a flat file for XML data, we have a quite fast storing (or retrieving) of whole documents. However, this storage format has many disadvantages, such as difficulty in accessing and updating (since the only way is to overwrite the whole file) data (Silberschatz et al., 2002). Furthermore, this approach encounters also security, concurrent access, atomicity and integrity problems.
- **LDAP Directories:** Currently, researchers have showed a steadily increasing interest in LDAP (Lightweight Directory Access Protocol) directories in order to effectively store XML documents (e.g., Marron &

Lausen, 2001). Several commercial companies offer LDAP support in their browsers and operating systems, making directory services a remarkable alternative to more traditional systems for the storage and efficient retrieval of information. According to this trend, XML documents are stored in LDAP directories which can be considered as a specialized database (Johner et al., 1998). Therefore, the internal storage model of this database system is defined in terms of LDAP classes and attributes[5].

The XML documents are organized in a hierarchical fashion, similar to the way files are organized in file system. In conjunction with the DSML (Directory Service Markup Language), which is a new standard for representing directory information as XML, the directory services can take advantage of XML's most powerful features. In particular, DSML bridges the gap between directory services and XML applications in a robust way. Today, several products support DSML, including Sun Microsystems, Microsoft, Oracle Corp., IBM, Hewlett-Packard, etc.

The main differences between directories and typical DBMSs are related to size and design issues. In fact, LDAP directories are generally smaller and less complex applications than DBMSs. More specifically, the LDAP directories are more widely distributed, more easily extended, replicated on a higher scale, and have a higher read-to-write ratio than typical DBMSs. On the other hand, the LDAP is a protocol for online directory services (storing and accessing heterogeneous entities over the Internet). It provides a standard model (the LDAP model) which has a hierarchical infrastructure. On the other hand, XML and LDAP have many similarities since, in LDAP, data are organized as a tree (where each node can contain data value and can act as a namespace for other nodes). This is quite close to XML since the XML data model is hierarchical in structure and usually implemented by considering the XML document as a tree structure. Therefore, the transformation from the XML data model to the LDAP data model is not a complex task. Figure 7 depicts the LDAP tree representation for our example XML document. Moreover, LDAP directories also provide several standard APIs that can be used for accessing the directory. Finally, in Marron and Lausen (2001), an LDAP-based system for storing their XML documents is proposed, and the results of their work have shown that LDAP directories reduce the workload and provide efficient performance for storing and retrieving XML data.

Figure 7: XML Data Representation in LDAP

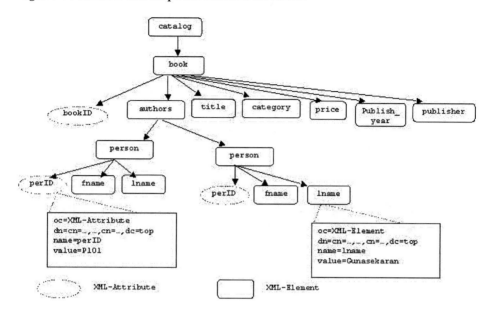

ACCESS CONTROL ISSUES
FOR XML DOCUMENTS

Even though much research effort has focused on implementing XML-based storage tools, the security of such implementations is still in primary research steps. Security of databases is guaranteed through the satisfaction of several needs: (a) *authentication*, (b) *authorization*, (c) *confidentiality*, (d) *integrity*, and (e) *non-repudiation*. Cryptography and digital signatures were the first steps toward authentication. Unfortunately, researchers have been engaged in the research of the rest of security issues (which are highly related to access control) only recently. Attacks against confidentiality, integrity and non-repudiation may result from a misfunctional access control (or authorization) mechanism which fails to protect document repositories from unauthorized accesses.

The need for a functional access control mechanism has become really significant since XML-based (or hypertext) documents have contributed to the enlargement of repositories. Such a fact has led to the distribution of protected documents to several physical locations which should be secured against unauthorized access. Moreover, since XML is a language for representing documents distributed through the Internet, they are stored in huge distributed databases which are connected via the World Wide Web. Although, that development has led to a worldwide exchange of knowledge, it has also increased the need for robust access control. Nowadays, web-based databases can be easily attacked by automated malicious software "traveling" through the Internet (such software owners may hide anywhere on the globe).

It is obvious that XML documents storage systems cannot be protected by conventional access control models such as *Mandatory Access Control (MAC)* and *Discretionary Access Control (DAC)*, since MAC protects only confined centralized environments (when a unique administrator is responsible for the protection of repositories from unauthorized users (Sandhu & Mason, 1993), and DAC might be a primitive solution (since the owner of each document is responsible for its protection) since it is inflexible, especially for huge heterogeneous repositories containing (numerous owners') documents.

Most recent authorization systems (and their XML-based storage environments) use mainly the idea of roles employed on user and groups. *User* is the individual connecting to the system, allowed to submit requests. *Group* is a set of users or other groups. *Role* is a named collection of privileges needed to perform specific activities in the system. The important benefit of role-based models is that they are *policy neutral*, i.e., they may enforce multiple policies and they are not associated with a particular security policy.

Role-based access control has been extensively studied by Osborn et al. (2000) and Sandhu et al. (1996), where a description of RBAC is given. One or more roles is assigned to users, and one or more permissions is assigned to roles.

A more modern idea is the concept of credentials, which are information concerning a user (Winslett et al., 1997). This information is provided by the client (subject) when (s)he subscribes to the system, and it is needed by the access control mechanism. Credentials can be stored into different files or organized into groups.

As it will be discussed later, all of the well-known storing environments adopt role-based access control which is employed by an access control system as shown in Figure 1. After the system grants access to the requested resource, the request is passed to the storage subsystem for further processing. An access control policy is governed by three issues: (a) *subjects*, which are the entities requesting access to protected resources; (b) *objects*, which are the protected resources; and (c) *authorization*, which are rules specifying which subject can access which object. An access control policy consists of several authorizations concerning a subject or an object. Next, we will comment on role-based security by extending our case study.

Authorization Subjects and Objects

A subject is usually identified by its identity or by the location from which it sends the request for a document (Damiani et al., 2001). Moreover, in order to simplify authorization administration and support more compact authorizations, subjects can be organized in hierarchies, where the effects of a policy imposed to a general subject propagates to its descendants. While many approaches adopt subject hierarchies (based on subject identities), some other research efforts support location-based hierarchies. Various XML-based access control models require XML-based presentation of the users' credentials since XML provides all the characteristics for organizing the unique features of subjects.

We have already mentioned that most XML-based databases adopt the idea of roles for organizing subjects. With respect to our book catalog, a role hierarchy is the one shown in Figure 8, where the root role refers to all the users who visit that digital library site (public). These users are further classified into subscribers and non-subscribers, while the subscribers are in turn further classified into the authors and the simple readers. Of course, such a functionality demands the subscription of subjects to the system (something that is not required from all applications). XML can be used to define such hierarchies by exploiting the idea of DTDs[6] (as shown in Figure 9), which depicts a DTD describing a category of users. This DTD describes the required data about a subscriber. The attributes of the core element subscriber are its ID and its *category*, which can take two values: *author* and *reader*. A subscriber must have a name and a credit card number, (s)he may have an e-mail address and work for a company, and (s)he must have at least one phone number.

Figure 8: Subject Hierarchy

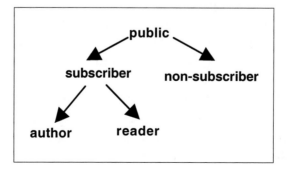

Also, we can define a non-subscriber by an empty DTD as:

```
<!DOCTYPE BOOKS SYSTEM "non_subscriber.dtd">
<!ELEMENT  non_subscriber empty>
```

The most common way of identifying XML protection objects is by path expressions which can identify elements and attributes under protection. The exploitation of a standard language like XPath[7] may prove to be highly advantageous because the syntax and the semantics of the language are already known by the potential users. An example of such an expression may be /book/ /person for the example of Figures 3 and 4.

The objects under protection may be: (a) all instances of a DTD, (b) whole documents, or (c) selected portions of a document (like elements or attributes). Referring to Figures 3 and 4, an object may be the whole document or a number of elements, like authors and title. Of course, an object may also be the whole DTD, such as the one in Figure 4. Authors in Akker et al. (2000) introduce the categorization of objects into sets in order to minimize the need to use multiple security policies for protecting them independently.

Authorizations

The basic issues in relation to the authorizations for XML documents include:

Policies

The policy is the core security issue in access control systems. An authorization policy consists of a list of authorizations defining which subject can take which action (over which object). A principle that should guide every access control system is the distinction between policy and mechanism. Policy is the logic which rules an access control system, while the mechanism implements (or enforces) that logic.

By XML-based access control systems, we refer to tools where policies protecting XML-based repositories are XML-defined and organized, and to tools where only the protected resources are organized by using XML features. The first version is more flexible and modern since it exploits the discussed features of XML.

Policies are most commonly divided into: (a) *positive*, where permissions are defined; and (b) *negative*, where denials are specified. Modern access control tools combine these two categories in favor of flexibility and expres-

Figure 9: A Subject DTD, XML Schema and an Instance

```
<!DOCTYPE BOOKS SYSTEM "subscriber.dtd">
<!ELEMENT subscriber (name,address,phone_number*,email?,company?,credit_card)>
<!ATTLIST subscriber credID ID #REQUIRED
          category (author|reader) #REQUIRED>
<!ELEMENT name (fname,lname)>
<!ELEMENT fname (#PCDATA)>
<!ELEMENT lname (#PCDATA)>
<!ELEMENT address (#PCDATA)>
<!ELEMENT phone_number (#PCDATA)>
<!ELEMENT email (#PCDATA)>
<!ELEMENT company (#PCDATA)>
<!ELEMENT credit_card (#PCDATA)>

<xsd:schema xmlns:xsd="http://www.w3.org/2001/XMLSchema">
  <xsd:element name="subscriber">
   <xsd:complexType>
      <xsd:sequence>
        <xsd:element name="name">
           <xsd:complexType>
             <xsd:sequence>
               <xsd:element name="fname" type="xsd:string"/>
               <xsd:element name="lname" type="xsd:string"/>
             </xsd:sequence>
           </xsd:complexType>
        </xsd:element>
        <xsd:element name="address" type="xsd:string"/>
        <xsd:element name="phone_number" type="xsd:string" minOccurs="1"/>
        <xsd:element name="email" type="xsd:string" minOccurs="0"/>
        <xsd:element name="company" type="xsd:string" minOccurs="0"/>
        <xsd:element name="credit_card" type="xsd:string" minOccurs="0"/>
        <xsd:element name="category">
         <xsd:simpleType>
          <xsd:restriction base="xsd:string">
            <xsd:enumeration value="author"/>
            <xsd:enumeration value="reader"/>
          </xsd:restriction>
         </xsd:simpleType>
        </xsd:element>
      </xsd:sequence>
      <xsd:attribute name="credID" type="ID" use="required"/>
   </xsd:complexType>
  </xsd:element>
</xsd:schema>

<subscriber="12345">
<subscriber category="author">
   <name>
      <fname>Omar</fname>
      <lname>Khalil</lname>
   </name>
   <phone_number>011111111</phone_number>
   <email>okhalil@csd.auth.gr</email>
   <credit_card>5555555</credit_card>
</subscriber>
```

siveness (e.g., Bertino et al., 2001a; Damiani et al., 2000; Castano & Ferrari, 2003).

Since, in XML-based systems, all of the protected resources are organized according to DTDs (and, therefore, in hierarchical format), another core issue concerning policies is their propagated effect. Great attention should be given to this feature since its inappropriate execution may lead to conflicts. The implicit propagation rule adopted by all the XML-based access control tools is that all DTD-level policies propagate to all DTD instances. Explicit propagation rules are based on the hierarchical organization of objects. Thus, most tools allow (or deny) the propagation of the effects of a policy under some condition. The approach, introduced by Kudo and Hada (2000), also allows the propagation to the top, where propagation takes effect to the parent elements. Of course, the occurrence of conflicts is inevitable and, at this point, *conflict resolution mechanisms* are triggered.

Since an authorization policy can be employed for the protection of grouped objects, it can also have an effect on grouped subjects. This feature is allowed where subjects are organized in hierarchies (as shown in Figure 8). Therefore, a policy referring to the root of a hierarchy propagates to all of its children down to the leaves. For example, in Figure 8, if a policy refers to "subscriber," then its effects propagate to both authors and simple readers by default, unless another policy prohibits this propagation.

According to the above discussed issues, a policy may contain authorizations of the form *<subject, object, mode, type, propagation>*. *Mode* specifies the action the subject can exercise on the object, and can take various values according to the implementation and the protected resources. For example, the most commonly used values for documents are those defined by Kudo and Hada (2000): *read*, *write*, *create* and *delete*. In our example, we will adopt the following modes: read and write. The parameter *type* may take either the value "+" (if the policy is positive) or "-" (if it is negative). Finally, the parameter *propagation* defines the type of propagation to be implemented. In order to simplify our example, we will only adopt two types: *prop* (propagation) and *no-prop* (no propagation).

The following are examples of policies specified according to the above approach:

```
(1) <//subscriber.[category="author"]/name/[fname="Omar"
        and lname="Khalil"], catalog.xml://person/
        [fname="Omar" and lname="Khalil"], write,
        +, prop>
(2) <//subscriber.[category="reader"], catalog.dtd, read,
        +,prop>
(3) <*,catalog.dtd,read,-,prop>
(4) <*,catalog.dtd,write,-,prop>
```

Tuple (1) specifies an authorization policy granting write access to author "Omar Khalil" on his books. Moreover, the policy propagates to all of the elements of the documents. The policy encoded by tuple (2) grants all readers the right to read all books. The last two tuples deny read and write access respectively to the public (which is depicted by an *).

Provisional Actions

Policies can be further supported with provisional actions. In Kudo and Hada (2000), four types of provisional actions have been introduced: (a) *log*, where the session should be logged for the request to be satisfied; (b) *encrypt*, where the returned resource view should be encrypted; (c) *verify*, where the signature of the subject should be verified; and (d) a combination of these.

As PUSH dissemination techniques (i.e., documents are distributed to users without prior request) have been gaining ground these years, a modern access control system should include such mechanisms so as to support this modern dissemination technique. Author-X (Bertino et al., 2001a) is a Java-based XML access control system satisfying such a need by using the idea of cryptography with several keys. The authors in Castano and Ferrari (2003) try to express policies used by Author-X.

Document View

The presentation of the requested object to the subject is another important activity performed by every access control model. After the object components accessible by the subject have been identified, a mechanism *prunes* the document tree so as to contain only those parts (and sometimes links) that the requesting subject is allowed to access. The resulting document is referred to as *document view*. A problem in such an approach is that a view may not be a valid document as it may not follow the DTD associated with the document from which it is derived (Damiani et al., 2000). A solution to this problem could be a loosened DTD, where the definition of the elements may be defined as optional and not as required. Such an approach prevents the subject from realizing whether some parts are missing or simply do not exist in the original document. According to Bertino et al. (2001a, 2001b), Castano and Ferrari (2003), and Kudo and Hada (2000), the resulting document may be encrypted if such a security action has been requested by the user.

IMPLEMENTATIONS

Some of the most popular database vendors (like *IBM*, *Microsoft* and *Oracle*) have developed database tools for the storage of XML documents, and several storage techniques have been adopted (in order to maximize functionality and performance). Moreover, for reasons of integrity, these indicative database systems are supported by access control mechanisms. Currently, the most widely adopted technology to enforce the security guarantees of the XML-based databases is the Microsoft .NET platform. Microsoft .NET has been recently proposed and has been adjusted to support XML Web Services. Its security mechanism is adopted by Oracle 9i, XIS and DB2, which have been designed to cooperate with Microsoft .NET technology.

The Microsoft .NET Platform

Microsoft .NET[8] is a technology for connecting people, systems and resources. The driving force that has led the Microsoft researchers in this direction was the need to build and use XML Web Services securely.

The increasing complication of some core tasks, (like security, data management, data storing) has dictated their decomposition into a number of more specialized functions. These "simple" functions are executed by XML Web Services, which Microsoft .NET technology fights to integrate. These XML Web Services may originate from various sources residing in distributed places all over the globe. Microsoft provides clients and servers with its own XML Web Services, but it is possible to combine them with others through the .NET platform. XML Web Services are characterized by:

- XML Web Services may be differently implemented and they may be placed in various locations, but they can cooperate through the use of a common communication protocol (e.g., SOAP).
- XML Web Services allow the definition of an interface for the communication of the user with them. The description of the steps needed to build interface applications is explained in an XML document called a Web Service Description Language (WSDL) document.
- XML Web Services are registered using Universal Discovery Description and Integration (UDDI) so that users can easily find them.

A general architecture of a .NET-based system showing its XML-based nature is presented in Figure 10. Such a technology would be totally incomplete if it did not offer guarantees. Therefore, Microsoft .NET contains software for covering authentication, authorization and cryptographic needs. As authentica-

Figure 10: The Basic Components of a .NET Architecture

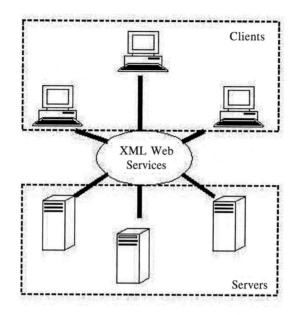

tion is beyond the scope of this chapter, we will focus on the second issue. Like most modern access control systems, .NET employs the idea of roles as subjects. After a user has logged on to the system, (s)he is assigned roles. Authorization policies expressed in .NET framework (i.e., the multilanguage used to build and execute XML and other web services and applications in .NET) define which role can perform which operations over which resources. Developers can sum up XML to express such policies, or they can simply tie their system (e.g., client or server) with existing Windows authorization mechanisms.

Moreover, the .NET technology employs evidence-based and code access security, which allows local administrators to protect resources from malicious code. In such a case, the subject is code and is identified using certain features (like the directory it resides, the Internet location originating from, its has value, etc.). Code access security disallows the execution of untrusted code even if the user executing it is trusted. Furthermore, such a functionality allows the developer to define permissions for mobile code which can be downloaded and executed by any user unknown to the developer at the designing phase.

A code access security policy system is governed by three core issues: (a) *evidence*, (b) *permissions*, and (c) *security policy*. *Evidence* is the information about the identity of code (called assembly). Evidence is connected with every assembly, and it is presented to the security system whenever an

Figure 11: How Permissions are Produced

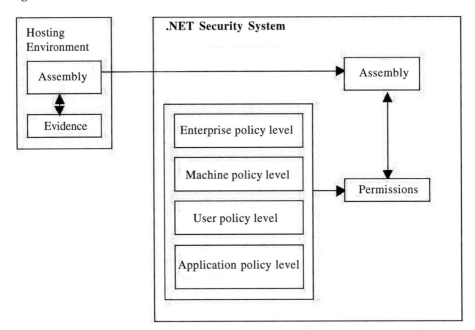

assembly is loaded into the runtime. *Permissions* represent authorizations to conduct a protected action (e.g., file or network access). Permissions may be grouped to form *permission sets*. Therefore, whenever an assembly requests access to a protected resource, the security system grants a permission set to it according to its evidence. Finally, a *security policy* integrates the two above issues by defining which permissions are given to an assembly according to its evidence. Policies are categorized into four levels:

- Enterprise policy level
- Machine policy level
- User policy level
- Application Domain policy level

The evidence, combined with the policies of each level, results in a permission set. The finite permission set arises through the intersection of the previous sets. Thus, in Figure 11, the function of the security system is depicted.

XML Storage Under DBMSs

Over the last years, many of the major database vendors (such as *IBM, Microsoft* and *Oracle*) have developed database tools to support XML documents. The goal of these tools is to provide secure data transfer from XML

Table 2: Storage in XML-Enabled Databases

PRODUCT	DBMS MODEL	STORAGE
Oracle 9i	Object-Relational	Data are stored as relational tables or as XML documents.
MS SQL Server 2000	Object-Relational	Each XML document is stored as relational table and an element is created for each row.
IBMs DB2	Object-Relational	Data are stored as relational tables or as XML documents.

documents to databases and vice versa. More specifically, XML database tools involve a set of processes for accessing the XML data, and such software can either be built into the object relational DBMSs or into a new data model (Native XML DBMSs). In this framework, the most well-known software tools that employ XML documents storage and access control can be categorized in the following types of databases:

- **XML-enabled DBMSs:** They provide various interfaces for extracting structured data from XML documents to be stored in DBMSs (according to their model). In this case, XML documents are stored in conventional DBMSs internally in the database. XML-enabled DBMSs also support services that do the reversible task, producing an XML document. This is done by using a query that can be expressed by the DBMS query language.

- **Native XML DBMSs:** They have been designed especially to store XML documents. XML plays a basic role in Native XML DBMSs since it is the only interface for storing the data. XML documents are stored in XML internally in the database. Therefore, the documents in native XML DBMSs are parsed and stored (as parsed).

- **Microsoft's (MS) SQL Server 2000[9]:** A relational database management system which provides a variety of tools for managing all aspects of databases. In particular, it provides support for XML data schemas, the ability to execute XPath (a language for addressing parts of an XML document) queries, and the ability to retrieve and create XML data (Rys, 2001). MS SQL Server 2000 has also added many new features which are focusing on XML support. Its utilities offer more flexibility for storing and structuring the XML documents. Each XML document is stored as a relational table, and an element is created for each row. Furthermore, the structure of data is transparent to users, who interact with the relational DBMS using only XML-based technologies. A disadvantage of such an approach is the increased overhead that has been associated with mapping and translating XML structured data into relational data. Another disadvantage is also the hierarchical structure of XML documents.

SQL Server is the only discussed database system containing its own access control system, as every modern tool authorization is based on roles. After a user has logged on to the system, (s)he is assigned a role which is granted some permissions. SQL Server supports several types of roles, which are:

- *Public role:* every user is assigned this role. It is a default role which cannot be deleted. Moreover, the administrator cannot de-assign or assign a subject with this role. Such a role is necessary in case the administrator could not think of a role during the design phase that would tie with an unknown user.

- *Predefined roles:* it is about roles with predefined permissions which cannot be given to other roles. For example, the administrator, who has some rights that no other subject should have.

- *User-defined:* roles of this type are defined by an administrator controlling a single database. Of course, they are local to the database in which they are created, and they do not have global effect.

- *Application-defined roles:* these roles are assigned to applications, making them able to substitute users and take over control.

The access control policies, which are determined by the local administrators, define which role is granted which permissions over which protected resources.

- **Oracle9i[10]:** Under Oracle, the XML documents can be stored either in a relational DBMS or in a file system. Therefore, Oracle can store and retrieve entire XML documents as columns, can access XML stored in external files (or on the Web), and can map XML document elements to tables and columns in the database. In particular, its architecture has a specific XML layer that supports a set of tools for managing XML documents. Moreover, the manufacturers of Oracle9i have also developed a high-performance, native XML storage and retrieval technology which is called *Oracle XML DB*. XML DB provides a unique ability to store and manage the XML documents under a standard XML data model. It provides several features for managing XML storage, such as XML schema, XML indexes, foldering (enable folders to map XML documents into database structure), etc. Furthermore, XML DB also supports access control policies by creating access control lists (for any XML object), and by defining the users' privileges in addition to the system-defined ones. Details for the Oracle XML data management system can be found in Banerjee et al. (2000).

Oracle 9i can excellently cooperate with Microsoft's .NET system and Windows 2000. Therefore, in order to achieve access control, one can build .NET clients able to cooperate with Oracle 9i database.

- **IBMs DB2[11]:** IBM DB2 provides a variety of features for storing data. This implementation offers support via a DB2 XML Extender product, which provides new operations for facilitating the storage and manipulation of XML documents. The XML Extender product serves as a repository for the management of DTDs. More specifically, it stores an XML document as a single column, or it maps the XML document to multiple tables and columns. In order to provide the structure of the generated document, a DTD is mapped against the relational tables using Data Access Definition (DAD). Also, IBM adopts .NET platform for access control.

CONCLUSION

This chapter has presented an overview for XML documents' storage and access control. More specifically, the most important policies for storage and accessing of XML data and storage are studied under several typical database environments (e.g., Relational, Object-Relational, Object-Oriented, etc.) and non-typical frameworks (such as LDAP). Then, we studied the main issues for the security of XML documents, since access control is essential in guaranteeing the security of such storage approaches. In particular, the most-well known access control and authorization models were presented through examples. Also, the chapter presented the most popular commercial tools for XML management with respect to their storage and access control techniques.

It is important to indicate that no definite guidelines have yet been proposed for selecting an optimal solution when storing and securing XML documents. In order to improve the management of XML documents, some issues should require further research. In particular, the storage of XML documents may be improved by using some data mining techniques (e.g., specific clustering algorithms). Furthermore, the XML management techniques should further extend existing access control policies in order to improve the security in XML documents accessing. Finally, the commercial DBMSs should be extended to support more sophisticated storage and access control techniques, such as integrated methods for locating and accessing of dynamic XML documents.

REFERENCES

Akker, T., Snell, Q. O., & Clemant, M. J. (2001). The YGuard access control model: Set-based access control. *Proceedings of the 6th ACM Symposium on Access Control Models and Technologies*, Chantilly, Virginia.

Amer-Yahia, S. & Fernandez, M. (2002, February/March). Techniques for storing XML. *Proceedings of the 18th International Conference on Data Engineering (ICDE 2002)*, San Jose, California.

Banerjee, S., Krishnamurthy, V., Krishnaprasad, R., & Murthy, R. (2000, February/March). Oracle8i-The XML enabled data management system. *Proceedings of the 16th International Conference on Data Engineering (ICDE)*, San Diego, California (pp. 561-568).

Bertino, E., Castano, S., & Ferrari, E. (2001). On specifying security policies for web documents with an XML-based language. *Proceedings of the 6th ACM symposium on access control models and technologies, Chantilly, Virginia* (pp. 57-65).

Bertino, E., Castano, S., & Ferrari, E. (2001, May/June). Securing XML documents with Author-X. *IEEE Internet Computing, 5*(3), 21-31.

Bohannon, P., Freire, J., Roy, P., & Simeon, J. (2002, May/June). From XML schema to relations: A cost-based approach to XML storage. *Proceedings of the 18th International Conference on Data Engineering (ICDE 2002)*, San Jose, California.

Castano, S. & Ferrari, E. (2003). Protecting datasources over the web: Policies, models, and mechanisms. In *Web-powered Databases* (chap. 11, pp. 299-330). Hershey, PA: Idea Group.

Castano, S., Fugini, M., Martella, G., & Samarati, P. (1994). *Database Security*. Reading, MA: Addison-Wesley.

Damiani, E., De Capitani di Vimercati, S., Paraboschi, S., & Samarati, P. (2000). Design and implementation of an access control processor for XML documents. *Proceedings of the 9th World Wide Web Conference (WWW9)*, Amsterdam, Holland.

Damiani, E., Samarati, P., De Capitani di Vimercati, S., & Paraboschi, S. (2001, November/December). Controlling access to XML documents. *IEEE Internet Computing, 5*(6), 18-28.

Damiani, E., Vimercati, S. D. C., Paraboshi, S., & Samarati, P. (2000). Securing XML documents. *Proceedings of the 7th International Conference on Extending Database Technology*, Konstanz, Germany.

Florescu, D. & Kossmann, D. (1999, May). *A performance evaluation of alternative mapping schemes for storing XML data in a relational database*. Rocquencourt, France: INRIA. (Technical Report No. 3680).

Hess, A., Schulz, H., & Brossler, P. (2000). *SHORE - A hypertext repository based on XML*. Southfield, USA: Software Design and Management. (Technical Report).

Howes, T. A., Smith, M. C., & Good, G. S. (1999). *Understanding and Deploying LDAP Directory Services*. USA: Macmillan Technical Publishing.

Johner, H., Brown, L., Hinner, F. S., Reis, W., & Westman, J. (1998, June). *Understanding LDAP*, International Technical Support Organization (Ed.), IBM.

Kanne, C. C. & Moerkotte, G. (2000, February/March). Efficient storage of XML data. *Proceedings of the 16th International Conference on Data Engineering (ICDE 2000)*, San Diego, California.

Khan, L. & Rao, Y. (2001, November). A performance evaluation of storing XML data in relational DBMS. *Proceedings of the 3rd ACM CIKM'01 Workshop on Web Information and Data Management (WIDM'01)*, Atlanta, Georgia.

Kudo, M. & Hada, S. (2000). XML document security based on provisional authorization. *Proceedings of the 7th ACM Conference on Computer and Communications Security*, Athens, Greece.

Marron, P. J. & Lausen, G. (2001). On processing XML in LDAP. In *Proceedings of the 27th conference on very large data bases (VLDB 2001)*, Rome, Italy, September 2001 (pp. 601-610).

McHugh, J., Abiteboul, S., Goldman, R., Quass, D., & Widom, J. (1997). Lore: A database management system for semi-structured data. *ACM SIGMOD Record*, 26(3), 54-66.

Moyer, M. J. & Ahamad, M. (2001). Generalized role-based access control. *Proceedings of the 21st International Conference on Distributed Computing Systems,* Mesa, Arizona.

Osborn, S., Sandhu, R., & Munawer, Q. (2000). Configuring role-based access control to enforce mandatory and discretionary access control policies. *ACM Transactions on Information and System Security*, 3(2), 85-106.

Rys, M. (2001, April). Bringing the Internet to your database: Using SQL Server 2000 and XML to build loosely-coupled systems. *Proceedings of the 17th International Conference on Data Engineering (ICDE)*, Heidelberg, Germany.

Sandhu, R. S. & Mason, G. (1993, November). Lattice-based access control models. *IEEE Computer, 26*(11), 9-19.

Sandhu, R. S., Coyne, E. J., & Feinstein, H. L. (1996, February). Role-based access control models. *IEEE Computer, 29*(2), 38-47.

Schmidt, A., Kersten, M., Windhouwer, M., & Waas, F. (2000, May). Efficient relational storage and retrieval of XML documents. *Proceedings of the 3rd International Workshop on the Web and Databases (WebDB 2000)*, Dallas, Texas.

Schoning, H. (2001, April). Tamino - A DBMS designed for XML. *Proceedings of the 17th International Conference on Data Engineering*, Heidelberg, Germany.

Shimura, T., Yoshikawa, M., & Uemura, S. (1999, August/September). Storage and retrieval of XML documents using object-relational databases. *Proceedings of the 10th International Conference and Workshop on Database and Expert Systems Applications (DEXA 1999)*, Florence, Italy.

Silberschatz, A., Korth, H., & Sudarshan, S. (2002). *Database System Concepts* (4th ed.). New York: McGraw Hill.

Tian, F., DeWitt, D. J., Chen, J., & Zhang, C. (2002). The design and performance evaluation of alternative XML storage policies. *ACM SIGMOD Record, 31*(1), 5-10.

Vakali, A. & Terzi, E. (2000). An object-oriented approach for effective XML data storage. *Proceedings of the ECOOP Workshop on XML Object Technology,* Cannes, France.

Winslett, M., Ching, N., Jones, V., & Slepchin, I. (1997). Using digital credentials on the world wide web. *Journal of Computer Security,* 5(3), 255-266.

Woo, T. Y. C. & Lam, S. S. (1993, November). A framework for distributed authorization. *Proceedings of the 1st ACM Conference on Computer and Communications Security,* Fairfax, Virginia.

Yoshikawa, M., Amagasa, T., Shimura, T., & Uemura, S. (2001). XRel: A path-based approach to storage and retrieval of XML documents using relational databases. *ACM Transactions on Internet Technology,* 1(1), 110-141.

Zhu, Y. & Lu, K. (2001. July). An effective data placement strategy for XML documents. *Proceedings of the 18th British National Conference on Databases (BNCOD),* Chilton, UK.

ENDNOTES

1   http://www.w3.org/TR/1998/REC-xml-19980210/
2   http://www.saxproject.org/
3   http://www.w3.org/DOM/
4   http://www.exceloncorp.com/xis/
5   More details about the architecture of the LDAP model and protocol are discussed by Howes et al. (1999).
6   We use DTDs instead of XML Schemas for their brevity
7   http://www.w3.org/TR/xpath
8   http://www.microsoft.com/net/
9   http://www.microsoft.com
10 http://technet.oracle.com
11 http://www-4.ibm.com
12 http://www.cse.unsw.edu.au/~soda/
13 http://www.xyleme.com/
14 http://www.ipedo.com/html/products.html
15 http://exist.sourceforge.net/
16 http://www.dbxml.org

APPENDIX A

In general, the most popular commercial native XML DBMSs can be classified into the following two categories with respect to their underlying storage model:

Storage Model: Tree Structure

*   **NATIX** (Kanne & Moerkotte, 2000)**:** It is the most well-known native repository approach for storing, retrieving and managing tree-structured XML documents. The basic idea of NATIX is to represent and store XML documents based on their tree structure, and it is oriented for research based implementations. The logical tree used for representing each XML document is split into sub-trees, based on certain criteria. These sub-trees are the basic storage and query units.
*   **SODA**[12]**:** It is another semi-structured DBMS tailored to manage XML information. In this system, the XML documents are stored in a single tree, which preserves all XML information and allows for efficient query and update operations, along with optimizations that are XML-oriented and that cannot be applied when conventional database schemes (like tables)

are used. SODA is oriented for both research and commercial based implementations. Moreover, SODA also provides secured access control and authorization. The component which is responsible for preserving the security of XML documents in the SODA database system is the access control manager.

- **Xyleme[13]:** A dynamic warehouse for XML documents of the web. More specifically, Xyleme is designed to store, classify, index, integrate, query and monitor the XML documents. The performance of Xyleme heavily depends on the efficiency of its repository, which is the *Natix*. As we referred above, in Natix, the XML documents are represented by using an ordered tree structure. In order to store XML documents, Xyleme uses a combination of the following two approaches. In the first, the XML documents are stored in a conventional DBMS. In the second, the documents are stored as byte streams. Therefore, data are stored as trees until a certain depth, where byte streams are used. The security of XML documents in Xyleme is guaranteed by using access control lists. Access permissions are stored with each document, and users only get to view the documents they have rights to. In addition, the top secure documents can also be stored in an independent partition.

Storage Model: Collection Structure

- **Ipedo[14]:** It is a native XML database that allows its users to quickly and easily build XML-based information management solutions. The Ipedo architecture is composed of several components that make the Ipedo XML database accessible through standard Java programming interfaces. It provides both document-level, as well as node-level, access to XML, and allows the users to organize XML documents by their schema. In particular, Ipedo supports a hierarchical storage engine which is highly optimized for XML information. The XML documents are organized into collections, which can be typed or un-typed. They are used to group related XML documents together. Typed collections contain a schema based on a DTD or XML Schema, and all documents within that collection must conform to that schema. Un-typed collections can hold any number of XML documents regardless of the relationships between the schemas of those documents. Furthermore, Ipedo provides a sophisticated access control mechanism (security manager) in order to support a high-level security of XML documents. In particular, the security manager manages access to system resources by providing username and password authentication. Ipedo has also been designed to cooperate with Microsoft .NET technology.

- **eXist**[15]**:** It is an Open Source native XML database which provides pluggable storage backends. According to this product, XML documents can be stored in the internal native XML database or an external relationship DBMS. XML can be stored either in the internal, native XML database or in an external relational DBMS. In eXist, the XML documents are stored using a DOM-tree (built from SAX-events) and are organized into hierarchical collections. Collections can be nested and are considered part of an XPath query string, so there is always a root collection. Indexes on collections may also be organized and, thus, the size of a collection may have a considerable impact on performance. As a disadvantage, eXist does not support direct manipulations of the DOM tree (like node insertions or removals). So, the XML documents should be deleted or updated as a whole. In order to ensure the integrity and compliance of XML documents, eXist supports an access control policy, which provides an interface to manipulate permissions and manage users. In particular, it organizes users into several groups, granting different permission sets for each one.

- **Tamino** (Schoning, 2001)**:** It is a modern database system that has been thoroughly designed for handling XML documents. In Tamino's database, the XML documents are stored in collections. More specifically, each XML document stored in Tamino resides in exactly one collection. In order to manage the XML documents effectively, Tamino supports a set of graphical tools. In addition, Tamino supports an XML-specific query language (Tamino-X-Query), which includes text retrieval facilities.

- **Xindice**[16]**:** It is an open source native XML database system which is still evolving. In this system, XML documents are queried and updated using XML technologies, the first of which is W3C specification known as XPath. Using XPath, it is possible to obtain a set of XML elements contained in a given XML document that conforms the parameters of the XPath query. In Xindice, XML documents are also organized using collections that can be queried as whole. A collection can be created either consisting of documents of the same type or a single collection can be created to store all documents together. Every XML document must be stored in at least one collection. While collections can be used strictly for organizational purposes, Xindice also allows for indexes to be created on collections to increase XPath performance. Moreover, Xindice supports a sophisticated mechanism for ensuring the integrity of XML documents. More specifically, Xindice provides an access control (on individual files or folders, by user based and/or group based) to XML documents.

Chapter V

Transformation of XML Schema to Object Relational Database

Nathalia Devina Widjaya, Monash University, Australia

David Taniar, Monash University, Australia

Johanna Wenny Rahayu, La Trobe University, Australia

ABSTRACT

XML (eXtensible Markup Language) is fast emerging as the dominant standard for describing data and interchanging data between various systems and databases on the Internet. It offers the XML schema definition language as formalism for defining the syntax and structure of XML documents, providing rich facilities for defining and constraining the content of XML documents. Nevertheless, to enable efficient business application development in large-scale e-commerce environments, XML needs to have databases to keep all the data. Hence, it will inevitably be necessary to use methods to describe the XML schema in the Object-

Relational Database (ORDB) formats. In this chapter, we present the way to transform the XML encoded format, which can be treated as a logical model, to the ORDB format. The chapter first discusses the modeling of XML and why we need the transformation. Then, a number of transformation steps from the XML schema to the Object-Relational Logical model and XML to ORDB are presented. Three perspectives regarding this conceptual relationship (aggregation, association and inheritance) and their transformations are mainly discussed.

INTRODUCTION

The eXtensible Markup Language (XML) is increasingly finding acceptance as a standard for storing and exchanging structured and semi-structured information (Conrad, Scheffner & Freytag, 2000). XML has emerged, and is gradually being accepted, as the standard for describing data and for interchanging data between various systems and databases on the Internet (Bray, Paoli & Sperberg-McQueen, 1998). The XML community has developed a number of schema languages for representing business vocabularies. The Document Type Definition (DTD) is the original XML schema language included in the XML 1.0 specification. However, many individuals have recognized the limitations of this DTD standard for supporting data interchange in global e-business applications. The new XML schema extends the capabilities for validating documents and exchanging information with other non-XML system components.

With the wide acceptance of the Object-Oriented conceptual models, more and more systems are initially modeled and being expressed with OO notation. This situation suggests the necessity to integrate the OO conceptual models and XML. The goal of this work is to present a coherent way to transform the XML schema into ORDB (Object-Relational Databases) using Oracle 9*i* features models (refer to Figure 1).

The emphasis of this chapter is only on the transformation of aggregation, association and inheritance relationships from XML schema to ORDB, in order to help people conveniently and automatically generate Oracle database. This transformation is important so that all tables created using XML schema can be transformed to the object-relational databases using Oracle format and features. This research consists of two parts. First is the transformation from XML schema into Object-Relational Logical model. Second is the transformation

Figure 1: Transformation from XML Schema to ORDB

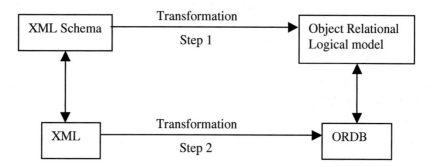

from XML into ORDB. The XML and ORDB come from XML schema and Object-Relational Logical model format.

This research is different with a transformation from a conceptual model into ORDB because this research discusses the transformation from XML schema format into ORDB. But, it has a similarity in the ORDB format because the XML schema adopts its features from the object-oriented conceptual model.

The work presented in this chapter is actually part of a larger research project on *Transformation from XML schema to Object-Relational Databases.* This project consists of three stages: (i) transformation association relationship from XML schema to Object-Relational Database; (ii) transformation inheritance relationship from XML schema to Object-Relational Database; and (iii) transformation aggregation relationship from XML schema to Object-Relational Database. The research results from the first and second stages have been reported in Widjaya, Taniar, Rahayu and Pardede (2002) and Widjaya, Taniar & Rahayu (2003). In this chapter, we focus on all three stages of the project.

BACKGROUND AND RELATED WORK
Object-Oriented: A Brief Overview

In 1970, there was only Relational Database Management System (RDBMS) (Dillon & Tan, 1993). Traditional RDBMSs perform well only when working on numeric data and characters stored in tables, what are often called "simple data types" (Stonebraker & Moore, 1996). Then, ORDBMS (Object-Relational Database Management System) came later to improve RDBMS's performance. Basically, the ORDBMS is the RDBMS with the object-oriented features. ORDBMS becomes popular because of the failure of ODBMSs, which have limitations that can prevent them from taking on enterprise-wide tasks. Therefore, by storing objects in the object side of the ORDBMS, but keeping the simpler data in the relational side, users may approach the best of both worlds. For the foreseeable future, however, most business data will continue to be stored in object-relational database systems.

Since ORDBMS has object-oriented features, we will discuss briefly about Object-Oriented Conceptual Model (OOCM). OOCM encapsulates the structural/static, as well as behavioral/dynamic, aspects of objects. The static aspects consist of the classes/objects and the relationship between them, namely *inheritance*, *association* and *aggregation*. The dynamic aspect of the OOCM consists of generic methods and user-defined methods. We only discuss the static aspects, since this is the topic that is relevant for this chapter. Static aspects in OOCM create objects and classes that also include decisions regarding their attributes. Furthermore, they also concern the relationship between objects. The basic segment of the object-oriented system is an object. An object is a data abstraction that is defined by: an object name as a unique identifier; valued attributes (instance variables), which give a state to the object; and methods or routines that access the state of the object.

In XML schema, there are static aspects from object-oriented conceptual models that we can find. The aggregation, association and inheritance relationships are the three OOCM features that we will discuss in this chapter.

The *aggregation* relationship (refer to Figure 2) represents a "part-of" relationship, indicating that a "whole" object consists of "part" objects (Dillon & Tan, 1993). Figure 2 shows us the aggregation relationship between the superclass and sub-classes. *C* is the "whole" object and *C*1, *C*2 and *C*3 are the "part" objects. This kind of relationship exists commonly in XML documents.

Figure 2: A One-Leveled Aggregation Relationship Rooted at C

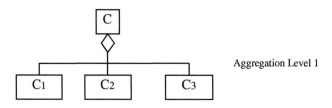

XML assumes that data is hierarchically structured. One element may contain sub-elements, which may sequentially contain other elements. ORDB in Oracle 9i also has a feature that can support aggregation relationship. Therefore, we can easily map aggregation relationship in XML schema onto ORDB in Oracle 9i.

In this chapter, we discuss two types of aggregations: *existence independent* and *existence dependent*. An existence independent aggregation relationship means that the sub-class can stand by itself, even if the superclass does not exist. On the other hand, existence dependent means that the sub-class is totally dependent on the superclass. Furthermore, we also look at two more types of aggregation relationship, i.e., ordered composition and homogeneous/ heterogeneous composition. We called the aggregation an ordered composition if it is a "whole" object composed of different "part" objects in particular order. In other words, the order of occurrence of the "part" objects in the composition is vital to the model. Homogeneous means one whole consists of several different types of "part" objects.

The *inheritance* relationship (refer to Figure 3) represents "inherited" relationship, indicating that an object or a relation inherits the attribute (and methods) of another object (Dillon & Tan, 1993). This kind of relationship exists commonly in XML documents. XML assumes that data is hierarchically structured. One element may contain sub-elements, which may sequentially contain other elements. ORDB in Oracle 9i also has a feature that can support inheritance relationships. Therefore, we can easily map inheritance relationships in XML schema onto ORDB in Oracle 9i. In this chapter, we discuss two types of inheritances: *single inheritance* and *multiple inheritance*. Single inheritance means the sub-class only has one superclass. Multiple inheritance means the sub-class has multiple superclasses.

The *association* relationship represents a "connection" between object instances. Basically, it is a reference, from one object to another, which provides access paths among objects in a system. Objects are connected

Figure 3: A One-Leveled Inheritance Relationship Rooted at C

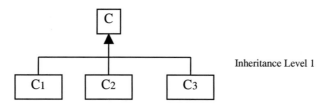

through an association link. The link can have a specified cardinality, e.g., one-to-one, one-to-many, and many-to-many. We will discuss this relationship further in this chapter.

Related Work

Most existing work has focused on a methodology that has been designed to map a relational database to an XML database for database interoperability. The schema translation procedure is provided with an EER (Extended Entity Relationship) model mapped into XML schema (Fong, Pang & Bloor, 2001).

There are many works that explain the mapping from relational databases to XML. Some of them still use DTD (Yang & Wang, 2001), and some of them use XML schema (Mani, Lee & Muntz, 2001). Since XML is rapidly emerging as the dominant standard for exchanging data on the WWW, the previous work already discussed mapping referential integrity constraints from Relational Database to XML, semantic data modeling using XML schemas, and enhancing structural mapping for XML and ORDB.

In addition, the study of the use of new scalar and aggregate functions in SQL for constructing complex XML documents directly in the relational engine has been done (Shanmugasundaram et al., 2001).

Relational and object-relational database systems are a well-understood technique for managing and querying such large sets of structured data. In Kletke and Meyer (2001), the writers wrote about how a relevant subset of XML documents and their implied structure can be mapped onto database structures. They suggest mapping DTDs onto object-relational database schemas and, to overcome the typical problems (large schemas), they suggested an algorithm for determining an optimal hybrid database schema.

The way to model XML and to transform the OO conceptual models into XML schema have been discussed in Xiao, Dillon, Chang & Feng (2001). The writers chose the OO conceptual model because of its expressive power for developing a combined data model. They come out with several generic-transforming rules from the OO conceptual model to XML schema, with the emphasis on the transformations of generalization and aggregation relationships. The XML schema code that is presented below in this chapter is adopted from the existing work that was done previously. In addition, our chapter is done to improve what has been done in Xiao, Dillon, Chang & Feng (2001).

The work reported in this chapter is distinguished from this work in the following aspects. First, we focus on the transformation from XML schema to ORDB. Second, our transformation target uses OO features in Oracle 9*i*, not just the general OO features. The similarity is we take aggregation, association and inheritance relationships into consideration.

TRANSFORMATION FROM XML SCHEMA TO ORDB: THE PROPOSED METHODOLOGY

In the following, we use XML schema and Oracle 9*i* to interpret the aggregation, inheritance, and association relationships in OO conceptual models. We discuss the transformation or mapping from XML schema to ORDB. In this section, we also validate the following documents against the schema. In addition to that, we also give the example of how to insert the data into the table after creating the table in Oracle 9*i*. The expressions that are commonly used for data types mapping from XML schema to ORDB in this chapter are String to Varchar2 and Decimal to Decimal(l,d), where l = length and d = decimal.

Aggregation Composition

As previously discussed, there are three types of aggregation composition that will be discussed in this chapter. The first one is ordered existence dependent composition; second is homogeneous existence dependent composition; and lastly, existence independent composition.

Existence Dependent (Ordered Composition)

The structure of XML schema for existence dependent is as below. Firstly, it creates the superclass element and categorizes it as a type. Then, under sequence, adds the sub-classes for that superclass element.

XML schema for existence dependent aggregation relationship:

```
<xsd:element name= "Invoice" type = "InvoiceType"/>
  <xsd:complexType name = "InvoiceType">
    <xsd:sequence>
      <xsd:element name = "Heading"type = "xsd:string">
      <xsd:element name = "Contact_Person" type = "ContactPersonType"/>
```

```
    <xsd:element name = "Items_Ordered" type = "xsd:string"/>
    <xsd:element name = "Total_Price" type = "xsd:decimal">
  </xsd:sequence>
    <xsd:attribute name = "heading_id" type = "xsd:
    integer" use = "required"/>
</xsd:complexType>
<xsd:complexType name = "ContactPersonType">
  <xsd:sequence>
    <xsd:element name = "Name"type = "xsd:string"/>
    <xsd:element name = "Address"type = "xsd:string"/>
    <xsd:element name = "PhoneNo"type = "xsd:decimal"/>
  </xsd:sequence>
    <xsd:attribute name = "contact_person_id" type =xsd:
     integer" use = "required"/>
</xsd:complexType>
```

From the XML schema above, we can look at the conceptual model behind it. Figure 4 shows the aggregation relationship from the Invoice. The diamond arrow shows the relationship from the superclass and the sub-class. Invoice is a composite class that consists of classes *Heading*, *Contact_Persons*, *Item_ordered* and *total_price*. This relationship is existence dependent aggregation since the sub-elements cannot exist if we remove the composite class.

The following steps generate a transformation from XML schema to Object-Relational Logical model in Oracle 9*i* for existence dependent aggregation relationship.

i.   For an aggregation relationship rooted at a composite class C, an element named C with a complex Type Ctype in XML schema (`<xsd:element name = "C" type = "Ctype">`) can be transformed by creating a cluster named C_cluster in Object-Relational Logical Model. Then, write the type of class C attributes (such as `c_id`) based on the attribute for that

Figure 4: An Aggregation Relationship Example

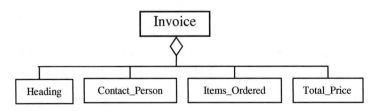

complex type in XML schemas. Usually it is in the *varchar2* format and the user will enter the length for it.

XML schema:
```
<xsd:element name= "Invoice" type = "InvoiceType" />
    <xsd:complexType name = "InvoiceType">
```

ORDB:
```
Create  Cluster  Invoice_Cluster
    (invoice_Id varchar2 (10));
```

ii.   Create a table for composite class *C* and the type of its attribute, which is exactly the same as `C_cluster` above and has Not Null besides the `C_id`, which means table invoice must have an id. Then, create a primary key for this table, which is usually `C_id`. Next, create a cluster, as *C* table attributes and the type will be `C_cluster (C_id)`.

ORDB:
```
Create  Table  Invoice
    (invoice_id        varchar2(10)  Not  Null,
      Primary Key  (invoice_id))
Cluster  Invoice_Cluster  (invoice_id);
```

iii. Based on each sub-element named C1 within the *complexType Ctype* in the XML schema (`<xsd:element name = "C1"type= "...">`), we need to create another table for each sub-element. Its attributes will consist of `C_id`, `C1_id` and other attributes that are relevant to C1. `C_id` and `C1_id` will be the primary key, and the foreign key will be *C_id references C (C_id)*. Next, create a cluster and its type that should be the same with the cluster that is created before, `C_cluster (C_id)`.

XML schema:
```
<xsd:sequence>
   <xsd: element name = "Heading"type = "xsd:string"/>
```

ORDB:
```
Create  Table  Heading
        (invoice_id varchar2 (10)  Not  Null,
        heading_id        varchar2 (10)  Not  Null,
        Heading           varchar2 (30),
```

```
        Primary Key (invoice_id, heading_id),
        Foreign Key (invoice_id) References In
        voice (invoice_id))
Cluster Invoice_Cluster (invoice_id);
```

iv.   Create index for C_cluster_index on cluster C_cluster

ORDB:

```
Create Index Invoice_Cluster_Index
     On Cluster Invoice_Cluster;
```

Below is the full example of the ORDB after XML schema transformation.

ORDB for existence dependent aggregation relationship:

```
Create Cluster Invoice_Cluster
     (invoice_id      varchar2 (10));
Create Table Invoice
     (invoice_id      varchar2 (10) Not Null,
     Primary Key   (invoice_id))
     Cluster     invoice_cluster (invoice_id);
Create Table Heading
     (invoice_id      varchar2 (10) Not Null,
     heading_id   varchar2 (10) Not Null,
     Primary Key (invoice_id, heading_id),
     Foreign Key (invoice_id) References In
voice (invoice_id))
Cluster       invoice_cluster (invoice_id);
Create Table Contact_Person
     (contact_person_id varchar2 (10) Not Null,
     invoice_id   varchar2 (10) Not Null,
     name         varchar2 (40),
     address      varchar2 (40),
     phone_no        number
     Primary Key (invoice_id, contact_person_id),
     Foreigh Key (invoice_id) References In
voice (invoice_id))
Cluster       invoice_cluster (invoice_id);
Create Table Item_Ordered
     (invoice_id       varchar2 (10) Not Null,
     item_ordered_Id varchar2 (10) Not Null,
     Primary Key   (invoice_id, item_ordered_id),
     Foreign Key   (invoice_id) References In
```

```
voice (invoice_id))
Cluster          invoice_cluster (invoice_id);
Create Table Total_Price
    (invoice_id      varchar2 (10) Not Null,
    total_price_ID  varchar2 (10) Not Null,
    Primary Key (invoice_id, total_price_id),
    Foreign Key (invoice_id) References In
voice (invoice_id)
Cluster          invoice_cluster (invoice_id)
Create Index Invoice_Cluster_Index On Cluster
Invoice_Cluster
```

Below is the XML and INSERT query for the existence dependent aggregation. In the XML, the tag is based on the element declaration in XML schema. Then, the words or numbers between the tags are the data that is going to be inserted into the table.

In the INSERT part, the element in the Insert query should exist as a table name that is created above. The data that is inserted between elements in the XML is written in the middle of the quotation mark in Insert query. The data in the Insert query should be entered by following the order of the attributes that are declared in the create table.

Common syntax ordered composition XML:
```
<A>     a     </A>
<B>
              <B1>    b   </B1>
              <B2>    c   </B2>
</B>
<C>
              <C1>    d   </C1>
              <C2>    e   </C2>
</C>
```

Common syntax ordered composition Insert query:
```
Insert into A values ('a')
Insert into B values ('b', 'c')
Insert into C values ('d', 'e')
```

The steps to transform from XML to ORDB Insert query are discussed:
i.   XML for existence dependent aggregation will be structured like above.

For every element that is a class (A, B, C), we insert the values to it (a, b, c). B *1* and *B 2* are the attributes for *B* class, since *B* has many attributes, that contain *b* and *c* values

ii.   For every class $(A, B$ and $C)$, we transform it into the Insert query by writing "Insert into *A* values." Then, for every value in the class, we insert it into the class by using (' '). If one class contains many attributes, we separate them by using a comma. If the data contains numbers only, we do not need to put the quotation mark.

For example: ('*a*', '*b*', '*c*')

XML for ordered composition (Example: Invoice case study):

```
<?xml version = "1.0" ?>
<Invoice Invoice_id = "1001">
        <Heading> This is Invoice 1 </Heading>
        <Contact_Person>
                <Name> John </Name>
                <Address>570 Lygon St</Address>
                <PhoneNo> 95086868</PhoneNo>
        </Contact_Person>
        <Item_Ordered>50</Item_Ordered>
        <Total_Price>40</Total_Price>
</Invoice>
```

INSERT for ordered composition (Example: Invoice case study):

```
Insert into Invoice Values (1001)
Insert into Heading Values ('This is Invoice 1')
Insert into Contact_Person Values(101, 1001, 'John', '570
Lygon St',95086868)
Insert into Item_Ordered Values ('This is Invoice 1', 50)
Insert into Total_Price Values (1001, 40)
```

Existence Dependent (Homogeneous Composition)

The structure of XML schema for existence dependent homogeneous composition is as below. First, it creates the superclass element and categorizes it as a type. Then, under the complex type, adds the sub-classes for that superclass element. Since this sub-class can occur for more than one time, we need to include minOccurs = "1" and maxOccurs = "unbounded." Last, add any attributes for that element.

Figure 5: A Homogeneous Composition Example

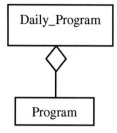

XML schema for existence independent homogeneous aggregation:

```
<xsd:element name = "Daily_Program"type = "DailyProgramType"/>
<xsd:complexType name = "DailyProgramType">
    <xsd:element name = "Program_Name"type = "xsd:string"
        minOccurs ="1"maxOccurs="unbounded"/>
    <xsd:attribute name = "program_id" type = "xsd:integer" use =
        "required">
    <xsd:attribute name = "daily_program_id" type = "xsd:integer"
        use = "required">
</xsd:complexType>
```

The XML schema above can be modeled using a conceptual diagram. Figure 5 shows the homogeneous existence independent aggregation relationship. This relationship means that the sub-classes can stand alone without the composite class. For example, *Programs* can exist without the *Daily_Program*. *Daily_Program* consists of several *Programs*.

We can generate a transformation for existence independent homogeneous aggregation relationship from XML schema to Object-Relational Logical model in Oracle 9*i* as follows:

i.   Each sub-element named C1 with a complex Type Ctype in XML schema
    (`<xsd:element name = "C1"type= ""... ." MinOccurs= "..."`
    `maxOccurs= "...">`) needs to be created as an object named C1.
    Then, write the type of C1 attributes (such as C1_id) based on the
    attribute for that complex type in XML schemas. Usually it is in the
    `varchar2` format, and the user will enter the length for it.

XML schema:
```
<xsd:element name = "Program" type = "xsd:string"
        minOccurs="1" maxOccurs="unbounded"/>
```

The *maxOccurs* explains the maximum number of *Programs* in *Daily_Program*. This may be a positive integer value or the word "unbounded" to specify that there is no maximum number of occurrences. The *minOccurs* shows the minimum number of times an element may appear. It is always less than or equal to the default value of *maxOccurs*, i.e., it is 0 or 1. Similarly, if we only specify a value for the *maxOccurs* attribute, it must be greater than or equal to the default value of *minOccurs*, i.e., 1 or more.

ORDB:
```
Create Or Replace Type Program As Object
        (Program_id varchar2 (10));
```

ii.   Create a table for composite class C1 (as a table of the object above).

ORDB:
```
Create Or Replace Type Program_Table As Table Of Program
```

iii.   For an existence independent aggregation relationship rooted at a composite class C, an element named C within the complexType Ctype in the XML schema (<xsd:element name = "C" type= "Ctype">) needs to created as an object named C. Its attributes will consist of c_id and other attributes that are relevant to it. c_id will be the primary key. Next, nest this table and store it as the table that is created before.

XML schema:
```
<xsd:element name = "Daily_Program"type ="DailyProgramType"/>
        <xsd:complexType name = "DailyProgramType">
```

ORDB:
```
Create Table Daily_Program
    (daily_program_id   varchar2(10) Not Null,
    program_name       Program_Table,
    Primary Key (daily_program_id))
    Nested Table program_name Store As
    Program_Table;
```

Next, is the full example of Object-Relational Logical model after it has been transformed from XML schema.

ORDB for existence dependent homogeneous aggregation:

```
Create Or Replace Type Program As Object
   (program_id   varchar2 (10));
Create Or Replace Type Program_Table As Table
Of Program
Create Table Daily_Program
   (daily_program_id   varchar2(10) Not Null,
   program_name         Program_Table,
   Primary Key (daily_program_id))
   Nested Table program_name Store As
Program_Table;
```

The following is the XML and INSERT query for the homogeneous independent aggregation. Similar to the explanation in ordered dependent aggregation, the tag in XML is based on the element declaration in XML schema. And, the words or numbers between the tags are the data that is going to be inserted into the table.

In the INSERT part, the element in the Insert query should exist as a table name that is created above. The data that wants to be inserted into the table is written in the middle of the quotation mark in Insert query. The data in the Insert query should be entered by following the order of the attributes that are declared in the create table. Since we use clustering techniques to create the aggregation, we are not creating a table to store nested data; instead, we are only creating a datatype and are storing an attribute of that datatype with a different name. Hence, while inserting data into a nested table, we actually store data in the object rather than in the table.

Common syntax for homogeneous composition for XML:

```
<A>
         <B>    b    </B>
         <B>    c    </B>
</A>
```

Common syntax homogeneous composition Insert query:

```
Insert into A values (1, 'b', ( B_Table (B (1, ' '))))
```

The following steps are for transforming from XML to ORBD Insert query homogeneous composition:

i.   In the existence dependent homogeneous aggregation, composite class
      contains several homogeneous sub-classes.
      In XML, *A* is the composite class, and *B* is the sub-class that contains
      some values.
ii.   In the Insert query, since the sub-class is inside the composite class, the
      insert query will look like the structure above.
iii. Since every table in Oracle needs to have an ID, in the Insert query, we
      put the ID for *A* and *B* table. That is the reason why, in the beginning of
      every table, there is a number that represents the ID table before the
      values.

*XML for homogeneous composition (Example:Daily Program case
study):*

```
<daily_program>
      <daily_program_id> 1 </daily_program_id>
      <program_id> 1 </program_id>
      <program_name>This is program 1</program_name>
</daily_program>
<daily_program>
      <daily_program_id> 1 </daily_program_id>
      <program_id> 2 </program_id>
      <program_name> This is program 2 </program_name>
</daily_program>
```

*INSERT for homogeneous composition (Example:Daily Program case
study):*

```
Insert into Daily_Program Values (1, 'This is program 1',
Program_Table(Program(1)));
Insert into Daily_Program Values (1, 'This is program 2',
Program_Table(Program(2)));
```

Existence Independent

      Below is the structure of XML schema for existence independent aggre-
gation. First, it creates the superclass element and categorises it as a type. Then,
under the complex type, we use 'choice' to refer to the sub-classes for
superclass element. Last, put attributes for each element, according to its
needs.

XML schema for existence independent aggregation relationship:

```
<xs:element name="Hamper" type ="HamperType">
  <xs:complexType>
```

```
    <xs:choice>
      <xs:element ref = "Biscuit"/>
      <xs:element ref = "Confectionary"/>
      <xs:element ref = "Deli"/>
    </xs:choice>
  </xs:complexType>
  </xs:element>

<xs:element name = "HamperType">
<xs:complexType>
    <sequence>
      <xs:element name = "hamper_id" type = "xs:string"/>
      <xs:element name="hamper_price" type = "xs:decimal"/>
    </sequence>
</xs:complexType>
</xs:element>

<xs:element name = "Biscuit">
<xs:complexType>
    <sequence>
      <xs:element name = "biscuit_id" type = "xs:string"/>
      <xs:element name = "biscuit_name" type ="xs:string"/>
      <xs:element name = "biscuit_price" type =
"xs:decimal"/>
    </sequence>
</xs:complexType>
</xs:element>
<xs:element name = "Confectionary">
<xs:complexType>
    <sequence>
      <xs:element  name  =  "confectionary_id"  type  =
"xs:string"/>
      <xs:element name = "confectionary _name" type =
      "xs:string"/>
      <xs:element name = "confectionary_price" type =
      "xs:decimal"/>
    </sequence>
</xs:complexType>
</xs:element>
<xs:element name = "Deli">
<xs:complexType>
    <sequence>
      <xs:element name = "deli_id" type = "xs:string"/>
      <xs:element name = "deli_name" type = "xs:string"/>
      <xs:element name = "deli_price" type = "xs:decimal"/>
```

```
    </sequence>
  </xs:complexType>
  </xs:element>
```

Based on the XML schema above, we try to draw the conceptual diagram for it. Figure 6 shows the existence independent aggregation relationship from the Hamper case study. The diamond arrow shows the relationship from the superclass to the sub-classes. Hamper is a composite class that consists of classes *Biscuit, Confectionary* and *Deli*. This relationship is existence independent aggregation since the sub-elements can exist by themselves even if we remove the composite class.

The following steps generate a transformation from XML schema to Object-Relational Logical model in Oracle 9*i* for existence independent aggregation relationship.

i.   For an aggregation relationship rooted at a composite class C, an element named C with a complex Type Ctype in XML schema (`<xsd:element name = "C" type = "Ctype">`) can be transformed by creating a table named C in ORDB. Then, write the type of class C attributes (such as `c_id`), based on the attribute for that Ctype in the XML schemas.

XML schemas:
```
<xs:element name="Hamper" type ="HamperType">
.......
.... ....
<xs:element name = "HamperType">
<xs:complexType>
   <sequence>
   <xs:element name = "hamper_id" type = "xs:string"/>
   <xs:element name = "hamper_price" type = "xs:decimal"/>
   </sequence>
</xs:complexType>
</xs:element>
```

Figure 6: An Existence Independent Composition Example

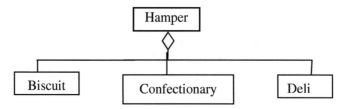

ORDB:

```
Create  Table  Hamper
   (hamper_id    varchar2(3) Not   Null,
   hamper_price Number,
   Primary Key  (hamper_id));
```

ii.   Create tables for each element under choice. The element reference under
      choice means that it refers to the details below, where the element name
      equals the element reference.

XML schema:

```
<xs:complexType>
<xs:choice>
   <xs:element ref = "Biscuit"/>
   <xs:element ref = "Confectionary"/>
   <xs:element ref = "Deli"/>
</xs:choice>
</xs:complexType>

<xs:element name = "Biscuit">
<xs:complexType>
<sequence>
      <xs:element name = "biscuit_id" type = "xs:string"/>
      <xs:element name = "biscuit_name" type ="xs:string"/>
      <xs:element  name  =  "biscuit_price"  type  =
"xs:decimal"/>
</sequence>
</xs:complexType>
</xs:element>
```

ORDB:

```
Create  Table  Biscuit
   (biscuit_id    varchar2(3) Not   Null,
   biscuit_name      varchar2(20),
   biscuit_price Number,
   Primary Key  (biscuit_id));
```

iii. Create the last table that we call an aggregate table, which will link the
      composite class with the sub-classes. Then, create the attributes for this
      class, which includes the id for the composite class, part_id and part_type.
      Lastly, create a primary key and a foreign key.

ORDB:

```
Create  Table  Aggregate
  (hamper_id    varchar2(3) Not  Null,
  part_id       varchar2(3) Not  Null,
  part_type     varchar2(20) Check
     (part_type In ('biscuit', 'confectionery', 'deli')),
     Primary  Key  (hamper_id, part_id),
     Foreign  Key  (hamper_id)  References hamper
(hamper_id));
```

Below is the mapping of Object-Relational Logical model for existence independent from the XML schema existence independent aggregation.

ORDB for existence independent aggregation:

```
Create  Table  Hamper
  (hamper_id    varchar2(3) Not  Null,
  hamper_price  Number,
  Primary  Key  (h_id));
Create  Table  Biscuit
  (biscuit_id      varchar2(3) Not  Null,
  biscuit_name  varchar2(20),
  biscuit_price Number,
  Primary  Key  (biscuit_id));
Create  Table  Confectionery
  (confectionery_id       varchar2(3)
  confectionery_name  varchar2(20),
  confectionary_price Number,
  Primary  Key  (confectionary_id));
Create  Table  Deli
  (deli_id         varchar2(3) Not  Null,
  deli_name        varchar2(20),
  deli_price       Number,
  Primary  Key  (deli_id));
Create  Table  Aggregate
  (hamper_id    varchar2(3) Not  Null,
  part_id       varchar2(3) Not  Null,
  part_type     varchar2(20)   Check
  (part_type In ('biscuit', 'confectionery', 'deli')),
  Primary  Key  (hamper_id, part_id),
  Foreign  Key  (hamper_id)  References hamper
(hamper_id));
```

Below is the XML and INSERT query for the existence independent aggregation. The steps for its transformation are also discussed.

Syntax for existence independent aggregation XML:

```
<A>
        <A1>    a    <A1>
        <A2>    b    <A2>
</A>

<B>
        <B1>    c    <B1>
        <B2>    d    <B2>
</B>
```

The steps below are for transforming from XML to Insert query homogeneous composition:

i.   In the existence independent homogeneous aggregation, composite class is defined at the top of XML (we use A as a variable that refers to a class and 'a', 'b' as its attributes). Therefore, for every data in XML, we convert it to INSERT query in Oracle by using the following format: INSERT into A values (a, b).

ii.   In XML, A is the composite class and B is the sub-class that contains some values. If there is more than one sub-class, there will be more XML code below its composite. Then, insert into the aggregation table using the following format: INSERT into Aggregate values ('a', 10000,'B'), which is the table to link the composite table with the sub-classes and does not exist in XML.

Syntax for existence independent aggregation INSERT table:

```
INSERT into A values ('a', 'b');
INSERT into B values ('c', 'd');
INSERT into Aggregate values ('a', 10000,'B');
```

XML for existence independent aggregation:

```
<Hamper>
    <hamper_id> 1 </hamper_id>
    <hamper_price> 20 </hamper_price>
```

```
<Biscuit>
   <biscuit_id>  10  </biscuit_id>
   <biscuit_name>  Arnold  </biscuit_name>
   <biscuit_price>  5.5  </biscuit_price>
</Biscuit>

<Confectionary>
   <confectionary_id>  100  </confectionary_id>
   <confectionary_name>  Casey  </confectionary_name>
   <confectionary_price>10.5</confectionary_price>
</Confectionary>

<Deli>
   <deli_id>  1000  </deli_id>
   <deli_name>  Demoi  </deli_name>
   <deli_price>  4  </deli_price>
</Deli>
</Hamper>
```

Insert query for existence independent aggregation:

```
INSERT into Hamper values (1, 10);
INSERT into Biscuit values (10, 'Arnold', 5.5);
INSERT into Confectionary values (100, 'Casey', 10.5);
INSERT into Deli values (1000, 'Demoi', 4.2);
INSERT into Aggregate values (1, 10000,'biscuit');
```

Association Transformation

The association transformation that will be presented in this chapter consists of three parts, i.e., one-to-one association relationship, one-to-many association relationship, and many-to-many association relationship.

One to One Association Relationship

The example that is used in this section is the relationship between lecture and office. We assume that one lecture can only have one office, and one office can only have one lecture. For one-to-one association relationship, it is important for us to determine the participation of the objects to decide the location of the primary keys in relational system. There are two types of participation: *total participation* and *partial participation*. Total participation is when the existence of an object is totally dependent on the other object, and the partial participation is when the existence of an object is partially dependent on the other object.

Below is the XML schema for one-to-one relationship. The characteristic of one-to-one relationship in XML schema is minOccurs = "0" maxOccurs = "1" for each element or class. The attributes for each element will be defined after the element.

XML schema for one-to-one relationship:

```
<element name = "lecture">
<complexType>
    <sequence>
    <element ref="office" minOccurs="0" maxOccurs= "1" />
    <element ref="lecture" minOccurs="0" maxOccurs= "1"/>
    </sequence>
    <attribute name = "lectureid" type = "string" use ="required"/>
    <attribute name = "lectureName" type = "string" use = "optional"/>
</complexType>
</element>
<element name = "office">
    <attribute name = "officeid" type = "string" use ="required"/>
</element>
```

Figure 7 shows the conceptual diagram from the XML schema above. From the XML schema, we would like to transform it to Object-Relational Logical model, and the procedures about how the transformation will work are explained next.

The steps below explain how to transform the one-to-one association relationship from XML schema to ORDB. (Refer to the full example following the steps.)

i.   From the XML schema, the total participation will be the element that has minOccurs ="0" maxOccurs ="1" next to it. Therefore, we need to create an object for office before we create an object for lecture. An element named 'Office' can be transformed by creating an object named 'Office_T' in ORDB. Then, write all the attributes for this element based on the attribute's name in that complexType.

ii.   Create another object named 'Lecture_T' in ORDB and write all the attributes for 'Lecture' element based on the attribute's name in 'Lecture' complexType. The minOccurs = 0 and maxOccurs = 1 in XML means that element D can contain 0 or 1 data. In ORDB, it will be

Figure 7: One-to-One Association

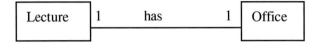

shown by using REF, so we create one attribute in 'Lecture_T' object named 'Lecture_Office' that refers to 'Office_T'.

iii. Lastly, we create one table for 'Lecture' and another one for 'Office'. Each table has its id and a primary key that refers to the id. Declare every id as a Not Null since it is required.

Below is the full example of ORDB for one-to-one relationship after the transformation.

ORDB for one-to-one relationship:

```
Create Or Replace Type Office_T As Object
   (office_id    varchar2 (10))
Create Or Replace Type Lecture_T As Object
   (lecture_id varchar2 (10),
   lecture_name  varchar2 (50),
   lecture_office Ref office_T)
Create Table Office Of Office_T
   (office_id    Not  Null,
   Primary Key (office_id));
Create Table lecture Of Lecture_T
   (lecture_id Not  Null,
   Primary Key (lecture_id));
```

This part describes the XML and INSERT query for the one-to-one association relationship. In the XML, the tag is based on the element declaration in XML schema. Then, the words or numbers between the tags are the data that will be inserted into the table.

In the INSERT part, the element in the Insert query should exist as a table name that is created before. The data that is inserted between elements in the XML is written in the middle of the quotation mark in Insert query. The data in the Insert query should be entered by following the order of the attributes that are declared in the create table. Furthermore, to link those two tables, we make reference to the table. We use the SQL query by selecting the reference from the other table.

Common syntax for XML one-to-one association relationship:

```
<A>
        <A1>    a    </A1>
        <A2>    b    </A2>
</A>
<B>
        <B1>    c    </B1>
</B>
```

Common syntax for Insert query one-to-one association relationship:

```
Insert into B values ('c');
Insert into A values ('a', 'b', (Select REF (a) from B a where a.Bid
= c));
```

Below are the steps of transformation from XML to Insert Query:

i.   When transforming one-to-one association relationship from XML to
       Insert query, first we insert the values for B class.

ii.   Then, we insert the values for A class and refer that class to B table with
       its id = c.

XML for one-to-one association relationship:

```
<lecture>
    <lectureid> 1090 </lectureid>
    <lectureName> Josep </lectureName>
</lecture>
<office>
    <officeid> 101 </officeid>
</office>
```

INSERT for one-to-one relationship:

```
Insert into office values (101);
Insert into lecture values (1090, 'Josep', (Select REF (a) From
office a Where      a.Officeid=101));
```

One-to-Many Association Transformation

The example that is used in this section is the relationship between customer and order (see Figure 8). One customer can have many orders, and one order belongs to only one customer.

Figure 8: One-to-Many Association

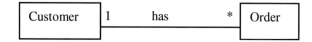

Let us look at the structure of XML schema for one-to-many relationship. Then, we can transform these structures to ORBD format.

XML schema for one-to-many relationship:

```
<xs:element name = "customer" type ="customerType"/ >
<xs:complexType name = "customerType">
   <xs:sequence>
      <xs:element name = "order" type= "orderType"
      minOccurs= "1" max Occurs = "unbounded" / >
   <xs:sequence>
   <xs:attribute name ="customerName"type="xs:string"/>
   <xs:attribute name = "shippingAddress"
   type="xs:string"/>
   <xs:attribute name="shippingCity" type="xs:string"/>
   <xs:attribute name ="shippingState"type= "xs:string"/>
   <xs:attribute name = "shippingPostalCode" type="xs:integer"/>
   <xsd:attribute name = "customer_id" type = "xsd: integer" use
   = "required"/>
</xs:complexType>
<xs:complexType name = "orderType">
   <xs:attribute name ="orderID" type="xs:integer"/>
   <xs:attribute name ="orderDate" type="xs:date"/>
</xs:complexType>
```

The following steps explain how to transform the one-to-many association relationship from XML schema to Object-Relational Logical model:

i.   For one-to-many association relationship, an element named C with a complex Type `Ctype` in XML schema (`<xsd:element name = "C" type= "Ctype">`) can be transformed by creating an object named `C_type` in ORDB. Then, write all the attributes for this element based on the attribute's name in that complex type.

XML schema:

```
<xs:element name = "customer" type = "customerType"/ >
<xs:complexType name = "customerType">
    <xs:attribute name = "customerName" type="xs:string"/>
    <xs:attribute name = "shippingAddress" type="xs:string"/>
    <xs:attribute name = "shippingCity"type="xs:string"/>
    <xs:attribute name = "shippingState" type="xs:string"/>
    <xs:attribute name = "shippingPostalCode" type="xs:integer"/>
    <xsd:attribute name = "customer_id" type = "xsd: integer" use
    = "required"/>
</xs:complexType>
```

ORDB:

```
Create Or Replace Type Customer_T As Object
    (customer_id           varchar2 (10),
    customer_name          varchar2 (50),
    shipping_address       varchar2 (100),
    shipping_city          varchar2 (20),
    shipping_state          varchar2 (20),
    shipping_postalcode     number)
```

ii. Since it is one-to-many relationship, there is another element (D), in the Ctype complex type under sequence compositor, that refers to another table. Create another object named D_type in ORDB, and write all the attributes for D element   based on the attribute's name in D complex type. The minOccurs = 1 and maxOccurs = unbounded in XML means that element D should contain one or more data. In ORDB, it will be shown by using REF, so we create one attribute in Dtype object named D_C that refers to Ctype.

XML schema:

```
<xs:sequence>
    <xs:element name = "order" type= "orderType" minOccurs= "1"
max Occurs =      "unbounded"/ >
</xs:sequence>
<xs:complexType name = "orderType">
    <xs:attribute name ="orderID" type="xs:integer"/>
    <xs:attribute name = "orderDate" type= "xs:date"/>
</xs:complexType>
```

ORDB:

```
Create Or Replace Type Order_T As Object
    (order_id        varchar2(10),
     order_date      date,
     order_customer Ref customer_T)
```

iii.   Last, we create one table for c and another one for d. Each table has its id and a primary key that refers to the id. Declared every id as a Not Null since it is required.

ORDB:

```
Create Table Customer Of Customer_T
    (customer_id     Not Null,
     Primary Key (customer_id));
Create Table Order Of Order_T
    (order_id     Not Null,
     Primary Key (order_id));
```

Below is a complete example of transformation from one-to-many association relationship XML schema into Object-Relational Logical model.

ORDB for one-to-many relationship:

```
Create Or Replace Type Customer_T As Object
    (customer_id         varchar2 (10),
     customer_name       varchar2 (50),
     shipping_address    varchar2 (100),
     shipping_city       varchar2 (20),
     shipping_state          varchar2 (20),
     shipping_postalcode number)

Create Or Replace Type Order_T As Object
    (order_id        varchar2(10),
     order_date      date,
     order_customer Ref customer_T)

Create Table Customer Of Customer_T
    (customer_id     Not Null,
     Primary Key (customer_id));
Create Table Order Of Order_T
    (order_id     Not Null,
     Primary Key (order_id));
```

Below is the XML and INSERT query for the one-to-many association relationship. Similar to the XML in one-to-one relationship, the tag is based on the element declaration in XML schema. Then, the words or numbers between the tags are the data that will be inserted into the table.

In the INSERT part, the element in the Insert query should exist as a table name that is created before. The data that is inserted between elements in the XML is written in the middle of the quotation mark in Insert query. If the data is a number, we do not use the quotation mark. The data in the Insert query should be entered by following the order of the attributes that are declared in the create table. Furthermore, to link those two tables, we make reference to the table. We use the SQL query by selecting the reference from the other table.

Common syntax for XML one-to-many relationship:

```
<A>
        <A1>    a    </A1>
        <A2>    b    </A2>
        <A3>    c    </A3>
</A>

<B>
        <B1>    d    </B1>
        <B2>    e    </B2>
</B>

<C>
        <C1>    f    </C1>
        <C2>    g    </C2>
</C>
```

Common syntax for XML one-to-many relationship:

```
Insert into A values (a_id, a, b, c);
Insert into B values (bid, d, e ) select REF (a) from A where a.A =
1;
Insert into C values (cid, f, g) select REF (a) from A where a.A =
1;
```

Transformation from XML to Insert query for one-to-many relationship:

i.   When transforming one-to-many association relationship from XML to Insert query, firstly, we insert the value of *A*. The values in the Insert query will start with its ID, *a*, *b*, *c*.

ii.   Then insert the values for *B*, *C* and etc., and refer to the *A* table, where the id is equal to the one that is required.

XML for one-to-many association relationship:
```
<customer customer_id = "1">
<customerName> Agus </customerName>
<shippingAddress> 570 Lygon St </shippingAddress>
<shippingCity>Carlton </shippingCity>
<shippingState>Victoria </shippingState>
<shippingPostalCode>3053 </shippingPostalCode>

<order>
   <orderID> 101 </orderID>
   <orderDate> 23/09/02 </orderDate>
</order>
<order>
   <orderID> 102 </orderID>
   <orderDate> 24/09/02 </orderDate>
</order>
</customer>
```

INSERT for one-to-many association relationship:
```
Insert into customer values (1, 'Agus', '570 Lygon St',
'Carlton',
'Victoria', 3053);
Insert into order values (101, '23/09/02', Select Ref (a)
From customer where a.customer = 1);
Insert into order values (102, '24/09/02', Select Ref (a)
From customer where a.customer = 1);
```

Many-to-Many Association Transformations

        The last association type is many-to-many relationship. The example that we use next is the relationship between student and course. Students can enroll in many courses, and one course can be enrolled in by many students. The characteristic of many-to-many association in XML schema is each element can have one or more data. The syntax to show that one element consists of one or more data is minOccurs = "1" maxOccurs = "unbounded." Figure 9 shows the conceptual diagram for this relationship.

Figure 9: Many-to-Many Association

XML schema for many-to-many relationship:

```
<xs:element name = "Department">
    <xs:complexType>
        <xs:sequence>
            <xs:element name = "students" minOccurs ="1"
                maxOccurs ="unbounded">
            <xs:complexType>
                <xs:sequence>
                    <xs:element ref = "student" minOccurs = "1"
                        maxOccurs = "unbounded"/>
                </xs:sequence>
                </xs:complexType>
            </xs:element>

        <xs:element name = "course" minOccurs ="1" maxOccurs
        = "unbounded">
            <xs:complexType>
              <xs:sequence>
            <xs:element ref = "course" minOccurs = "1" maxOccurs
            ="unbounded" />
            </xs:sequence>
                </xs:complexType>
                </xs:element>
            </xs:sequence>
        </complexType>
    </xs:element>

<xs:element name = "student">
    <xs:complexType>
        <xs:sequence>
            <xs:element name = "studentname" type ="xs:string" />
            <xs:element name = "course">
                <xs:complexType>
                    <xs:attribute name ="refCourseID" type= xs:string" />
                </xs:complexType>
            </xs:element>
            </xs:sequence>
            <xs:attribute name = "studentid" type = "xs:string"/>
        </xs:complexType>
</xs:element>
```

```
<xs:element name = "course">
   <xs:complexType>
      <xs:sequence>
         <xs:element name = "coursename" type = "xs:string"/>
         <xs:element name = "student">
            <xs:complexType>
               <xs:attribute name ="refstudentID"type="xs:string"/>
            </xs:complexType>
         </xs:element>
      </xs:sequence>
      <xs:attribute name = "courseid" type = "xs:string" />
   </xs:complexType>
</xs:element>
```

There are three steps to transform many-to-many relationship from XML schema to Object-Relational Logical model:

i.   In the XML schema for many-to-many relationship, we can find the element name that has `minOccurs = "1"` max `Occurs = "unbounded"`. Those elements need to be created as objects in ORDB. Then, write all its attributes based on the attribute name under the element or based on all the elements between `<xs:sequence>` and `</xs:sequence>`.

XML schema:

```
<xs:element name = "Department">
   <xs:complexType>
      <xs:sequence>
      <xs:element name = "students" minOccurs ="1"

      maxOccurs ="unbounded">
         <xs:complexType>
            <xs:sequence>
               <xs:element ref="student" minOccurs = "1"
                   maxOccurs = 'unbounded' />
            </xs:sequence>
         </xs:complexType>
   </xs:element>
         <xs:element name = "course" minOccurs ="1" maxOccurs =
         "unbounded">
            <xs:complexType>
               <xs:sequence>
                  <xs:element ref = "course" minOccurs = "1"
            maxOccurs ='unbounded' />
```

```
        </xs:sequence>
            </xs:complexType>
        </xs:element>
      </xs:sequence>
    </complexType>
</xs:element>
```

ORDB:

```
Create Or Replace Type Student_T As Object
(student_id        varchar2 (10),
 student_name varchar2 (30))

Create Or Replace Type Course_T As Object
(course_id         varchar2(10),
 course_name       varchar2 (30))
```

ii.   In the XML schema, each element will be linked to another element by using the attribute name that refers to another element ID. For those two elements in XML schema, we need to create tables for each of them in ORDB. Then, write the type of its attributes (such as `student_id`) and declare it as a `Not Null`. Create its id as the primary key for that table.

XML schema:

```
<xs:element name = "student">
    <xs:complexType>
      <xs:sequence>
        <xs:element name="studentname"type="xs:string"/>
            <xs:element name = "course">
          <xs:complexType>
            <xs:attribute name ="refCourseID" type=
                "xs:string"/>
        </xs:complexType>
      </xs:element>
      </xs:sequence>
      <xs:attribute name = "studentid" type = "xs:string"/>
    </xs:complexType>
</xs:element>

<xs:element name = "course">
    <xs:complexType>
```

```
        <xs:sequence>
          <xs:element name = "coursename" type ="xs:string"/>
          <xs:element name = "student">
            <xs:complexType>
              <xs:attribute name ="refstudentID" type=
              "xs:string" />
            </xs:complexType>
          </xs:element>
        </xs:sequence>
        <xs:attribute name = "courseid" type = "xs:string" />
      </xs:complexType>
  </xs:element>
```

ORDB:
```
Create Table Student Of Student_T
        (student_id        Not Null,
         Primary Key (student_id));
Create Table Course Of Course_T
        (course_id        Not Null,
         Primary Key (order_id));
```

iii.   Since it is many-to-many relationship, we need to create another table (for this example, we called it `enrols_in` table) to keep the relationship between the two connected tables in ORDB. This table will have the two table names as its attribute and reference to its object that is created before.

ORDB:
```
Create  Table  Enrolls_in
(student        Ref   Student_T,
course  Ref   Course_T);
```

Below is the full example of ORDB for many-to-many relationship based on the XML schema above:

ORDB for many-to-many relationship:
```
Create  Or  Replace  Type Student_T As  Object
    (student_id           varchar2 (10),
     student_name      varchar2 (30))
Create  Or  Replace  Type Course_T As  Object
    (course_id        varchar2(10),
     course_name          varchar2 (30))
```

```
Create Table Student Of Student_T
    (student_id          Not  Null,
    Primary  Key (student_id));
Create Table Course Of Course_T
    (course_id          Not  Null,
    Primary  Key (order_id));
Create  Table  Enrolls_in
    (student     Ref      Student_T,
    course       Ref      Course_T);
```

Below is the XML and INSERT query for the many-to-many association relationship. In the XML, the tag is based on the element declaration in XML schema. Then, the words or numbers between the tags are the data that is going to be inserted into the table.

In the INSERT part, the element in the Insert query should exist as a table name that is created before. The data that is inserted between elements in the XML is written in the middle of the quotation mark in Insert query. The data in the Insert query should be entered by following the order of the attributes that are declared in the create table. Furthermore, to link those two tables, we make another table (middle table). We use the SQL query by selecting the reference from the other two tables that are created before.

Common syntax for many-to-many XML association:

```
<A>
        <A1>    a    </A1>
        <A2>    b    </A2>
</A>
<B>
        <B1>    c    </B1>
        <B2>    d    </B2>
</B>
```

Common syntax for many-to-many Insert Query association:

```
Insert into A values (a, b)
Insert into B values (c, d)
Insert into A_B values (Select Ref (a) From A where a.A
= a, Select Ref (b) From B where b.B = c)
```

The following are the steps to transform many-to-many association relationships from XML to Insert query:

1.   Start from the beginning of the XML, insert the values in the Insert query based on the element in the XML.
2.   Since it is many-to-many relationships, in the insert query, we need to have a middle table that will link from many classes to other classes. The middle class does not exist in XML. When inserting the values in middle table, we need to refer to the *B* table and *A* table, where the id is the same with the one that is required.

XML for many-to-many relationship:

```
<Department>
      <student>
        <studentid> 123456 </studentid>
        <studentname>      Nathalia </studentname>
      <course>
        <courseid> 1212 </courseid>
      </course>
      <course>
        <courseid> 1234 </courseid>
      </course>
      </student>
      <student>
        <studentid> 123457 </studentid>
        <studentname> Josep </studentname>
      <course>
        <courseid> 1212 </courseid>
      </course>
      <course>
        <courseid> 1234 </courseid>
      </course>
      </student>
</Department>
```

INSERT for many-to-many association relationship:

```
Insert into Student values (123456, 'Nathalia')
Insert into Student values (123457, 'Josep')
Insert into Course values (1212, 'Business System')
Insert into Course values (1234, 'Engineering')
Insert into Enrolls_in values (Select Ref (a) From Student
where
a.student = 123456, Select Ref (b) From Course where b.course
= 1212)
Insert into Enrolls_in values (Select Ref (a) From Student
    where a.student = 123456, Select Ref (b) From Course
    where b.course = 1234)
```

```
Insert into Enrolls_in values (Select Ref (a) From Student
   where a.student = 123457, Select Ref(b) From Course
   where b.course = 1212)
Insert into Enrolls_in values (Select Ref (a) From Student
   where a.student = 123457, Select Ref(b) From Course
   where b.course = 1234)
```

Inheritance Transformation

Inheritance transformations that will be discussed in this chapter are single and multiple inheritance relationship.

Single Inheritance Relationship Transformation

There are three types of single inheritance relationship. The first one is union inheritance implementation. It declares that the union of a group of sub-classes constitutes the entire membership of the superclass. In union inheritance, we know that every object in the superclass is an object of at least one of the sub-classes. The second one is the mutual exclusion inheritance implementation. This type of inheritance declares that a group of sub-classes in an inheritance relationship is pairwise disjointed. The last type of single inheritance is partition inheritance implementation. It declares that a group of sub-classes partitions a superclass.

In this example, we will use the mutual exclusion single inheritance implementation. Account class is the superclass and it has two sub-classes, which are saving account and current account. Before we look at the transformation steps from XML schema into Object-Relational Logical model, let us have a look at the structure of XML schema for single inheritance relationship.

XML schema for single inheritance relationship:
```
<xsd:complexType name="AccountType"/>
<xsd:Sequence>
   <xsd:element name = "AccountNo" type = "xsd:integer"/>
   <xsd:element name = "Name" type = "xsd:string"/>
   <xsd:element name = "Balance" type =  "xsd:decimal"/>
   </xsd:sequence>
   </xsd:complexType>

   <xsd:element  name  =  "Saving  Account"  type  =
"SavingAccountType"/>
   <xsd:complexType name = "SavingAccountType/>
      <xsd:complexContent>
```

```
      <xsd:Extension base = "AccountType">
      <xsd:element name = "InterestRate" type ="xsd:decimal"/>
      </xsd:extension>
   </xsd:complexcontent>
</xsd:complextType>
<xsd:element   name   =   "CurrentAccount"   type   =
"CurrentAccountType"/>
<xsd:complexTypename= "CurrentAccountType"/>
   <xsd:complexContent>
   <xsd:extension base = "AccountType">
   <xsd:element name = "OverDraftLimite" type =
   "xsd:decimal"/>
   </xsd:extension>
</xsd:complexContent>
   </xsd:complexType>
```

Figure 10 is the conceptual model for a mutual exclusion single inheritance based on the XML schema above. There are three steps to transform the XML schema into Object-Relational Logical model in Oracle 9*i*.

i. For the superclass C in the generalization relationship, create it as an object based on a complexType name C in XML schema. Then, create its attributes based on the element name in XML schema after `<xsd:sequence>`. Add another attribute, called C_type, and write Not Null beside it.

XML schema:
```
<xsd:complexType   name="AccountType"/>
   <xsd:Sequence>
   <xsd:element name = "AccountNo" type ="xsd:integer"/>
   <xsd:element name = "Balance" type = "xsd:decimal"/>
   </xsd:sequence>
</xsd:complexType>
```

ORDB:
```
Create Or Replace Type Account_T As Object
   (AccountNo    varchar2 (10),
   Name          varchar2 (20),
   Balance       number,
   Account_Type varchar2 (10) Not Final)
```

ii. In the XML schema, there is an extension base <xsd:extension base=Ctype> to show that the element name mentioned previously, is

Figure 10: A Mutual Exclusion Generalization Example

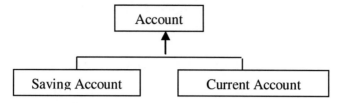

inheritance with Ctype. Create a table for superclass C and create attributes for it (such as C_id and assign it as a Not Null). For every element that is inheritance with the superclass and null, we need to check whether it has C_type in it. Then, create a primary key for that table (such as C_id).

XML schema:

```
<xsd:element name = "Saving Account" type =
"SavingAccountType"/>
    <xsd:complexType name = "SavingAccountType/>
    <xsd:complexContent>
    <xsd:Extension base = "AccountType">
    <xsd:element name = "InterestRate" type =
    "xsd:decimal"/>
    <xsd:element name = "CurrentAccount" type
    ="CurrentAccountType"/>
    <xsd:complexTypename="CurrentAccountType"/>
    <xsd:complexContent>
    <xsd:extension base = "AccountType">
```

ORDB:

```
Create Table Account Of Account_T
     (AccountNO  varchar2 (10)  Account_Type
         Check (account_type in ('Saving_ account',
         'Current_account', 'Null'))
     Primary key (AccountNo));
```

iii.   Next, use 'under' to show the inheritance relationship for its sub-class and the superclass in the Oracle. Declare its attributes type based on the element name under the sub-class section in the XML schema.

ORDB:

Create or Replace Type Saving_account_T **Under** Account
   (interest_rate number)

Below is the full example of single inheritance relationship mapping result
in ORDB.

ORDB for single inheritance relationship:
```
   Create Or Replace Type Account As Object
    (AccountNo      varchar2 (10)
    Name            varchar2 (20)
    Balance         number
    Account_Type    varchar2 (10) Not Final)
   Create Table Account_T of account
    (AccountNo  varchar2 (10)
    Account_Type
       CHECK (account_type In ('Saving_Account',
       'Current_Account',  'Null'))
    Primary key (id));
   Create or Replace Type Saving_account_T UnderAccount
    (Interest_rate number)
   Create or Replace Type Current_account_T Under Account
    (OverDraftLimite    number)
```

Below is the XML and INSERT query for the single inheritance relationship. In the XML, the tag is based on the element declaration in XML schema.
Then, the words or numbers between the tags are the data that will be inserted
into the table.

In the INSERT part, the element in the Insert query should exist as a table
name that is created above. The data that is inserted between elements in the
XML is written in the middle of the quotation mark in the Insert query for string
type and without quotation mark for number or integer. The data in the Insert
query should be entered by following the order of the attributes that are
declared in the create table.

Common syntax for single inheritance relationship for XML:
```
<AD>
<A>
        <B>   b   </B>
        <C>   c   </C>
</A>
```

```
<D>
          <E>    e    </E>
          <F>    f    </F>
</D>
</AD>
```

Common syntax for single inheritance relationship for Insert query:

```
Insert into AD_T values (A('b', 'c'));
Insert into AD_T values (D('e', 'f'));
```

The steps below are for transforming from XML to Insert query for the single inheritance relationship:

1. In the single inheritance relationship, the superclass contains several sub-classes. In XML, *AD* is the superclass; and, *A* and *D* are the sub-classes that contain some values.

2. In the Insert query, since the sub-class is inside the composite class, the insert query will look like the syntax above. The superclass in XML will be the one that the Insert query will insert the data into. Then, write down the sub-class and put another bracket to insert the data for that class.

XML for single inheritance relationship:

```
<SavingAccount>
    <AccountNo>  123999011    </AccountNo>
    <Name>  John Smith    </Name>
    <Balance>  10000  </Balance>
    <InterestRate>  0.05    </InterestRate>
</SavingAccount>

<CurrentAccount>
    <AccountNo>  123999011    </AccountNo>
    <Name>  John Smith    </Name>
    <Balance>  10000  </Balance>
    <OverDraftLimit>  5000 </OverDraftLimit>
</CurrentAccount>
```

Insert for single inheritance relationship:

```
    Insert into Account_T Values (Saving_account (123999011, 'John
Smith',    10000, 0.05));
```

```
Insert into Account_T Values (Current_account (123999011, 'John
Smith', 10000, 5000));
```

Multiple Inheritance

The example that we use for this transformation is Administration class. Administration is the superclass, and it has two sub-classes, which are project assistant and coordinator. ISI People class can be said to be inheriting from overlapping classes because, basically, an ISI People can be a Project Assistant who is also a coordinator member. Although Oracle has added some inheritance features in its Oracle 9 version, it still does not have a facility for handling multiple inheritance. The best way to handle multiple inheritance from overlapping classes is to use one table for each superclass and one table for the sub-class.

Before describing the transformation steps from XML schema into Object-Relational Logical model, we present the XML schema for multiple inheritance relationship.

XML schema for multiple inheritance relationship:

```
<xsd: complexType name = "Administrator">
<xsd: sequence>
<xsd: element name = "id" type = "xsd: string"/>
<xsd: element  name = "name" type = "xsd: string"/>
<xsd: element name = "address" type = "xsd:string"/>
</xsd:sequence>
</xsd:complexType>

<xsd: complexType name = "ProjAssistant">
   <xsd:complexContent>
   <xsd:extension base = "Admin">
      <xsd: sequence>
         <xsd: element name = "Project" type = "xsd:
         string"/>
      </xsd: sequence>
   </xsd:extension>
   </xsd:complexContent>
</xsd:complexType>

<xsd: complexType name = "Coordinator">
   <xsd: complexContent>
      <xsd:extension base = "Admin"/>
   </xsd: complexContent>
</xsd:complexType>
```

```
<xsd: element name = "Coordinator" type = "Coordinator"/>
<xsd: element name = "ProjAssistant" type = "ProjAssistant"/>
<xsd: element name = "ISIPeople">
  <xsd: complexType>
  <xsd: choice minOccurs = "0" maxOccurs = "unbounded">
     <xsd: element ref = "Coordinator"/>
     <xsd: element ref = "ProjAssistant"/>
  </xsd: choice>
  </xsd: complexType>
</xsd:element>
```

By looking at the structure of multiple inheritance in XML schema, we can draw the conceptual diagram for it. Figure 11 shows the conceptual model of multiple inheritance relationship based on the XML schema above.

There are three steps to transforming the XML schema into Object-Relational Logical model in Oracle 9*i*.

i.   For the superclass C in the generalization relationship, create it as a table based on a complexType name C in XML schema. Then, create its attributes based on the element name in XML schema after `<xsd:sequence>`. The id for each table needs to be created as a Not Null. In the create table for the superclass, create a primary key and put "id" as its primary key.

XML schema:
```
<xsd: complexType name = "Administrator">
<xsd: sequence>
<xsd: element name = "id" type = "xsd: string"/>
<xsd: element  name = "name" type = "xsd: string"/>
<xsd: element name = "address" type = "xsd:string"/>
</xsd:sequence>
</xsd:complexType>
```

ORDB:
```
Create  Table Administrator
    (id         VARCHAR2 (10) NOT NULL,
     name       VARCHAR2 (20),
     address    VARCHAR2 (35),
     Primary Key (id));
```

ii.   In the XML schema, there is an extension base <xsd:extension base=Ctype> to show the element name that is mentioned before it and

Figure 11: Multiple Inheritance

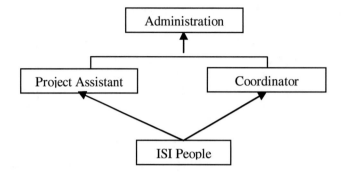

its inheritance with Ctype. Create a table for sub-class C1 and create its attributes (such as C_id and assign it as a Not Null). Then, create two keys, one is primary key and the other is foreign key, that refer to the superclass id.

XML schema:

```
<xsd: complexType name = "ProjAssistant">
   <xsd:complexContent>
   <xsd:extension base = "Admin">
     <xsd: sequence>
        <xsd: element name = "Project" type = "xsd:
        string"/>
     </xsd: sequence>
   </xsd:extension>
   </xsd:complexContent>
</xsd:complexType>

<xsd: complexType name = "Coordinator">
   <xsd: complexContent>
     <xsd:extension base = "Admin"/>
   </xsd: complexContent>
</xsd:complexType>
```

ORDB:

```
Create  Table  ProjAssistant
    (id          VARCHAR2 (10) NOT NULL,
    project     VARCHAR2 (40),
```

```
Primary Key (id),
Foreign Key (id) References Administrator (id) On
Delete
Cascade) ;
```

```
Create Table Coordinator
   (id    VARCHAR2 (10) NOT NULL,
   Primary Key (id),
   Foreign Key (id) References Administrator (id) On
   Delete
   Cascade);
```

iii.   Lastly, create the table for the sub-class that has multiple parents. This table also has two keys, primary key and foreign key, that refer to the superclass C id.

XML schema:
```
<xsd: element name = "ISIPeople">
  <xsd: complexType>
  <xsd: choice minOccurs = "0" maxOccurs = "unbounded">
    <xsd: element ref = "Coordinator"/>
    <xsd: element ref = "ProjAssistant"/>
  </xsd: choice>
  </xsd: complexType>
</xsd:element>
```

ORDB:
```
Create Table ISIPeople
    (id    VARCHAR2 (10) NOT NULL,
    Primary Key (id),
    Foreign Key (id) References Administrator (id)
    On Delete
    Cascade);
```

Below is the full example of multiple inheritance relationship in ORDB after it is transformed from XML schema.

ORDB for multiple inheritance relationship:
```
Create Table Administrator
   (id         VARCHAR2 (10) NOT NULL,
   name        VARCHAR2 (20),
   address     VARCHAR2 (35),
   Primary Key (id)) ;
```

```
Create Table ProjAssistant
   (id        VARCHAR2 (10) NOT NULL,
   project    VARCHAR2 (40),
   Primary Key (id),
   Foreign Key (id) References Administrator (id) On
   Delete
   Cascade)  ;

Create Table Coordinator
   (id      VARCHAR2 (10) NOT NULL,
   subject  VARCHAR2 (25),
   Primary Key (id),
   Foreign Key (id) References Administrator (id) On
   Delete
   Cascade)  ;

Create Table ISIPeople
   (id       VARCHAR2 (10) NOT NULL,
   office    VARCHAR2 (10),
   Primary Key (id),
   Foreign Key (id) References Administrator (id) On
   Delete  Cascade);
```

Common syntax for multiple inheritance relationship for XML:

```
<AD>
 <A>
       <B>   b   </B>
       <C>   c   </C>
 </A>

 <D>
       <B>   b   </B>
       <E>   e   </E>
 </D>

 <F>
       <B>   b   </B>
       <G>   g   </G>
 </F>
</AD>
```

Common syntax for multiple inheritance relationship for Insert query:

```
Insert into A values ('b', 'c');
Insert into D values ('b', 'e');
Insert into F values ('b', 'g');
```

The steps below are for transforming from XML to Insert query for the multiple inheritance relationship:

i.   In the multiple inheritance relationship, the subclass has two superclasses. In XML, *AD* is the superclass; and, *A* and *D* are the sub-classes that contain some values. *F* is the sub-class that has two superclasses, which are *A* and *D*.

ii. When doing the transformation from XML to Insert query, each class in XML will be treated as a table in the Insert query, and all the values in the XML will be inserted in that table according to its order.

Below is the XML and INSERT query for the single inheritance relationship.

XML for multiple inheritance relationship:

```
<Administrator>
    <id> 123 </id>
    <name> Josep </name>
    <address> 570 Lygon St </address>
<ProjAssistant>
    <id> 123 </id>
    <name> Josep </name>
    <address> 570 Lygon St </address>
    <project> computer project </project>
</ProjAssistant>
<Coordinator>
    <id> 123 </id>
    <name> Josep </name>
    <address> 570 Lygon St </address>
    <subject> mathematics </subject>
</Coordinator>
<ISIPeople>
    <id> 123 </id>
    <name> Josep </name>
    <address> 570 Lygon St </address>
    <office> B506 </office>
<ISIPeople>
</Administrator>
```

Insert query for multiple inheritance relationship:

```
Insert into Administrator Values (123, 'Josep', 570 Lygon
St');
Insert into ProjAssistant Values  (123, 'Josep', '570 Lygon
St','computer project');
Insert into Coordinator Values (123, 'Josep', '570 Lygon
St','mathematics');
Insert into ISIPeople Values (123, 'Josep', 570 Lygon St',
'B506');
```

CONCLUSION AND FUTURE WORK

In this chapter, we have investigated the transformation from XML schema to the ORDB by using Oracle 9*i*. We emphasised the transformation of *aggregation*, *association* and *inheritance relationships* to help people easily understand the basic object conceptual mapping that we proposed. This transformation is important because people always eliminate the object-oriented conceptual features when they transform XML schema to the database.

Our research gives better solutions in transforming XML schema into ORDB, rather than the XML features that Oracle 9*i* has. Oracle 9*i* can only convert all the data or query result in XML format, but it does not deal with the type of database that is used, such as relational database or object-oriented database, like we do. This transformation can be applied on any XML documents that use XML schema.

Our future work is being planned to investigate more transformation from XML schema to ORDB for other XML schema features that have not been discussed in this chapter. In addition, further research should be done to create a query from XML schema to get the data from the Oracle 9*i* databases.

REFERENCES

Bray, T., Paoli, J., & Sperberg-McQueen, C. M. (eds.). (1998). *Extensible markup language (XML) 1.0. W3C*. Available at: http://www.w3c.org/TR/REC-xml.

Conrad, R., Scheffner, D., & Freytag, J. C. (2000). *XML Conceptual Modeling Using UML*. Berlin: HU Berlin, Institute of Computer Science (Technical Report).

Dillon, T. & Tan, P. L. (1993). *Object-oriented Conceptual Models*. New York: Prentice Hall.

Fong, J., Pang, F., & Bloor, C. (2001). Converting relational database into XML document. In *Proceedings of the 12th International Workshop on Database and Expert Systems Applications* (pp. 61-65).

Klettke, M. & Meyer, H. (2001). XML and object-relational database system. *Lecture Notes in Computer Science* (Vol. 1997, pp. 151-170). Berlin: Springer-Verlag.

Mani, M., Lee, D., & Muntz, R. (2001). Semantic data modelling using XML schemas. *Lecture Notes in Computer Science* (Vol. 2224, pp. 149-163). Berlin: Springer-Verlag.

Shanmugasundaram, J. et al. (2001). Efficiently publishing relational data as XML documents. *The VLDB Journal*, 10, 133-154.

Stonebraker, M. & Moore, D. (1996). *Object-relational DBMSs: The Next Great Wave*. San Francisco, CA: Morgan Kaufmann.

Widjaya, N. D., Taniar, D., & Rahayu, J. W. (2003). Inheritance relationship transformation of XML schemas to object-relational databases. *Proceedings of the 4th International Conference on Intelligent Data Engineering and Automated Learning (IDEAL 2003),* Hong Kong.

Widjaya, N. D., Taniar, D., Rahayu, J. W., & Pardede, E. (2002). Association relationship transformation of XML schemas to object-relational databases. *Proceedings of the 4th International Conference on Information Integration and Web-based Applications and Services (IIWAS 2002)*.

Xiao, R., Dillon, T., Chang, E., & Feng, L. (2001). Modelling and transformation of object-oriented conceptual models into XML schema. *Lecture Notes in Computer Science* (Vol. 2113, pp. 795-804). Berlin: Springer-Verlag.

Yang, X. & Wang, G. (2001). Efficiently mapping referential integrity constraints from relational databases to XML. *Lecture Notes in Computer Science* (Vol. 2151, pp. 338-351). Berlin: Springer-Verlag.

Yang, X. & Wang, G. (2001). Mapping referential integrity constraints from relational databases to XML. *Lecture Notes in Computer Science* (Vol. 2118, pp. 329-340). Berlin: Springer-Verlag.

SECTION III

WEB INFORMATION EXTRACTION

Chapter VI

A Practical Approach to the Derivation of a Materialized Ontology View

Carlo Wouters, La Trobe University, Australia

Tharam Dillon, University of Technology Sydney, Australia

Johanna Wenny Rahayu, La Trobe University, Australia

Elizabeth Chang, Curtin University, Australia

Robert Meersman, Vrije Universiteit Brussel, Belgium

ABSTRACT

The success of the semantic web depends largely on how well ontologies can be utilized and formulated. Interoperability between systems using different versions of the same ontology is essential, and this implies the need for a regulated derivation of materialized ontology views (which can be considered a modified version of an ontology). This chapter applies the formalisms for such a derivation process to a practical example, emphasizing the possibility for automation, and also for optimization, to develop a high-quality derived ontology.

INTRODUCTION

In recent years, the unstructured storage of data, especially on the World Wide Web, and the difficulties experienced with retrieving relevant data with the existing search engines, have triggered new research aimed at ameliorating information retrieval and storage. New ways of storing information meant for the internet were developed, such as XML (W3C, 1999a), HTML[a] (Fensel, Decker, Erdmann, & Studer, 1998), DTD and RDF (W3C, 1999b). These languages provide a tool to store the information in a structured way, but, with that, another problem arose; everyone was free to develop their own taxonomy of how they want to categorize their information. Some examples can be found in Heflin, Hender and Luke (1999) and Harmelin and Fensel (1999). It is clear that widely accepted standards should be used as metadata to define how the actual information is split up, no matter what language or syntax is used to implement this. These widespread standards are formulated as ontologies. In the initial and very broad definition (Gruber, 1993a, 1993b), an ontology is a specification of a conceptualization of a problem domain.

The first wave of ontology applications and researchers mainly concentrated on getting an effective system up, and solving the apparent issues that had been holding back knowledge acquisition from the Internet and related resources. A number of these have turned out to be beneficial, but without any of them clearly standing out, and no single standard has been agreed upon (Hovy, 1998). Since then, we have seen the merging of some of the standards — e.g., OIL incorporating elements of OKBC (Fensel et al., 2000), XOL and RDF, Ontolingua using KIF (Genesreth, 1991; Genesreth & Fikes, 1992; Gruber, 1992) — and diversification of others.

Now that the first generation of ontology applications has settled in, more complicated issues and considerations have reared their heads, such as the quality of ontologies in all their facets (see Colomb & Weber, 1998; Guarino & Welty, 2002; Hahn & Schnattinger, 1998; Kaplan, 2001; Holsapple & Joshi, 2002). Improvements need to be made to the systems that are already in place, and theoretical and practical modifications are required for versioning, maintenance and distribution of ontologies. Furthermore, a continuing integration of different existing systems is needed.

Ontologies tend to grow larger, to a point where, ideally, the entire world is modeled in one super-ontology (Lenat, 1995), providing great compatibility and consistency across all sub-domains. But practically, it introduces the new problem of being too vast to be used in its entirety by any application. Considering the Internet as a data repository, it seems clear that users with a very slow or costly connection to this repository might opt to get a local, modified copy of the repository to base views upon and to query in other ways. It seems highly unlikely that someone will be able to copy the entire contents of the World Wide Web to a local repository, and even more unlikely that all this data will actually be used in whatever application the user might intend it to be used for. If a business just needs access to information on shares, it would not benefit from all the other information that their local copy would contain. This is just one of the many reasons why a complete ontology might not be a valid structuring option for certain users. Another reason can be found in varying levels of security and confidentiality — not necessarily every user of an ontology has the same access rights, and using a smaller ontology, merely containing the appropriate parts of the base ontology, might enable local copies. Efficiency of querying repositories might be another reason for having a simplified, local version of an ontology; and many more can be found. A lot of research is carried out trying to solve the various problems that arise from impractical or unmanageable large ontologies, such as research on the management, modification, merging and versioning of ontologies (see Hovy, 1998; McGuinness, Fikes, Rice, & Wilder, 2000; Klein, Fensel, Kiryakov, & Ognyanov, 2002; Klein & Fensel, 2001; Noy & Klein, 2002; Heflin & Hendler, 2000; Heflin, Hendler, & Luke, 1999; Wouters, Dillon, Rahayu, & Chang, 2002).

It is imperative that when an ontology view is derived, the quality of the resulting ontology is as high as possible. First of all, this is done by ensuring that the intentions of the ontological engineer are satisfied, and the resulting design is a consistent, cohesive, complete, and well-formed ontology. Secondly, a fine-tuning process further enhances the quality of the ontology view, i.e. ensuring that the obtained solution is one of the most efficient, flexible, simple, versatile, etc. solutions. The derived materialized ontology view should be usable as the base for an independent system, i.e., be an ontology in its own right.

In this chapter, a practical approach is taken to demonstrate the entire process of deriving a materialized ontology view. A particular case is examined and used to explain, in plain language, the meaning and intention of the rules that are the foundation of the theoretical research. In the next section, some of the theoretical background behind the derivation process and the optimization schemes in particular is given. This chapter does not aim to justify these formalisms — these can be found in Wouters et al. (2003) — but rather demonstrates the practical usefulness and automation possibilities of these formalisms. Another emphasis is the optimization, as it results in a high-quality ontology. A high-quality of the obtained materialized ontology view is ensured by the optimization schemes. Finally, a brief outline of future research will be given, eventually leading up to an integrated transformation environment for ontologies, interfacing with existing international standards.

BACKGROUND

In this chapter the practical application of a derivation process formalism is the main focus, but, before the practical side can be explored, first, a brief summary of the theoretical background needs to be presented, which is done in this section. Where possible, the mathematical background and formal rules are left out and replaced by a plain text explanation that serves to provide a better intuitive understanding. The downside to this is the lack of a rigorous justification of each step taken in algorithms. However, as mentioned before, the justification is not the aim of this chapter, and including it here would distract from the subject at hand, i.e., how such theories and algorithms can be used in a real example to obtain a high-quality result. For the mathematical formalisms, we refer the reader to Wouters et al. (2003). In this section, the main focus goes to the definition of an ontology, firstly, and to the introduction of optimization schemes, secondly.

Ontology Definition

Throughout this chapter, an understanding of some key elements of an ontology is necessary; and so, it becomes imperative to start with a formal definition of an ontology as it is used in this context. It should be noted that more elaborate definitions are possible, but the definition presented here serves the purpose of deriving a high-quality materialized ontology view.

Intuitively, ontologies conceptually represent a perceived world through concepts (here, set C), attributes (set A), and relationships (set B). Concepts may represent the different higher-level components of this world, and each component may have attributes (represented through attribute mapping *attr*). These attributes may be derived from the characteristics of components of the world. Relationships may also hold between these concepts. Both sets M are cardinality sets, linked to either attributes (M_a) or relationships (M_b).

For practical reasons, only binary relationships are considered here. Note that binary relationships are most frequent currently in modeling. Unary models are not modeled, since these are taken care of by forming subtypes. N-ary relationships are not considered as transformation of this type of relationship to

Figure 1: Definition of Ontology (Wouters et al., 2003)

We define
 An ontology $O \in \vartheta \Leftrightarrow O \equiv <C, A, attr, B, M_a, M_b>$
with
 $C = finite \wedge C \neq \emptyset$
 $A = finite$
 $attr: C \rightarrow 2^A$
 $B \subseteq C \times C \wedge B = B_s \cup B_i \cup B_{agg}$
 $M_a: attr \rightarrow card^2$
 $M_b: B \rightarrow card^4$
 $\forall a \in A, \exists c \in C: a \in attr(c)$
 $\exists$ an Ontology Graph G_O for O

binary relationships is possible. For a more comprehensive treatment of arity of relationships, see Nijssen and Halpin (1989) and Halpin (1995).

An Ontology Graph is defined as a graph that is made up of the concepts of an ontology, with its vertices and relationships as its edges. One restriction that is very important here is that an Ontology Graph always has to be an interconnected graph (containing only one proper component) (see Von Staudt (1847) and Biggs, Lloyd and Wilson (1976). As a result, a valid ontology has to have a graph mapping that is one interconnected component. Separate components will be referred to as islands in an ontology. The result of this requirement in the definition is demonstrated in, where the whole diagram is the representation of an invalid ontology, or two valid ontologies. In other words, the whole is not considered an ontology (because not all concepts have a semantic connection with all other concepts). Although not a distinction in a number of standards, this restriction, nonetheless, allows for automation that would be a lot more complex otherwise, if possible at all.

The relationships that are considered in set *B* are further split up into three categories: inheritance relationships (B_i); aggregation relationships (B_{agg}); and association relationships (B_s). More information will be provided on these sets when they are used, but, semantically, they hold the same meaning as in Object-Oriented Modeling (Rumbaugh, 1991; Rumbaugh, Jacobson, & Booch, 1999).

Figure 2: Two Valid Ontologies (1 and 2), but Together Resulting in Invalid Ontology

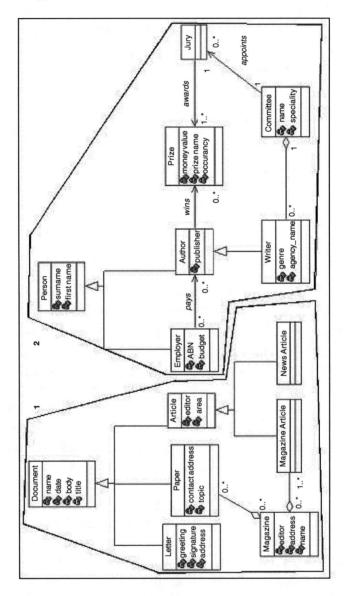

Representing the Ontology

Following Spyns, Meersman and Mustafa (2002), the 'semantics' of an ontology is the range of interpretation mapping of an application environment onto an ontology. Note that the semantics of the real world problem are replaced by an ontology. Some examples of an application environment are

RDBMS, software applications, documents, website, etc. While it is recognized that there are important differences between an ontology and a conceptual model, for the purpose of deriving sub-ontologies, these are immaterial. Frequently, a conceptual model can be considered to be an ontology expressed in a chosen syntax. However, this syntax should not impact the definitions and theorems presented, and, for the purpose of this chapter, this difference is irrelevant.

Throughout this chapter, the Unified Modeling Language (UML) (see (Rumbaugh, Jacobson, & Booch, 1999) is sometimes used to graphically represent an ontology, but it is not the intention to show the suitability of UML for the modeling of ontologies. UML is merely a convenient modeling notation that, for practical reasons, was chosen to highlight aspects of ontologies. There should be no confusion as to the difference of the ontology and the modeling notation used to represent it, and by no means is it the intention of the authors to promote this modeling notation to a higher status. UML is used to represent object-oriented models, and, as our definition of an ontology has concepts (similar to classes), attributes, and relationships, it was found convenient to use this easy to read data model to illustrate aspects of semantics of ontologies. One could, however, choose any alternative notation such as semantic nets (Feng, Chang, & Dillon, 2002) to illustrate the issues.

Besides UML, a number of other possibilities exist to graphically represent an ontology (or certain aspects of it). Some modeling languages are briefly discussed here, and some references are given for the interested reader to learn more about these tools.

The oldest and widely accepted standard of Entity Relationship Model (ER Model) (see Chen, 1976) has been around since the '70s, and has proven its usefulness to graphically represent the design of a Relational Database. One of the advantages ER has is that it stays very close to its intended implementation platform (Relational Databases). This contributed to the vast success of ER, as it is easy to use, read, and understand by designers who are familiar with Relational Databases. However, to represent ontologies, this advantage becomes a disadvantage because ontology designs and representations should emphasize the semantics of the model, and should be completely abstracted and independent from the implementation platform. Another downside to using ER is its limited expressiveness.

Another standard that can be considered for ontology representation is the Object Role Modeling (ORM) (see Nijssen & Halpin, 1989; Halpin, 1995). ORM provides a fact-based approach to designing, which leads to a model that is easier to understand and use by domain experts who are unfamiliar to software engineering or data modeling. Domain experts can give facts about the domain in plain language (e.g., "Book A is written by Author X"), and these can be used to shape the model (in our case, this model represents the ontology that is the conceptualization of the particular problem domain). When applied rigorously, ORM leads to a very precise representation of the problem domain (called the *Universe of Discourse - UoD*), with much more semantic significance than an ER model could ever entail. The reasons for not using this representation language in this chapter are bifold: (i) the resulting representation tends to be larger in ORM than the corresponding UML diagram; and (ii) because of the specific treatment of attributes and their connection to concepts (called *attribute mapping* throughout this chapter), UML graphically represents all the necessary key-components, while there would be an overload of information in the ORM representation that is not relevant to the research described in this chapter.

The last standard that is discussed here is a newer standard, called *Semantic Net* (Feng et al., 2002). This methodology focuses on the modeling of XML documents, and is split up into a semantic level and a schema level part. The semantic level closely resembles the needed setup for an ontology modeling tool, and can be used as such. However, to be used in this chapter, several extensions to this standard are required. The standard can not be used in its current form. Another disadvantage is its similarity to ORM in regards to how attributes — and attribute mappings — are modeled. As mentioned previously, attributes and their specific connections are treated in an automated processing way, so there is no need to explicitly depict these connections through a connecting line, as is done in ORM and Semantic Net. In UML, attributes reside in the container that is a class (or concept, in the terminology used in this chapter), but no actual line between the two is visible.

The authors would like to emphasize that the reasons for using UML solely apply to this chapter and to the research discussed herein, and that, for other situations, the choice of modeling tool would likely be different. Even extension of the optimizations schemes that are central to the derivation process might make another representation language more suitable.

Optimization Schemes

The intention of the processes that are introduced here is to go from a certain ontology — referred to as base ontology — to a derived ontology, which is a materialized ontology view[2] of the base ontology. This materialized ontology view always has a certain semantic connection to the base ontology, but what this connection is can differ from one solution to another. Or, to be precise, depending on how an ontology engineer defines the connection, a different view will be obtained. The optimization schemes that are introduced in this section provide the 'language' in which the type of semantic link between the base and derived ontology can be expressed. They are set up in a way that makes it easy for nonexperts to utilize them as well.

An optimization scheme always needs a solution set as an input. This solution set is nothing more than a labeled ontology. The output of an optimization scheme is one or multiple solution sets. The labeling of an ontology applies mainly to concepts, attributes and relationships. For attribute mappings, automatic derivation from the labeling of attributes and concepts proves sufficient. There is no labeling necessary for cardinalities, as their specific semantic connection with other ontological elements does not make them require a labeling.

In a less abstract way, this means that every concept, attribute and relationship gets a certain tag. The options for these tags are "deselected," "selected" and "void." An element that is tagged (or labeled) as "selected" is an element that decidedly needs to be present in the materialized ontology view, while "deselected" means exactly the opposite, i.e., the element should definitely not be a part of the solution. Naturally, "void" indicates that no decision has been made yet. In practice, most of the elements will start out with a "void" labeling, but in the end, no "void" tags should be present anymore. Putting all the selected elements together gives us a valid materialized ontology view. Throughout this chapter, selected elements are circled and deselected elements are crossed out in their UML representation.

Every optimization scheme has a different emphasis, and provides a set of rules and/or algorithms of how to go from the base ontology to an (intermediate) solution set for a materialized ontology view. For instance, the first optimization scheme that should be applied to every base ontology is called a "requirement consistency optimization scheme" (RCOS). This optimization scheme ensures that there are no contradictions in the labeling. To demonstrate how the rules are formulated mathematically, we set up RC Rule 1 (Figure 3).

In this case, the rule states that no relationship can be labeled "selected" if one of the concepts it is connecting is deselected. This rule arises from the fact that the relationship can only be in the end solution (in unmodified form) as long as both concepts that it connects are there as well; but, one of these concepts cannot be a part of the solution if it is labeled "deselected." In short, this is a contradiction in what is wanted in the end solution, and is prevented by this rule.

Figure 3: RC Rule 1 (Wouters et al., 2003)

> *Given an ontology $O=<C, A, attr, B, M_a, M_b>$ with a labeling*   (1)
> *δ applied to O*
> *$\forall b \in B: \delta_C(\pi_1(b))=deselected \vee \delta_C(\pi_2(b))= deselected$*
> *$\Rightarrow \neg(\delta_B(b)= selected)$*

The following section will introduce a practical example and then discuss the optimization schemes it uses to get to an optimized materialized ontology view, where the preference for optimization is obtaining a simplified version of the base ontology.

OPTIMIZATION SCHEMES ALGORITHMS: A WALKTHROUGH CASE STUDY

This section demonstrates the optimization schemes in action by means of a practical walkthrough. At the start of each section, the actual optimization scheme will be explained without going into too much mathematical detail. The original algorithm is given, in appropriate formalism. Their meanings are elaborated when applying them to the practical examples.

The first task that the ontology engineer has to complete is to decide what kind of optimization is desirable. There are a couple of optimization schemes that are always necessary in a chain of schemes, but mostly these can be freely selected and put in a certain order. Note that using the same optimization schemes but in a different order might result in a different materialized ontology view. Such an ordering is referred to as a priority list of optimization schemes, and represents the sequence in which the optimization schemes are applied. Note that the word "priority" here refers to a sequential or chronological priority, i.e., a higher priority means an optimization scheme is applied before another scheme with a lower priority. In the priority list, this translates to firstly applying the optimization scheme with priority "1," then the one with "2," etc. Here, the following priority list was decided on:
1.   RCOS (Requirement Consistency)
2.   WFOS (Well Formedness)

3.   SCOS (Semantic Completeness)
4.   ESOS (Extreme Simplicity)
5.   WFOS (Well Formedness)

Note that it is possible to have the same optimization scheme more than one time in a priority list. The priority list given here can be interpreted as first applying the RCOS, and then using that output solution set as the input solution set for the WFOS, and so forth. The first two schemes are a standard choice, as is the last scheme, and, for normal use, they always appear in those positions. The first one ensures that there are no inconsistencies in what a labeling of an ontology specifies, as that would make it impossible to determine a optimized solution. The second scheme makes sure that the following schemes can rely on a well-formed ontology in the solution set (this occasionally is a requirement for the input of an optimization scheme). The last scheme (again WFOS) guarantees that the result is, in fact, a valid ontology. Usually, changes that are made will not render the ontology invalid, but it is a possibility; having the WFOS as a last step prevents the end result from being invalid. The two middle schemes (3 and 4) are the heart of this particular derivation process. In plain words, the ontology engineer requests the simplest solution that is semantically complete. More information on the meaning of this is provided throughout the next sections.

Firstly, the scenario that will be used as an example is introduced, together with the initial requirements labeling. Together, they make up the initial solution set that is used as the input for the first optimization scheme. Every optimization scheme will be explained and applied in a separate section, following the order of the priority list. As the entire process can become quite lengthy, especially when written down, non-interesting or irrelevant steps receive a quick mention without further scrutiny. This allows us to focus on the more important steps, particularly those leading to modifications.

Illustrative Case Study

The first step in this practical walkthrough is the introduction of the base ontology. As mentioned, this is the original ontology that is used as a starting point to derive a materialized ontology view. The reasons for such a derivation can be many, as was indicated in the introduction, and one is chosen here as an example. Note that often these reasons will partly — or even completely — determine the priority list of optimization schemes.

Let us consider here the case of a magazine publisher which uses an ontology as the basis of its knowledge information system. This publishing

Figure 4: UML Representation of the Base Ontology

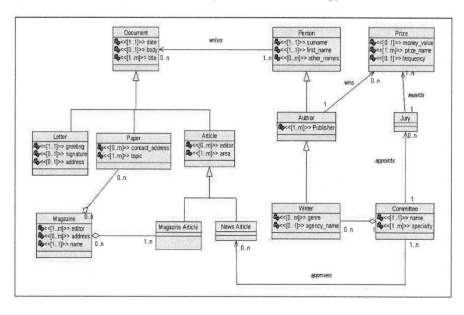

company has a number of daughter companies, some of which publish magazines themselves. One of the daughter companies specializes in analyzing which magazines won what prizes, when they were won, the consistency throughout time, and so forth. They do not want, nor do they require, all the information modeled in the basis ontology as used by the main publisher, and because the daughter company is located in a remote office, a local copy of the ontology (and data) is needed. In Figure 4, a UML representation of relevant aspects of the base ontology as used by the main publisher is shown. This ontology is part of the solution set that is used as the initial input for the first optimization scheme. However, as specified earlier, a labeling needs to be introduced as well. Note that, by default, we always use a "void" labeling for every element, so even if no labeling is specified, this default labeling enables the optimization schemes to use the base ontology as an input solution set. However, in our example, we will slightly modify this default labeling to demonstrate how and why this is done.

The publishing company is not prepared to give all the information it possesses. For instance, it considers the Committee information it has as not being appropriate for the statistical center to use. This translates into a "deselected" labeling of this concept. After discussion with the statistical center, the publisher decides to not put any restriction on the attributes of the concept "Committee," but still not allow the concept itself to be taken in the

Figure 5: UML Representation of the Ontology and Initial Labeling

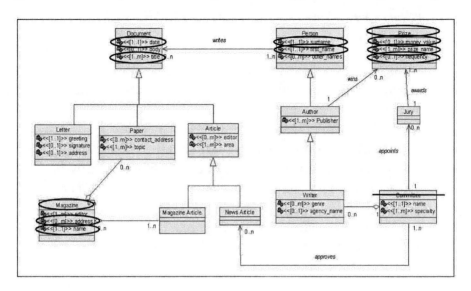

ontology view, as this might give an insight into its inner workings. It wants to prevent this in case someone gets a hold of this local copy of the ontology.

Once the stats center has set out its main focus, it has some initial elements in the ontology of which it is certain should be present in the solution as well. These elements are labeled as "selected." For instance, the concept "Prize," together with all its attributes, is considered crucial for the materialized ontology view, and thus, these elements are selected. A resulting initial labeling is introduced in Figure 5, where the selected elements are circled, and the deselected elements are crossed out. The void elements are all the other (unmarked) elements. There are 11 selected elements and one deselected element.

As was mentioned in the labeling section, an automated attribute mapping is applied here. This means that the connections between concepts and attributes (not explicitly shown as such in UML, but an attribute inside a concept, 'belongs' to that concept, and that is a connection) do not have to be labeled by a person, but that their default mapping is modified automatically to enforce the concept, attribute, and relationship labeling.

This automation of the mapping consists of the application of two rules:

- *If there is an attribute mapping between a selected concept and a selected attribute, this mapping receives a "selected" label as well.*

- *If the concept or attribute of a certain attribute mapping is labeled "deselected", this mapping becomes deselected as well.*

An example of this is that attributes which 'belong' to "Prize" all are selected, as is the concept itself, and thus, all the mappings between them become selected as well (note that this cannot be easily shown in UML notation).

Requirement Consistency Optimization Scheme (RCOS)

The requirement consistency optimization scheme checks the input labeling of the base ontology to see that there are no contradictions. There are a total of four rules that will ensure this consistency, and each one is briefly discussed next. The first rule was already given as an example, but is repeated here:

- *No relationship can be labeled "selected" if one of the concepts it is connecting is deselected.*

The explanation for this rule was given earlier. In our initial labeling, there are no contradictions to this rule. There is a deselected concept ("Committee") with a number of relationships that connect it, but none of those relationships (e.g., from "Committee" to "Jury") has a "selected" label. In fact, nothing was specified about any of these relationships, so they still have their default labeling, i.e., "void."

The second rule is the equivalent of the first rule in regards to attribute mappings:

- *For every attribute mapping with a deselected concept or a deselected attribute, the label of the mapping itself cannot be "selected."*

Although there is a deselected concept ("Committee") in our example, it does not have any "selected" labels for its attribute mappings (as they were done by the automated attribute mapping).

The third rule puts a stricter requirement on the attribute mapping, saying:

- *If an attribute is selected, its attribute mapping cannot be deselected.*

Again, as we applied the automated attribute mapping, this is never the case here.

The fourth rule we use here is a bit more complicated, and uses the notion of a path. Without going into the formal definition (Wouters, 2003), a path is defined as the chain of relationships that connect two concepts, where the end concept of one relationship is the start concept of the following relationship in the chain. Also, the same relationship can only appear once in the chain.

Usually, the emphasis of a path lies with the first and last concept it visits, as these are the two that are connected by the path. Sometimes, restrictions are used on all the other concepts that are part of the connection, and on the relationships that form the chain as well. In these cases, the path will be a specialized path and will get a different name (e.g., proper path). More information on these paths will be given in the ESOS section.

- *If an attribute is selected, but the concept it 'belongs' to is deselected, there is a path to a concept that is not deselected. The path can only contain relationships with a label other than "deselected."*

In this scenario, there is no attribute selected with a deselected concept, so the solution set complies with this fourth rule as well.

Well Formedness Optimization Scheme (WFOS)

In this optimization scheme, the emphasis is on the well formedness of the resulting solution set. With well formedness, we mean being a valid ontology according to the definition of an ontology given earlier. The input solution set is a labeled ontology, where only the "selected" and "void" labels are considered toward a well formed output. As we are certain the deselected elements have to be left out of a final solution, the WFOS checks whether at least one possible solution that is valid can still be reached by using all selected elements and none, some, or all void elements.

There are five rules that need to be adhered to before the solution set is considered well formed, but we disregard the first rule, as it has no importance in the context of our scenario. These rules follow directly from our ontology definition. To ensure that the resulting solution set is in accordance with all these rules, algorithms are used per rule to go through the solution set and modify it to get to a correct end result. To demonstrate the formal algorithms, the second rule for the WFOS is given here in its original form, together with its algorithm in the original form. Although not easy to read, this is a very convenient and exact method to use once an implementation of these algorithms is needed (i.e., a kind of pseudo-code) (Figure 6).

- *If a concept is deselected, all attributes belonging to it, together with their attribute mappings, should be deselected.*

If an input solution set does not satisfy this rule, a change in the solution set needs to be made so that the resulting output solution set does satisfy it. In this

Figure 6: WF Rule 2

> *Given an ontology O=<C, A, attr, B, Ma, Mb> with a*   (2)
> *labeling δ applied to O and an attribute mapping*
> $t\delta_C(\pi_1(t))=$ *deselected* $\Rightarrow \delta_A(\pi_2(t))=$ *deselected* $\wedge \delta_{attr}(t)=$ *deselected*

case, it means that if we have a deselected concept that has attributes and/or attribute mappings that are not deselected, they can either be: (i) relabeled "deselected" as well, i.e., a modification in labeling of the ontology; or (ii) the attributes can be linked to another concept that does not have a "deselected" label, i.e., the attribute mappings are replaced with new ones that link the attributes to another concept. Which one of these solutions is appropriate, is decided through the use of following algorithm Figure 7, as well as executing the modification.

From here onward, a plain English explanation will be given as to how to go about dealing with the modification of the solution set, i.e., either the ontology or the labeling, without going into too much detail. For the algorithm in Figure 7, the following interpretation and application is given: Going through all the deselected concepts (in our example, there is only "Committee"), we have to consider the connected attributes and the connecting attribute mappings. If any of these is not labeled "deselected," at least one proper path[1] starting from the concept has to be found. If there are multiple proper paths, the most appropriate path is chosen (appropriateness or strength will be discussed later). The most appropriate path here consists of a single relationship — the

Figure 7: The Algorithm for Well Formedness Rule 2 (Wouters et al., 2003)

1.   While ($\exists t \in$ attr: $\delta_C(\pi_1(t)) ==$ 'deselected' $\wedge$ ($\delta_A(\pi_2(t)) \neq$ 'deselected' $\vee \delta_{attr}(t) \neq$ 'deselected'))
     1.1.   if there is no proper path p from c to another concept c_i that is not 'deselected' ($\delta_C(c_i) \neq$ 'deselected')
          1.1.1.   if ($\delta_A(a) ==$ 'void')   // never 'selected' because RC4
               1.1.1.1. $\delta \leftarrow \xi_A^\delta(a,$ 'deselected')
     1.2.   else (there is one (p) or more ($\{p_1, p_2, ..., p_n\}$) proper paths)
          1.2.1.   if multiple paths
               1.2.1.1.   p $\leftarrow$ BEST_PATH($\{p_1, p_2, ..., p_n\}$)
          1.2.2.   loop i from 1 to n   // with $p=b_1b_2...b_n$
               1.2.2.1.   O $\leftarrow \xi_A^O(b_i, t)$
               1.2.2.2.   t $\leftarrow$ t'   // t' is constructed in Attribute Distribution Rule

Figure 8: Distributed Attributes due to WF Rule 2

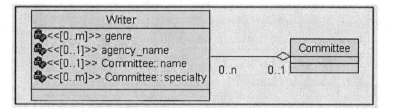

aggregation between "Writer" and "Committee." For every relationship in the path, a transformation is applied, and the result serves as the input for the next relationship in the path. As there is only one relationship in the path here, a single transformation is adequate to obtain the new ontology result. The formal notation of this transformation can be found in line 1.2.2.1 in Figure 7, and means that the attribute mapping (t) is shifted along the relationship (b_i), resulting in a new ontology. A part of this new ontology (the modified part) is shown in Figure 8. There were a total of two transformations here (one for each attribute mapping). If no proper path is found, the attributes and attribute mappings get a modified labeling that gives them all a "deselected" tag.

The third Well Formedness Rule (WF Rule 3) states:

- *If an attribute is deselected, its attribute mapping should also be deselected.*

Figure 9: Modified Labeling after WFOS (Output Labeling)

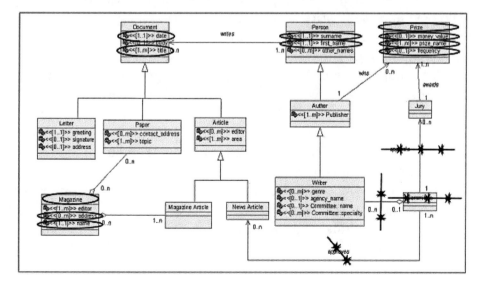

Because the automated attribute mapping was applied in our example, this rule is always adhered to, and does not require further testing.

The fourth rule for Well Formedness (WF Rule 4) deals with deselected concepts:

- *If a concept is deselected, all the relationships that connect it to another concept should be labeled "deselected" as well.*

Only the deselected concepts have to be considered here, which means that, in our example, we only have to look at "Committee." This concept has three relationships connected to it. For these relationships, a transformation of the labeling will be applied, modifying their labels to "deselected." Note that the modification of the labeling can only be done if the relationships have a "void" label, but because RCOS is run before this optimization scheme, there is never a selected relationship connected to a deselected concept, so the additional check for this case does not need to be performed here.

The resulting labeling can be interpreted from Figure 9.

For the last rule (WF Rule 5), Ontology Graphs become important, and this arises directly out of the ontology definition:

- *There has to be a valid Ontology Graph for the elements labeled "selected" and "void."*

This means that for the vertices, we take the concepts that have a label other than "deselected," and for the edges, the relationships that have a label other than "deselected," and we check whether they are a valid Ontology Graph. Remember that the important restriction that was set on a valid Ontology Graph was that it is a completely interconnected graph, i.e., there are no 'islands' in the graph. We can use Kruskal's Algorithm for minimal spanning trees in graphs (see Kruskal, 1956) to determine whether there is a valid Ontology Graph solution. Because Kruskal uses weighted graphs, all relationships are allocated the same weight (e.g., one). Although not occurring in our example, it might be possible that two concepts have more than one relationship between them. We note that Kruskal's algorithm provides an acyclic solution, terminating when an edge addition leads to a cycle. Where there are two relationships between two concepts, this inevitably leads to a cycle. Kruskal's algorithm will pick one of them, allowing us to satisfy the well formedness condition. What the particular solution from applying this algorithm would be is not important at this stage; we just want to ensure there is at least one possibility for a solution. The end result of the algorithm is checked with:

- If V=E+1 there is no island
- If V≠E+1 there are islands

Applying that algorithm here results in V=E+1, so no modifications need to be made. Note that the inequality can be substituted with V>E+1, as the other case (V<E+1) would mean there has to be a cycle somewhere, and Kruskal always prevents this.

Semantic Completeness Optimization Scheme (SCOS)

As the name already indicates, the SCOS aims to produce a semantic complete solution set. The idea of semantic completeness can be interpreted in a variety of ways, but here it is considered as the inclusion of defining elements of selected elements in the input solution set. A defining element is a relationship, concept or attribute that is essential to the semantics of a concept; and, in our research, the types are super-concepts (i.e., inheritance relationship), part aggregates (i.e., aggregation relationship), and attributes with a minimum cardinality different than zero. Note that for both inheritance and aggregation relationships, the defining aspect only applies in one direction. This will become clearer while applying the resulting algorithms to the solution set. Firstly, the initial rule is explained:

Figure 10: Inheritance Relationships in the Ontology

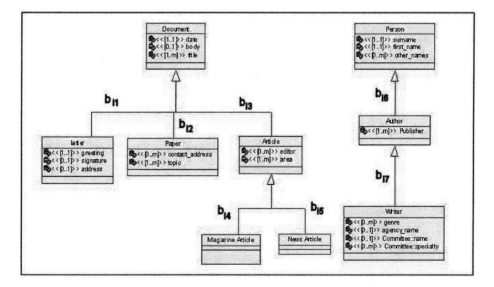

- *If a concept is selected, all its super-concepts, and the inheritance relationships between the concepts and its super-concepts, have to be selected as well.*

In our example model, there are seven binary relationships. To facilitate the explanation, these relationships have been isolated and identified (from b_{i1} to b_{i7}) in Figure 10. The algorithm for compliance with the rule utilizes a temporary set that starts out with all the inheritance relationships in it, and ends when this set is empty. Every iteration, one element is deleted from the set (this does not affect the actual ontology; it is only from the temporary set that these elements are deleted). In our example, it means we will have seven iterations, as we identified seven relationships. Instead of listing all the iterations, a couple will be demonstrated so that the workings of the algorithm become clear.

Iteration 1 (starts with $\{b_{i1}, b_{i2}, ..., b_{i7}\}$):
Take the first element of the temporary set: b_{i1}
Does the sub-concept of b_{i1}, i.e., "Letter," have any sub-concepts itself?
    No
Is "Letter" labeled as "selected?" No
Remove b_{i1} from the temporary set
Iteration 2 (starts with $\{b_{i2}, b_{i3}, ..., b_{i7}\}$):
    Take the first element of the temporary set: b_{i2}
    Does the sub-concept of b_{i2}, i.e., "Paper," have any sub-concepts itself? No
    Is "Paper" labeled as "selected?" No
    Remove b_{i2} from the temporary set
Iteration 3 (starts with $\{b_{i3}, b_{i4}, ... b_{i7}\}$)
    Take the first element of the temporary set: b_{i3}
Does the sub-concept of b_{i3}, i.e., "Article," have any sub-concepts itself?
    Yes, e.g., b_{i4}
Does the sub-concept of b_{i4}, i.e., "Magazine Article," have any sub-concepts itself? No
            Is "Magazine Article" labeled as "selected?" No
            Remove b_{i4} from the temporary set

The iterations continue in this way until the temporary set is empty. Note here that in our example, iteration 4 would have started with the set $\{b_{i3}, b_{i5}, b_{i6}, b_{i7}\}$, so b_{i3} is still there, but b_{i4} is removed. The end result of this algorithm in our example is that nothing changes in the solution set.

Figure 11: Concepts and Binary Aggregation Relationships in Ontology

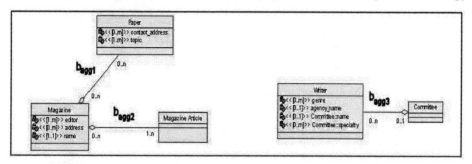

The second rule considers the aggregation relationship:
- If a concept is selected, all the aggregate part-of concepts of this concept, together with the aggregation relationship, have to be selected as well.

Only three aggregation relationships can be found, and these are shown in Figure 11, and given an identifier for easy reference. The algorithm that is used for these relationships is very similar to the one used for the inheritance relationship, but as there are some changes it brings to our example, it is given here.

Iteration 1
Take the first element of the temporary set: b_{agg1}
Is the whole-concept, i.e., "Magazine," a part-concept of another concept? No
Is "Magazine" labeled as "selected?" Yes
Make b_{agg1} selected, as well as the part concept ("Paper")
Remove b_{agg1} from temporary set
Iteration 2
Take the first element of the temporary set: b_{agg2}
Is the whole-concept, i.e. "Magazine," a part-concept of another concept? No
Is "Magazine" labeled as "selected?" Yes
Make b_{agg2} selected, as well as the part concept ("Magazine Article")
Remove b_{agg2} from temporary set
Iteration 3
Take the first element of the temporary set: b_{agg3}

Figure 12: Modified Labeling after First Round of SC Rule 2

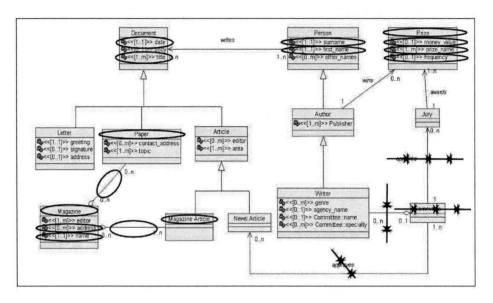

Is the whole-concept, i.e. "Committee," a part-concept of another concept? No
Is "Committee" labeled as "selected?" No
     Remove b_{agg3} from the temporary set

Some changes were made in the labeling of the solution set during these three iterations, and the resulting labeling can be seen in Figure 12.

The third and final rule for the SCOS states:

- *If a concept is selected, all the attributes it 'possesses' with a minimum cardinality other than zero and their attribute mappings should be selected as well.*

The algorithm that ensures the compliance to this rule has to loop through all the selected concepts, and, for each one of these, check the attributes. An extract of the application of the algorithm to our example is given next (only two of the four selected concepts are shown):

Concept "Magazine"
     What attributes of this concept have a minimum cardinality other than zero? "editor" and "name"

Figure 13: New Selected Labeling for "Magazine" and "Paper" Concept after First Round of SC Rule 3

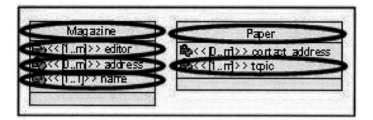

Are they deselected? No
Are they selected? "name" is
        Do not consider "name" anymore
Change the labeling to "selected" for the "editor" and its attribute mapping
Concept "Paper"
What attributes of this concept have a minimum cardinality other than zero? "topic"
Is it deselected? No
Is it selected? No
Change the labeling to "selected" for the attribute and its attribute mapping

For the two other selected concepts, no changes in the labeling of the solution set needs to be introduced anymore, and Figure 13 shows the impact of this algorithm on the attribute labeling.

Although there are only three rules with algorithms for this optimization scheme, and all three have been applied, this is not the end of the SCOS. All the smaller algorithms are contained in a bigger "while" loop, indicating that the entire process (all three algorithms) needs to be reapplied if any changes occurred in the solution set (including the labeling) during the application of the algorithms. As this was the case in our example, we have to do a second round with the SCOS algorithms. As all algorithms have been demonstrated, it suffices to show an example of the impact of the second round, rather than going through all the algorithms again.

For the inheritance relationship algorithm, we start with the same temporary set, and, thus, have seven iterations. The first iteration is the same as in the previous round, but the second iteration is different, and is given here:

Figure 14: Resulting Labeling after SCOS

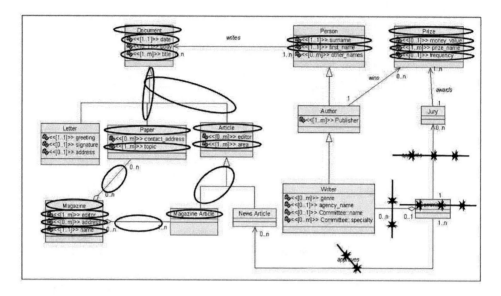

Iteration 2 (starts with {b_{i2}, b_{i3}, ..., b_{i7}}):
   Take the first element of the temporary set: b_{i2}
   Does the sub-concept of b_{i2}, i.e. "Paper," have any sub-concepts itself? No
   Is "Paper" labeled as "selected?" Yes
        Make b_{i2} and "Document" selected if they are not so already
   Remove b_{i2} from the temporary set

Going through all the algorithms in the same fashion results in a number of additional changes, so a third round is required. In this third round, no further changes need to be made in our example, and so there is no need for a fourth round. The final result of all these changes is presented in Figure 14.

Extreme Simplicity Optimization Scheme (ESOS)

The ESOS is the optimization scheme to obtain a compact result. On the Internet, ontologies tend to become extremely large, and being able to cut down these ontologies to smaller materialized views is something a lot of implementations and distributed systems will have to do at some stage. The ESOS results in a minimum number of concepts, attributes and relationships being kept in the

Figure 15: Labeled Ontology Graph before ESOS

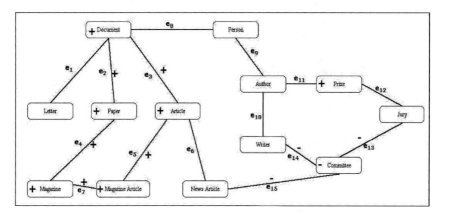

materialized ontology view, while ensuring its validity at the same time. The interconnectivity of the mapped Ontology Graph can be an obstacle for this validity.

For this optimization scheme, the separate rules will not be given, as the solution algorithms combine all these rules. A first solution utilized Kruskal's algorithm (see Kruskal, 1956) to get to a result, but because of the different nature of the concepts due to their mapping, this solution was abandoned, and a second algorithm was proposed. This algorithm will be applied on the example here.

As mentioned before, it is the ontology graph part of the definition that poses a problem, or rather that has a major influence on the solution; so first, all the concepts are taken and put into vertices, and the relationships are mapped onto edges. The labeling is included ("+" and "-" for "selected" and "deselected" respectively). The result is presented in Figure 15. A preprocessing step changes the labeling of all the void attributes and attribute mappings to a "deselected" labeling (as we want a simple solution, we just leave out the attributes that are not really necessary).

In the explanation of the algorithm, we consider the connectivity of a vertex to be the number of edges it is connected with. If no labeling is presented next to the vertex or edge, it has a "void" labeling. Note also that changes made by the algorithm are not solely made to the labeling, but sometimes to the actual ontology itself (which is different from the previous optimization schemes, where changes were made only to the labeling, not the actual ontology). The resulting solution set might have different elements altogether, and because it is

Figure 16: Indication of Initial Substitute Triples (One Possibility)

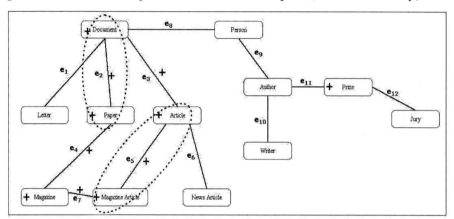

very decisive, no more "void" labels will be present, i.e. the algorithm decides for every element whether it should be there or not, while other algorithms often did not have an 'opinion' about certain elements.

The first step in the algorithm is removing all the deselected elements, so this means "Committee," and all the edges connected to it, are removed. In the output solution set, they will still be there with their "deselected" labeling, but for the algorithm, they are temporarily removed from the ontology graph.

Between all of the remaining steps, a check is always made. This check is to remove an edge if there is already an edge between the same vertices with a lower weight (the weights will be discussed further). If two equal weights are encountered, the solution set is split up into two solution sets, one for each

Figure 17: Modified Graph with Double Edge Between Vertices

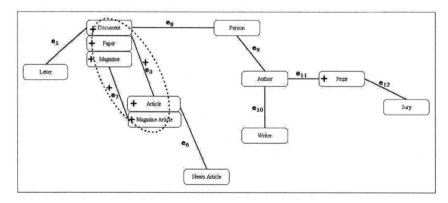

Figure 18: Graph Result after Substitution of Selected Triples

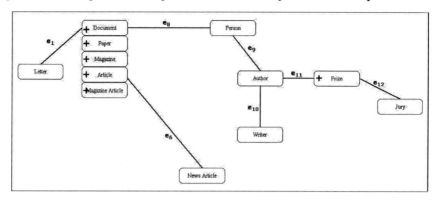

possibility. The output of this algorithm can be a number of equivalent solution sets (rather than always a single solution set). Note that removing means removing from the temporary Ontology Graph and giving a "deselected" label to the element, but the element is not removed from the ontology.

The next step is to go through to graph, and replace all the combinations of two positive vertices connected by a positive edge by just one vertex. Two such combinations are indicated in Figure 16. There are different combinations that can be chosen initially, but they will all lead to the same result, so an arbitrary selection can be made.

Figure 16 has also already removed the deselected elements. The resulting modified graph, with already a new combination indicated, is shown in Figure 17. For reasons of clarity, we have left the names of the combined vertices in the new vertex, but during the rest of the algorithm, these combined vertices are considered one normal vertex.

Figure 19: Graph Result after Deletion of Connectivity = 1 and Void Vertices

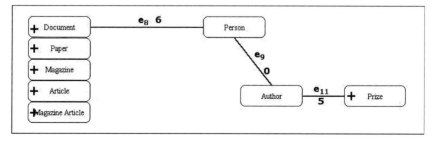

Table 1: Possible Weights Distribution According to Cardinalities

Cardinality	Weight
Inheritance/aggregation	0
(1,1)	1
(1, m)	2
(0, 1)	3
(0, m)	4

The same step is repeated until there are no more combinations of two positive vertices connected by a positive edge to be found. Sometimes it might occur that there are two edges between the positive vertices. If both edges are positive (e.g., Figure 17), both edges are left out of the graph, but no modification is made to the actual labeling for the solution set. If one is positive, but the other is void, they are both left out, but the void edge invokes a modification on the labeling of the represented relationship. In other words, the relationship that was mapped onto the edge gets a "deselected" label.

The next step is to look at all the vertices that have a "void" label and a connectivity of one. All these vertices, together with their connected edge, are removed as well (again, this means temporarily removed, and a "deselected" labeling for the mapped relationships and concepts). Applying this to our example, we go from Figure 18 to Figure 19.

In Figure 19, weights are introduced into the system as well. As they only become important now, they are calculated in this step, rather than at the start of the algorithm. This results in fewer calculations, so less stress on a system. The way the weights are calculated here is simple but effective, and is done by adding the corresponding weights for the cardinalities or type of the relationships that are mapped onto the edges. Table 1 presents the scale used in our example.

For the redistribution of attributes, the weights will be split up into directional weights, but for now, cardinalities for both directions of a relationship are considered in the total weight for the mapped edge.

Something else that needs to be considered here is the distribution of the attributes. As mentioned before, all the attributes (and their attribute mappings) with a "void" label have this label changed to a "deselected" label. Intuitively, this means that, if they are not really necessary, the simplest solution is to leave them out of the solution. There are, of course, some selected attributes as well,

Figure 20: Indication of Void Vertex with Connectivity = 2

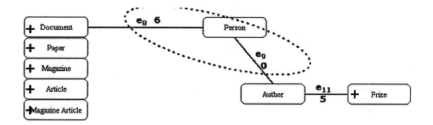

and they can belong to concepts with a "void" or "selected" labeling. In the second case, there is no change, but in the case of a "void" concept, there potentially is a redistribution needed of those selected attributes (and, thus, a change in the ontology, with the deletion of the attribute mappings, and the introduction of new attribute mappings). In the following step, this will occur in our example, and how the algorithm deals with this is shown then.

The next step is another replacement. This time, the combination of a "void" vertex with connectivity of two, and with both connecting edges having a "void" label as well, is replaced by a new relationship, connecting the two target vertices of the edges that connect the "void" vertex in question. Visually, this is a lot easier to comprehend, and Figure 20 shows such a combination.

However, the concept "Person" had a number of selected attributes, so the redistribution of these attributes is needed. For this redistribution, the weights are split up in weights in both directions of the edges. Then, the directional weights are added separately into each direction until a selected vertex is reached. For more complex weighted graphs, Dijkstra (1959) can be used to

Figure 21: Calculation of Lowest Cost for Distribution of Selected Attributes of "Person"

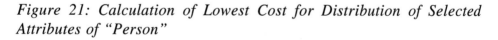
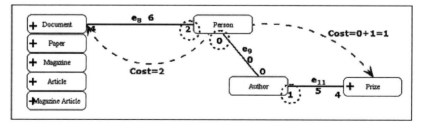

Figure 22: Resulting Graph after Substitution

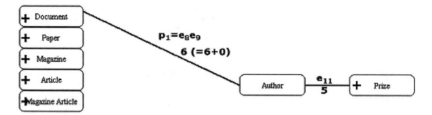

resolve the lowest cost. Then, the lowest cost path is used to redistribute the attributes. A more complex but correct method for redistribution is to wait until the entire labeling for concepts is modified by the algorithm, and then to apply this redistribution by lowest cost. It requires more system resources, however, and for this example, the result is the same.

Applied to our example, we get resulting costs for redistribution as shown in Figure 21, concluding the cost is lower to redistribute the attributes to "Prize."

Getting back to the step that was being demonstrated, we now replace the combination by a single edge that corresponds to a path. This path is converted into a single relationship in the solution set, and is given a "selected" labeling. Figure 22 shows the resulting graph, and the new relationship can be seen in Figure 24 (end result).

This process is repeated until there are no more void vertices with a connectivity of two. The final result for our example has removed all the void vertices, and the result for the process is shown in Figure 23. Note that it is possible to have to go through void vertices with a connectivity higher than two,

Figure 23: Resulting Ontology Graph after ESOS

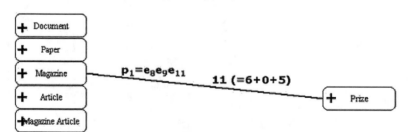

and, for these, the conversion to selected elements is usually the solution, except in a couple of exceptional cases.

The elements that have been modified in the solution set due to the processing of the ontology graph are included in a final solution. As indicated previously, there are no more "void" labels after the ESOS, only "selected" and "deselected." In the solution, only the selected elements are important, as they constitute a solution for the optimized materialized ontology view.

As we have already discussed the WFOS, that is applied to this solution set once more, and because it does not enforce any changes anymore (in our example), we have omitted this step from this chapter. It can be tested be reapplying the appropriate section to the solution set we have obtained now.

Resulting Materialized Ontology View

At the end of the sequence of optimization schemes dictated by the priority list, the final output is another solution set. This solution set — as every solution set — consists of an ontology and a labeling. For the final solution, the selected elements from the ontology are taken to construct a new ontology. This new

Figure 24: UML Representation of the Resulting Ontology after ESOS

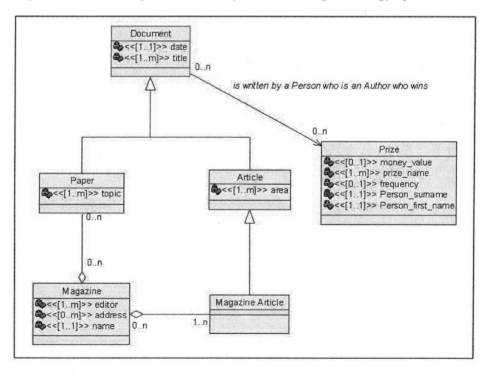

ontology is, in fact, a valid materialized ontology view of the base ontology, optimized according to the specific requirements the user has provided (through the initial labeling and priority list). As discussed previously, because the last optimization scheme was WFOS (ensuring well formedness), we know that the resulting materialized ontology view is, in fact, a valid ontology in its own right. For our example, the resulting materialized ontology view is shown in Figure 24. As the base ontology (Figure 4) was fairly small, arriving at this result could have been achieved by visually checking the relationships, and by trying to match a result to the requirements set out initially. However, ontologies that require materialized ontology views typically are a lot more complex, containing more concepts, and even more relationships, making the manual derivation tedious and sometimes near impossible to carry out (without any test to see whether the result is optimized or not).

As can be seen from the UML representation (and from the information provided during the derivation process), the end result is a valid materialized ontology view, and can be used as an independent local system, while maintaining a very simple mapping onto the original ontology. The local system would also be able, without any problems, to import appropriate data that is structured using the base ontology, even if new ontological elements were introduced. In our example, such a new ontological element is the relationship between Prize and Document.

CONCLUSION

In this chapter, we introduced a derivation process to construct optimized materialized ontology views. There are two main emphases covered throughout this chapter: automation of the process and high-quality of the resulting ontology view. Clearly, the benefits of a derivation process like this are immense, as they not only enable non-experts to derive a high-quality materialized ontology view to use for their own system (e.g., here the needs for the optimization could be interpreted from a plain sentence like, "We want a simple solution that is semantically complete."), but also to do this with only minimal human intervention. All the algorithms presented here can be easily automated, and are designed to be. Some conflicting situations might still have to be resolved by humans, but besides these exceptions, the priority list of optimization schemes and optional initial requirements are enough for the algorithms to produce a high-quality result.

Because of the diversity in reasons why a materialized ontology view needs to be extracted, it is hard to provide a single high-quality method of obtaining a result. The optimization schemes provide the ideal compromise. They are easy building blocks that can be used by non-experts (they merely need to be put in certain order), but at the same time, experts with new needs can construct their own algorithms, resulting in new optimization schemes. These new schemes can be readily plugged into the system already in place, and seamlessly, these new needs are met by the system.

Currently, a framework is being developed that provides a plugin architecture for optimization schemes. A simple communication between the framework and various dynamic optimization scheme modules is reached by using the solution sets as described in this chapter. Solution sets provide the input and output of an optimization scheme, resulting in the compatibility of the output of any solution set to be used as the input of another optimization scheme.

In future work, the library of diverse optimization schemes will be expanded, enabling a very versatile set of tools to derive independent materialized views from base ontologies, thus enabling the semantic web to distribute ontologies with easy (or no) mappings to one another. Import/export layers already enable this system to incorporate multiple standards, as long as they allow for a formulation in DTD/XML. This provides compatibility with standards such as OWL (see W3C, 2002a, 2002b) and DAML-OIL (Berners-Lee & Al, 2001). The data available, although structured according to different ontologies, will no longer be incompatible, and this will contribute to the success of the semantic web.

ACKNOWLEDGMENT

The findings presented in this chapter rely on research that has partly been funded by Victorian Partnership for Advanced Computing (VPAC) Grant EPPNLA090.2003.

REFERENCES

Berners-Lee, T., et al. (2001). *Reference description of the DAML+OIL ontology markup language.*

Biggs, N. L., Lloyd, E. K., & Wilson, R. J. (1976). *Graph Theory 1736-1936.* Oxford, UK: Clarendon Press.

Chen, P. P. (1976). The entity-relationship model: Toward a unified view of data. *ACM Transaction on Database Systems*, 1(1), 9-36.

Colomb, R. M. & Weber, R. (1998). Completeness and quality of an ontology for an information system. *Proceedings of the International Conference on Formal Ontology in Information Systems*, Trento, Italy.

Dijkstra, E. (1959). A note on two problems in connection with graphs. *Numerische Mathematik*, 1, 269-271.

Feng, L., Chang, E., & Dillon, T. (2002). A semantic network based design methodology for XML documents. *ACM Transactions on Information Systems*, 20(3).

Fensel, D., et al. (2000). OIL in a nutshell. *Proceedings of the 12th International Conference on Knowledge Engineering and Knowledge Management Methods,* Juan-Les-Pins, France.

Fensel, D., Decker, S., Erdmann, M., & Studer, R. (1998). Ontobroker: Or how to enable intelligent access to the WWW. *Proceedings of the 11th Knowledge Acquisition for Knowledge-Based Systems Workshop*, Banff, Canada.

Genesereth, M. R. (1991). Knowledge interchange format. In *Proceedings of the 2nd international conference on principles of knowledge representation and reasoning*. San Francisco, CA: Morgan Kaufmann.

Genesereth, M. R. & Fikes, R. (1992). *Knowledge Interchange Format, version 3.0, Reference Manual*. Stanford, CA: Stanford University, Computer Science Department.

Gruber, T. R. (1992). *Ontolingua: A Mechanism to Support Portable Ontologies*. Stanford, CA: Stanford University, Knowledge Systems Laboratory.

Gruber, T. R. (1993a). Toward principles for the design of ontologies used for knowledge sharing. In N. Guarino & R. Poli (Eds.), *Formal Ontology in Conceptual Analysis and Knowledge Representation*. Deventer: Kluwer Academic.

Gruber, T. R. (1993b). A translation approach to portable ontology specifications. *Knowledge Acquisition*.

Guarino, N. & Welty, C. (2002). Evaluating ontological decisions with OntoClean. *Communications of the ACM*, 45(2), 61-65.

Hahn, U. & Schnattinger, K. (1998). Towards text knowledge engineering. *Proceedings of the 15th National Conference on Artificial Intelligence,* Madison, Wisconsin.

Halpin, T. (1995). *Conceptual Schema and Relational Database Design* (2nd ed.). New York: Prentice Hall.

Harmelen, F. Van & Fensel, D. (1999). Practical knowledge representation for the web. *Proceedings of the International Joint Conferences on Artificial Intelligence.*

Heflin, J. & Hendler, J. (2000). Dynamic ontologies on the web. *Proceedings of the American Association for Artificial Intelligence Conference,* Menlo Park, California.

Heflin, J., Hendler, J., & Luke, S. (1999). Coping with changing ontologies in a distributed environment. In *Proceedings of the American Association for Artificial Intelligence Conference, Workshop on Ontology Management.* Cambridge, MA: MIT Press.

Heflin, J., Hendler, J., & Luke, S. (1999). *SHOE: A Knowledge Representation Language for Internet Applications.* College Park, MD: University of Maryland, Department of Computer Science.

Holsapple, C. W. & Joshi, K. D. (2002). A collaborative approach to ontology design. *Communications of the ACM,* 45(2), 42-47.

Hovy, E. H. (1998). Combining and standardizing large-scale, practical ontologies for machine translation and other uses. *Proceedings of the First International Conference on Language Resources and Evaluation,* Granada, Spain.

Kaplan, A. N. (2001). Towards a consistent logical framework for ontological analysis. *Proceedings of the International Conference on Formal Ontology in Information Systems.*

Klein, M. & Fensel, D. (2001). Ontology versioning for the semantic web. *Proceedings of the International Semantic Web Working Symposium,* California.

Klein, M., Fensel, D., Kiryakov, A., & Ognyanov, D. (2002). Ontology versioning and change detection on the web. In *Proceedings of the 13th International Conference on Knowledge Engineering and Knowledge Management, Siguenza, Spain.* Berlin: Springer-Verlag.

Kruskal, J. B. J. (1956). On the shortest spanning subtree of a graph and the traveling salesman problem. In *Proceedings of the American Mathematics Society,* 1956(7), 48-50.

Lenat, D. B. (1995). Cyc: A large-scale investment in knowledge infrastructure. *Communications of the ACM, 38*(11).

McGuinness, D. L., Fikes, R., Rice, J., & Wilder, S. (2000). An environment for merging and testing large ontologies. In *Proceedings of the Seventh International Conference on Principles of Knowledge Representation and Reasoning.* San Francisco, CA: Morgan Kaufmann.

Nijssen, G. M. & Halpin, T. (1989). *Conceptual Schema and Relational Database Design: A Fact-Oriented Approach*. New York: Prentice Hall.

Noy, N. F. & Klein, M. (2002). Ontology evolution: Not the same as schema evolution. *Stanford Medical Informatics*.

Rumbaugh, J. (1991). *Object-oriented Modeling and Design*. New York: Prentice Hall.

Rumbaugh, J., Jacobson, I., & Booch, G. (1999). *Unified Modeling Language Reference Manual*. New York: Addison-Wesley.

Spyns, P., Meersman, R., & Mustafa, J. (2002). Data modelling versus ontology engineering. *SIGMOD, 2002* (special issue, pp. 14-19).

Staudt, G. K. C. von. (1847). *Geometrie der Lage*. Nurnberg, Germany.

W3C. (1999a). *Extensible markup language (XML) 1.0*. W3C Recommendation.

W3C. (1999b). *Resource description framework (RDF) model and syntax specification*. W3C Recommendation.

W3C. (2002a). *OWL web ontology language 1.0 abstract syntax*. W3C working draft.

W3C. (2002b). *OWL web ontology language 1.0 reference*. W3C working draft.

Wouters, C., Dillon, T., Rahayu, W., & Chang, E. (2002). A practical walkthrough of the ontology derivation rules. *Proceedings of DEXA 2002*, Aix-en-Provence.

Wouters, C., Dillon, T., Rahayu, W., Meersman, R., & Chang, E. (2003). *Transformational processes for ontology view specification*. Submitted for publication.

ENDNOTES

[1]   A proper path only contains non-deselected relationships and intermediate concepts with a "void" label.

[2]   A materialized ontology view of a base ontology is a (valid) ontology that consists solely of projections, copies, compressions, and/or combinations of elements of the base ontology, presenting a varying and/or restricting perception of the base ontology, without introducing new semantic data.

Chapter VII

Web Information Extraction via Web Views

Wee Keong Ng, Nanyang Technological University, Singapore

Zehua Liu, Nanyang Technological University, Singapore

Zhao Li, Nanyang Technological University, Singapore

Ee Peng Lim, Nanyang Technological University, Singapore

ABSTRACT

With the explosion of information on the Web, traditional ways of browsing and keyword searching of information over web pages no longer satisfy the demanding needs of web surfers. Web information extraction has emerged as an important research area that aims to automatically extract information from target web pages and convert them into a structured format for further processing. The main issues involved in the extraction process include: (1) the definition of a suitable extraction language; (2) the definition of a data model representing the web information source; (3) the generation of the data model, given a target source; and (4) the extraction and presentation of information according to a given data model. In this chapter, we discuss the challenges of these issues and the approaches that current research activities have taken to revolve these issues. We propose several classification schemes to classify existing approaches of information extraction from different perspectives. Among the existing works, we focus on the WICCAP system — a software system that enables ordinary end-users to obtain information of interest in a simple and efficient manner by constructing personalized web views of information sources.

INTRODUCTION

The World Wide Web has become such a successful channel in delivering and sharing information that people are getting used to searching the Web as the first resort for information. As the amount of data accessible via the Web grows rapidly, the weaknesses of traditional ways of browsing and searching the Web become more and more apparent (Laender, 2002a). Browsing requires users to follow links and to read (usually) long web pages, thus making it tedious and difficult to find a particular piece of information. Keyword searching usually returns massive irrelevant information, along with some useful information hidden in the long list of search results. Even with improved search engines, such as Google, that return accurate results, a large number of web pages cannot be indexed by these engines. Therefore, users surfing the Web with these traditional facilities have been facing the information overload problem; they are overloaded with too much irrelevant information.

As HTML web pages are designed to be viewed by humans, most of the HTML syntax is for presentation purposes and does not contain much semantic meaning; this makes automatic access by software applications difficult. However, there is an increasing demand to turn web data into structured and machine-readable formats so that further processing, such as integration, filtering and customized visualization, can take place.

To address the problems mentioned above, over the past few years, some web information extraction (IE) systems (mainly in the form of wrappers) (see Adelberg, 1998; Ashish, 1997; Baumgartner, 2001; Crescenzi, 2001; Hammer, 1997; Kushmerick, 2000; Liu, 2000; Liu, 2002; Liu 2002a; Mecca, 1999) have been developed to automatically extract target information from the Web and convert the extracted data into some structured format. The approaches taken by these systems differ greatly, ranging from Natural Language Processing (NLP) to machine learning to database techniques. Despite the differences in approaches, there are several common issues that these systems need to address: (1) the definition of a suitable extraction language; (2) the definition of a data model representing the web information source; (3) the generation of data models, given a target source; and (4) the extraction and presentation of the information according to a given data model.

Objectives

This chapter aims to provide an in-depth analysis of the above issues and of how the existing approaches address them. This chapter is not intended to be a simple survey of existing web IE systems, which has been done in Laender (2002a), where a brief description of those systems is given and a simple classification is proposed. The focus of this chapter is to look into the details of each important issue mentioned above, to discuss how the issue can be handled, and to analyze approaches taken by current systems and how effective they are in solving the problems. In addition, several classification schemes are proposed in order to classify these existing systems and to help understand the issues that they try to resolve.

To further illustrate the issues, a detailed description of one of the systems called WICCAP (see Li, 2001; Liu, 2002) is provided. The aim of the WICCAP system is to enable ordinary users to create their own views of the target web sites in a simple and easy manner so that information extraction from web sites can be performed automatically.

It should also be pointed out that the focus of this chapter is on academic research projects. For a brief survey on related commercial products, the readers are referred to Kuhlins (2002).

Outline of Chapter

The remainder of this chapter starts with the discussion of the various issues of web information extraction systems, including different aspects of designing a data extraction grammar, characteristics of a data model, algorithms for generating data models and extraction expressions, and various miscellaneous issues. Several classification schemes are then proposed to categorize existing web IE systems. Then, one particular system is presented, which is the WICCAP system. We describe the approach taken by this system and how it addresses the various issues mentioned above. The chapter ends with a conclusion and future research directions for web information extraction systems.

ISSUES

The kernel of a web IE system what is termed a wrapper. A wrapper is capable of automatically extracting semi-structured data from the Web and transforming the extracted data into a structured format. In addition, a web IE system might also have modules to build the extraction rules used by wrappers, as well as modules to verify and maintain wrappers.

Due to the size and complexity of the Web, it is impossible to develop one IE system that extracts all kinds of data from the Web and is suitable to all kinds of users. Although traditional relational database techniques can be used to process structured information online, they are not suitable for processing heterogeneous web data sources such as HTML, XML, ps files, etc. To extract various kinds of data accurately, researchers are resorting to ideas from different areas such as database, NLP (natural language processing), etc.

In this section, we describe the issues in IE system development and the methods IE systems exploit to solve these issues. At the end of the section, we classify existing IE systems into various categories based on different facets of these systems.

Data Extraction Language

Given a set of web documents, wrapping these documents typically requires three steps. First, wrappers should be able to download documents from the Web. We can view the Web as a directed graph. Each web document, or segment of it, can be treated as one data node in this graph. Nodes are connected through hyperlinks. In addition to a simple hyperlink, sometimes we must submit FORMs or execute scripts in web pages to get these URI. We call all these URIs obtained from "FORMs," scripts as inter-page links. As the first step, a wrapper must have the ability to download web pages from a given inter-page link.

Secondly, every web IE system needs a data extraction language that defines the syntax of the extraction rules, which, in turn, determine how the extraction should be performed. In some systems, this language grammar may be implicitly defined, while other systems formally define their extraction languages explicitly.

Finally, wrappers have to reorganize the data nodes extracted and represent them as a structured format. Depending on the users' interest, the extracted data can be reorganized into traditional relational database, object-oriented database, XML documents, etc.

Depending on the specific wrapper implementation, the three steps above might not be performed in the order that they are presented. A wrapper can download a web page, extract all URI strings in this page in the second step, and then execute step 1 to download all web pages pointed to by these URIs. The following elaborates these three steps in detail.

Crawl Related Features

In order to accurately extract information from the web, IE systems must have the ability to access services available on the Web, typically web pages. Services on the Web have properties of wide area distribution, unreliability, various security models, etc. Those characteristics must be addressed when we do an extraction task, otherwise the wrappers will be prone to failure. The robustness of a wrapper lies in:

- *The types of services that it supports.* The most frequently used protocols include HTTP, HTTPS and FTP. Most existing web IE systems support only HTTP. But, this might be considered as an implementation issue in some systems.

- *Network exceptions it can handle.* In a web IE system, failure to download a specified web page may mean the failure of all extraction tasks. It is a good idea to let the user explicitly specify what the system should do when it encounters exceptions such as server failure, service timeout, etc. Wrappers can reload a web page, retry a request, or use a backup data source to make themselves more robust.

Most IE systems encapsulate the web access function and process all kind of services and exceptions implicitly. But some systems do allow users to control what to do when problems occur. WebL (Kistler, 1998) is a programming language for the Web in which developers can implement the web data extraction function by hand coding. In this language, users can bind an exception handler with each service access operation.

Other important features are the support for following hyperlinks, the ability to handle HTML Form elements, and script in web pages. Without the ability to follow hyperlinks, the wrapper will be restricted to extracting data from a single web page. In most web sites, useful information is usually located in different web pages. For example, newspaper web sites typically have a list of headlines with links to the web pages containing the detail stories. Therefore, being able to extract information across multiple web pages (i.e., following hyperlinks among web pages) is very important in a useful wrapper.

In other cases, such as user login and search form, wrappers have to first fill in HTML Forms before they can reach the correct web page. Few systems are capable of handling such situations. The WICCAP Data Model (Liu, 2002) proposed in the WICCAP system, includes a group of elements dedicated to the HTML Form elements. When encountering such elements, the extraction agent in WICCAP simulates the form-filling action by popping up a dialog box and submitting it to the remote server after the user fills it up. In W4F (Sahuguet, 2001), a Form Wizard was provided to facilitate the specification of rules involving HTML Forms.

Sometimes URIs are returned by a script function when we click a hyperlink, button or invoke an event on a DOM node bonded with an event handler script; so it's also important for an IE system to support the event mechanism of web pages. Again, this might be perceived as an implementation issue by systems focusing on the extraction or integration of data. However, as more and more web pages are relying on JavaScript or VBScript to provide very interactive web pages, a truly robust wrapper system has to pay more attention to such a feature.

Data Extraction Rules

The most important function of a wrapper is to extract information. Wrappers must be able to recognize, locate and extract data from the web pages downloaded by the previous step. Such capabilities rely on the data extraction rules, which is the knowledge provided by knowledge engineer or generated using machine learning techniques.

Much research has been done in the area of how to represent this knowledge using various methods. Some literatures discuss how to use NLP-related techniques (Cali, 1998; Ribeiro-Neto, 1999) and how to process web data to make it processable to an NLP system (Soderland, 1997; Soderland, 1995) and generate knowledge used by an NLP system. Chang (2001) devised a method learn rules generated by PAT trees (Morrison, 1968). Rajaraman et al. (2001) applied data graph algorithms to process graphic skeletons, which is a kind of data extraction knowledge. Others tried to apply grammar induction in rules generation (Kosala, 2002; Kosala, 2000; Chidlovskii, 2000; Kushmerick, 2000; Muslea, 1999). Grammar induction and many other approaches generate rules that can be formally analyzed using formal language theory.

The traditional IE community mainly uses NLP techniques to learn extraction rules and extract relevant data from free text documents (Appelt, 1999).

Such techniques, including word segmentation, speech tagging, word sense tagging, syntactic analysis, and ontology analysis, have been used to build the relations among phrases and syntactic elements. For the extraction of semi-structured data, the contents in documents show some special structural information; and the grammar and syntactic information are difficult to figure out. Soderland introduced Webfoot (Soderland, 1997), which is a step in this direction. It pre-processed semi-structured documents and made them processable by CRYSTAL (Soderland, 1995), which is an NLP system. RAPIER (Cali, 1998) is a relation rules-based system capable of learning the relations among data blocks in freetext documents.

Hidden Markov models methods (Seymore, 1999) have been used in the NLP area. They can also deal with HTML documents, especially in some sophisticated situations such as error codes in HTML pages. They use statistical models, which can describe the appearance probability of data fields.

Approaches originated from NLP seldom use structure information of HTML pages. On the contrary, such structure information often makes syntactic analysis even more difficult. To make full use of such information, Kushmerick (2000) (2000b) (1999) introduced six classes of wrapper rules. The simplest one is Left-Right class. It can extract contents, appearing in a tabular format with K columns, by scanning the left delimiter and right delimiter of each column, one by one. LR can only extract flat format data, and is too simple to extract information from many web sites. Kushmerick extended LR classes to Head-Open-Close-Left-Right-Tail (HOCLRT) to prune those texts that could potentially be confusing.

The pioneering work by Kushmerick cannot handle sources with nested structure and missing and varying-order attributes. SoftMealy (Hsu, 1998) is able to handle these exceptional cases, but it requires seeing all possible special cases (missing attributes or out of order attributes) in the training phase in order to induce a correct wrapper. STALKER (Muslea, 2001) provides a more expressive extraction language by allowing disjunction and multiple patterns for locating information.

Data Extraction Schema

At the end of the extraction, a data model is required to capture the organization or structure of the extracted information. This data model should reflect the users' understanding of the structure of the data to be extracted. It may also imply the way that the extracted data will be stored, although the approach to data storage can vary with different implementation.

Some IE systems still remain in prototype phase. They only export the data blocks extracted from a data source; they need other tools to map these extracted parts to a physical storage schema.

In some cases, users want to perform a select, join, or reconstruction operation on extracted data. It is easier and more stable to implement systems supporting these features based on relational database. Using RDBMS, we can leverage some other advantages such as portability and scalability. Over the Internet, most data are still stored in relational databases, and web documents are generated by applying templates to the relational database. From this point of view, wrapping web data is just like finding out the templates and is a kind of reverse engineering of semi-structured data. VDB (Gupta, 1998) is a virtual relational database management system. It wraps web data and stores them in a relational format. Source Description Language (SDL), defined in VDB, can describe web sites and map them to RDBMS. WebSources (Bright, 1999) defines a query language that can return relational data from semi-structured data sources.

XML has become the de facto standard of data exchange, and some users are using it for data storage, as well. More and more web sites use XML to represent their web pages. Some IE systems [WICCAP, XWrap (Liu, 2000) and DEByE (Laender, 2002)] directly store the extracted data as XML documents. Minerva (Crescenzi, 1998) needs users to write code manually to describe how to generate XML output. Lixto (Baumgartner, 2001) allows users to specify a mapping between the final XML output and the extracted data in a transformation step. W4F (Sahuguet, 2001) provides mapping wizards to let users indicate how to map extracted data to output XML.

Wrapper Rules Generation

To construct a wrapper, the naive way is to have an expert user manually write the required extraction rules and compose the data structure for organizing the extracted data. This turns out to be too time-consuming and restrictive. Wrapper Generation (WG) appears as a field independent of the traditional IE community, with the aim of extracting and integrating data from web-based semi-structured data (Muslea, 1998). Wrappers work as the kernel of information mediators between users and a large number of heterogeneous data sources (see Florescu, 1998; Mecca, 1998; Gupta, 1998). In this field, wrappers typically process semi-structured texts, generated from structured databases, based on given templates or rules. One of the challenges is how to figure out the implicit rules hidden inside web pages.

There are two basic approaches to building data extraction rules, namely the *Knowledge Engineering Approach* and the *Machine Learning Approach* (Appelt, 1999). The first method requires a person called a 'knowledge engineer,' who is familiar with the IE system, to develop the rules. On the contrary, the Machine Learning Approach doesn't need users to deal with how the IE system works in detail and develop rules manually. If it is a supervised machine learning approach, users need to have some knowledge related to the data sources, and know how to annotate these data, instead of having detailed knowledge of the IE system itself. Fed with annotated data, the IE system will learn the extraction rules. For unsupervised machine learning methods, even the annotation work is not necessary.

Webfoot (Soderland, 1997) preprocesses semi-structured documents and makes them processable by CRYSTAL. One of the important features of CRYSTAL (Soderland, 1995) is to automatically induce a dictionary of "concept-node-definitions" (CN) to identify relevant information from a training set. CN is a concept in the University of Massachusetts' BADGER sentence analyzer, used to perform selective concept extraction. Webfoot's idea is quite simple: It uses page layout cues to divide a web document text into sentence-length segments of text. The text segments are logically coherent and can be used as input to the CRYSTAL system. In another paper, Soderland (1999) introduced WHISK. WHISK can induce regular like expression from tagged text. It also has a strong relation with NLP techniques, and can deal with processed free text documents.

RAPIER (Cali, 1998) is a relation rule-based system. Its original target is free text documents. It learns relation rules based on the assumption that the text has three fields around the target phrase: Pre-filler Pattern, Filler Pattern and Post-filler Pattern. The rules RAPIER learned specify a relation of items that can match these three patterns. RAPIER uses an inductive logic programming method to do bottom-up maximal pattern searches, followed by compressing and generalizing. It can make use of limited syntactic and semantic information to extract single-slot data (Muslea, 1999) from free text documents, and can be extended to process semi-structured text if we treat tags as these relation patterns.

SRV (Freitag, 1998) is a system that exploits multi classifiers (ROTE, Bayes classifier, and a relational rule learner that does a top-down induction similar to FOIL) to extract single-slot data by transforming a single-slot extraction problem to a classification problem. It uses the quantity statistic capability of ROTE and Bayes classifier to count the term frequency, and uses relation learning method to find the relation among them. SRV also originates from the NLP community, but there is some research focusing on how to classify semi-structured text (Yang, 2002) that can be used in combination with it. SRV and RAPIER are both designed to extract single-slot data. RAPIER can be extended to extract multi-slot data by using more delimiter patterns instead of three patterns. How to extend SRV to multi-slot extraction is much more complex intuitively. The rules learned by CRYSTAL and RAPIER support multi-slot data extraction inherently.

Minerva (Crescenzi, V., 1998) requires users to write programming language-like codes to tell the system how to extract data. Some other systems (Mecca, 1999; Bright, 1999; Gupta, 1998; Baumgartner, 2001; May, 1999) can only generate extraction rules by hand, i.e., using KE methods. KE methods are tiresome, but they can deal with very complex web pages if the knowledge engineer is an expert in a related area.

Another group of systems, including Lixto, WICCAP, DEByE, and XWrap, provide visual support to help users build extraction rules. Various facilities that induce simple rules from marked examples are also provided by these systems. Many other IE systems use grammar induction methods to learn rules. WIEN (Kushmerick, 2000) first labels input web pages in tabular formats, then tries to induce delimiters around these labels. These delimiters can be organized to extract information from similar web pages.

IEPAD (Chang, 2001) first encodes HTML input as a tokens sequence. It treats the sequence as a string and builds a PAT tree of this string. And then, finding the most frequent sub-TOKEN sequence becomes an easy task because we can find repeated HTML hierarchical patterns in a web page. Such patterns can be used to extract data from HTML pages where the data appears in the form of a record list, such as the books list on the Amazon web site.

Wrapper Maintenance

The wrappers that we have discussed so far extract data based on the rules that can identify context around the target data blocks. Much research effort is dedicated to generate rules, while only a few literatures, e.g., (Kushmerick, 2000b; Kushmerick, 1999b; Lerman, 2003), mention how to maintain these rules when the target web sites or web pages change. This usually leaves the constructed wrappers vulnerable to the changes of the data sources.

Since predicting layout changes is almost impossible, web IE systems usually have to passively regenerate the data extraction rules after some changes occur. It would be useful to find methods to verify whether rules are still extracting the right data. When the wrapper is known to fail in the process of extraction, it then needs to recognize layout modification and re-induce rules.

Kushmerick (2000) (1999b) devised a domain-independent heuristic algorithm—RAPTURE—to verify wrappers. This is based on the assumption that if a wrapper is still working correctly, it can extract identical or similar output from different versions of the same web data source. RAPTURE uses several features, such as word count and the mean word length, to measure similarity of the wrapper output. It calculates the similarity of two outputs by using a regression testing paradigm. In Lerman (2003), the authors also used a similar statistic method to measure the similarity of features extracted from different output.

The work done by Cohen (1999) and Lerman (2003) suggests how to re-induct wrappers when they find wrappers incorrect. The main idea is to learn new wrapper rules, test the similarity of outputs, and then choose the newly generated wrapper that can extract the most similar output. In all these literatures, the features selected are very simple, and how to compare the extracted structures has not been considered.

Miscellaneous

We have introduced issues from wrapper generation to wrapper maintenance. In the life cycle of a wrapper, there are still some other issues. IE systems act as mediators between users and web sites. Worthy of further study is how to provide a friendly interface to other systems, and how to use those other systems' features to extend IE systems application areas.

The strategies of generating extraction rules using machine learning require users to give a training example. The efforts required for marking examples sometimes may be very large. How to automatically prepare web pages and annotate them is a big challenge. Golgher (1998) used an ontological dictionary (boostrapping repository) to evaluate whether there exists interesting information in sample web pages, and then to assemble these parts into an example set.

Some literatures (Lin, 2002; Wang, 2002; Embley, 1999) discuss pre-process training set, clear data source. Lin et al. (2002) introduced an algorithm, based on Shannon's information uncertainty formula, to calculate features entropy in web pages. It detects which tables in HTML pages from the same web site include informative data instead of redundant content such as advertisements. It stems words in web pages and deletes words in the stoplist. The word frequency and weight are used as features. The features selection method is relatively simple compared to Wang's, which makes use of layout features. Wang (2002) suggested using Support Vector Machine (SVM) and decision trees to classify tables based on the features in tables and to find interesting tables. Embley et al. (1999) introduced an algorithm that combines several individual heuristics to discover the boundaries of records within a web document. It uses HTML Tags appearance information and ontology knowledge to determine which parts of HTML pages are informative.

There are still many other issues we have not mentioned in this section, e.g., integrating extracted data, presentation techniques, incrementally storing changing part in web pages, etc. IE systems development is still an open area in which various issues are to be studied.

Summary

Due to the diverse techniques used by the existing systems and the different purposes that these systems have been developed for, it is difficult to provide a single classification scheme that categorizes all existing systems appropriately. Summarizing all the issues we discussed above, we propose a multifaceted scheme in an attempt to characterize these systems.

- *Data Source Type*. Web information extraction tools are mostly developed for extracting data from semi-structured documents. All web IE systems we discuss here have the ability to process HTML documents, but there are still large quantities of free text documents, such as email, newsgroup articles, etc. Some other semi-structured documents are not represented using HTML format, e.g., ps files. We categorize IE systems into three kinds, depending on the data source they support: HTML-MIX (HTML, free text, etc.); HTML (HTML only); or special semi-structured documents. In Table 1, we use HTMLMIX, HTML and SPEC to represent these three categories, respectively.

- *Data Extraction Rules Type*. Some systems define a procedural language and ask users to write codes in that language to tell wrappers how to extract information. Many IE systems generate and use rules which are formally equivalent to formal language and automata. We can call them Automata Rules. Some IE systems are originated from NLP systems, and they use a pattern dictionary to match data sources and extract information. Statistical methods, e.g., Hidden Markov Model, also find their application in IE.

- *Rules Generation Method*. Knowledge Engineering method is a manual rule generation method used by some systems. Researchers have also developed machine learning algorithms to do this hard and tedious work of generating extraction rules. Supervised learning needs users to prepare training sets, while unsupervised learning can generate rules full-automatically. We use KE, SML and USML to represent the three kinds of methods, respectively.

- *User Interface.* Some IE systems only include a kernel to extract information corresponding to given rules. Others provide a visual interface to help users annotate training sets, generate rules, and monitor extracted data. Some systems provide a programming interface to query extracted information. We use three categories — No, Visual and API — to represent the three kind of IE systems in Table 1.
- *Output Data Model.* Depending on the kind of output data model an IE system uses, we can categorize it into a flat, relational, hierarchical or XML class.
- *Scope.* Some systems can recognize structure relations in a web site scope, while some others can only find relations among data blocks in a text fragment, a web page, or a set of web pages.

Table 1: Classification of IE Systems

IE systems	Data Source Type	Data Extraction Rules type	Rules Generation Method	User Interface	Output Data Model	Scope
WICCAP	HTMLMIX	AUTOMATA	KE+SML	Visual	XML	Web Sites
HRHYPER	HTMLMIX	AUTOMATA	SML	No	hierarchical	Single Page
Lixto	HTML	AUTOMATA	KE	Visual	XML	Web Sites
MHLL	HTMLMIX	AUTOMATA	KE	API	hierarchical	Single Page
WHISK	THMLMIX	DICTIONARY	SML	No	hierarchical	Single Page
STALKER	HTMLMIX	AUTOMATA	SML	Visual	flat	Page Set
MSE	HTML	AUTOMATA	USML	No	flat	Page Set
IBWI	HTMLMIX	AUTOMATA	SML	No	hierarchical	Single Page
TSIMMIS	HTMLMIX	AUTOMATA	KE	API	hierarchical	Web Sites
SoftMealy	HTMLMIX	AUTOMATA	SML	No	flat	Single Page
BYU	HTMLMIX	ONTOLOGY	KE	No	flat	Single Page
NoDoSE	HTML	AUTOMATA	KE	Visual	XML	Single Page
W4F	HTML	AUTOMATA	KE	API+Visual	XML	Web Sites
RoadRunner	HTML	AUTOMATA	USML	No	hierarchical	Page Set
T-wrappers	HTMLMIX	AUTOMATA	USML	No	hierarchical	Single Page
WhizBang	HTML	AUTOMATA	SML	No	hierarchical	Web Sites
MINERVA	HTMLMIX	CODE	KE	API	relational	Web Sites
RAPIER	HTMLMIX	AUTOMATA	SML	No	flat	Single Page
Webfoot	HTMLMIX	DICTIONARY	SML	No	flat	Single Page
VDB	SPEC	AUTOMATA	KE	API+Visual	relational	Web Sites
XWRAP	HTML	AUTOMATA	SML	Visual	XML	Page Set
BWI	HTMLMIX	AUTOMATA	SML	No	flat	Page Set
EDITOR	HTMLMIX	AUTOMATA	KE	No	hierarchical	Page Set
WebSources	HTML	AUTOMATA	KE	API	relational	Page set
IEPAD	HTML	PAT tree	PAT tree	N/A	flat	Single Page

THE WICCAP SYSTEM

In this section, we present WICCAP[1], a software system that empowers users to build their own views of web sites. WICCAP provides a comprehensive architecture covering each stage in the full life cycle of web information extraction. Here, we choose WICCAP as an example to explain how to apply these techniques, introduced before, in real application environments.

We propose a data model to represent web sites from the logical point of view and to provide a set of tools to automate the construction of the data models. An information extraction agent has been implemented to allow users to create their views of the target web sites, based on the data models previously defined, and to extract the information from the web site according to the defined views. As a last step, a flexible presentation toolkit has been designed to present the information in a manner that is programmable by the users.

The primary goal of WICCAP is to overcome the information overload problem. As a by-product, the extracted information can also be used for integration, query processing, or other general purposes that deal with structured data.

Motivation

As we mentioned before, with the explosion of the Web, information available from web sites is usually overwhelming to users surfing the sites. The majority of the users who are suffering from this information overload problem are ordinary home users who do not have much technical knowledge.

From the users' point of view, a lot of information presented in a web site is not of their interest. This may include auxiliary and additional information, such as advertisements. But, quite often, some of the core contents that the web site is providing do not interest the users, either. Users, when surfing a web site, usually have in mind what they want to see, i.e., they have their own view of the web site. Therefore, a tool that enables these users to specify their views of web sites, and that automatically constructs the views for the users, would help to solve the information overload problem because users will no longer be overloaded with information they are not interested in.

It is, thus, important to enable these users to create their customized views of web sites such that they only see what they want, in the way they prefer. Moreover, such personalized web views should be created in as easy a manner as possible so that ordinary web surfers are able to accomplish this task.

Some web portals, such as My Yahoo![2], try to handle this problem by allowing users to specify the contents and even layout of the front page that the users see when they log in. Such self-design functionality may help to reduce the amount of inappropriate core contents, but still leaves most of the auxiliary information, especially advertisements, untouched. The amount of freedom given to the users to control the personalization of content differs from site to site, but it is usually limited. Some other web sites pro-actively provide additional personalization services, such as product recommendation (e.g., Amazon.com[3]), to users by observing users' past behaviors and discovering patterns. Such services may be helpful, but often do not reflect the real needs of the users because they come from the web sites maintainers instead of from the users themselves.

Over the past couple of years, some *information extraction* (IE) systems (wrappers and agents) (Adelberg, 1998; Baumgartner, 2001; Crescenzi, 2001; Embley, 1999; Liu, 2000; Sahuguet, 2001) have been proposed to automatically extract target information from the Web, and to transform the information into a structured or semi-structured format for further processing. An important step toward the automatic extraction of information is the generation of wrappers, which involves the issues discussed in last section. However, to ordinary web surfers, the step of building a wrapper is very difficult because, although these users know what information they want to view, they usually do not know how to extract this information due to the lack of relevant technical knowledge. As a result, ordinary users are forced to accept data models pre-built by expert users, which may not reflect what they really want.

Meanwhile, information presented in a web site is usually organized according to a certain logical structure that corresponds to people's common perception. However, most existing IE systems do not make use of this fact to improve the intuitiveness of their data models. On the contrary, the information extracted by these systems is modeled in proprietary ad-hoc data structures that do not truly reflect the original logical view of the web site. This renders the resulting data models not intuitive to most users, and makes customization of user views difficult.

The WICCAP Approach

In this section, we propose a novel approach to combine these two aspects of web site personalization and information extraction. A software framework, called the WICCAP system, has been implemented. It enables ordinary users to create personalized views of web sites in a simple and flexible manner. The aim of WICCAP is to provide fast and flexible ways of customizing views of web sites while keeping this task simple and easy to perform. To achieve this: (1) one or more global logical views of a target web site is first constructed; (2) based on these global views, different users create their own views that only contain the portions that they are interested in; (3) users also specify how and when their views should be visually shown to them. With these three steps, and with the help of the tools provided by the WICCAP system, users are able to easily and quickly design their preferred views of web sites.

One of the key contributions of our approach is the explicit separation of the tasks of information modeling and information extraction. This is important because it essentially allows ordinary users to perform the task of creating customized web views that was previously very difficult for them. More specifically, in WICCAP, expert users specify how to extract information, and ordinary end users decide what to extract and how and when to present the extracted information. In this way, we allow users to extract accurately and exactly what they want. This is in contrast with existing IE systems, where the person who creates the data model and specifies the extraction details is the person who wants to extract information, which might eventually lead to the extraction of inaccurate information (due to lack of knowledge, when done by ordinary users) or undesired information (due to misunderstanding of needs, when done by expert users).

One important distinction from the IE systems mentioned earlier is that WICCAP is designed to deal with information at site-level, as opposed to page-level for most of other systems. Information presented within one page is usually limited. The efforts required to locate the target pages within a site are often not trivial. Therefore, the ability to model the web site as a whole is desirable since it gives users an overall view of the web site and, at the same time, allows them to pinch down to each individual piece of information without much difficulty. In addition, our proposed data model represents web sites from a logical point of view and completely separates the information from the physical location of web pages. It not only makes the data model intuitive to users, but also reduces, or even eliminates, the efforts that users previously had to spend following hyperlinks to reach a web page, because users are simply not aware of the actual physical location of the web pages when they are presented with the final customized views.

Another contribution of the WICCAP system is the rich set of tools that has been implemented to facilitate the various tasks required to create a user-customized view of a web site. Providing easy-to-use tools that reduce the technical requirement to a minimum is crucial for a system that targets ordinary home users. Each of the tools is designed to accomplish a specific goal that is in line with the individual step outlined earlier. The tools may be used by a single user or by several users who collaboratively create the desired views. The most important tools that have been implemented are: the *Mapping Wizard*, which helps to quickly generate a global view of a given web site; the *Network Extraction Agent*, that enables users to create personalized views of web sites; and the WIPAP, which allows a flexible way of presenting the views.

WICCAP Architecture

The WWW Information Collection, Collaging and Programming (WICCAP) system is designed to allow ordinary users to access information from the Web in a simple and efficient manner. The basic idea of the WICCAP system is to empower users to create their own views of web sites. In WICCAP, a personalized web view of a web site refers to the user's preference on, not only what contents they want to see from the web site, but also the way that the information is delivered to them (i.e. in what format and layout, and at what time and frequency).

To make it simple and manageable, the process of creating user views is divided into three steps: *modeling* the complete web site with its logical view, *customizing* the user views according to the defined model, and *defining* the way that the view is delivered to the user. The architecture of the WICCAP system is designed to accommodate these three steps by introducing a three-layer structure, with each layer corresponding to one of the three steps (Figure 1).

The separation of the whole process into three steps is important to the goal of enabling ordinary users to make full use of the system. In WICCAP, there are two groups of target users. The information modeling task, especially the sub-task of specifying the extraction details, which requires certain technical knowledge, is meant to be performed by expert users; whereas the view customization and presentation tasks can be invoked by ordinary users, whose main interests are to obtain information without worrying about the technical details. In this way, the system enables ordinary users to use the system easily while still maintaining high accuracy of the extracted information and high efficiency of the data model creation process.

Figure 1 shows the three main components of the WICCAP system: *Mapping Wizard*, *Network Extraction Agent* (NEA), and *Web Information Programmer And Player* (WIPAP). The Mapping Wizard takes in information of a particular web site and produces global logical views of the web site (or,

Figure 1: Architecture of the WICCAP System

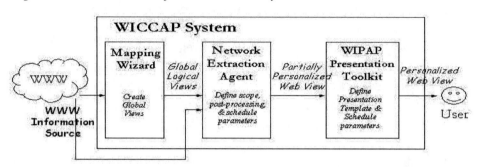

what we call mapping rules). Note that there might be more than one logical view for one web site if we look at the web site from different angles or with different purposes. With these logical views of the web site, the Network Extraction Agent component then allows users to customize these views based on their preferences, extracts the desired information from the web site, and performs post-processing on the extracted contents. Finally, the WIPAP Presentation Toolkit allows users to define the way they want the information to be delivered, and applies different presentation styles and templates to present the information in personalized ways.

Intermediate information, such as the global views and personalized web views, are stored using XML documents together with XML schemas that define their formats. The three components together form a channel through which information is transformed from the raw hyperlinked web pages into a personalized web view. The final output, Personalized Web View, could be in any format, ranging from static HTML pages to animated Flash clips, depending on the implementation of the last layer.

The tasks of the information modeling and extraction are explicitly separated into two modules: namely, Mapping Wizard and Network Extraction Agent. The Mapping Wizard is designed to be used by expert users who are knowledgeable enough to quickly and accurately derive the logical data models. NEA and WIPAP, on the other hand, are designed to be easy-to-use for general public users who only know what information they want to extract but not how. In this way, the system allows most users to extract the information they want, while freeing them from the tedious and difficult process of specifying the extraction rules. To put it simply, the WICCAP system separates the *what* and the *how*. It allows users to say *"To extract the headlines of the World News from BBC News Online"* instead of *"To extract the contents between* *the every <TD> and </TD> in the second TABLE in the web page http://news.bbc.co.uk/."*

Dividing the whole system into three layers allows for the reusability of intermediate results and for easy integration with other systems. The intermediate result of each module is stored as XML documents, along with well-defined XML Schemas. Applications with XML knowledge will be able to process these results easily. One example is that an information integration system can take the global logical views of multiple web sites (the output of the first layer) and integrate them to allow uniform access.

WICCAP **Data Model**

When extracting data from web sites, it would be useful to have a complete logical model representing the target web site, and to specify the target portions based on this model instead of on the actual web pages. The central idea of the WICCAP system is based on this. To accommodate this idea, we propose a data model called the WICCAP Data Model (WDM). This section provides a brief overview of WDM. A more detailed discussion can be found in Liu (2002).

In most current web information extraction systems, when defining a data model, users usually have to directly specify which portion of a web page within a web site is the target information. The separate pieces of target information are later organized in some manner to make them more readable and accessible. The data model produced in this manner is usually not intuitive to other users, especially to ordinary users who have no knowledge of the extraction process.

The WICCAP Data Model views information to be extracted from a different angle. It relates information from a web site in terms of a *commonly perceived logical structure*, instead of physical directory locations. As mentioned earlier, different pieces of information in a web site are usually related to each other through a certain logical structure that is hidden from the inter-linking of multiple web pages. This hidden logical structure is usually apparent to most users, and when users look at a web site, they tend to perceive the information as organized in this logical structure.

For instance, when a newspaper web site is mentioned, users generally think of a site that has a list of sections such as World News, Local News, and Sports News; each section may have subsections and/or a list of articles, each of which may have a number of information, including the title, the abstraction or summary, the article itself, and maybe other related articles. This hierarchy of information (Figure 2) is the commonly perceived structure of a newspaper web site, which most users are quite familiar with.

Figure 2: Logical View of BBC News Online

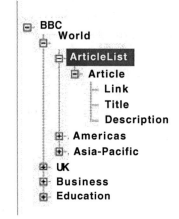

The logical model is essentially a tree, where each node represents a logical concept perceived by the user. The organization of individual tree nodes into a tree forms the logical skeleton of the target web site. This logical structure is what the users of the next layer in WICCAP (for information extraction) will be operating on. In order to allow extraction to occur, each tree node has a *Mapping* attribute that associates the node with the corresponding data in the actual web site. This *Mapping* attribute is, in fact, the extraction rule(s) that enable the extraction agent to perform the actual extraction of information.

An important feature of WDM is that it is able to model information not only in a single web page, but also in a set of web pages. This set of web pages may or may not have similar layout structures in terms of HTML syntax. It could be a small collection of several web pages located in the same directory, the whole web site, or pages across several web sites, so long as all pages together form an unified logical view. Typically, WDM will be used to model a web site or a self-contained portion of a large web site.

WDM Schema and Mapping Rule

The WICCAP Data Model consists of two main components: WDM schema and Mapping Rule. A WDM schema defines the possible structure that a mapping rule could have; while a mapping rule is an instance of the WDM schema, similar to the Object-Class relationship in the object-oriented concept.

W_DM schema was first designed to describe the logical structure of a category of web sites that exhibit similar logical views (Liu, 2002). We have extended and generalized the definition of W_DM schema to make it suitable for representing the logical view of any web site. Thus, there is now only one global W_DM schema that defines the syntax that all mapping rules should follow. The W_DM schema is defined using XML Schema (XML SCHEMA, 2003).

A *mapping rule* of a web site refers to a specific W_ICCAP Data Model that describes that particular web site's logical structure using the W_DM schema. It represents the logical structure of a particular web site and the detailed definition of the mapping between logical elements and the actual web pages for a specific web site. A mapping rule is defined as a normal XML document, with the corresponding XML schema as its definition. Since a mapping rule is an XML document, it is structured, interoperable, and easy to process.

WDM Elements

The elements defined by the W_ICCAP Data Model can be classified into two groups: elements for logical modeling purpose and elements for mapping purpose. The former refers to the elements constituting the logical tree, whereas the latter refers to the group of elements defining the mapping between the logical element and the actual web data to be extracted.

There are four elements for logical modeling: *Item*, *Record*, *Region*, and *Section*. These elements serve to represent some logical concepts in a W_ICCAP Data Model. But the actual semantic meaning of each element in different models depends on the web sites. This semantic meaning can be partially reflected by setting the values of attributes, such as "Name" or "Desc." Each element also has a Mapping attribute that describes how to link the element to the corresponding portion on the web site.

With all the four logical elements, the logical view of a web site can be composed. However, this is just a representation of the users' perception of the web site. It does not contain any instruction that allows the extraction of data to occur. To make it possible, we defined a set of elements dedicated for mapping from the logical tree node to the corresponding portion within the actual web site. These elements are the basic constructs of the extraction rules used in the W_ICCAP Data Model.

The W_DM elements for mapping purposes include: *Locator*, *Link*, *Form*, and *Mapping*.

A *Locator* is the fundamental element of the W_DM schema that locates a portion of information within a web page. A *Link* represents a hyperlink in the actual web page. It can be *Static* (a simple fixed URL), *Dynamic* (obtained by using a Locator), or *Form. Form* is defined as catering to a special category of HTML tags: FORM and other related HTML elements.

An example of a Locator is:

```
<Locator Type="ByPattern">
  <LocatorPattern>
    <BeginPattern Repeat="2">
        <![CDATA[ <TD> ]]>
    </BeginPattern>
    <EndPattern><![CDATA[ </TD> ]]></EndPattern>
  </LocatorPattern>
</Locator>
```

Applying this Locator to the following HTML segment:

```
<TD>something to be ignored</TD>
<TD>something to be extracted</TD>
```

the target information located by this Locator is the text "something to be extracted." Note that how the begin and end patterns and the "Repeat" attribute are combined to locate the information. "<![CDATA[" and]]>" are special symbols in XML syntax, and are used to enclose a text string that may contain special characters, such as "<" and ">".

A Link element such as the following:

```
<Link>
  <Locator Type="ByPattern">
    <LocatorPattern>
      <BeginPattern>
          <![CDATA[ <a href=" ]]>
      </BeginPattern>
      <EndPattern><![CDATA[ "> ]]></EndPattern>
    </LocatorPattern>
  </Locator>
</Link>
```

when applied to the following HTML segment:

```
<a href="some_webpage.htm">
```

will retrieve the text "some_web page.htm". Because the Locator is embedded within a Link, this text string will be treated as a hyperlink.

As shown above, the Locator allows one to navigate anywhere within a single page, while Link enables one to jump from one page to another. Mapping combines these two basic elements to enable navigation throughout the entire web resource. Mapping allows a W$_{DM}$ element to jump through arbitrary levels of links and, essentially, makes it possible to separate logical elements from the physical structure defined by the hierarchy of links.

Combining the definition of all the logical and mapping elements described, we obtain the complete W$_{DM}$ schema. All the mapping rules are instances of this W$_{DM}$ schema. In a mapping rule, every logical element, which is shown in the logical tree view as a node, should have a Mapping element as its attribute to indicate how to get to this node in the actual web site. When each logical element that constitutes a logical structure is augmented with a Mapping element, this logical structure is considered a complete mapping rule. This mapping rule can be used to extract of information.

Mapping Wizard

In W$_{ICCAP}$, users do not create the web views directly from the web site. Instead, they do it based on a global logical view of the web site. Therefore, the first step is to create global logical views of the target web site. There might be more than one such logical view that models the target web site, each from a different angle. But any of these logical views is supposed to be complete, in the sense that each view covers all the information that the users might want to see from one angle. This is why they are called global logical views.

The manual process of creating any kind of data model for web information sources, including the W$_{ICCAP}$ Data Model, is tedious and slow. This fact holds even for experienced users. Therefore, it is important that facilities are available to automate the process as much as possible. The Mapping Wizard is designed for this reason. Its goal is to facilitate and automate the process of producing a mapping rule for a given web site. To achieve this goal, we define a formal process of producing a mapping rule and provide tools to automate this process.

It should be noted that the Mapping Wizard is convenient for use by expert users with relevant knowledge about extracting information from HTML pages. However, some of these features could still be used by ordinary users, especially the step for constructing the basic logical structure, as will be shown later.

Formal Process

The proposed formal process of producing a mapping rule consists of four stages: Logical Structure Construction, Extraction Rule Definition, Mapping Rule Generation, and Testing and Finalization.

Logical Structure Construction. This is the process of building up the logical tree, e.g., the one shown in Figure 2. The user begins by supplying a starting address of a target web site, which is usually the home URL of a web site such as "http://news.bbc.co.uk." The basic logical organization, then, can be figured out either by using knowledge about the web site or by navigating throughout the web site. The details of how to map each node to the actual web pages will be done only in the second step.

This step can be performed by ordinary users because it does not involve the technical details of the extraction. Another reason is that ordinary users might have a better understanding of the web site's logical structure, which might lead to a more complete and intuitive logical view.

Extraction Rule Definition. At this step, the user supplies the Mapping Wizard with the necessary information to link the logical structure to the physical web site. This includes specifying the Mapping attributes of various main tree nodes.

Although, by using the assistant tools, as will be described later, the user may not need to touch the underlying mapping rule. Knowledge about basic HTML syntax is required in order to obtain an accurate data model. It is suggested that this task be performed by a user with sufficient technical knowledge, so that any fine-tuning can be done to improve the accuracy of the resulted mapping.

Mapping Rule Generation. When all the mapping information has been specified, the Mapping Wizard automatically generates the mapping rule according to the tree structure and all the tree nodes' properties. It validates all the information and produces the mapping rule according to the syntax defined in the WDM Schema.

Testing and Finalization. Once the mapping rule is generated, the Mapping Wizard performs the actual extraction using the generated mapping rule and shows the result to the user for verification. Debugging information will also be provided, if any error occurs.

If it is confirmed that the generated mapping rule indeed represents the logical structure of the web site, the user can finalize it. The finalized mapping rule, i.e., the global logical view, can either be put into a repository or can be delivered to the user of the Network Extraction Agent, the next layer in the WICCAP architecture.

GUI and Assistant Tools

This section briefly describes the GUI and the tools that are provided to aid the creation of mapping rules. A more detailed discussion of the tools provided by the Mapping Wizard can be found in Liu (2002a).

Figure 3: Mapping Wizard

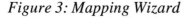
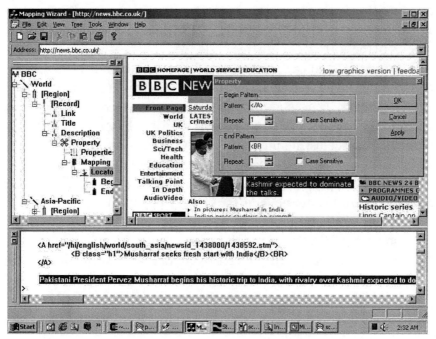

The Graphical User Interface of the Mapping Wizard is depicted in Figure 3. Based on this GUI, a set of assistant tools is provided to help to automate the process of generating a global logical view. These tools are the crucial components that make the Mapping Wizard practically useful.

We believe that, in practice, it is not possible to have a single tool that fully automates the whole logical view generation process; this process is usually complex and requires human intervention from time to time. In the Mapping Wizard, instead of trying to provide a single tool, a set of tools has been built to address different aspects of the problem. We identify the main difficulties and bottlenecks that slow down the overall process and develop tools to accelerate those parts, one by one. In this way, the efficiency of the overall process is improved, and the time required to generate a global logical view for a given web site is greatly reduced.

The `Pattern Searching Tool` is similar to the "Search" function that most text editors provide. It allows searching of certain text patterns, both within the HTML source and on the web browser view. The `Pattern Induction Tools` are the most useful ones among all the assistant tools provided. They are developed to release users from manually looking at the HTML source to figure out the patterns that enclose the target information. The user only needs to highlight the information; the Mapping Wizard will apply a brute force algorithm to derive the starting pattern and ending pattern that enclose this part of the HTML source. The result is stored in the Mapping property of the corresponding tree node.

The `Section Extraction Tool` is developed to find out all the possible Section nodes in the same level and derive the Mapping properties for them with a single click. The section extraction tool is supported by several heuristics that exploit common patterns for menus used in the HTML page. With the help of this tool, the user just highlights the area of the sections; the Mapping Wizard will automatically derive the section nodes and insert them into the logical tree. The `Structure Copier` is used to copy the structure of the constructed tree node Section to other tree nodes in the same level, assuming that the same sub-tree structure will fit into those nodes with little modification.

Combining all the assistant tools to create a mapping rule, the user first uses the `Section Extraction Tool` to generate all the Sections, uses the `Pattern Induction Tools` to identify various tree nodes under the first Section, then activates the Structure Copier to copy the structure of the first Section to other Sections. After some modification on the rest of the Sections, a mapping rule is generated.

Network Extraction Agent

Once a global logical view has been constructed using the Mapping Wizard, other users can create personalized views of the web site based on this global view. The Network Extraction Agent (NEA), as shown in Figure 4, is the component that is responsible for helping users customize the views and manage extraction jobs that retrieve data from a web site based on the personalized web views. The view created by the NEA is "customized" in the sense that users are allowed to choose, from within the global view, what to remove and what to keep, as well as how often the view should be refreshed with the actual web site. In addition, post-processing functions provided by the NEA give users more control over how the view should be "fine-tuned" to achieve exactly what the users want.

As mentioned earlier, this module is intended to be used by ordinary users. It has been designed to be simple, user-friendly, and easy-to-use, such that ordinary users who do not possess much technical knowledge of information extraction will be able to use it. Users are expected to use NEA together with WIPAP (discussed in next section) to produce the final personalized web view.

Unlike other similar systems, the extraction functionalities in WICCAP are separated from the extraction rules, i.e., mapping rules, and are placed in NEA.

Figure 4: Network Extraction Agent

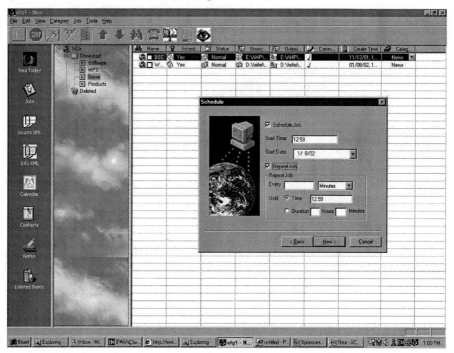

The NEA contains generic codes that are capable of understanding any mapping rule and performing extraction according to the definition in the rule. The advantage of having a separate extraction module is that it allows the data model to be defined in an open format for other applications to process, and makes it easy for the extraction module to incorporate extra functionalities such as the post-processing of extracted contents.

Information Extraction

The most important job of the NEA is to accurately extract information specified in the personalized web views. The NEA performs information extraction according to the definition in the mapping rule. For example, to extract the following Item:

```
<Item Type="Title" Description="This is the title of the
news">
    <Mapping>
      <Locator Type="ByPattern">
        <LocatorPattern>
          <BeginPattern>
            <![CDATA[ <B class="h*** ]]>
```

```
            </BeginPattern>
            <EndPattern> <![CDATA[ </B> ]]> </EndPattern>
          </LocatorPattern>
        </Locator>
      </Mapping>
    </Item>
```

from the following HTML segment:

```
<A  href="/sport3/worldcup2002/hi/matches_wallchart/
argentina_v_england/newsid_2028000/2028137.stm">
    <b class="h1">Eriksson: Best is still to come
    </B><BR>
    </A>
```

the N~EA~ extracts the target information by first locating the BeginPattern "<B class="h1">" and the EndPattern "</B>," and then extracting the text between these two patterns. Here, the "*" in the BeginPattern serves as a single character wildcard. The text enclosed by these two strings is the information to be extracted. The final extracted result is: `"Eriksson: Best is still to come"`.

Other parts of the mapping rule are executed in a similar manner. When the extracted information is specified as a Link, the N~EA~ interprets the extracted text as a URL and fetches the web page from this URL. The retrieved web page then becomes the current extraction target.

Web View Management

In the N~EA~, each personalized web view that the user created is also termed as an extraction job, since each view is for extracting information from the web site according to the definition of the view. The N~EA~ provides tools for creating and managing web views. It should be noted that the views created here are, by definition, not the final web views because they do not contain the information about how they should be presented to the users (defined in the next layer). Nevertheless, without loss of ambiguity, we still refer them as personalized web views, since they are actually views that are "customized" based on the global ones.

The user creates a new view by selecting a global view and by specifying what nodes are to be extracted. For example, from the BBC News Online web site, the user may indicate that he or she is only interested in retrieving Sports News and World News. Besides defining the scope of extraction, the user is also provided with options to specify how frequently the job should be performed. Based on these options, the Job Scheduling Engine will then decide when and how often to extract information.

An execution job can be started either manually, by the user, or automatically, by the Job Scheduling Engine. Once started, the execution job is under the control of the Job Execution Engine, which will extract the information according to the mapping properties specified in the mapping rule. The Job Execution Engine manages jobs in a multi-threaded mode, such that multiple extraction jobs can be executed concurrently and performance can be maximized.

Usually, for each user, there is more than one personalized web view, since the user is likely to be interested in information from multiple sources. Even for a global view of the same web site, different web views may be created by supplying different extraction scope or scheduling properties. In NEA, all extraction jobs are assigned with categories by users. These categories are further organized into a hierarchy to allow easy navigation of categories and jobs. The category hierarchy and details of jobs are displayed in a Windows Explorer-like User Interface (see Figure 4), so that it looks familiar to most Microsoft Windows users.

Post-Processing

Merely extracting the information from the original web site may not satisfy the user, since he or she may not be interested in all the information extracted. The NEA provides post-processing functionalities to allow further constraints to be placed on the created views. The constraints added to the views constitute parts of the final personalized web views.

Filtering

NEA allows the views constructed from the extraction results to be filtered based on simple text matching of certain attributes. The attributes to be searched are identified from the WDM schema and selected by the user. The user specifies the search conditions, such as "Keep only news articles with the word 'World Cup' in the title or description" or "Remove all product information from Dell which have a value of more than $1,000 in the price attribute." Filtering conditions are specified using the Filter Dialogs. The current implementation uses a simple filter which keeps only information that contains the specified keywords in the specific field.

Incremental Updating

Most users are used to receiving notification of new emails. The same expectation applies here, where users may expect to see only "new" news in a newspaper web site or to only be informed about the newly published papers in digital libraries. To provide such a feature, the NEA is designed with an incremental updating ability. Information is first extracted and stored in a temporary work space, and then compared with the previous extraction result to determine whether the content is new. The user is notified only if the information on the web site has been updated. The whole process appears to the user as if the content is incrementally updated according to changes on the web site.

Consolidation

Sometimes, information from multiple sources describes similar or the same things. This is especially true if the user has web views for both the Washington Post and CNN web sites, as the headline news will likely be the same. In this situation, the user may instruct the NEA that these two views are similar and instruct it to combine them to form an integrated one, so that when information in the two views is detected to be similar, it is presented as one piece instead of two. This is called Consolidation. It relies on similarity detection algorithms to determine whether two key attributes are similar. The current algorithm implemented uses Latent Semantic Indexing (Berry, 1995) to determine the similarity between two items.

Supporting HTML Form Query

The WICCAP Data Model has defined a special group of elements to cater to HTML Form and other related HTML tags. When the NEA encounters such elements in the mapping rule, it will dynamically construct a dialog box at runtime according to the attributes in the mapping rule. Figure 5 shows the search form used in a BBC News Advanced Search. At the top is the actual HTML web page that contains the form, and the bottom is the constructed form dialog in NEA. Each HTML form element (e.g., Select, TextField) has a corresponding counterpart in the constructed dialog. The layout of elements in the dynamic dialog may not be exactly the same as that of the web page, but all the visible elements will be arranged in a manner that looks similar to the original page.

The user's input to the dynamic dialog box is used to construct the complete query string by combining the action URL of the original HTML Form

Figure 5: Dynamic Construction of Form

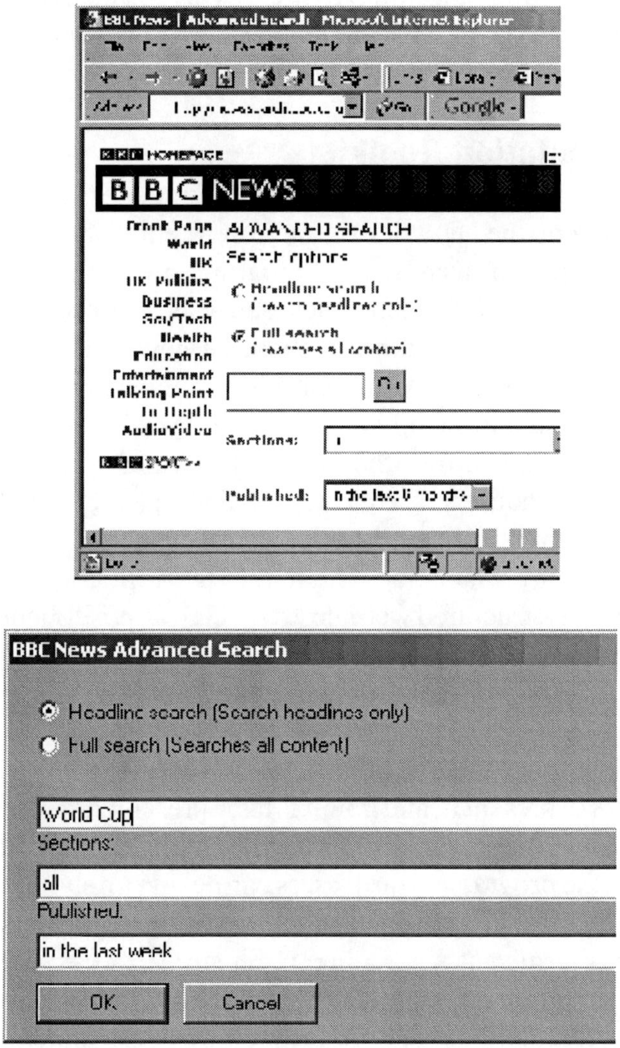

and the name and value pairs of all input elements. This URL is then posted to the remote web server, and the returned web page is processed like other normal static web pages. The extraction process is then continued.

This ability to directly handle Forms is important for a web IE system due to the extensive use of Forms in web sites. Typical usages of Forms include search functions of web sites and user login authentication. Without the direct support of HTML Forms, it might be very difficult to retrieve information from these sites. Support of Form is also one of the characteristics that distinguishes the WICCAP system from other similar systems, as currently only few of the related systems (see Atzeni, 1997; Sahuguet, 2001) take Forms into consideration or directly incorporate them into their systems.

WIPAP Presentation Toolkit

The tool of Web Information Player and Programmer (WIPAP) deals with the views created by the Network Extraction Agent. Using the WIPAP, the views are further customized by incorporating information about how to present the views (presentation templates) and when to present them (presentation schedule). With this added information, the views are now considered as the final personalized web views that can be consumed by the users.

The WIPAP presentation toolkit is the most flexible layer in the WICCAP architecture. With the views from the previous layer, there might be many ways of presenting them to the users. Therefore, potentially many different implementations of the third layer might be possible, each of them focusing on a different aspect of information presentation. This may range from a single web page, to a well-organized re-structured web site, to special purpose client-side applications. In our current implementation, the third layer has been implemented as a Windows application, with the aim of presenting the views in an animated and interesting manner.

The current implementation of WIPAP allows users to control *what* is to be presented, *when* to present it, and *how* it is to be presented. This information is incorporated into the personalized web view with the help of the Program Wizard. Using the program wizard, users can design a detailed schedule of how each of the views should be presented, and in what order and frequency. This schedule is termed as a Presentation Program because it is rather similar to a TV program schedule. The role of the program wizard is to guide users to create presentation programs in a step-by-step manner. The Presentation Engine then takes the defined presentation program and executes it according to the schedule specified in the program.

Note that in this layer, a view is associated with a frequency of how often it should be presented to the user. As discussed earlier, this frequency is different from the one defined in the NEA. It only refers to the user's preference of how often he or she wants to see the view, whereas the one defined earlier determines how often the view should be updated from the remote web site.

In the current implementation, a presentation program can contain more than one view, but at any point in time, only one view will be presented. In future implementations, presenting multiple views at the same time might be possible

Figure 6: WIPAP System

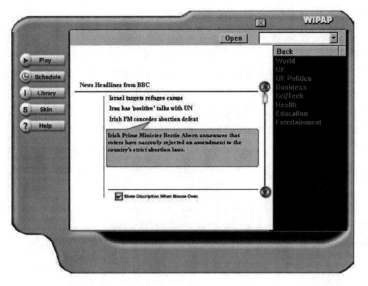

if efficient ways of designing the layout of different views are provided. This will indirectly help to achieve integration among multiple web site views to a certain extent.

Macromedia Flash is used in WIPAP to display information. Flash is chosen because of its ability to display content in a nice, animated and appealing way. Several generic Flash container clips are implemented using ActionScript, the scripting language of Flash. These clips are called `Presentation Templates`. Different presentation styles are associated with different templates, and these templates are capable of taking in the information to be presented from the XML document at runtime and displaying it according to the specified style. Users will be able to choose a presentation template from the list. The `Template Manager` allows more templates to be incorporated at runtime, making the system more extensible.

Besides the implementation of a desktop application, alternative implementations on the web platform and PDAs are currently being designed and developed.

Figure 6 is a snapshot of the WIPAP system at runtime. The design criteria of WIPAP's GUI is quite similar to that of NEA, which is to make the application appear user-friendly and simple to use for ordinary users. The appearance of WIPAP looks like the Windows Media Player. However, this is just one of skins available in WIPAP. Users are allowed to change this appearance by selecting another skin.

Summary of WICCAP

In this section, we introduce a novel system for enabling ordinary end-users to create their preferred views of web sites. The proposed WICCAP system lets users perform this task in three steps: creating global logical views of web sites, customizing the global views, and specifying the way the views will be displayed. Tools have been implemented to automate and facilitate the three steps. We have also proposed a data model that allows the information from the Web to be viewed from its logical structure.

The three steps are decoupled, and each step can be performed by a user that is most suitable for the job, i.e., expert users specify the technical details, while end-users indicate the preference on the views. With this strategy, we are able to achieve our goal of empowering ordinary users to create their personalized views of web sites in a simple and efficient way.

Other future work includes maintenance of views in the face of change. This may involve change detection at the source web site and change propagation to individual personalized web views. Support for the integration of views across multiple web sites is another important area to work on. We plan to allow for the creation of views that integrate global views from several web sites. We are also looking at alternate implementations of the last layer for presenting the extracted information in different ways, and to different platforms and devices.

CONCLUSION

In this chapter, we have discussed the important issues involved in designing Information Systems that extract data from the Web. As we have seen, most of the issues have not been fully explored by existing literatures, and there is still room for improvement or for brand new algorithms and systems to appear. Among them, wrapper maintenance is of particular importance. The main challenges are how to accurately detect the failure of a wrapper, and how to make use of the old extraction rules and extracted data to quickly re-derive a new wrapper. Another related problem is how to derive the wrapper of a web source, given the wrapper of a similar web source. This problem is also important because web sites of the same category, for example, all online newspaper web sites, usually exhibit similar logical structures and even similar extraction clues.

We have also described the WICCAP system as a web IE system that enables users to create personalized web views. WICCAP takes a three-layer approach to turn the difficult problem of web information extraction into something that can be performed by ordinary users. Web views are, in fact, wrappers with personalization of the content to be extracted, the schedule of extraction, and the modes and schedule of information presentation. The step-by-step wizard for creating web views releases users from the technical details, and helps users overcome the information overload problem.

We believe that the issues of web IE systems are challenging enough to make web information extraction remain an important research area under the topic of Web Information Systems.

REFERENCES

Adelberg, B. (1998). NoDoSE - A tool for semi-automatically extracting semi-structured data from text documents. In *Proceedings of the 1998 ACM SIGMOD International Conference on Management of Data,* Seattle, Washington, June 1998 (pp. 283-294).

Appelt, D. E. & Israel, D. (1999). *Introduction to information extraction technology.* Tutorial of the 16th International Joint Conference on Artificial Intelligence (IJCAI-99).

Ashish, N. & Knoblock, C. A. (1997). Semi-automatic wrapper generation for Internet information sources. *ACM SIGMOD Record,* 26(4), 8-15.

Atzeni, P., Mecca, G., & Merialdo, P. (1997). To weave the web. In *Proceedings of the international conference on very large data bases (VLDB 1997),* Athens, Greece, August 1997 (pp. 206-215).

Baumgartner, R., Flesca, S. & Gottlob, G. (2001). Visual web information extraction with Lixto. In *Proceedings of the 27th International Conference on Very Large Data Bases (VLDB 2001),* Rome, Italy, September 2001 (pp. 119-128).

Berry, M. W., Dumais, S. T., & Letsche, T. A. (1995, December). Computational methods for intelligent information access. *Proceedings of Supercomputing '95,* San Diego, California.

Bright, L., Gruser, J. R., Raschid, L., & Vidal, M. E. (1999). A wrapper generation toolkit to specify and construct wrappers for web accessible data sources (Web-Sources). *International Journal of Computer Systems Science and Engineering,* 14(2), 83-97.

Cali, M. E. & Mooney, R. J. (1998). Relational learning of pattern-match rules for information extraction. *Working Notes of the AAAI Spring Symposium on Applying Machine Learning to Discourse Processing* (pp. 6-11). Menlo Park, CA: AAAI Press.

Chang, C. H. & Lui, S. C. (2001). IEPAD: Information extraction based on pattern discovery. In *Proceedings of the 10th International World Wide Web Conference (WWW 10),* Hong Kong, China, May 1-5, 2001 (pp. 681-688). New York: ACM Press.

Chidlovskii, B., Ragetli, J., & Rijke, M. D. (2000). Wrapper generation via grammar induction. In *Proceedings of the 11th European Conference on Machine Learning,* Barcelona, Spain, May 31-June 2, 2000 (Vol. 1810, pp. 96-108). Berlin: Springer-Verlag.

Cohen, W. & Jensen, L. (2001, August). A structured wrapper induction system for extracting information from semi-structured documents. *Proceedings of the International Joint Conference on Artificial Intelligence (IJCAI-2001) Workshop on Adaptive Text Extraction and Mining,* Seattle, Washington.

Cohen, W. W. (1999). Recognizing structure in web pages using similarity queries. In *Proceedings of the 16th National Conference on Artificial Intelligence and the 11th Conference on Innovative Applications of Artificial Intelligence (AAAI/IAAI),* Orlando, Florida, July 18-22, 1999 (pp. 59-66).

Crescenzi, V. & Mecca, G. (1998). Grammars have exceptions. *Information Systems,* 23(8), 539-565.

Crescenzi, V., Mecca, G., & Merialdo, P. (2001). RoadRunner: Towards automatic data extraction from large web sites. In *Proceedings of the 27th International Conference on Very Large Data Bases (VLDB 2001),* Rome, Italy, September 2001 (pp. 109-118).

Embley, D. et al. (1999). Conceptual-model-based data extraction from multiple record web pages. *Data and Knowledge Engineering,* 31(3), 227-251.

Embley, D., Jiang, S., & Ng, Y. (1999). Record-boundary discovery in web documents. In *Proceedings of the ACM SIGMOD International Conference on Management of Data* (pp. 467-478).

Florescu, D., Levy, A. Y., & Mendelzon, A. O. (1998). Database techniques for the world wide web: A survey. *SIGMOD Record,* 27(3), 59-74.

Freitag, D. (1998). Multistrategy learning for information extraction. In *Proceedings of the 15th International Conference on Machine Learning* (pp. 161-169). San Francisco, CA: Morgan Kaufmann.

Freitag, D. & Kushmerick, N. (2000). Boosted wrapper induction. In *AAAI/IAAI,* 577-583).

Golgher, P. B., Silva, A. S. D., Laender, A. H. F., & Ribeiro-Neto, B. A. (2001). Bootstrapping for example-based data extraction. In *Proceed-*

*ings of the 2001 ACM CIKM International Conference on Informa-
tion and Knowledge Management,* Atlanta, Georgia, November 5-10,
2001 (pp. 371-378). New York: ACM Press.

Gupta, A., Harinarayan, V., & Rajaraman, A. (1998). Virtual database
technology. *Proceedings of the 14th International Conference on
Data Engineering,* Orlando, Florida, February 23-27, 1998.

Hammer, J., Molina, H. G., Cho, J., Crespo, A., & Aranha, R. (1997).
Extracting semistructured information from the web. In *Proceedings of
the Workshop on Management of Semistructured Data,* Tucson,
Arizona, May 1997 (pp. 18-25).

Hammer, J., Molina, H.G., Nestorov, S., Yerneni, S., Breunig, M., &
Vassalos, V. (1997). Template-based wrappers in the TSIMMIS system. In *Proceedings of the 1997 ACM SIGMOD International Conference on Management of Data,* Tucson, Arizona, May 1997 (pp. 532-
535).

Hsu, C. N. & Dung, M. T. (1998). Generating finite-state transducers for
semistructured data extraction from the web. *Information Systems,*
23(8), 521-538.

Kistler, T. & Marais, H. (1998). WebL - a programming language for the web.
In *Proceedings of WWW7* (Vol. 30, 1-7) of Computer Networks, pp.
259-270).

Kosala, R. & Blockeel, H. (2000). Instance-based wrapper induction. In
*Proceedings of the 10th Belgium-Dutch Conference on Machine
Learning* (pp. 61-68).

Kosala, R., Bussche, J. V. D., Bruynooghe, M., & Blockeel, H. (2002).
Information extraction in structured documents using tree automata
induction. In *Proceedings of the 6th European conference (PKDD-02)*
(LNCS, pp. 299-310).

Kuhlins, S. & Tredwell, R. (2002, September). Toolkits for generating
wrappers — A survey of software toolkits for automated data extraction
from websites. *Proceedings of Net.ObjectsDays 2002.*

Kushmerick, N. (1999). Gleaning the web. *IEEE Intelligent Systems,* 14(2),
20-22.

Kushmerick, N. (1999). Regression testing for wrapper maintenance. In
*Proceedings of the 16th National Conference on Artificial Intelli-
gence and the 11th Conference on Innovative Applications of Artificial Intelligence (AAAI/IAAI),* Orlando, Florida, July 18-22, 1999 (pp.
74-79).

Kushmerick, N. (2000). Wrapper induction: Efficiency and expressiveness. *Artificial Intelligence*, 118(1-2), 15-68.

Kushmerick, N. (2000). Wrapper verification. *Proceedings of World Wide Web*, 3(2), 79-94.

Laender, A. H. F., Ribeiro-Neto, B. A., & Silva A. S. D. (2002). DEByE — Data extraction by example. *Data and Knowledge Engineering*, 40(2), 121-154.

Laender, A. H. F., Ribeiro-Neto, B. A., Silva, A. S. D., & Teixeira, J. S. (2002). A brief survey of web data extraction tools. *ACM SIGMOD Record*, 31(2), 84-93.

Lerman, K., Knoblock, C., & Minton, S. (2003). Wrapper maintenance: A machine learning approach. *Journal of Artificial Intelligence Research, 18*, 149-181.

Li, F. F., Liu, Z. H., Huang, Y. F., & Ng, W. K. (2001). An information concierge for the web. In *Proceedings of the 1st International Workshop on Internet Bots: Systems and Applications (INBOSA 2001)* and the *12th International Conference on Database and Expert System Applications (DEXA 2001),* Munich, Germany, September 2001 (pp. 672-676).

Lin, S. H. & Ho, J. M. (2002). Discovering informative content blocks from web documents. *Proceedings of the International Conference on Knowledge Discovery and Data Mining (SIGKDD-02)*.

Liu, Z., Li, F., & Ng, W. K. (2002). Wiccap data model: Mapping physical websites to logical views. In *Proceedings of the 21st International Conference on Conceptual Modelling (ER 2002),* Tempere, Finland, October 2002 (pp. 120-134).

Liu, Z., Li, F., Ng, W. K., & Lim, E. P. (2002). A visual tool for building logical data models of websites. In *Proceedings of the 4th ACM CIKM International Workshop on Web Information and Data Management (WIDM 2002),* McLean, Virginia, November 2002 (pp. 92-95).

Liu, L., Pu, C., & Han, W. (2000). XWRAP: An XML-enabled wrapper construction system for web information sources. In *Proceedings of the 16th International Conference on Data Engineering (ICDE 2000),* San Diego, California, February 2000 (pp. 611-621).

May, W., Himmer̈oder, R., Lausen, G., & Lud̈ascher, B. (1999). A unified framework for wrapping, mediating and restructuring information from the web. In *Advances in Conceptual Modeling: ER '99 Workshops on Evolution and Change in Data Management, Reverse Engineering in Information Systems, and the World Wide Web and Conceptual*

Modeling, Paris, France, November 15-18 1999 (Vol. 1727 of LNCS, pp. 307-320). Berlin: Springer-Verlag.

Mecca, G. & Atzeni, P. (1999). Cut and Paste. *Journal of Computer and System Sciences*, 58(3), 453-482.

Mecca, G., Atzeni, P., Masci, A., Merialdo, P., & Sindoni, G. (1998). The araneus web-base management system. In *Proceedings of the SIGMOD conference*, (pp. 544-546).

Morrison, D. R. (1968). Patricia - practical algorithm to retrieve information coded in alphanumeric. *Journal of the ACM*, 15(4), 514-534.

Muslea, I. (1998). *Extraction patterns: From information extraction to wrapper generation.* Los Angeles, CA: University of Southern California, Information Sciences Institute. (Technical Report).

Muslea, I. (1999). Extraction patterns for information extraction tasks: A survey. In *Proceedings of the Workshop on Machine Learning for Information Extraction,* Orlando, Florida, July 1999 (pp. 1-6).

Muslea, I., Minton, S., & Knoblock, C. A. (1999). A hierarchical approach to wrapper induction. In *Proceedings of the 3rd International Conference on Autonomous Agents (Agents'99),* Seattle, Washington (pp. 190-197). New York: ACM Press.

Muslea, I., Minton, S., & Knoblock, C.A. (2001). Hierarchical wrapper induction for semi-structured information sources. *Autonomous Agents and Multi-agent Systems*, 4(1/2), 93-114.

Rajaraman, A. & Ullman, J. D. (2001). Querying websites using compact skeletons. In *Proceedings of the 20th ACM SIGACT-SIGMOD-SIGART Symposium on Principles of Database Systems (PODS)*, Santa Barbara, California, May 21-23, 2001. New York: ACM Press.

Ribeiro-Neto, B. A., Laender, A. H. F., & Silva, A. S. D. (1999). Extracting semi-structured data through examples. *Proceedings of the 1999 ACM International Conference on Information and Knowledge Management (CIKM)* (pp. 94-101). New York: ACM Press.

Sahuguet, A. & Azavant, F. (2001). Building intelligent web applications using lightweight wrappers. *Data and Knowledge Engineering,* 36(3), 283-316.

Seymore, K., McCallum, A., & Rosenfeld, R. (1999). *Learning hidden Markov model structure for information extraction.* AAAI'99 Workshop on Machine Learning for Information Extraction.

Soderland, S. (1997). Learning to extract text-based information from the world wide web. In *Proceedings of Knowledge Discovery and Data Mining* (pp. 251-254).

Soderland, S. (1999). Learning information extraction rules for semi-structured and free text. *Machine Learning*, 34(1/3), 233-272.

Soderland, S., Fisher, D., Aseltine, J., & Lehnert, W. (1995). CRYSTAL: Inducing a conceptual dictionary. In *Proceedings of the 14th International Joint Conference on Artificial Intelligence (IJCAI)* (pp. 1314-1319). San Francisco, CA: Morgan Kaufmann.

Thomas, B. (1999). Anti-unification based learning of t-wrappers for information extraction. *Proceedings of the Workshop on Machine Learning for Information Extraction.*

Thomas, B. (2000). Token-templates and logic programs for intelligent web search. *Journal of Intelligent Information Systems*, 14(2-3), 41-261.

Wang, Y. L., Hu, J. Y., & Ramakrishnan, I. V. (2002). A machine learning based approach for table detection on the web. In *Proceedings of the 11th International World Wide Web Conference (WWW2002)*, Honolulu, Hawaii, May 7-11, 2002. New York: ACM Press.

XML Schema. Retrieved 2003 from: http://www.w3.org/XML/Schema/.

Yang, Y. M., Slattery, S., & Ghani, R. (2002). A study of approaches to hypertext categorization. *Journal of Intelligent Information Systems*, 18(2-3), 219-241.

ENDNOTES

[1]   Web Information Collection, Collaging and Programming (Wiccap) is an on-going project in CAIS, NTU. Presently, it is not publicly available.

[2]   http://my.yahoo.com

[3]   http://www.amazon.com

SECTION IV

WEB INFORMATION MINING

Chapter VIII

A Knowledge-Based Web Information System for the Fusion of Distributed Classifiers

Grigorios Tsoumakas, Aristotle University of Thessaloniki, Greece

Nick Bassiliades, Aristotle University of Thessaloniki, Greece

Ioannis Vlahavas, Aristotle University of Thessaloniki, Greece

ABSTRACT

This chapter presents the design and development of WebDisC, a knowledge-based web information system for the fusion of classifiers induced at geographically distributed databases. The main features of our system are: (i) a declarative rule language for classifier selection that allows the combination of syntactically heterogeneous distributed classifiers; (ii) a variety of standard methods for fusing the output of distributed classifiers; (iii) a new approach for clustering classifiers in order to deal with the semantic heterogeneity of distributed classifiers, detect their interesting similarities and differences, and enhance their fusion; and (iv) an architecture based on the Web services paradigm that utilizes the open and scalable standards of XML and SOAP.

INTRODUCTION

Recently, the enormous technological progress on acquiring and storing data in a digital format has led to the accumulation of significant amounts of personal, business and scientific data. Advances in network technologies and the Internet have led to the availability of much of these data online. Personal text, image, audio and video files are today accessible through web pages, peer-to-peer systems, and FTP archives. Businesses have transferred their enterprise systems online, providing their customers information and support of excellent quality in a low-cost manner. Huge scientific data from physics experiments, astronomical instruments, and DNA research are being stored today in server farms and data grids, while, at the same time, software technology for their online access and integration is being developed. Today, the grand challenge of Machine Learning, Knowledge Discovery, and Data Mining scientists is to analyze this distributed information avalanche in order to extract useful knowledge.

An important problem toward this challenge is that it is often unrealistic to collect geographically distributed data for centralized processing. The necessary central storage capacity might not be affordable, or the necessary bandwidth to efficiently transmit the data to a single place might not be available. In addition, there are privacy issues preventing sensitive data (e.g., medical, financial) from being transferred from their storage site.

Another important issue is the syntactic and semantic heterogeneity of data belonging to different information systems. The schemas of distributed databases might differ, making the fusion of distributed models a complex task. Even in a case where the schemas match, semantic differences must also be considered. Real-world, inherently distributed data have an intrinsic data skewness property. For example, data related to a disease from hospitals around the world might have varying distributions due to different nutrition habits, climate and quality of life. The same is true for buying patterns identified in supermarkets at different regions of a country.

Finally, systems that learn and combine knowledge from distributed data must be developed using open and extensible technology standards. They must be able to communicate with clients developed in any programming language and platform. Inter-operability and extensibility are of primal importance for the development of scalable software systems for distributed learning.

The main objective of this chapter is the design and development of WebDisC, a knowledge-based Web information system for the fusion of classifiers induced at geographically distributed databases. Its main features are: (i) a declarative rule language for classifier selection that allows the combination of syntactically heterogeneous distributed classifiers; (ii) a variety of standard methods for fusing the output of distributed classifiers; (iii) a new approach for clustering classifiers in order to deal with the semantic heterogeneity of distributed classifiers, detect their interesting similarities and differences, and enhance their fusion; and (iv) an architecture based on the Web services paradigm that utilizes the open and scalable standards of XML and SOAP.

In the rest of this chapter, we initially present the technologies that constitute the Web services framework and are at the core of the WebDisC system. We then give background information on classification, classifier fusion, and related work on distributed classifier systems. Subsequently, we describe the architecture, main functionality, and user interface of the WebDisC system, along with the X-DEVICE component of the system and the proposed classifier clustering approach. Finally, we conclude this work and pose future research directions.

WEB SERVICES

A Web service is a software system, identified by a URI, whose public interfaces and bindings are defined and described using XML. Its definition can be discovered by other software systems. These systems may then interact with the Web service in a manner prescribed by its definition, using XML-based messages conveyed by Internet protocols (Champion et al., 2002).

The use of the Web services paradigm is expanding rapidly to provide a systematic and extensible framework for application-to-application (A2A) interaction, built on top of existing Web protocols and based on open XML standards. Web services aim to simplify the process of distributed computing by defining a standardized mechanism to describe, locate, and communicate with online software systems. Essentially, each application becomes an accessible Web service component that is described using open standards.

The basic architecture of Web services includes technologies capable of:
- Exchanging messages.
- Describing Web services.
- Publishing and discovering Web service descriptions.

Exchanging Messages

The standard protocol for communication among Web services is the Simple Object Access Protocol (SOAP) (Box et al., 2000). SOAP is a simple and lightweight XML-based mechanism for creating structured data packages that can be exchanged between network applications. SOAP consists of four fundamental components: an envelope that defines a framework for describing message structure; a set of encoding rules for expressing instances of application-defined data types; a convention for representing remote procedure calls and responses; and a set of rules for using SOAP with HTTP. SOAP can be used with a variety of network protocols, such as HTTP, SMTP, FTP, RMI/IIOP, or a proprietary messaging protocol.

SOAP is currently the de facto standard for XML messaging for a number of reasons. First, SOAP is relatively simple, defining a thin layer that builds on top of existing network technologies, such as HTTP, that are already broadly implemented. Second, SOAP is flexible and extensible in that, rather than trying to solve all of the various issues developers may face when constructing Web services, it provides an extensible, composable framework that allows solutions to be incrementally applied as needed. Thirdly, SOAP is based on XML. Finally, SOAP enjoys broad industry and developer community support.

SOAP defines four XML elements:

- *env:Envelope* is the root of the SOAP request. At the minimum, it defines the SOAP namespace. It may define additional namespaces.
- *env:Header* contains auxiliary information as SOAP blocks, such as authentication, routing information, or transaction identifier. The header is optional.
- *env:Body* contains one or more SOAP blocks. An example would be a SOAP block for RPC call. The body is mandatory and it must appear after the header.
- *env:Fault* is a special block that indicates protocol-level errors. If present, it must appear in the body.

SOAP is used in WebDisC for the exchange of messages between the Portal and the distributed classifiers. Examples of those messages can be found in Figures 9, 10, and 11.

Describing Web Services

The standard language for formally describing Web services is Web Services Description Language (WSDL). WSDL (Chinnici et al., 2002) is an XML document format for describing Web services as a set of endpoints operating on messages containing either document-oriented or procedure-oriented (RPC) messages. The operations and messages are described abstractly and then bound to a concrete network protocol and message format to

Figure 1: WSDL Service Implementation and Interface Definitions

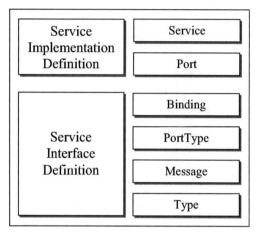

define an endpoint. Related concrete endpoints may be combined into services. WSDL is sufficiently extensible to allow description of endpoints and their messages regardless of what message formats or network protocols are used to communicate. A complete WSDL definition of a service comprises a service interface definition and a service implementation definition, as depicted in Figure 1.

A service interface definition is an abstract or reusable service definition that may be instantiated and referenced by multiple service implementation definitions. A service interface definition can be thought of as an IDL (Interface Definition Language), Java interface, or Web service type. This allows common industry standard service types to be defined and implemented by multiple service implementers.

In WSDL, the service interface contains elements that comprise the reusable portion of the service description: *binding*, *portType*, *message*, and *type* elements. In the *portType* element, the operations of the Web service are defined. The operations define what XML messages can appear in the input, output, and fault data flows. The *message* element specifies which XML data types constitute various parts of a message. The *message* element is used to define the abstract content of messages that comprise an operation. The use of complex data types within the message is described in the *type* element. The *binding* element describes the protocol, data format, security and other attributes for a particular service interface (*portType*).

The service implementation definition describes how a particular service interface is implemented by a given service provider. It also describes its location so that a requester can interact with it. In WSDL, a Web service is modeled as a *service* element. A *service* element contains a collection of *port* elements. A port associates an endpoint (e.g., a network address location) with a *binding* element from a service interface definition.

Examples of WSDL definitions for all WebDisC Web services can be found in WebDisC (2003).

Publishing and Discovering Web Service Descriptions

While there are some established standards for Web service description and communication, the publishing and discovery of Web services can be implemented with a range of solutions. Any action that makes a WSDL document available to a requestor, at any stage of the service requestor's lifecycle, qualifies as service publication. In the same way, any mechanism that allows the service requestor to gain access to the service description and make it available to the application at runtime qualifies as service discovery.

The simplest case of publishing a Web service is a direct publish. This means that the service provider sends the service description directly to the service requestor. This can be accomplished using an email attachment, an FTP site, or even a CDROM distribution. Slightly more dynamic publication uses Web Services Inspection Language (WSIL) (Brittenham, 2001). WSIL defines a simple HTTP GET mechanism to retrieve Web services descriptions from a given URL. Another means of publishing service descriptions available to Web services is through a Universal Description, Discovery and Integration (UDDI) registry (Bellwood et al., 2002). There are several types of UDDI registries that may be used, depending on the scope of the domain of Web services published to it. When publishing a Web service description to a UDDI registry, complete business context and well thought out taxonomies are essential if the service is to be found by its potential consumers.

The X-DEVICE system (Bassiliades et al., 2003a) is used in WebDisC for registering and discovering Web services for distributed classification. More details are given later in the chapter.

CLASSIFIER FUSION: METHODS AND SYSTEMS

This section introduces the learning task of classification, the rationale for classifier fusion, established methods, and existing systems that perform classifier fusion.

Classification

Supervised classification is one of the most common machine learning and data mining tasks (Saitta, 2000). It deals with the problem of identifying interesting regularities between a number of independent variables and a target or dependent categorical variable in a given data set. For example, given a set of training instances $(x_{i1}, x_{i2}, ..., x_{ik}, y_i)$, $i = 1..N$, the task is to compute a classifier, or model, or a concept that approximates an unknown function $y=f(x)$, that correctly labels any instance drawn from the same source as the training set.

There exist many ways to represent a classification model and many more algorithms to generate it. Typical classifier learning approaches include concept learning, neural networks, decision trees, rule learning, Bayesian learning, and instance-based learning. All these approaches construct models that share the common ability to classify previously unknown instances of a domain based on instances of the same domain that were used for their training.

The output of a classifier can be: (i) the label of a class; (ii) rankings for all the classes; and (iii) measures of uncertainty, such as belief, confidence, probability, possibility, plausibility, or other for each class. Consider, for example, a domain for predicting tomorrow's weather with three possible classes: sunny, windy, and rainy. The corresponding output for the three types of classifiers could be: (i) sunny; (ii) 1 - sunny, 2 - windy, 3 - rainy; and (iii) 0.8 - sunny, 0.5 - windy, 0.1 - rainy. Classifiers that output class labels are commonly called hard classifiers, while classifiers that output measures of uncertainty are called distribution/soft classifiers. Classifiers that output rankings are not so common in the machine learning literature.

Another distinction among classifiers is whether they are homogeneous or heterogeneous. There are two forms of classifier heterogeneity. According to the first, two classifiers are considered homogeneous if they are created using the same learning algorithm. For example, a naive Bayes classifier and a decision list are heterogeneous classifiers, while two neural networks are homogeneous classifiers. Another form of heterogeneity is based on the schema of the training data of the two classifiers. For example, two decision trees both predict tomorrow's weather, but one is based on temperature and wind speed, while the other is based on atmospheric pressure and humidity. Both are considered heterogeneous classifiers. In this chapter, the term heterogeneity will be used with the latter meaning.

Fusion Methods

Classifier Fusion has been a very active field of research in the recent years. It was used for improving the classification accuracy of pattern recognition systems because single classification learning algorithms were approaching their limits. It was also used as a method for scaling up data mining to very large databases through combining classifiers trained in parallel from different parts of the database. Finally, it was used for learning from geographically distributed databases, where bandwidth or privacy constraints forbid the gathering of data in a single place, through the fusion of locally learned classification models.

There are two general groups of Classifier Fusion methods. The first group encompasses methods that combine the outputs of the classifiers, while the second group deals with the structure of the multiple classifier system. We will focus on the former group of methods, as WebDisC implements some of them and provides the necessary infrastructure for implementing the rest.

Methods that fuse classifier outputs can be further categorized based on two properties. The first is the classifier output type on which they can operate, and the second is the need for training data for the fusion process. According to these, Table 1 presents the main methods. WebDisC currently implements the simple methods of Majority Voting and the Sum, Product, Min, Max, and Median rules.

Majority Voting works for both hard and distribution classifiers. In the latter case, the class with the maximum certainty measure receives one vote, breaking ties arbitrarily. The Sum, Min, Max, Prod, and Median rules apply to distribution classifiers only. An interesting study of these rules for classifier combination can be found in Kittler et al. (1998).

Let $C = \{C_1, C_2, ..., C_N\}$ be a set of classifiers, and $L = \{L_1, L_2, ..., L_K\}$ be a set of class labels. Hard classifiers receive an input instance x and output an element of the set L. Distribution classifiers receive an input instance x and output a k-dimensional vector $C_i(x) = [c_{i,1}(x), c_{i,2}(x), ..., c_{i,k}(x)]$, where $c_{i,j}(x)$ is the certainty measure that classifier C_i gives to label L_j.

For the Majority Voting combination of hard classifiers, the output is the element of set L that got the most votes (outputs) from the N classifiers. For the Sum, Min, Max, Prod, and Median rules, the output is a k-dimensional vector $[r_1(x), r_2(x), ..., r_k(x)]$, where:

$$r_i(x) = op(c_{1,i}(x), c_{2,i}(x), ..., c_{N,i}(x))$$

Table 1: Classifier Fusion Methods

Output	Re-Training	
	Yes	No
Label	Knowledge-Behavior Space (Huang & Suen, 1995)	Majority Voting (Lam & Suen, 1995)
Ranking	The Highest Rank Logistic Regression Intersection of Neighborhoods Union of Neighborhoods	Borda Count
Distribution	Stacked Generalization (Wolpert, 1992) Dempster-Shaffer Combination (Rogova, 1994) Fuzzy Templates (Kuncheva et al., 1995) Fuzzy Integrals (Tahani & Keller, 1990)	Sum, Product, Min, Max, Median rules (Kittler et al., 1998)

and *op* is the respective operation (average, minimum, maximum, product, and median).

Fusion Systems

Despite the availability of many classifier fusion methods, there are few systems that implement such methods in a distributed database scenario. A reason is that most of these methods were used for pattern recognition tasks, where data are usually gathered at a single place and there are no distributed computing requirements. In the following paragraphs, we summarize some of the most important work on system development aimed at classifier learning and combination from distributed data.

A system that learns and combines classifiers from distributed databases is Java Agents for Meta-Learning (JAM) (Stolfo et al., 1997). It is implemented in Java and uses the Java technology of Remote Method Invocation (RMI) for distributed computing. An important limitation to the extensibility of the system is the fact that clients have to be written in Java. Therefore, JAM is bound to be a closed system that is intended for use in a group of firmly-coupled distributed databases. Furthermore, in contrast to WebDisC, it cannot be used for the fusion of heterogeneous classifiers.

A CORBA infrastructure for distributed learning and meta-learning is presented in Werges and Naylor (2002). Although CORBA is a standard-based distributed object technology, it has been surpassed by the Web services technology. In addition, the presented infrastructure is very complex, as the client developers have to implement a lot of different interfaces. The lack of open standards, such as XML and SOAP, and the complexity of the system hinder its extensibility. Furthermore, like JAM, it combines homogeneous classifiers.

Another system that is built using CORBA technology is MAS (Botia et al., 2001). This is a sophisticated system with some interesting features that add to its extensibility. These include a common services interface for all learning agents and an X.500-based directory service as a repository for the system components. However, as stated above, these standards have been surpassed by Web services technologies which are open, scalable and extensible.

THE WebDisC SYSTEM

WebDisC is a knowledge-based Web information system for the fusion of classifiers induced at geographically distributed databases. The architecture of WebDisC is based on the new and promising Web services paradigm. It further encompasses a Web-based interface that allows users to interact with the system through guided procedures. Its main functionality includes: (i) a declarative rule language for classifier selection that allows the combination of syntactically heterogeneous distributed classifiers; (ii) a variety of standard methods for fusing the output of distributed classifiers; and (iii) a new approach for clustering classifiers in order to deal with the semantic heterogeneity of distributed classifiers, detect their interesting similarities and differences, and enhance their fusion. The rest of this section describes the architecture, functionality, methodologies, and user interface of the system.

Architecture and Main Functionality

The architecture of WebDisC comprises three basic components as depicted in Figure 2: (i) Clients; (ii) The Portal; and (iii) WebDisC Nodes.

The WebDisC Nodes

WebDisC Nodes are databases located at different geographical areas, along with local classification models that were induced from those databases using a machine learning/data mining algorithm.

WebDisC Nodes expose the following web services:
- *wsClassify* takes as input the attribute-value pairs of an unclassified example and outputs the classification result.
- *wsGetClassifier* takes an empty input and returns the classifier of the WebDisC Node in PMML format (Data Mining Group, 2002).

Figure 2: The Architecture of WebDisC

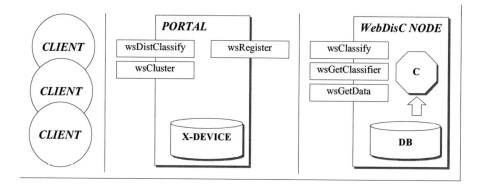

- *wsGetData* returns a vector of tuples from the WebDisC Node's database. It takes as input an integer indicating the number of tuples that will be transferred.

Notice that the WSDL descriptions for all the Web services of our system can be found in (WebDisC, 2003).

The Portal

The Portal is the coordinating component of the system. It consists of the X-DEVICE deductive XML database system and the following Web services: *wsRegister*, *wsDistClassify*, and *wsCluster*. In addition, it offers a Web-based interface for thin client access that also implements the fusion methods.

X-DEVICE's main purpose is the storage of meta-data regarding the distributed classifiers that are registered with WebDisC. These meta-data include: description, names and types of the input and output attributes, name of learning algorithm, ability to handle missing values, and the URI of the Web services.

Figure 3 shows the DTD for the classifier's meta-data, which also define the type of objects that are stored in X-DEVICE for each classifier, according to the XML-to-object mapping scheme of X-DEVICE (see Figure 8). Notice that the actual XML Schema data types for *attType* and *address* elements are *xs:anyType* and *xs:anyURI*, respectively. Figure 4 shows sample meta-data for a classifier registered in X-DEVICE, according to the DTD of Figure 3. More on X-DEVICE will be presented in the corresponding section.

Figure 3: DTD for Classifier Metadata

```
<!ELEMENT classifier (name, description, address,
                      classificationMethod, acceptsMissingValues,
                      classificationAttribute, inputAttribute*)>
<!ELEMENT name (#PCDATA)>
<!ELEMENT description (#PCDATA)>
<!ELEMENT address (#PCDATA)>
<!ELEMENT classificationMethod (#PCDATA)>
<!ELEMENT acceptsMissingValues (#PCDATA)>
<!ELEMENT classificationAttribute (attName, attName)>
<!ELEMENT inputAttribute (attName, attType)>
<!ELEMENT attName (#PCDATA)>
<!ELEMENT attType (#PCDATA)>
```

wsRegister is the Web service that WebDisC Nodes use in order to register with the system. This service takes as input the classifier meta-data of a WebDisC Node and adds them within X-DEVICE (see Figure 9).

wsDistClassify, implements a new approach for distributed classification. It takes as input the name of the dependent attribute and the names and values of some independent attributes of an unclassified example. It also takes as input the name of a predefined method or a set of user-defined X-DEVICE rules that specifies a strategy for selecting the classifiers that should be used for classifying this example, amongst all suitable classifiers. The selection strategies offered by the system, along with the specifications for describing user-defined strategies,

Figure 4: Sample Classifier Metadata

```
<classifier>
  <name>Classifier1</name>
  <description>A local classifier that uses a Decision Tree</description>
  <address>http://startrek.csd.auth.gr/Classifier1</address>
  <classificationMethod>Decision Tree</classificationMethod>
  <acceptsMissingValues>true</acceptsMissingValues>
  <classificationAttribute>
    <attName>loan</attName>
    <attType>xs:string</attType>
  </classificationAttribute>
  <inputAttribute>
    <attName>income</attName>
    <attType>xs:integer</attType>
  </inputAttribute>
  <inputAttribute>
    <attName>card</attName>
    <attType>xs:string</attType>
  </inputAttribute>
  <inputAttribute>
    <attName>home</attName>
    <attType>xs:string</attType>
  </inputAttribute>
</classifier>
```

are further explained later in this chapter. The service retrieves from X-DEVICE the URIs and SOAP messages of the selected classifiers and calls the *wsClassify* Web service of the distributed classifiers, passing the names and values of the corresponding independent attributes as arguments. The output of the service is a list of the collected results.

wsCluster implements a new approach for clustering distributed classifiers. It takes as input a list of URIs that corresponds to a group of *N* classifiers, that all share the same input and output attributes, and calls their *wsGetData* and *wsGetClassifier* services. It so retrieves the actual classifiers and necessary data to centrally run the clustering algorithm that is explained in the *Clustering Distributed Classifiers* section. The output of the service is the clustering result in the form of a vector of size *N*, with numbers indicating the cluster of each classifier.

Finally, the Portal offers a Web-based user interface with guided procedures for using the system. Users of WebDisC can select from the main page one of the tasks of classification or clustering and are directed to the corresponding pages. Data are entered via dynamically created HTML forms from classifier meta-data stored in the X-DEVICE system. Classification and clustering results are also presented in the Web-browser. Java servlets handle the form input data and the preparation of results. The user interface is detailed in the following subsection.

The Clients

Thick clients (applications) that want to exploit the functionality of WebDisC can directly use the Portal's *wsDistClassify* and *wsCluster* Web services. In addition, thin clients (Web browsers) can access the functionality of WebDisC by visiting the system's Web pages and performing one of the tasks through guided procedures.

User Interface

The main Web page of WebDisC allows users to select either the main task of classification or that of clustering.

Classification

The classification data entry page contains a form where users can fill in the details of the example to be classified and a form for selecting or entering the classifier selection strategy. Figure 5 shows this page completed with values for a specific domain regarding the approval of a loan application.

Figure 5: Example of the Classification Data Entry Web Page of WebDisC

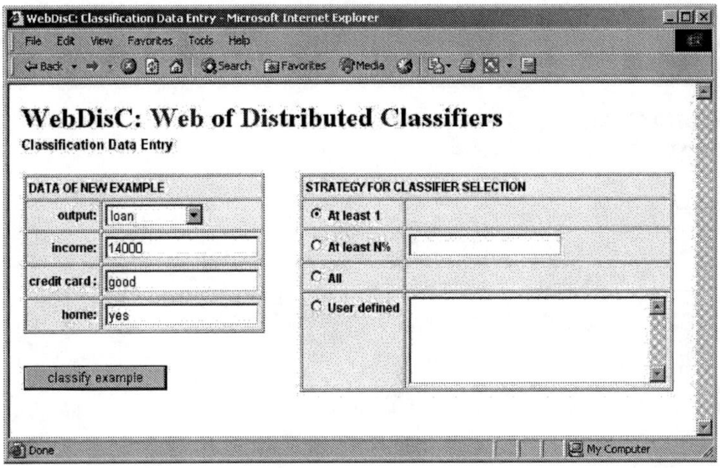

In the general case, users first select one of the available output attributes from a combo-box. The entries of this combo-box are dynamically created from the meta-data of the registered classifiers using a simple X-DEVICE query. Once an output attribute has been selected, the page reloads with a table containing the names of all the input attributes that can be used to predict this output attribute. Again, this is performed dynamically through a simple X-DEVICE query. Users can fill in the values for these attributes in the corresponding text-boxes. If an attribute value is left unspecified, then it is ignored.

After entering the data of the example, users can select one of the default classifier selection strategies or enter their own using the X-DEVICE query language. The default strategies are: (i) select the classifiers that have at least one input attribute in common with the attributes of the new example; (ii) select the classifiers that have at least N% of their input attributes in common with the attributes of the new example; and (iii) select the classifiers that have all their input attributes in common with the attributes of the new example. The last strategy selects homogeneous classifiers.

After selecting a strategy, users can press the *classify example* button, which calls the *wsClassify* service of the Portal through a Java servlet, passing the entered data and the selection strategy as arguments. The classification results that the *wsClassify* service outputs are subsequently visualized on another Web page by a table with a row for each classifier result. An example of such a table, filled in with values for the loan application example, is depicted in Figure 6.

Figure 6: Example of the Classification Results Web Page of WebDisC

CLASSIFIER DESCRIPTION	INPUT			LOAN		CL	ON
	income	card	home	yes	no		
Bank A Headquarters	x	x		0.6	0.4	-	☑
Bank A Loan Assesment Unit 1	x	x	x	0.8	0.2	1	☑
Bank A Loan Assesment Unit 2	x	x	x	0.7	0.3	1	☑
Bank B Headquarters	x		x		x	-	☑
Bank B Loan Assesment Unit	x	x	x		x	2	☑
Bank C Headquarters		x	x	x		-	☑
Bank C Loan Assesment Unit	x	x	x	x		1	☑
COMBINATION				x			

FUSION METHOD
- ○ Majority Voting
- ○ Sum Rule
- ○ Min Rule
- ○ Max Rule
- ○ Product Rule
- ○ Median Rule

[Fuse]

In this example, seven classifiers from three different banks registered with WebDisC match the input data that the user entered. The loan assessment units of the banks have homogeneous classifiers that take as input all three attributes, while the headquarters of each bank have classifiers that use a different combination of input attributes. Furthermore, we notice that only bank A uses classifiers that output distributions, while the rest use classifiers that output class labels. Another thing that can be noticed is that banks A and C output a *yes* decision to the loan application, while bank B classifiers output a *no* decision. Column *CL* of the table concerns the clustering process and will be subsequently explained.

At the bottom of the page, there is a *fuse* button which users can press for combining the results of classifiers. The users can select one of the five supported combination methods, as explained in the *Classifier Fusion: Methods and Systems* section. By default, all classifiers are selected for participating in the combination. To exclude one or more classifiers, users can uncheck the check box in the last column (*ON*) of the table. When the *fuse* button is pressed, the page reloads with the fusion result presented in the final row of the classifier results table, as depicted in Figure 6. In this example, the Majority Voting decision is *yes*, as five out of the seven classifiers output *yes*. If one of the other fusion methods were selected, then the classifiers of banks B and C would not have taken part in the fusion because they are not distribution classifiers, as these methods demand.

Clustering

The clustering page contains a combo-box for selecting the output attribute, similarly to the classification page. Upon selecting this attribute, the page reloads with a table that has a row for each group of homogeneous classifiers that can predict it. The content of this table is dynamically calculated through a simple query to X-DEVICE. Each row describes the input attributes of the classifier group and has a radio button next to it so that only one group can be selected.

Figure 7 shows the clustering page for the loan application example of the previous section. There are four groups of homogeneous classifiers. The first corresponds to classifiers from the four loan assessment units, while the rest correspond to classifiers from each of the bank headquarters.

Pressing the cluster button at the bottom of the page will call the *wsCluster* service of the Portal passing as parameters the URLs of the classifiers that belong to the selected group. The result of the clustering process will be stored,

Figure 7: Example of the Clustering Web Page of WebDisC

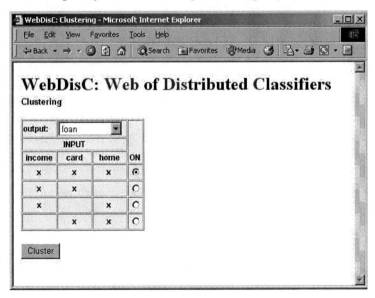

along with the classifier meta-data, in X-DEVICE for future use in a classification process. Going back to Figure 6, we can see the result of clustering the four loan assessment units of the banks. Column CL of the table has as value for each classifier, the number of the cluster to which it belongs. We can see that there are two groups. One contains the classifiers from the loan assessment units of banks A and C, and the other contains the classifier from the loan assessment unit of bank B.

Classifier clustering aims at discovering semantic differences that arise from the geographical distribution of the databases. Using the above example, banks A and C could belong to poorer countries than bank B, and thus, consider the income of the example as high enough for the loan to be granted. Bank B, however, considers the income low for granting the loan. In this case, bank B classifiers should never be fused with bank A and C classifiers due to semantic differences of the classification models. Having performed the clustering process, the user of WebDisC has gained this knowledge and can avoid fusing classifiers belonging to different clusters. Details of the clustering algorithm can be found in the *Clustering Distributed Classifiers* section.

THE X-DEVICE COMPONENT

In this section, we initially present an overview of the X-DEVICE system, a deductive object-oriented XML database system (Bassiliades et al., 2003a) that is used as a Web service registry component for the WebDisC system. Then, we describe in detail the functionality of X-DEVICE within WebDisC.

Overview of the X-DEVICE System

In X-DEVICE, XML documents are stored into the OODB by automatically mapping the DTD to an object schema. Furthermore, X-DEVICE employs a powerful rule-based query language for intelligently querying stored web documents and data and for publishing the results. X-DEVICE is an extension of the active object-oriented knowledge base system DEVICE (Bassiliades et al., 2000). DEVICE integrates deductive and production rules into an active OODB with event-driven rules (Diaz & Jaime, 1997) on top of Prolog. This is achieved by translating the condition of each declarative rule into a set of complex events that is used as a discrimination network to incrementally match the condition against the database.

The advantages of using a logic-based query language for XML data come from the well-understood mathematical properties and the declarative character of such languages, which both allow the use of advanced optimization techniques, such as magic-sets. Furthermore, X-DEVICE, compared to the Xquery (Boag et al., 2002) functional query language, has a more high-level, declarative syntax. This syntax allows users to express everything that XQuery can express, but in a more compact and comprehensible way, with the powerful addition of general path expressions, which are due to fixpoint recursion and second-order variables.

XML Object Model

The X-DEVICE system translates DTD definitions into an object database schema that includes classes and attributes, while XML data are translated into objects. Generated classes and objects are stored within the underlying object-oriented database ADAM (Gray et al., 1992). The mapping of a DTD element to the object data model depends on the following:

- If an element has PCDATA content (without any attributes), it is represented as a string attribute of the class of its parent element node. The name of the attribute is the same as the name of the element.

- If an element has either (a) children elements or (b) attributes, then it is represented as a class that is an instance of the xml_seq meta-class. The attributes of the class include both the attributes of the element and the children elements. The types of the attributes of the class are determined as follows:

  • Simple character children elements and element attributes correspond to object attributes of string type. Attributes are distinguished from children elements through the att_lst meta-attribute.

  • Children elements that are represented as objects correspond to object reference attributes.

The order of children elements is handled outside the standard OODB model by providing a meta-attribute (elem_ord) for the class of the element that specifies the correct ordering of the children elements. This meta-attribute is used when (either whole or a part of) the original XML document is reconstructed and returned to the user. The query language also uses it.

Alternation is also handled outside the standard OODB model by creating a new class for each alternation of elements, which is an instance of the xml_alt meta-class, and it is given a unique system-generated name. The attributes of this class are determined by the elements that participate in the alternation. The structure of an alternation class may seem similar to a normal element class; however, the behavior of alternation objects is different because they must have a value for exactly one of the attributes specified in the class.

The mapping of the multiple occurrence operators, such as "star" (*), etc., are handled through multi-valued and optional/mandatory attributes of the object data model. The order of children element occurrences is important for XML documents. Therefore, the multi-valued attributes are implemented as lists and not as sets.

Figure 8 shows the X-DEVICE representation of the XML document in Figure 4.

XML Deductive Query Language

X-DEVICE queries are transformed into the basic DEVICE rule language and are executed using the system's basic inference engine. The query results are returned to the user in the form of an XML document. The deductive rule language of X-DEVICE supports generalized path and ordering expressions, which greatly facilitate the querying of recursive, tree-structured XML data and the construction of XML trees as query results. These advanced expressions are implemented using second-order logic syntax (i.e., variables can range over class and attribute names) that have also been used to integrate heterogeneous schemata (Bassiliades et al., 2003b). These XML-aware constructs are translated through the use of object meta-data into a combination of (a) a set of first-order logic deductive rules, and/or (b) a set of production rules so that their conditions query the meta-classes of the OODB, they instantiate the

Figure 8: X-DEVICE Representation of the XML Document in Figure 4

```
object              1#classifier
   instance         classifier
   attributes
   name                              'Classifier1'
      description                    'A local classifier that uses a Decision Tree'
      address                        'http://startrek.csd.auth.gr/Classifier1'
      classificationMethod          'Decision Tree'
      acceptsMissingValues          true
      classificationAttribute       2#classificationAttribute
      inputAttribute                [3#inputAttribute,4#inputAttribute,5#inputAttribute]

object              2#classificationAttribute    object              3#inputAttribute
   instance         classificationAttribute          instance         inputAttribute
   attributes                                         attributes
      attName          loan                              attName          income
      attType          xs:string                         attType          xs:integer

object              4#inputAttribute             object              5#inputAttribute
   instance         inputAttribute                   instance         inputAttribute
   attributes                                         attributes
      attName          card                              attName          home
      attType          xs:string                         attType          xs:string
```

second-order variables, and they dynamically generate first-order deductive rules.

In this section, we mainly focus on the use of the X-DEVICE first-order query language to declaratively query the meta-data of the classifier Web services that are represented as XML documents. More details about DE-VICE and X-DEVICE can be found in Bassiliades et al. (2000) and Bassiliades et al. (2003a). The general algorithms for the translation of the various XML-aware constructs to first-order logic can be found in X-DEVICE (2002).

In X-DEVICE, deductive rules are composed of condition and conclusion. The condition defines a pattern of objects to be matched over the database, and the conclusion is a derived class template that defines the objects that should be in the database when the condition is true. For example, rule R4 (see next subsection) defines that: An object with attribute `classifierID` with value `CL`, and attribute `address` with value `URL`, exists in class `candidate_classifier` if there is an object with OID `I` in class `init_candidate` with an attribute method that its value equals string "At least one," an attribute `address` with value `URL`, and an attribute `classifierID` with value `CL`, which points to an object of class `classifier` which, in turn, has an attribute `acceptsMissingValues` with value "true."

Actually, rule R4 selects all the initial candidate classifiers if the selection method requires at least one input attribute common to the user's classification request, and if the classifier accepts missing values for some of its input attributes. Class `candidate_classifier` is a derived class, i.e., a class whose instances are derived from deductive rules. Only one derived class template is allowed at the THEN-part (head) of a deductive rule. However, many rules can exist with the same derived class at the head (e.g., rules R15 and R16). The final set of derived objects is a union of the objects derived by all the rules.

The syntax of such a rule language is first-order. Variables can appear in front of class names (e.g., `I`, `CL`), denoting `OID`s of instances of the class, and inside the brackets, denoting attribute values, i.e., object references (`CL`) and simple values (`URL`), such as integers, strings, etc. Variables are instantiated through the ":" operator when the corresponding attribute is single-valued, and through the "∋" operator when the corresponding attribute is multi-valued. Conditions can also contain comparisons between attribute values, constants and variables. Negation is also allowed if rules are safe, i.e., variables that appear in the conclusion must also appear at least once inside a non-negated condition.

Path expressions can be composed using dots between the "steps," which are attributes of the interconnected objects which represent XML document elements. For example, rule R2 generates the set of initial candidate classifiers by selecting all the registered classifiers that have at least one input attribute common to the user's classification request. The object that represents the user's request is C@classify and, in order to retrieve names of input attributes, the query navigates from classify through inputVector and inputPair to attName.

The innermost attribute should be an attribute of "departing" class, i.e., inputVector is an attribute of class classify. Moving to the left, attributes belong to classes that represent their predecessor attributes. Notice the right-to-left order of attributes, contrary to the common C-like dot notation, that stress out the functional data model origins of the underlying ADAM OODB (Gray et al., 1992). Under this interpretation, the chained "dotted" attributes can be seen as function compositions.

A query is executed by submitting the set of stratified rules (or logic program) to the system, which translates them into active rules and activates the basic events to detect changes at base data. Data are forwarded to the rule processor through a discrimination network (much like in a production system fashion). Rules are executed with fixpoint semantics (semi-naive evaluation), i.e., rule processing terminates when no more new derivations can be made. Derived objects are materialized, and are either maintained after the query is over or discarded on user's demand. X-DEVICE also supports production rules, which have at the THEN-part one or more actions expressed in the procedural language of the underlying OODB.

The main advantage of the X-DEVICE system is its extensibility; it allows the easy integration of new rule types, as well as transparent extensions and improvements of the rule matching and execution phases. The current system implementation includes deductive rules for maintaining derived and aggregate attributes. Among the optimizations of the rule condition matching is the use of a RETE-like discrimination network, extended with reordering of condition elements, for reducing time complexity, and virtual-hybrid memories, for reducing space complexity (Bassiliades & Vlahavas, 1997). Furthermore, set-oriented rule execution can be used for minimizing the number of inference cycles (and time) for large data sets (Bassiliades et al., 2000).

More examples of the X-DEVICE language will be presented and explained in the sequel when needed for the description of the WebDisC functionality.

X-DEVICE Functionality in WebDisC

In this subsection, we describe in detail the functionality of the X-DEVICE system within the WebDisC system, as it has been previously presented in the WebDisC system architecture.

Classifier Registration

The initial task that X-DEVICE performs within WebDisC is to register the meta-data for the classifiers of the WebDisC Nodes. The DTD of the classifiers' meta-data has been given in Figure 3. The WSDL description for the *wsRegister* service is shown in WebDisC (2003). New WebDisC Nodes are sent in a SOAP message that contains their meta-data. A sample SOAP message is shown in Figure 9. The schema of the incoming SOAP message is determined at the input message of the corresponding port type of the WSDL description.

Figure 9: Sample SOAP Message for Registering a Classifier

```
<SOAP-ENV:Envelope xmlns:xs="http://www.w3.org/2001/XMLSchema"
                   xmlns:SOAP-ENV="http://schemas.xmlsoap.org/soap/envelope/"
                   xmlns:m0="http://startrek.csd.auth.gr/wsRegister.xsd">
  <SOAP-ENV:Body>
    <m:Register xmlns:m="http://startrek.csd.auth.gr/wsRegister.wsdl">
      <classifierName>Classifier1</classifierName>
      <classifierDescription>
          A local classifier that uses a Decision Tree
      </classifierDescription>
      <address>http://startrek.csd.auth.gr/Classifier1</address>
      <classificationMethod>Decision Tree</classificationMethod>
      <acceptsMissingValues>true</acceptsMissingValues>
      <inputAttribute>
          <m0:attName>income</m0:attName>
          <m0:attType>xs:integer</m0:attType>
      </inputAttribute>
      <inputAttribute>
          <m0:attName>card</m0:attName>
          <m0:attType>xs:string</m0:attType>
      </inputAttribute>
      <inputAttribute>
          <m0:attName>home</m0:attName>
          <m0:attType>xs:string</m0:attType>
      </inputAttribute>
      <classificationAttribute>
          <m0:attName>loan</m0:attName>
          <m0:attType>xs:string</m0:attType>
      </classificationAttribute>
    </m:Register>
  </SOAP-ENV:Body>
</SOAP-ENV:Envelope>
```

Input SOAP messages are stored within the X-DEVICE system using the schema for the SOAP message found in the corresponding WSDL description. However, the top-level element node of the input SOAP message is linked to an instance of the `input_soap_message` class, through the OID of the object-element node and its attribute content.

The following X-DEVICE rule Rl iterates over all incoming SOAP messages that register a new classifier and generates a new classifier object for each one of them.

```
R1:
if   I@input_soap_message(content:R) and
     R@register(classifierName:Name,classifierDescription:Desc,
                address:Address,classificationMethod:Method,
                acceptsMissingValues:AMV,
                classificationAttribute:CA,inputAttribute:IA)
then classifier(name:Name,description:Desc,address:Address,
                classificationMethod:Method,acceptsMissingValues:AMV,
                classificationAttribute:CA,inputAttribute:IA)
```

Actually, rule Rl transforms the XML data of SOAP messages (Figure 9) into classifier meta-data (Figure 4), stored as a set of objects (Figure 8).

Classifier Selection

One very important task of X-DEVICE is the selection of classifiers that are relative to the user's request. Initially, rule R2 below pre-selects all classifiers that have at least one input attribute `Att` common to the input SOAP message for the *wsDistClassify* service.

```
R2:
if   I@input_soap_message(classify:C) and
     C@classify(select:Method,classificationAtt:CAtt,
                attName.inputPair.inputVector:Att) and
     CL@classifier(address:URL,attName.inputAttribute=Att,
                   attName.classificationAttribute=CAtt)
then init_candidate(method:Method,classifierID:CL,address:URL)
```

Figure 10 shows an example of such a SOAP message. Notice that the classification attribute `CAtt` of the registered classifier must also coincide with the requested classification attribute. The selection strategy `Method` provided by the user is kept, along with the initial set of candidate classifiers, in order to be used for the next step of classifier selection.

Furthermore, all the input attributes of the input SOAP message that match some of the initial set of candidate classifiers are also kept as instances of the `candidate_atts` class, using rule R3.

```
R3:
if    I@input_soap_message(inputPair.inputVector.classify э P) and
      P@inputPair(attName:Att,attValue:Val) and
      IC@init_candidate(classifierID:CL) and
      CL@classifier(attName.inputAttribute=Att)
then  candidate_atts(classifierID:CL,attribute:Att,value:Val)
```

The above classes, `init_candidate` and `candidate_atts`, constitute the programming interface for the rules that implement the classifier selection strategy. Some of these strategies, such as *At least one*, *All*, and *At least N%*, are provided by the system. A knowledgeable user can also use the X-DEVICE language to provide his/her own selection strategy.

Rule R4 below implements the selection of a classifier that has at least one common input attribute with the input SOAP message. Notice that the set of the initially selected candidate classifiers already satisfies the above requirement; therefore, the following rule just checks whether a classifier accepts missing input values, and then copies its OID and address to the output interface class `candidate_classifier`.

```
R4:
if    I@init_candidate(method='At least one',classifierID:CL,address:URL) and
      CL@classifier(acceptsMissingValues='true')
then  candidate_classifier(classifierID:CL,address:URL)
```

The selection of the classifiers that have all their input attributes present at the input SOAP message needs a more complicated treatment. Rule R5 iterates over all initial candidate classifiers and excludes the ones that have an input attribute not present at the input SOAP message (instances of `candidate_atts` class). Then, rule R6 copies, to the `candidate_classifier` class, the OID and address of the initial candidate classifiers that have not been excluded by rule R5.

```
R5:
if    I@init_candidate(method='All',attName.inputAttribute.classifierID:Att)
and
      not C@candidate_atts(classifierID=CL,attribute=Att)
then  exclude_candidate(classifier:I)
```

Figure 10: Sample SOAP Message for Classifying an Example through the wsDistClassify Service

```
<SOAP-ENV:Envelope
xmlns:SOAP-ENV="http://schemas.xmlsoap.org/soap/envelope/"
xmlns:m0="http://startrek.csd.auth.gr/wsDistClassify.xsd">
   <SOAP-ENV:Body>
      <m:Classify xmlns:m="http://startrek.csd.auth.gr/wsDistClassify.wsdl">
         <inputVector>
            <inputPair>
             <m0:attName>income</m0:attName>
             <m0:attValue>14000</m0:attValue>
            </inputPair>
            <inputPair>
             <m0:attName>card</m0:attName>
             <m0:attValue>good</m0:attValue>
            </inputPair>
            <inputPair>
             <m0:attName>home</m0:attName>
             <m0:attValue>yes</m0:attValue>
            </inputPair>
         </inputVector>
         <classificationAtt>loan</classificationAtt>
         <select>At least one</select>
      </m:Classify>
   </SOAP-ENV:Body>
</SOAP-ENV:Envelope>
```

```
R6:
if   C@init_candidate(method='All',classifierID:CL,address:URL) and
     not Cl@exclude_candidate(classifier=C)
then candidate_classifier(classifierID:CL,address:URL)
```

Finally, the selection of a classifier, when the input SOAP message has at least N% of the input attributes of the classifier, needs aggregate functions. These functions count the total number of input attributes of the classifier (rule R7) and the total number of the input attributes of the classifier that are present at the input SOAP message (rule R8). Rule R9 retrieves the two numbers, calculates their ratio, and compares it to the user-supplied percentage. Notice that the selected classifier needs to accept missing values. All three rules make use of the prolog{} construct of X-DEVICE to call out arbitrary Prolog goals.

The addresses of the final set of candidate classifiers are returned to the

```
R7:
if   I@init_candidate(method=N,attName.inputAttributes.classifierID:Att) and
     prolog{number(N)}
then candidate_total_atts(classifier:I,atts_no:count(Att))
```

```
R8:
if    I@init_candidate(method=H,classifierID:CL) and
      C@candidate_atts(classifierID=CL,attribute:Att) and
      prolog{number(N)}
then  candidate_existing_atts(classifier:I,atts_no:count(Att))


R9:
if    C@init_candidate(method=N,classifierID:CL,address:URL) and
      CL@classifier(acceptsMissingValues='true') and
      CT@candidate_total_atts(classifier=C,atts_no:Total) and
      CE@candidate_existing_atts(classifier=C,atts_no:Existing) and
      prolog{number(N),P is 100*Existing/Total,P>=N}
then  candidate_classifier(classifierID:CL,address:URL)
```

requesting application, along with the corresponding SOAP messages that should be sent to the *wsClassify* services of the WebDisC Nodes. Figure 11 shows such a message.

The result is returned as an XML document, and is calculated by the rules R10 to R14. Rule R10 creates a classify object that points to a selected classifier object. Notice the use of the exclamation mark (!) in front of an attribute name to denote a system attribute, i.e., an auxiliary attribute that will not be a part of the query result. Rule Rll constructs a `classifyPair` object for each attribute-value pair of each selected classifier.

Rule R12 creates a `classifyVector` object for each selected classifier and links it with the corresponding `classifyPair` objects. The `list(CP)` construct in the rule conclusion denotes that the attribute `classifyPair` of the derived class `classifyVector` is an attribute whose value is calculated by the aggregate function `list`. This function collects all the instantiations of the variable `CP` (since many input attributes can exist for each classifier) and stores them, under a strict order, into the multi-valued attribute `classifyPair`. Notice that the values of the rest of the variables at the rule conclusion define a GROUP BY operation. More details about the implementation of aggregate functions in X-DEVICE can be found in Bassiliades et al. (2000) and Bassiliades et al. (2003a).

Rule R13 links the `classifyVector` object with the corresponding `classify` object through a derived attribute rule, which defines a new attribute `classifyVector` for class `classify`. The values for this attribute are derived by this rule. Objects of class `classify` that do not satisfy the condition of this class will have null value for this attribute. More details on derived attribute rules can be found in Bassiliades et al. (2000).

Figure 11: Sample SOAP Message for Classifying an Example through the wsClassify Service

```
<SOAP-ENV:Envelope
xmlns:SOAP-ENV="http://schemas.xmlsoap.org/soap/envelope/"
xmlns:m0="http://startrek.csd.auth.gr/wsClassify1.xsd">
  <SOAP-ENV:Body>
    <m:Classify xmlns:m="http://startrek.csd.auth.gr/wsClassify1.wsdl">
      <classifyVector>
        <classifyPair>
          <m0:attName>income</m0:attName>
          <m0:attValue>14000</m0:attValue>
        </classifyPair >
        <classifyPair >
          <m0:attName>card</m0:attName>
          <m0:attValue>good</m0:attValue>
        </classifyPair>
      </classifyVector>
    </m:Classify>
  </SOAP-ENV:Body>
</SOAP-ENV:Envelope>
```

Finally, rule R14 constructs the top-level XML element of the result, which is the SOAP message built for each classifier, augmented by the address of the classifier. The keyword `xml_result` is a directive that indicates to the query processor that the encapsulated derived class (`output_soap_message`) is the answer to the query. This is especially important when the query consists of multiple rules, as in this case.

```
R10:
if    C@candidate_classifier(classifierID:CL)
then classify(!classifierID:CL)


R11:
if    CL@classify(!classifierID:CL1) and
      A@candidate_atts(classifierID=CL1,attribute:Att,value:Val) and
then classifyPair(!classifierID:CL1,attName:Att,attValue:Val)


R12:
if    CP@classifyPair(!classifierID:CL,attName:Att,attValue:Val)
then classifyVector(!classifierID:CL,classifyPair:list(CP))


R13:
if    CL@classify(!classifierID:CL1) and
      CV@classifyVector(!classifierID=CL1) and
then CL@classify(classifyVector:CV)
```

```
R14:
if   CL@classify(!classifierID:CL1) and
     C@candidate_classifier(classifierID=CL1,address:URL)
then xml_result(output_soap_message(!address:URL,classify:CL))
```

Further selection strategies can be defined by the user, who must supply a complete set of X-DEVICE rules that start from the initial set of candidate classifiers, filter out some of them based on arbitrary criteria, and calculate the final set of candidate classifiers. The user should utilize the following classes as input to his/her query:

- `init_candidate(method, classifierID, address)`. Holds all the registered classifiers that share an input attribute with the incoming request. Attribute method stores the selection strategy of the request; `classifierID` points to the OID of the `classifier` object; and address holds the URL address of the corresponding *wsClassify* Web service. Attribute method has a value of user for user-defined selection strategy.

- `candidate_atts(classifierID, attribute, value)`. Holds all the input attributes and values of the input SOAP message that are shared with some registered classifier. Attribute `classifierID` points to the OID of the `classifier` object; `attribute` holds the name of the input attribute; and `value` holds the value of the input attribute.

The user-defined X-DEVICE query should return the set of selected classifiers as instances of the `candidate_classifier(classifierID, address)` derived class. Attribute `classifierID` points to the OID of the `classifier` object, and `address` holds the URL address of the corresponding *wsClassify* Web service. However, the user can avoid using the above output class altogether if he/she makes some use of the pre-defined selection strategies, as the following example shows.

We assume that a user wants to define a new selection strategy so that a classifier can be selected if at least one of the following conditions is true:

- The classification methodology is "Neural Network" and the input attribute "coverage" is at least 50%; or
- The classification methodology is "Decision Tree" and the input attribute "coverage" is at least 75%.

The following two rules use the `init_candidate` input class and copy an instance of this class to a new instance by changing the selection strategy from user (the name of the user-defined strategy) to the appropriate *At least N%* strategy, according to the classification method of the classifier. Notice that the user need not directly involve output class `candidate_classifier`, but only indirectly by re-feeding the `init_candidate` class.

```
R15:
if   I@init_candidate(method=user,classifierID:CL,address:URL) and
     CL@classifier(classificationMethod='Neural Network')
then init_candidate(method=50,classifierID:CL,address:URL)
```

```
R16:
if   I@init_candidate(method=user,classifierID:CL,address:URL) and
     CL@classifier(classificationMethod='Decision Tree')
then init_candidate(method=75,classifierID:CL,address:URL)
```

Finding Homogeneous Classifiers

One of the tasks of X-DEVICE is to provide to the *wsCluster* service the groups of homogeneous classifiers, i.e., the group of classifiers that have exactly the same input and classification attributes, using the following rules:

```
R17:
if   C@classifier(classificationAttribute:CA,inputAttribute:IA) and
     not G@group(classificationAttribute=CA,inputAttribute≡IA)
then group(classificationAttribute:CA,inputAttribute:IA)
```

```
R18:
if   G@group(class ificationAttribute:CA,inputAttribute:IA) and
     C@classifier(classificationAttribute=CA,inputAttributes≡IA)
then G@group(classifiers:list(C))
```

Rule R17 iterates, over all classifiers and copies, the classification and input attributes to an instance of group class. Notice that the group is only created if it does not already exist. In order to compare the multi-valued attribute `inputAttribute`, we use the same-set operator (≡), since the order of elements in each list may vary. Rule R18 iterates all the "similar" classifiers for each created group, and keeps their OID in the classifiers attribute of group, using the `list` aggregate function. Therefore, the group class has three attributes: `classificationAttribute`, `inputAttribute`, and `classifiers`; the two latter are multi-valued attributes.

Querying Registered Classifiers

The Web services of the portal might query X-DEVICE about the stored meta-data of the registered classifiers. The following is an example that generates the list of input attributes that are relevant for each classification attribute. This query is used by the portal to adjust dynamically the classification input page (see Figure 5).

```
R19:
if   C@classifier(attName.classificationAttribute:CA) and
     not Cl@corresponding_attributes(classificationAttribute=CA)
then corresponding_attributes(classificationAttribute:CA)
```

```
R20:
if   Cl@corresponding_attributes(classificationAttribute:CA) and
     C@classifier(attName.classificationAttribute=CA,attName.inputAttribute:IA)
then Cl@corresponding_attributes(inputAttribute:set(IA))
```

Rule R19 creates an instance of `corresponding_attributes` class for each distinct classification attribute, and stores the name of the attribute in the attribute `classificationAttribute`. Rule R20 iterates over all distinct classification attributes, i.e., all instances of class `corresponding_attributes`, and then retrieves all the input attributes of all the classifiers that have the same classification attribute. These input attributes are stored in the multi-valued attribute `inputAttribute`, using the set aggregate function. This function is similar to `list`, the only difference being that no duplicate values are stored inside the set, which is implemented as a Prolog list.

Finally, rule R21 creates a single instance of the class `all_classification_attributes` that holds a list (set) of all the distinct classification attributes. This query is also used by the portal to dynamically generate the values of the pull-down menu (Figure 5) of the classification data entry page.

CLUSTERING DISTRIBUTED CLASSIFIERS

The proposed approach of classifier clustering is based on the notion of classifier distance, its efficient calculation for all pairs of classifiers, and a clustering algorithm that takes as input the distances and outputs the clusters.

```
R21:
if    C@classifier{attName.classificationAttribute:CA}
then  all_classification_attributes{classAtt:set{CA}}
```

Classifier Distance

We here define classifier distance as a measure of how different two classification models are, and we propose its empirical measurement based on the classifiers' predictions in instances with known classes of an independent data set. By independent, we mean a data set whose instances were not part of the classifiers' training set. This will ensure unbiased results, as the predictions of classifiers on their training data tend to be optimistic.

If all classifiers are distribution classifiers, then we propose the use of distance measures, such as Euclidean Distance, Canberra Distance, and Czekanowski Coefficient (Krzanowski, 1993). In this case, the distance of two classifiers is defined as the average distance of their output vectors with respect to all instances of the independent data set.

If all classifiers are hard classifiers, then some measures that can be used for calculating classifier (dis)similarity are Yule's Q statistic, the correlation coefficient, the disagreement measure, and the double-fault measure (Shipp & Kuncheva, 2002).

If mixed types of classifiers are used, then one could adapt the distribution classifiers to the statistics for hard classifiers by using the class of maximum support, breaking ties arbitrarily. Another solution is to adapt the hard classifiers to the measures for distribution classifiers by giving a support of "1" to the predicted class and "0" to the rest. However, this will produce artificially increased distances between two classifiers of different type.

The proposed empirical evaluation of classifier distance exhibits the following beneficial properties:

- *Independence of the classifier type*. It is able to measure the distance of two classification models, whether they are decision trees, rules, neural networks, Bayesian classifiers, or other. This is useful in applications where different types of learning algorithms might be used at each distributed node.

- *Independence of the classifier opacity.* It is able to measure the distance of two classification models, even if they are black boxes, providing just an output with respect to an input. This is useful in applications where the models are coming from different organizations that might not want to share the details of their local models.

Distance Calculation

WebDisC uses the disagreement measure for classifier distance because (i) it is simple and fast to compute; (ii) it can be computed incrementally; (iii) it gives a value that directly expresses the distance of two classifiers that can be used without any transformation for the clustering process; and (iv) it can be used for mixed types of classifiers.

The following equation defines the disagreement measure for two hard classifiers, C_x and C_y, and a data set D with M instances:

$$d_D\left(C_x,C_y\right)=\frac{\sum_{i=1}^{M}\delta_{x,y}^i}{M}$$

where $\delta_{x,y}^i$ equals 1 if classifiers C_x and C_y have different output on tuple i, and 0 otherwise.

The algorithm in Figure 12 shows the actual distance calculation process. Let D be the union of the N data samples that the *wsCluster* Web service of the Portal gathers through the *wsGetData* Web service of the WebDisC Nodes. Let DC be the list of the N classifiers that the *wsCluster* Web service of the Portal gathers through the *wsGetClassifier* Web service of the WebDisC Nodes. For every instance of D, we calculate the output of all classifiers; and then we update the disagreements for each pair of classifiers, based on their output. In the end, the disagreements are normalized with respect to the number of instances that were used for calculating them. The final output of the algorithm is a vector *Dist*, with the distance for each pair of classifiers based on the disagreement measure.

Clustering

Having calculated the pairwise distances of all distributed classifiers, we proceed by clustering them using hierarchical agglomerative clustering. We chose this clustering algorithm because it does not require the user to specify the number of clusters, which is completely unknown; and it uses the pairwise distances of objects, which have already been computed for the distributed classifiers, as explained in the previous section.

The clustering algorithm takes three inputs. The first input is the distance vector calculated by the algorithm in Figure 12. The second input is the method for evaluating inter-cluster distances. There are various methods that could be used here, including single linkage, complete linkage, Ward's method, and weighted average linkage (Kaufmann & Rousseeuw, 1990). WebDisC uses the weighted average linkage method. The third input is a cutoff value that determines when the agglomeration of clusters will stop in order to produce the final clustering result.

That final clustering result is stored within the X-DEVICE system, along with the meta-data of the classifiers. This knowledge can be used to guide the selection of the distributed classifiers that will participate in a combination as explained in *The WebDisC System* section.

CONCLUSION AND FUTURE TRENDS

This chapter has presented the WebDisC system, an approach for the fusion of distributed classifiers based on Web services. Its main advantage over state-of-the-art systems for distributed classification is its versatility, interoperability, and scalability, which stems from the use of open and extensible standards based on XML for web-based distributed computing. The use of the XML-based PMML language for classifier exchange further adds to the inter-operability of WebDisC. Clients can be easily developed in any programming language and operating system that is web-aware.

From the point of view of classifier fusion methodology, WebDisC currently supports simple techniques that do not require re-training of a complex classification model. Yet, it provides the necessary infrastructure, through the *wsGetData* and *wsGetClassifier* Web services, for the implementation of any classifier fusion methodology that requires re-training. Adding methodologies demands the extension of the Portal's Java servlets, while the WebDisC Nodes do not require any modification at all. This shows that

Figure 12: Classifier Distance Calculation Algorithm

```
Input:
    D: an array of M instances (union of N data samples)
    C: an array of N classifiers
Output:
    Dist: an array of  N(N-1)/2  distances
Begin
  For i ← 1 to M
  begin
      // calculate the output of classifiers
      For x ← 1 to N
          O[x] ← C[x](D[i]);

      // update distances
      index ← 1;
      For x ← 1 to N-1
          For y ← x+1 to N
          begin
              If O[x] ≠ O[y] Then
                  Dist[index] ← Dist[index]+1
              index ← index+1
          end
      end

  // normalize distances
  For index ← 1 To  N(N-1)/2

          Dist[index] ← Dist[index]/M;
End
```

WebDisC is a highly scalable and extensible system for classifier fusion.

In addition, WebDisC implements a novel approach toward the detection of interesting similarities and differences among homogeneous classifiers. Clustering the distributed classifiers provides useful knowledge for guiding the selection of classifiers that will participate in the fusion process, thus enhancing the quality of the final classification results.

Furthermore, the X-DEVICE deductive object-oriented database system for XML data provides powerful mechanisms for querying the registered classifiers. Heterogeneous and homogeneous classifiers can be easily selected and fused through the use of the standard classifier selection strategies. The users of the system can also fine-tune the selection of classifiers that will participate in the fusion process, according to their requirements.

In the future, we intend to extend the system with more complex fusion methodologies that require re-training. We will also investigate the implementation of such methodologies under the constraint of avoiding moving raw data from the distributed databases (Tsoumakas & Vlahavas, 2002) in order to avoid increased network communication overhead.

We also intend to enrich the user-interface of WebDisC with a user-profiling system. Its purpose will be to keep the history of the user-defined classifier selection strategies for each different user of WebDisC. This way, strategies that have been successfully used in the past by a user can be retrieved and re-used in the future.

Finally, we intend to address syntactic and semantic heterogeneity problems that arise from the possibly different schemas of the distributed databases by empowering WebDisC with domain-specific ontologies. This is an important future trend in Web information systems development that is driven by the Semantic Web vision.

ACKNOWLEDGMENTS

Dr. Nick Bassiliades was supported by a postdoctoral scholarship from the Greek Foundation of State Scholarships (F.S.S. - I.K.Y.)

REFERENCES

Bassiliades, N. & Vlahavas, I. (1997). Processing production rules in DE-VICE, an active knowledge base system. *Data and Knowledge Engineering*, 24(2), 117-155.

Bassiliades, N., Vlahavas, I., & Elmagarmid, A. K. (2000). E-DEVICE: An extensible active knowledge base system with multiple rule type support. *IEEE Transactions on Knowledge and Data Engineering*, 12(5), 824-844.

Bassiliades, N., Vlahavas, I., & Sampson, D. (2003a). Using logic for querying XML data. In D. Taniar & W. Rahayu (Eds.), *Web-Powered Databases* (pp. 1-35). Hershey, PA: Idea Group.

Bassiliades, N., Vlahavas, I., Elmagarmid, A. K., & Houstis, E. N. (2003b). InterBase-KB: Integrating a knowledge base system with a multi-database system for data warehousing. *IEEE Transactions on Knowledge and Data Engineering*, 15(5), pp 1188-1205.

Bellwood, T. et al. (2002). *UDDI version 3.0*. Retrieved May 15, 2003, from: http://uddi.org/pubs/uddi-v3.00-published-20020719.htm.

Boag, S., Chamberlin, D., Fernandez, M. F., Florescu, D., Robie, J., & Simeon, J. (2002). *XQuery 1.0: An XML query language*. Retrieved May 15, 2003, from: http://www.w3.org/TR/xquery/.

Botia, J. A., Gomez-Skarmeta, A. F., Velasco, J. R., & Garijo, M. (2001). A proposal for meta-learning through a MAS (multi-agent system). In T. Wagner & O. F. Rana (Eds.), *Infrastructure for Agents* (Vol. 1887 of LNAI, pp. 226-233).

Box, D. et al. (2000). *Simple Object Access Protocol (SOAP) version 1.1*. Retrieved May 15, 2003, from: http://www.w3.org/TR/SOAP/.

Brittenham, P. (2001). *An overview of web services inspection language*. Retrieved May 15, 2003, from: http://www.ibm.com/developerworks/webservices/library/ws-wsilover.

Champion, M., Ferris, C., Newcomer, E., & Orchard, D. (2003). *Web services architecture*. Retrieved May 15, 2003, from: http://www.w3.org/TR/ws-arch/.

Chinnici, R., Gudgin, M., Moreau, J., & Weerawarana, S. (2002). *Web services description language (WSDL) version 1.2 working draft*. Retrieved May 15, 2003, from: http://www.w3.org/TR/wsdll2/.

Data Mining Group web site. (2002). Retrieved May 15, 2003, from: http://www.dmg.org/.

Diaz, O. & Jaime, A. (1997). EXACT: An extensible approach to active object-oriented databases. *VLDB Journal*, 6(4), 282-295.

Gray, P. M. D., Kulkarni, K. G., & Paton, N. W. (1992). *Object-oriented Databases: A Semantic Data Model Approach*. New York: Prentice Hall.

Huang, Y. S. & Suen, C. Y. (1995). A method for combining multiple experts for the recognition of unconstrained handwritten numericals. *IEEE Transactions on Pattern Analysis and Machine Intelligence*, 17, 90-93.

Kaufmann, L. & Rousseeuw, P. J. (1990). *Finding Groups in Data: An Introduction to Cluster Analysis*. Hoboken, NJ: Wiley InterScience.

Kittler, J., Hatef, M., Duin, R. P. W., & Matas, J. (1998). On combining classifiers. *IEEE Transactions on Pattern Analysis and Machine Intelligence*, 20(3), 226-238.

Krzanowski, W. J. (1993). *Principles of Multivariate Analysis: A User's Perspective*. Oxford, UK: Oxford Science Publications.

Kuncheva, L.I., Kounchev, R. K., & Zlatev, R. Z. (1995). Aggregation of multiple classification decisions by fuzzy templates. In *Proceedings of the 3rd European Congress on Intelligent Technologies and Soft Computing (EUFIT'95)* (pp. 1470-1474).

Lam, L. & Suen, C. Y. (1995). Optimal combinations of pattern classifiers. *Pattern Recognition Letters*, 16, 945-954.

Rogova, G. (1994). Combining the results of several neural network classifiers. *Neural Networks*, 7, 777-781.

Saitta, L. (2000). *Machine learning: A technological roadmap*. Amsterdam: University of Amsterdam. (Technical Report)

Shipp, C. A. & Kuncheva, L. I. (2002). Relationships between combination methods and measures of diversity in combining classifiers. *Information Fusion*, 3(2), 135-148.

Stolfo, S. J., Prodromidis, A. L., Tselepis, S., Lee, W., & Fan, D. W. (1997). JAM: Java agents for meta-learning over distributed databases. In *Proceedings of the AAAI-97 Workshop on AI Methods in Fraud and Risk Management*.

Tahani, H. & Keller, J. M. (1990). Information fusion in computer vision using the fuzzy integral. *IEEE Transaction on Systems, Man and Cybernetics*, 20, 733-741.

Tsoumakas, G. & Vlahavas, I. (2002). Effective stacking of distributed classifiers. In *Proceedings of the 15th European Conference on Artificial Intelligence*, (pp. 340-344).

WebDisC web site. (2003). Retrieved May 15, 2003, from: http://lpis.csd.auth.gr/systems/webdisc.html.

Werges, S. C. & Naylor, D. L. (2002). Corba infrastructure for distributed learning and meta-learning. *Knowledge-Based Systems*, 15, 139-144.

Wolpert, D. (1992). Stacked generalization. *Neural Networks*, 5, 241-259.

X-DEVICE web site. (2002). Retrieved May 15, 2003, from: http://lpis.csd.auth.gr/systems/x-device.html.

Chapter IX

Indexing Techniques for Web Access Logs

Yannis Manolopoulos, Aristotle University of Thessaloniki, Greece

Mikolaj Morzy, Poznan University of Technology, Poland

Tadeusz Morzy, Poznan University of Technology, Poland

Alexandros Nanopoulos, Aristotle University of Thessaloniki, Greece

Marek Wojciechowski, Poznan University of Technology, Poland

Maciej Zakrzewicz, Poznan University of Technology, Poland

ABSTRACT

Access histories of users visiting a web server are automatically recorded in web access logs. Conceptually, the web-log data can be regarded as a collection of clients' access-sequences, where each sequence is a list of pages accessed by a single user in a single session. This chapter presents novel indexing techniques that support efficient processing of so-called pattern queries, which consist of finding all access sequences that contain a given subsequence. Pattern queries are a key element of advanced analyses of web-log data, especially those concerning typical navigation schemes. In this chapter, we discuss the particularities of efficiently processing user access-sequences with pattern queries, compared to the case of searching unordered sets. Extensive experimental results are given, which examine a variety of factors and illustrate the superiority of the proposed methods over indexing techniques for unordered data adapted to access sequences.

INTRODUCTION

Web servers have recently become the main source of information on the Internet. Web access logs record the access history of users who visit a web server. Each web-log entry represents a single user's access to a web resource (HTML document, image, CGI program, etc.) and contains the client's IP address, the timestamp, the URL address of the requested resource, and some additional information. Conceptually, the web-log data can be regarded as a collection of clients' access-sequences, where each sequence is a list of pages accessed by a single user in a single session. Extraction of user access-sequences is a required pre-processing step in advanced analyses of web logs (called web-log mining), and it involves data cleaning and techniques of forming user sessions (see Cooley, Mobasher, & Srivastava, 1999; Lou, Liu, Lu, & Yang, 2002).

One of the most popular data mining problems in the context of web-log analysis is discovery of access patterns (Chen, Park, & Yu, 1998; Pei, Han, Mortazavi-Asl, & Zhu, 2000). Each access pattern is a sequence of web pages which occurs frequently in user access-sequences. Sequential access-patterns provide information about typical browsing strategies of users visiting a given website, e.g., "10% of users visited the page about a palmtop X, and later a page about a docking cradle for the palmtop X." After some frequently occurring sequences have been discovered, the analyst should be able to search for user access-sequences that support (i.e., contain) the patterns. The latter operation finds several applications, e.g., searching for typical/atypical user access-sequences.

Moreover, web-log mining algorithms, such as WUM (Spiliopoulou & Faulstich, 1998), use templates to constrain the search space and to perform more focused mining, according to the user's requirements. For instance, the user may specify the mining of sequences containing the subsequence <A *B *C>. Thus, a selection of the user access-sequences can be performed to collect those satisfying the given template. In the following, we refer to these types of queries over the database of user access-sequences as pattern queries.

Since web logs tend to be large, a natural solution to support efficient processing of pattern queries would be indexing web access-sequences.

Unfortunately, no indexes specific for this purpose have been proposed before, and existing indexing techniques for single-valued and set-valued attributes are not applicable or are inefficient, as they do not take ordering into consideration. These techniques can be applied merely to locate sequences built from the same set of elements as the query sequence, likely introducing many false drops if the actual task is a subsequence search.

In this chapter, we describe indexing methods for large collections of access sequences extracted from web access logs. The target of the chapter is twofold. First, it intends to clarify the particularities of efficiently processing user access-sequences with pattern queries, compared to the case of searching unordered sets. It will demonstrate how these particularities make the existing (traditional) solutions inadequate, and will show how they call for different index structures and searching algorithms. The second objective of this chapter is to organize recent research that has been conducted in the area of pattern queries (to a significant extent by authors of this chapter) and to present it in an integrated and comparative way. The key concept is the development of a family of methods, based on signatures capturing the presence of certain elements in a sequence as well as the ordering between the sequence elements (a factor that has not been examined by existing signature schemes). Emphasis is placed on scalability to web-logs' sizes. Extensive experimental results are given, which examine a variety of factors and illustrate the superiority of the proposed methods over indexing techniques for unordered data adapted to access sequences.

The rest of this chapter is organized as follows. We start with the introduction to web-log analysis, the reasons for indexes for web logs, and the critique of existing indexing techniques. This is followed by the description of the family of novel sequence-indexing methods for pattern queries. Next, the experimental results on the comparison of the described methods are presented. Finally, the discussion of possible future trends and some conclusions are given.

ANALYSIS OF WEB ACCESS LOGS

Each access to a web resource made by a browser is recorded in the web server's log. An example of the log's contents is depicted in Figure 1. Each entry represents a single request for a resource and contains the IP address of the requesting client, the timestamp of the request, the name of the method used and the URL of the resource, the return code issued by the server, and the size

Figure 1: An Example of a Web Log

```
150.254.31.173   -- [21/Jan/2003:15:48:52 +0100] "GET /mmorzy " 301 328
150.254.31.173   -- [21/Jan/2003:15:48:52 +0100] "GET /mmorzy/index.html " 200 9023
150.254.31.173   -- [21/Jan/2003:15:48:52 +0100] "GET /mmorzy/acrobat.gif " 304
144.122.228.120  -- [21/Jan/2003:15:48:56 +0100] "GET /imgs/pp1.gif " 200 2433
150.254.31.173   -- [21/Jan/2003:15:48:58 +0100] "GET /mmorzy/research.html " 200 8635
60.54.23.11      -- [21/Jan/2003:15:48:59 +0100] "GET /mmorzy/db/slide0003.htm " 200
24808
150.254.31.173   -- [21/Jan/2003:15:49:03 +0100] "GET /mmorzy/students.html " 200 7517
150.254.31.173   -- [21/Jan/2003:15:49:08 +0100] "GET /mmorzy/db_course.html " 200 10849
144.122.228.120  -- [21/Jan/2003:15:49:16 +0100] "GET /reports/repE.html " 200 76685
150.254.31.173   -- [21/Jan/2003:15:49:22 +0100] "GET /mmorzy/html.gif " 200 1038
150.254.31.173   -- [21/Jan/2003:15:49:22 +0100] "GET /mmorzy/zip.gif " 200 1031
144.122.228.120  -- [21/Jan/2003:15:50:03 +0100] "GET /imgs/polish.gif " 200 109
```

of the requested object (for brevity, we omit additional details recorded in the log, such as the protocol or the detailed identification of the browser).

Information stored in the web log can be directly used for simple statistical analyses in order to derive such measures as frequency of accesses to particular resources, numbers of accesses from individual network addresses, number of requests processed in a time unit, etc. However, for advanced and reliable analyses of the way users navigate through the website, information from the log needs processing and cleansing before it can be used. Several requests can have identical timestamps because they represent accesses to different elements of a single web page (in our example, the second entry represents an access to a web page `index.html`, whereas the third entry represents a retrieval of the image `acrobat.gif`, which is probably displayed on that page). Secondly, different records in a web log can have identical IP address and still refer to different users. For example, some users may access the web page from behind a proxy server. Some access paths might not be recorded in the log because browsers cache recently visited pages locally. In order to use the web log for advanced analysis, it must be transformed into a set of clients' access-sequences, where each sequence describes a navigation path of a single user during a single session. Interesting descriptions of web-log transformation and cleansing techniques can be found in Cooley et al. (1999).

Figure 2 presents an example client sequence derived from the web log from Figure 1. This sequence represents the session of a student who started from the teacher's main page (`index.html`) and navigated to a research page (`research.html`). The next request was made for the page containing information for students (`students.html`), and from there, the student went to the database course page (`db_course.html`). The analysis of the website's structure revealed that there was no link between `research.html` and `students.html`, so probably the student used the browser's back button.

Figure 2: An Example of a Client's Access Sequence

```
/mmorzy/index.html → /mmorzy/research.html → /mmorzy/students.html →
/mmorzy/db_course.html
```

A client's sequences extracted from the web log can be stored in a database and further analyzed to discover common access patterns. Such frequent patterns, which are subsequences occurring in a large fraction of the client's sequences, are called sequential patterns (Agrawal & Srikant, 1995). Sequential patterns can be used in several ways, e.g., to improve website navigation, to personalize advertisements, to dynamically reorganize link structure and adapt website contents to individual client requirements, or to provide clients with automatic recommendations that best suit customer profiles. Interpretation of discovered access patterns involves extracting access sequences that contain a given pattern (subsequence). If no indexes are available for the web log, such an operation requires a costly sequential scan of the whole web-log data. Another example of an operation that would benefit from web-log indexes is focused pattern mining that is to be confined to access sequences which contain a given subsequence (Spiliopoulou & Faulstich, 1998).

REVIEW OF EXISTING INDEXING TECHNIQUES

Traditional database systems provide several indexing techniques that support single tuple access based on single attribute value. The most popular indexes include B-trees (Comer, 1979), bitmap indexes (Chan & Ioannidis, 1998), and R-trees (Guttman, 1984). Contemporary database systems allow for storage of set-valued attributes, either in the form of abstract data types (ADTs) or nested tables. However, traditional indexes do not provide mechanisms to efficiently query such attributes, despite of the fact that the need for subset search operators has been recognized (Graefe & Cole, 1995). Indexing of set-valued attributes was seldom researched and resulted in few proposals.

The first access methods for set-valued attributes were developed in the area of text retrieval systems. Signature files (Faloutsos & Christodoulakis, 1984) and signature trees (S-trees) (Deppisch, 1986) utilize the idea of superimposed coding of bit vectors. Each element is represented by a fixed-width signature, with m bits set to '1.' Signatures are superimposed by a bitwise

OR operation to create a set representation. Signatures can be stored in a sequential signature file or a signature tree, or they can be stored using extendible signature hashing. Implementation details and performance evaluation of different signature indexes can be found in Helmer (1997) and Helmer and Moerkotte (1999). Improved methods for signature tree construction were proposed in Tousidou, Nanopoulos and Manolopoulos (2000).

Another set-indexing technique, proposed initially for text collection indexing, is inverted file (Araujo, Navarro, & Ziviani, 1997). Inverted file consists of two parts: the vocabulary and the occurrences. The vocabulary contains all elements that appear in indexed sets. A list of all sets containing a given element is maintained along with each element. All lists combined together form the occurrences. Inverted files are very efficient for indexing small and medium-sized collections of elements. An exhaustive overview of text indexing methods and pattern matching algorithms can be found in Baeza-Yates and Ribeiro-Neto (1999).

Indexing of set-valued attributes attracted the attention of researchers from the object-oriented database systems domain. These studies resulted in the evaluation of signature files in an object-oriented database environment (see Ishikawa, Kitagawa, & Ohbo, 1993; Nørvåg, 1999) and in the construction of the nested index (Bertino & Kim, 1989).

An interesting proposal stemmed from a modification of a well-known R-tree index, namely a Russian Doll tree (RD-tree) (Hellerstein & Pfeffer, 1994). The structure of the tree reflects a transitive containment relation. All indexed sets are stored in tree leafs, while inner nodes hold descriptions of sets contained in the child nodes. Descriptions can be complete representations of bounded sets, signatures or Bloom filter (Bloom, 1970) representations, range set representations, or hybrid solutions.

The first proposals of specialized indexes for set-valued attributes in the domain of data mining were formulated by Morzy and Zakrzewicz (1998). Two indexes were presented: a group bitmap index and a hash group bitmap index. The first index uses a complete and exact representation of indexed sets, but results in very long index keys. Every set is encoded as a bitmap of length n, where n denotes the number of all possible items appearing in the indexed sets. For each set, the i-th bit is set to '1' if this set contains item i. A subset search using a group bitmap index consists in bitwise comparison of index bitmaps, with the bitmap representing the searched subset. A hash group bitmap index uses a technique similar to Bloom filter. It represents indexed sets approximately, by hashing set elements to a bitmap of fixed length. The length of this bitmap is usually much smaller than the number of all possible elements. This technique allows some degree of ambiguity, which results in false drops and implies the verification of answers obtained from the index.

All indexing techniques for set-valued attributes do not consider the ordering of elements within the set. Therefore, those indexes are not suitable for sequence queries. However, set-indexing techniques can be applied to locate sequences built from the same elements as a given query sequence. Using those indexes for a subsequence search requires an additional post-processing step, in which all answers returned from the index are checked for a real containment of the searched sequence, and all sequences containing the searched elements in a wrong sequence, so-called false drops, are pruned. The number of false drops can be huge when compared to the number of correct answers, so this verification step adds significant overhead to query processing and will likely lead to unacceptable response times for sequential queries (for sequential patterns, many sequences contain searched elements but not necessarily in the correct order). Nevertheless, such an adaptation of set-oriented indexes can be considered a natural reference point for evaluating the performance of novel sequence-indexing techniques.

SEQUENTIAL DATA INDEXING METHODS FOR PATTERN QUERIES

In this section, we provide a formal definition of a pattern query over a database of web-log sequences, and describe sequential data indexing methods to optimize pattern queries. The indexing methods are built upon the concepts of equivalent sets, their partitioning, and their approximations.

Basic Definitions

Definition 1 (Pattern query). Let I be a set of *items*. A *data sequence X* is defined as an ordered list of items. Thus, $X = <x_1 x_2 ... x_n>$, where each $x_i \in I$ (x_i is called an *element* of X). We say that a data sequence $X = <x_1 x_2 ... x_n>$ *is contained* in another data sequence $Y = <y_1 y_2 ... y_n>$ if there exist integers $i_1 < i_2 < ... < i_n$ such that $x_1 = y_{i1}, x_2 = y_{i2}, ..., x_n = y_{in}$.

Given a database D of data sequences and a data sequence Q, a *pattern query* consists of finding in D all data sequences that contain Q. In other words, a pattern query formulates a problem of finding all data sequences containing a set of user-defined elements in a specified order.

Definition 2 (Equivalent set). In order to represent data sequences in a compact way, we introduce the concept of an *equivalent set*.

An *item mapping function* $f_i(x)$, where $x \in I$, is a function which transforms a literal into an integer value (we assume that I may contain any type of literals). Henceforth, we assume that literals are mapped to consecutive positive integers starting from 1, although any other mapping can be followed.

An *order mapping function* $f_o(x,y)$, where $x, y \in I$ and $f_o(x,y) \neq f_o(y,x)$, is a function which transforms an item sequence $<x\ y>$ into an integer value. It has to be noticed that the intuition for the use of $f_o(x, y)$ is that it takes into account the ordering, i.e., $f_o(x, y) \neq f_o(y, x)$. Henceforth, we assume order mapping functions of the form $f_o(x,y) = a * f_i(x) + f_i(y)$, where a is greater than the largest $f_i(x)$ value (i.e. $f_o(x,y) \neq f_o(y,x)$ and f_o values are always larger than f_i values).

Given a sequence $X = <x_1 x_2 \dots x_n>$, the *equivalent set E of X* is defined as:

$$E = \left(\bigcup_{x_i \in X} \{f_i(x_i)\} \right) \cup \left(\bigcup_{x_i, x_j \in X,\ i<j} \{f_o(x_i, x_j)\} \right)$$

where: f_i is an item mapping function and f_o is an order mapping function.

Example 1: For instance, for $I = \{A, B, C, D, E\}$, we have $f_i(A) = 1, f_i(B) = 2, f_i(C) = 3, f_i(D) = 4, f_i(E) = 5$, and $f_o(x, y) = 6 * f_i(x) + f_i(y)$ (e.g., $f_o(A,B) = 8$). Given a sequence $X = <A, C, D>$, using the mapping functions that were described above, we get: $E = (\{f_i(A)\} \cup \{f_i(C)\} \cup \{f_i(D)\}) \cup (\{f_o(A, C)\} \cup \{f_o(A, D)\} \cup \{f_o(C, D)\}) = \{1, 3, 4, 9, 10, 22\}$.

According to Definition 2, an equivalent set is the union of two sets: the one resulting by considering each element separately, and the other from considering pairs of elements. $S(E)$ denotes the former set, consisting of values of f_i, and $P(E)$ the latter set, consisting of values of f_o. Based on Definition 2, it is easy to show the following.

Corollary 1. Let two sequences Q, P and the corresponding equivalent sets E_Q and E_P. If Q is contained by P, then $E_Q \subseteq E_P$.

Therefore, equivalent sets allow us to express a pattern query problem as the problem of finding all sets of items that contain a given subset (note that Corollary 1 is not reversible in general). Also, it is easy to see that if $E_Q \subseteq E_P$, then $S(E_Q) \subseteq E_P$ and $P(E_Q) \subseteq E_P$.

Equivalent Set Signatures

Equivalent sets can be efficiently represented with *superimposed signatures*.

A signature is a bitstring of L bits (L is called signature *length*) and is used to indicate the presence of elements in a set. Using a hash function, each element of a set can be encoded into a signature that has exactly m out of L bits equal to '1' and all other bits equal to '0'. The value of m is called the *weight* of the element. The signature of the whole set is defined as the result of the superimposition of all element signatures (i.e., each bit in the signature of the set is the logical OR operation of the corresponding bits of all its elements). Given two equivalent sets E_1, E_2 and their signatures $sig(E_1)$, $sig(E_2)$, it holds that $E_1 \subseteq E_2 \Rightarrow sig(E_1)$ AND $sig(E_2) = sig(E_1)$.

Signatures provide a quick filter for testing the subset relationship between sets. Therefore, if there exist any bits of $sig(E_1)$ that are equal to '1,' and the corresponding bits of $sig(E_2)$ are not also equal to '1,' then E_1 is not a subset of E_2. The inverse of the latter statement, however, does not hold in general, and, evidently, *false drops* may result from collisions due to the superimposition. To verify a drop (i.e., to determine if it is an actual drop or a false drop), we have to examine the corresponding sequences with the containment criterion. In order to minimize the number of false drops, it has been proved (Faloutsos & Christodoulakis, 1984) that, for sets of size T, the length of the signatures has to be equal to: $L = m * T / \ln 2$.

Henceforth, we assume that m is equal to 1 [based on the approach from Helmer and Moerkotte (1997)], and the signature of the element x is the binary representation of the number $2^{x \bmod L}$ (with the least significant bit on the left). Given a collection of sequences, in the following section we examine effective methods for organizing the representations of the patterns, which consist of signatures of equivalent sets.

Family of Sequence Indexing Methods

We describe three methods of sequential data indexing to optimize pattern queries: SEQ(C) — which uses complete signatures of equivalent sets; SEQ(P) — which uses signatures of partitioned equivalent sets; and SEQ(A) — which uses signatures of approximated equivalent sets. Next, we discuss the possibility of extending the methods with advanced tree structures to store the signatures.

A Simple Sequential Index (SEQ(C) – "Complete")

Let D be the database of sequences to be indexed. A simple data structure for indexing elements of D is based on the paradigm of signature file (Faloutsos & Christodoulakis, 1984), and is called SEQ(C) ("SEQ" denotes that the structure is sequential, and "C" that it uses a complete signature representation for the equivalent set). It corresponds to the direct (i.e., naive) use of signatures of equivalent sets. The construction algorithm for SEQ(C) is given in Figure 3a ($sig(E)$ is the signature of equivalent set E).

Example 2: Let us consider the following example of SEQ(C) index entry construction. Assume the data sequence to be indexed is $X = <A, C, D, E>$. Assume the set I of items and item mapping functions and order mapping functions from Example 1, and $L=10$.
The equivalent set for the data sequence X is the following: $E = \{f_i(A), f_i(C), f_i(D), f_i(E), f_o(A,C), f_o(A,D), f_o(A,E), f_o(C,D), f_o(C,E), f_o(D,E)\}$ $= \{1, 3, 4, 5, 9, 10, 11, 22, 23, 29\}$
Therefore, the SEQ(C) index entry will consist of the following signature (starting with the least significant bit): $sig(E) = 1111110001$.

The algorithm for querying the structure for a given sequence Q is given in Figure 3b. Initially (step 1), the equivalent set, E_Q, of Q is calculated. Then, each signature in the structure is examined against the signature $sig(E_Q)$ (step 4, where "AND" denotes the bitwise AND of the signatures). The verification of each drop is applied at steps 5-7. The result, consisting of the sequences from D that satisfy query Q, is returned in set R.
The cost of the searching algorithm can be decomposed as follows:
(1)   *Index Scan cost (I/O)*: to read the signatures from the sequential structure.
(2)   *Signature Test cost (CPU)*: to perform the signature filter test.
(3)   *Data Scan cost (I/O)*: to read patterns in case of drops.
(4)   *Verification cost (CPU)*: to perform the verification of drops.

The signature test is performed very fast; thus, the corresponding cost can be neglected. Since the drop verification involves a main memory operation, it is much smaller compared to the Index and Data Scan costs that involve I/O. Therefore, the latter two costs determine the cost of the searching algorithm. Moreover, it is a common method to evaluate indexing algorithms by comparing the number of disk accesses (see, e.g., Faloutsos & Christodoulakis, 1984; Helmer & Moerkotte, 1997; Tousidou, Nanopoulos, & Manolopoulos, 2000).

Figure 3: SEQ(C) Method: (a) Construction Algorithm (b) Search Algorithm

1. $F = \emptyset$	1. E_Q = Equivalent_Set(Q)
2. **forall** $P \in D$	2. $R = \emptyset$
3. E = Equivalent_Set(P)	3. **forall** $<s$, pointer(P)$> \in F$
4. $F = F \cup \{<sig(E), pointer(P)>\}$	4. **if** (s AND $sig(E_Q)$) = $sig(E_Q)$
5. **endfor**	5. Retrieve P from D
	6. **if** Q *is contained in* P
	7. $R = R \cup \{P\}$
	8. **endif**
	9. **endif**
	10. **endfor**
(a)	(b)

For SEQ(C), the calculation of L (signature length) is done using the expected size of equivalent sets $|\overline{E}|$ (in place of T). Since $|\overline{E}|$ grows rapidly, L can take large values, which increases the possibility of collisions during the generation of signatures (i.e., elements that are hashed into the same position within signatures). Collisions result in false drops due to the ambiguity that is introduced (i.e., we cannot determine which of the elements that may collide in the same positions of the signature are actually present). Thus, a large Data Scan cost for the verification step incurs. Moreover, large sizes of equivalent sets increase the Index Scan cost (because they result in larger L values and, consequently, in an increase in the size of the index).

Due to the drawbacks described above, in the following, we consider the SEQ(C) method as a base to develop more effective methods. Their main characteristic is that they do not handle at the same time the complete equivalent set (i.e., all its elements) for the generation of signatures so as to avoid the described deficiencies of SEQ(C).

Partitioning of Equivalent Sets (SEQ(P) – "Partitioned")
   In Zakrzewicz (2001) and Morzy, Wojciechowski and Zakrzewicz (2001), a partitioning technique is proposed that divides equivalent sets into a collection of smaller subsets. With this method, large equivalent sets are partitioned into smaller ones. Thus, in the resulting signatures, we have a reduced collision probability, fewer false drops, and a reduced Data Scan cost.

Definition 3 (Partitioning of equivalent sets). Given a user-defined value β, the equivalent set E of a data sequence P is partitioned into a collection of $E_1, ..., E_p$ subsets: (1) by dividing P into $P_1, ..., P_p$ subsequences such that $\bigcup_{i=1}^{p} P_i = P$, $P_i \cap P_j = \emptyset$ for $i \neq j$; and (2) by having E_i be the equivalent set of P_i, where $|E_i| < \beta$, $1 \leq i \leq p$.

According to Definition 3, we start from the first element of P being the first element of P_1. Then, we include the following elements from P in P_1, while the equivalent set of P_1 has size smaller than β. When this condition does not hold, we start a new subsequence, P_2. We continue the same process until all the elements of P have been examined.

We denote the above method as SEQ(P) (P stands for partitioning). The construction algorithm for SEQ(P) is analogous to the one of SEQ(C), depicted in Figure 3a. After step 3, we have to insert:

3a. Patrition E into $E_1, ..., E_p$

and step 4 is modified accordingly:

4. $F = F \cup \{<sig(E_1), ..., sig(E_p), pointer(P)>\}$

Example 3: Let us consider the following example of SEQ(P) index entry construction. Assume the data sequence to be indexed is $X = <A, C, D, E>$. Assume the set I of items and item mapping functions and order mapping functions from Example 1, $\beta=4$ and $L=4$.

The data sequence X will be split into the following two data sequences: $X_1 = <A, C>$ and $X_2 = <D, E>$.

Next, we give the equivalent sets for the two data sequences. Notice the sizes of both sequences do not exceed β.
$E_1 = \{f_i(A), f_i(C), f_o(A,C)\} = \{1, 3, 9\}$
$E_2 = \{f_i(D), f_i(E), f_o(D,E)\} = \{4, 5, 29\}$

Therefore, the SEQ(P) index entry will consist of the following signatures:
$sig(E_1) = 0101$
$sig(E_2) = 1100$

The search algorithm for SEQ(P) is based on the following observation (Morzy et al., 2001): For each partition of an equivalent set E, a query pattern

Figure 4: SEQ(P) Method: Search Algorithm

```
1. R = Ø
2. forall Equivalent Sets E = E₁ … Eₚ stored as <sig(E₁), …, sig(Eₚ), pointer(P)>
3.       startPos = 0
4.       for (i=1; i ≤ p and startPos ≤ |Q|; i++)
5.              endPos = startPos
6.              contained = true
7.              while (contained == true and endPos ≤ |Q|)
8.                     E_Q = Equivalent_Set(Q[startPos, endPos])
9.                     if sig(E_Q) AND sig(E_i) = sig(E_Q)
10.                           endPos++
11.                    else
12.                           contained = false
13.                    endif
14.             endwhile
15.             startPos = endPos
16.       endfor
17.       if startPos > |Q|
18.              Retrieve P from D
19.              if Q is contained in P
20.                     R = R ∪ {P}
21.              endif
22.       endif
23. endfor
```

Q can be decomposed into a number of subsequences. Each subsequence is separately examined against the partitions of E. The algorithm is depicted in Figure 4.

We assume that an equivalent set is stored as a list that contains the signatures of its partitions, along with a pointer to the actual sequence (step 1). At steps 4-16, the query pattern is examined against each partition, and the maximum query part that can be matched by the current partition is identified. The part of query sequence Q from *startPos* to *endPos* is denoted as $Q[startPos, endPos]$. At the end of this loop (step 17), if all query parts have been matched against the partitions of the current equivalent set (this is examined at step 17 by testing the value of *startPos* variable), then the verification step is performed at steps 18-20.

SEQ(P) partitions large equivalent sets in order to reduce their sizes and, consequently, the Data Scan cost (because it reduces the possibility of collisions within the signatures, thus, it results in fewer false drops). However, since a separate signature is required for each partition of an equivalent set, the total size of the stored signatures increases [the length of each signature, in this case, is determined keeping in mind that the size of each partition of the equivalent set is equal to β (Definition 3)]. Thus, the Index Scan cost may be increased (using very small values of β and, thus, very small signature lengths for each partition, so as not to increase Index Scan cost, has the drawback of significantly increasing the false drops and the Data Scan cost).

Using Approximations of Equivalent Sets (SEQ(A) – "Approximate")

In Nanopoulos, Zakrzewicz, Morzy and Manolopoulos (2003), a different method for organizing equivalent sets is proposed. It is based on the observation that the distribution of elements within sequential patterns is skewed, since the items that correspond to frequent subsequences [called *large*, according to the terminology of Agrawal and Srikant (1995)] have larger appearance frequency. Therefore, the pairs of elements that are considered during the determination of an equivalent set are not equiprobable.

Due to the above, some pairs have much higher co-occurrence probability than others. The sizes of equivalent sets can be reduced by taking into account only the pairs with high co-occurrence probability. This leads to approximations of equivalent sets, and the resulting method is denoted as SEQ(A) ("A" stands for approximation). The objective of SEQ(A) is the reduction in the sizes of equivalent sets (so as to reduce Data Scan costs), with a reduction in the lengths of the corresponding signatures (so as to reduce the Index Scan costs).

Recall that $P(E)$ denotes the part of the equivalent set E, which consists of the pairwise elements. Also, $supp_D(x, y)$ denotes the support of an ordered pair (x, y) in D (i.e., the normalized frequency of sequence $<x\ y>$ (Agrawal & Srikant, 1995)), where $x, y \in I$ and the pair $(x, y) \in P(E)$. The construction algorithm for SEQ(A) is depicted in Figure 5.

SEQ(A) reduces the sizes of equivalent sets by considering for each element $i \in I$, only k most frequent ordered pairs, with i as the first element. In step 2 of the algorithm, those frequent pairs are discovered and represented in the form of NN sets containing k most frequent successors for each element. In steps 8-10, the NN sets are used to filter out infrequent pairs.

Example 4: Let us consider the following example of SEQ(A) index entry construction. Assume the data sequence to be indexed is $X = <A, C, D,$

Figure 5: SEQ(A) Method: Construction Algorithm

---

1. **forall** $i \in I$

2.   find $NN(i) = \{i_j \mid i_j \in I, 1 \le j \le k, i_j \ne i, \forall l \notin NN(i) \; supp_D(i, i_j) \ge supp_D(i, l)\}$

3. **endfor**

4. $F = \emptyset$

5. **forall** $P \in D$

6. $E = \text{Equivalent\_Set}(P)$

7.   **forall** $(x, y) \in P(E)$

8.   **if** $y \notin NN(x)$

9.   remove pair (x, y) from E

10.   **endif**

11.   **endfor**

12. $F = F \cup \{<sig(E), \text{pointer}(P)>\}$

13. **endfor**

$E>$. Assume the set I of items and item mapping functions and order mapping functions from Example 1, $k=1$ and $L=10$. Given are the following support values for the element pairs: $supp_D(D,E) = 0.280$, $supp_D(E,B) = 0.220$, $supp_D(A,C) = 0.120$, $supp_D(C,E) = 0.101$, $supp_D(A,D) = 0.075$, $supp_D(C,D) = 0.053$, $supp_D(A,E) = 0.040$, $supp_D(B,A) = 0.037$, and, for the other pairs, i.e, (A,B), (B,C), (B,D), (B,E), (C,A), (C,B), (D,A), (D,B), (D,C), (E,A), (E,C), (E,D) the support values less than 0.037.

Based on the support values of the element pairs, we construct the NN sets for each item. Each NN set contains only one item ($k=1$) which forms the strongest pair:

$NN(A) = \{C\}$, $NN(B) = \{A\}$, $NN(C) = \{E\}$, $NN(D) = \{E\}$, $NN(E) = \{B\}$

The equivalent set will not represent the pairs which are not represented in the NN sets:

$E = \{f_i(A), f_i(C), f_i(D), f_i(E), f_o(A,C), f_o(C,E), f_o(D,E)\} = \{1, 3, 4, 5, 9, 23, 29\}$

Therefore, the SEQ(A) index entry will consist of the following signature:

$sig(E) = 0101110001$.

The search algorithm of SEQ(A) is analogous to that of SEQ(C). However, step 1 of the algorithm depicted in Figure 3b has to be modified accordingly (identical approximation has to be followed for the equivalent set of a query pattern):

1. E_Q=Equivalent_Set(Q)
1a. **forall** $(x, y) \in P(E_Q)$
1b. **if** $y \notin NN(x)$
1c.   remove pair (x, y) from E_Q
1d.   **endif**
1e. **endfor**

During the generation of the approximation of the query's equivalent set, the NN sets are used, which implies that they have to be kept in memory. However, this presents a negligible space overhead.

Lemma 1. The SEQ(A) algorithm correctly finds all sequences that satisfy a given pattern query.

Proof. Let Q denote a pattern query and E_Q denote its equivalent set. Also, let S denote a sequence for which Q is contained in S, and let E_S denote its equivalent set. As described (see Corollary 1), it holds that $E_Q \subseteq E_S$, $S(E_Q) \subseteq S(E_S)$ and $P(E_Q) \subseteq P(E_S)$.

In SEQ(A), let us denote E'_Q and E'_S the equivalent sets of Q and S respectively, under the approximation imposed by this algorithm. From the construction method of SEQ(A), we have that $S(E'_Q) = S(E_Q)$ and $S(E'_S) = S(E_S)$. Therefore, $S(E'_Q) \subseteq S(E'_S)$.

Focusing on the pairwise elements, let an element $\xi \in P(E_S) - P(E'_S)$ (i.e., ξ is excluded from $P(E'_S)$ due to step 9 of SEQ(A)). We can have two cases:
(1)   If $\xi \in P(E_Q)$, then $\xi \in P(E_Q) - P(E'_Q)$ (i.e., ξ is also excluded from $P(E'_Q)$, due to the construction algorithm of SEQ(A) - see Figure 5). Therefore, SEQ(A) removes the same elements from $P(E'_Q)$ and $P(E'_S)$. Since $P(E_Q) \subseteq P(E_S)$, by the removal of such x elements, we will have $P(E'_Q) \subseteq P(E'_S)$.
(2)   If $\xi \notin P(E_Q)$, then the condition $P(E'_Q) \subseteq P(E'_S)$ is not affected, since such elements excluded from $P(E'_S)$ are not present in $P(E_Q)$, and, thus, in $P(E'_Q)$.

From both the above cases, we have $P(E'_Q) \subseteq P(E'_S)$.
Conclusively, $S(E'_Q) \cup P(E'_Q) \subseteq S(E'_S) \cup P(E'_S)$, which gives $E'_Q \subseteq E'_S$. Hence, we have proved that (Q is contained in S) $\Rightarrow (E'_Q \subseteq E'_S)$, which

guarantees that SEQ(A) will not miss any sequence S that satisfies the given pattern query (this can be easily seen in a way analogous to Corollary 1).

From the above it follows that, although the SEQ(A) method is based on the concept of approximation, no loss in precision is triggered (evidently, there is no reason to measure the precision/recall, since the method is always accurate). On the other hand, SEQ(A) and all other SEQ algorithms are based on signatures. Therefore, they may incur false drops, i.e., the fetching of sequences for which their signatures satisfy the query condition but the actual sequences do not. The number of false drops directly affects the Data Scan cost, since the fetching of a large number of sequences requires more I/O operations.

The Data Scan cost of SEQ(A) is reduced, compared to SEQ(C), due to the fewer false drops introduced by the drastic reduction in the sizes of equivalent sets. This is examined, experimentally, in the next section. It should be noted that the selection of the user-defined parameter k for the calculation of the NN set in algorithm of Figure 5 has to be done carefully. A small k value will remove almost all pairs from an equivalent set and, in this case, the Data Scan cost increases (intuitively, if the equivalent set has very few elements, then the corresponding signature will be full of 0s, thus, the filtering test becomes less effective). In contrast, a large k value will present a similar behavior as the SEQ(C) algorithm, since almost all pairs are considered. The tuning of the k value is examined in the next section.

Moreover, differently from SEQ(P), the Index Scan cost for SEQ(A) is reduced because smaller signatures can be used for the equivalent sets (due to their reduced sizes) and no partitioning is required. Thus, SEQ(A) combines the advantages of both SEQ(P) and SEQ(C).

Using Tree Structures to Store Signatures

SEQ(C), SEQ(P), and SEQ(A) assume that the elements of F (computed signatures together with pointers to data sequences) are to be stored in a sequential signature file. Nevertheless, SEQ(A) (and SEQ(C)) lead to one signature for each equivalent set. As a consequence, improved signature indexing methods are applicable in these cases, for instance, the S-tree (Deppisch, 1986).[1] By using a tree structure, we can avoid checking each signature during the search of those that satisfy the subset criterion (so as to answer the corresponding pattern query).

The S-tree is a height-balanced tree, having all leaves at the same level. Each node contains a number of pairs, where each pair consists of a signature and a pointer to the child node. In an S-tree, the root can accommodate at least two and at most M pairs, whereas all other nodes can accommodate at least m and at most M pairs, where $1 \leq m \leq M/2$.

Example 5: Let us consider the following example of S-tree construction. Assume that the index type is SEQ(C) and the data sequences to be indexed are the following:

$$X_1=<A,B,D> \ X_2=<C,D> \ X_3=<A,E> \ X_4=<A,C,D>$$
$$X_5=<A,D> \ X_6=<B,D> \ X_7=<B,C,E> \ X_8=<A,D,E>.$$

Assume also that the item mapping functions and order mapping functions are the same as in Example 1, and that L=10. The equivalent sets for data sequences are the following:

$$E_1=\{1,2,4,8,10,16\} \ E_2=\{3,4,22\} \ E_3=\{1,5,11\} \ E_4=\{1,3,4,9,10,22\}$$
$$E_5=\{1,4,10\} \ E_6=\{2,4,16\} \ E_7=\{2,3,5,15,17,23\} \ E_8=\{1,4,5,10,11,29\}$$

The signatures corresponding to the equivalent sets are presented below:

$$sig(E_1)=1110101010 \ \ sig(E_2)=0011100000 \ \ sig(E_3)=0100010000$$
$$sig(E_4)=1111100001$$
$$sig(E_5)=1100100000 \ \ sig(E_6)=0010101000 \ \ sig(E_7)=0011010100$$
$$sig(E_8)=1100110001$$

In Figure 6, an example of an S-tree with three levels is depicted. The nodes at the data level, which are depicted with a dashed line, represent the indexed equivalent sets. The leaves contain the signatures of equivalent sets. The signatures are assigned to the S-tree leaves in a random order. The signatures in internal nodes are formed by superimposing the signatures of their children nodes. For instance, the two signatures of node n_3 are superimposed to form the signature 0111110000 that is stored in the parent node n_1. It has to be noticed that, due to the hashing technique used to extract the object signatures, and due to the superimposition of child signatures, the S-tree may contain duplicate signatures corresponding to different objects.

Successful searches in an S-tree (for equivalent sets that are supersets of the query equivalent set) proceed as follows. First, we compute the signature of the query equivalent set. Next, we start from the root of the S-tree, comparing the query signature with the signatures in the root. For all signatures

Figure 6: Example of a Signature Tree

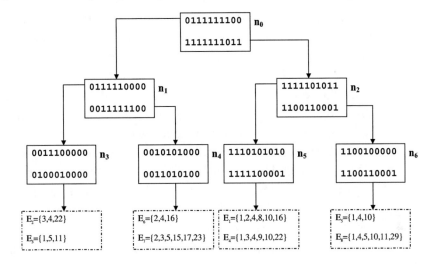

of the root that contain 1s, at least at the same positions as the query signature, we follow the pointers to the corresponding children nodes. Evidently, more than one signature may satisfy this requirement. The process is repeated recursively for all these children, down to the leaf level, following multiple paths. Thus, at the leaf level, all signatures satisfying the subset query are found, leading to the data nodes, whose equivalent sets are checked so as to discard the false drops.[2] In case of an unsuccessful search, searching in the S-tree may stop early at some level above the leaf level (this happens when the query signature has 1s at positions, where the stored signatures have 0s).

The S-tree is a dynamic structure that allows for insertions/deletions of signatures. In Nanopoulos, Zakrzewicz, Morzy and Manolopoulos (2002), the organization of signatures is done with the use of enhanced signature-tree indexing methods, based on Tousidou et al. (2000) and Nanopoulos and Manolopoulos (2002). The advantages of the latter approaches over the original S-tree (Deppisch, 1986) are with respect to the split policy that is used. Due to space restrictions, more details can be found in Tousidou et al. (2000) and Nanopoulos and Manolopoulos (2002).

Finally, we have to notice that both the approximation method and the method that uses the complete representation of equivalent sets can use an S-tree structure. Nevertheless, in the following, we mainly focus on the use of S-trees for the approximation method because the method that uses the complete representation tends to produce saturated signatures (full of 1s), which does not yield S-trees with good selectivity.

PERFORMANCE RESULTS

In this section, we present the experimental results concerning the performance of the examined sequence indexing methods, namely SEQ(C), SEQ(P), and SEQ(A). As we mentioned earlier, to the best of our knowledge, no other sequence-indexing methods applicable to web-log data have been proposed so far. Therefore, as a reference point, from existing indexing methods we choose one of the set-indexing methods — hash group bitmap index (Morzy & Zakrzewicz, 1998). This method can be applied to subsequence searches in the following manner. The index is built on sets of elements forming web-log sequences. Then, it can be used to locate sequences built from the same elements as the query sequence. The hash group bitmap index, similarly to our sequence indexing methods, can return false drops, so the results obtained by using it have to be verified (in the original proposal by using the subset test). Since we apply this index for subsequence search, in the verification step, the subsequence test with the query sequence is performed. We can consider this approach as a sequence indexing method based on generating signatures directly from sets of elements forming access sequences, ignoring the ordering of elements. In our performance study, the latter method is denoted as SEQ(U) ("U" stands for unordered). It should be noted that by comparing to an adaptation of a set-indexing method that is based on the same idea as the three proposed sequence-indexing methods, we can evaluate the advantages of taking element ordering into account. Finally, we examine the method that combines the approximation technique and the indexing with signature trees (this method is denoted as TREE(A)).

All methods were implemented in Visual C++, and the experiments were run on a PC with 933 MHz Intel Pentium III Processor, 128 MB RAM, under the MS Windows 2000 operating system. For the experiments, we used both synthetic and real data sets. The former are detailed in the sequel (i.e., we describe the synthetic data generator). Regarding the latter, we have tested several real web access logs. For brevity, we present results on the *ClarkNet* web log[3], which, after cleansing, contained 7200 distinct URLs organized into 75,000 sequences.

Table 1 summarizes the parameters that are used henceforth.

Synthetic Data Generation

In order to evaluate the performance of the algorithms over a large range of data characteristics, we generated synthetic sets of user sequences. Our data generator considers a model analogous to the one described in Agrawal and

Table 1: Summary of the Parameters Used

Symbol	Definition
I	Domain of items (distinct pages).
M	Number of possible frequent sequences.
N	Number of sequences in the data set.
S	Average length of sequences.
k	Number of most frequent successors considered for each item (for the approximation method).

Srikant (1995). Following the approach of Zakrzewicz (2001) and Morzy et al. (2001) (so as to examine the worst case for equivalent sets), we consider sequences with elements being single items (singletons). Our implementation is based on a modified version of the generator developed in Nanopoulos, Katsaros and Manolopoulos (2003), which was used to produce synthetic web-user traversals that consist of single items (see also Morzy et al., 2001).

The generator builds a pool of sequences, each being a sequence of pair-wise distinct items from a domain I. The length of each such sequence is a random variable that follows Poisson distribution with a given mean value. A new pool sequence keeps a number of items from the previous one, determined by the correlation factor. Since we are interested in the effects of item ordering within sequences, we modified the generator of Nanopoulos et al. (2002) so as to perform a random permutation of the common items before inserting them in the new pool sequence. This results in sequences that contain items with different ordering, thus, examining the impact of this factor. The rest of each sequence is formed by selecting items from I with uniform distribution. Each sequence in the pool is associated with a weight. This weight corresponds to its selection probability and is a random variable that follows exponential distribution with unit mean (weights are normalized in the sequel so that the sum of the weights for all paths equals 1). A user sequence is created by picking a sequence from the pool and tossing an M-sided weighted coin (M is the pool size), where the weight for a side is the probability of picking the corresponding pool sequence. In each user sequence, a number of random items from I (i.e., following uniform distribution) are inserted to simulate the fact that pool sequences are used as seeds and should not be identical to the resulting user sequences. The length of the sequence determines this number, which is a random variable following Poisson distribution with a given mean value denoted as S. The total number of generated sequences is denoted as N. Each result presented in the following is the average of five generated data sets, and, for each data set, we used 100 queries for each case (e.g., query size, number of sequences, etc.).

Results with Synthetic Data

In this section, we are interested in comparing all methods against several data characteristics. For this reason, we used synthetic data sets. In order to present the results more clearly, we focus on the SEQ algorithms, whereas results on the combination of the approximation technique with tree structures (i.e., TREE(A)) are given separately in the following section. This is because our objective is to examine the effectiveness of the approximation technique and, since SEQ(A) and TREE(A) use the same approximation technique, they lead to the same gains with respect to the data-scan cost.[4]

First, we focus on the tuning of k for SEQ(A). We used data sets with S set to 10, $|I|$ set to 1,000 and N equal to 50,000. We measured the total number of disk accesses (cost to scan both the index and the data) with respect to the length of the query sequences. The results for SEQ(A) with respect to k are depicted in Figure 7, where k is given as a percentage of $|I|$. As shown, for small values of k (less than 5%), SEQ(A) requires a large number of accesses because very small equivalent sets are produced that give signatures with almost all bits equal to '0.' Thus, as has been explained, the filtering of SEQ(A) becomes low and the cost to scan the data increases. On the other hand, for large k values (more than 20%), very large equivalent sets are produced, and SEQ(A) presents the drawbacks of SEQ(C). The best performance results occurred when setting k to 10% of $|I|$, which is the value used henceforth.

Our next experiments consider the comparison of SEQ methods. We used data sets that were similar to the ones used in the previous experiment. We used the following signature sizes: for SEQ(C), equal to 96 bits; for SEQ(P) and SEQ(A), equal to 64; and for SEQ(U), equal to 32. For SEQ(A), k was set to 10 percent of $|I|$, and for SEQ(P), β was set to 44 (among several examined values, the selected one presented the best performance). We measured the number of activated user sequences in the database. This number is equal to the total number of drops, i.e., the sum of actual and false drops. Evidently, for the same query, the number of actual drops (i.e., user sequences that actually satisfy the query) is the same for all methods. Therefore, the difference in the number of activated user sequences directly results from the difference in the number of false drops. The results are illustrated in Figure 8a (the vertical axis is in logarithmic scale). In all cases, SEQ(A) outperforms all other methods,

Figure 7: Tuning of k

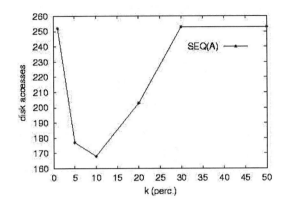

indicating that its approximation technique is effective in reducing the cost to scan the data through the reduction of false drops.

Since the query performance depends both on the cost to scan the data and the index contents, for the case of the previous experiment, we measured the total number of disk accesses. The results are depicted in Figure 8b, with respect to the query size (i.e., the number of elements in the query sequence).

Focusing on SEQ(P), we see that, for all query sizes, it performs better than or almost the same as SEQ(C). Especially for medium size queries, the performance difference between the two methods is larger. This is due to the reduced, for these cases, cost to scan the data (fewer false drops, as also given in Figure 8a), and resulted from the partitioning technique. Moving on to SEQ(U), we observe that, for medium query sizes, it is outperformed by SEQ(P); but, for very small and large ones, it performs better. These two cases present two different situations (see also the following experiment): (1) For very small queries (e.g., of size two), many signatures are activated and a large part of the database is scanned during verification. Hence, a large cost to scan the data is introduced for all methods. This can be called a "pattern explosion" problem. (2) For large queries (with size comparable to *S*), there are not many different user sequences in the database with the same items but with different ordering. Therefore, ignoring the ordering does not produce many false drops. In this case, a small number of signatures are activated, and all methods have a very small and comparable cost to scan the data. Since, at these two extreme cases, both SEQ(P) and SEQ(U) have comparable Data Scan cost, SEQ(P) loses out due to the increased Index Scan cost incurred through the use of larger signatures (SEQ(U) does not use equivalent sets, thus, it uses 32-bit signatures; in contrast SEQ(P) uses for a 64-bit signature for each partition, thus, the total

Figure 8: Comparison of Methods: (a) Number of Activated User Sequences in the Database w.r.t. Query Size (b) Disk Accesses w.r.t. Query Size

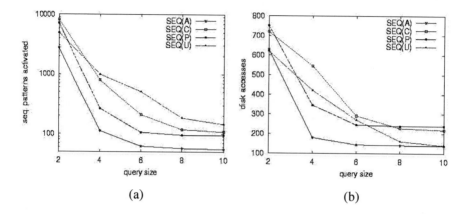

(a)   (b)

size is a multiple of 64-bits).

Turning our attention to SEQ(A), we observe that it significantly outperforms SEQ(C) and SEQ(P) for all query sizes. Regarding the two extreme cases, for the "pattern explosion" problem, SEQ(A) does not present the drawback of SEQ(C) and SEQ(P). In this case, it performs similarly to SEQ(U), which uses much smaller signatures. The same applies for the very large queries. For all the other cases, SEQ(A) clearly requires a much smaller number of disk accesses than SEQ(U).

Our next series of experiments examines the sensitivity of the methods. We first focus on the effect of S. We generated data sets, with the other parameters being the same as the previous experiments, and we varied the length S of sequences (the signature lengths were tuned against S). The resulting numbers of disk accesses are depicted in Figure 9a, for query size equal to $S/2$ in each case. Clearly, the disk accesses for all methods increase with increasing S. SEQ(A) performs better than all other methods, and it is not affected by increasing S as much as the other methods. SEQ(P) presents the second best performance. It has to be noticed that, for large values of S, the performance of SEQ(C) degenerates rapidly.

We also examined the effect of the cardinality of I (domain of items). For this experiment, S was set to 10, and the average query size was equal to five. The other parameters in the generated data sets were the same as those in previous experiments, and we varied I. The results are shown in Figure 9b. As shown, for all methods, very small values of $|I|$ (e.g., 100) require a much larger number of disk accesses. This is due to the larger impact of ordering, since more

Figure 9: Effect of: (a) S (b) |I|

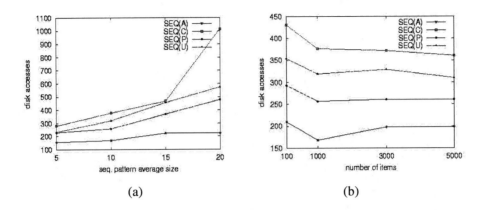

(a)   (b)

permutations of the same sets of items appear within sequences. SEQ(A) presents significantly improved performance compared to all other methods, whereas SEQ(P) comes second best.

Finally, we examined the scalability of the algorithms with respect to the number *N* of sequences. The rest parameters for the generated data sets were analogous to the ones in the experiments depicted in Figure 8, with varying *N*. The results are depicted in Figure 10a. As shown, for all methods, the disk accesses increase in terms of increasing *N*. SEQ(A) compares favorably with the remaining algorithms, whereas SEQ(P) comes second best. As in all previous results, SEQ(C) presents the worst performance.

Results with Real Data

We now move on to examine the *ClarkNet* real web-log. Based on the previous results on synthetic data, we focus on the two most promising methods, namely (1) the partitioning, and (2) the approximation of equivalent sets. Moreover, we also considered the use of tree indexes for the signatures. Nevertheless, as described, the partitioning method (1) results in multiple signatures for each equivalent set, which can only be stored one after the other in a sequential file (i.e., SEQ(P) algorithm). In contrast, the approximation method (2) leads to only one signature for each equivalent set. Therefore, the latter signatures can be easily indexed with a tree structure for signatures, e.g., the S-tree (Deppisch, 1986). We used the approximation method and the improved S-tree variation proposed in Tousidou et al. (2000), and the resulting method is denoted as TREE(A) (i.e., approximation + a tree structure).

The results for the comparison between SEQ(P) and TREE(A), with

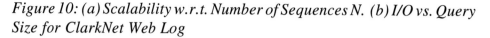

Figure 10: (a) Scalability w.r.t. Number of Sequences N. (b) I/O vs. Query Size for ClarkNet Web Log

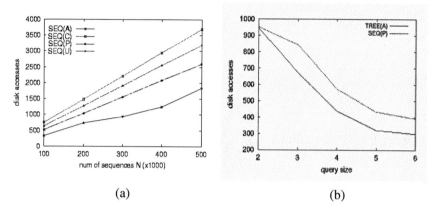

(a)   (b)

respect to query size (i.e., number of items in the query sequence), are given in Figure 10b. Evidently, TREE(A) significantly outperforms SEQ(P) in all cases. Only for very small queries (i.e., with two elements), do the methods present comparable performance, since a large number of the stored signatures and sequences are invoked by such queries (i.e., they have very low selectivity).

In summary, the approximation method has the advantage of allowing for a tree structure to index the signatures, which further reduces the cost to read the signatures. In combination with the reduced cost of scanning the data sequences due to lower number of false drops, the approximation method offers the best performance for large, real web logs.

FUTURE TRENDS

Analysis of the behavior of clients visiting a particular website is crucial for any companies or organizations providing services over the Internet. Understanding of clients' behavior is a key step in the process of improving the website. Nowadays, the information on how users navigate through a given web service is typically available in the form of web access logs. Knowing the limitations of web server logs, in the future, we may observe a tendency to log more accurate and complete information at the application server level. Nevertheless, after some preprocessing, the data to be analyzed by advanced tools (e.g., data mining tools) will have the form of a large collection of sequences stored in a company's database or data warehouse. A typical operation in the context of such data sets is searching for sequences containing a given subsequence. We believe that exploiting advanced indexing schemes, like those presented in this chapter, will be necessary to guarantee acceptable processing times.

Having this in mind, in the future, we plan to continue our research on sequence indexing, extending the most promising technique proposed so far, i.e., the method based on approximations of equivalent sets. We plan to examine alternative approximation schemes, such as: (1) global frequency threshold for ordered pairs of elements within a sequence (using most frequent pairs instead of most frequent successors for each item); and (2) information-content measures (considering only pairs that carry more information than others).

CONCLUSION

We considered the problem of efficient indexing of large web access logs for pattern queries. We discussed novel signature-encoding schemes, which are based on equivalent sets, to consider the ordering among the elements of access sequences, which is very important in the case of access logs. We have presented a family of indexing methods built upon the concept of equivalent sets. The performance of the proposed methods has been examined and compared, experimentally, with real and synthetic data. We tested the impact of query size, the tuning of the encoding schemes, and the scalability. These results illustrate the superiority of the proposed methods over existing indexing schemes for unordered data adapted to access sequences.

REFERENCES

Agrawal, R. & Srikant, R. (1995). Mining sequential patterns. In P. S. Yu & A. L. P. Chen (Eds.), *Proceedings of the 11th International Conference on Data Engineering* (pp. 3-14). Taipei, Taiwan: IEEE Computer Society.

Araujo, M. D., Navarro, G., & Ziviani, N. (1997). Large text searching allowing errors. In R. Baeza-Yates (Ed.), *Proceedings of the 4th South American Workshop on String Processing,* Valparaiso, Chile (pp. 2-20). Quebec, Canada: Carleton University Press.

Baeza-Yates, R. & Ribeiro-Neto, B. (1999). *Modern Information Retrieval.* New York: Addison-Wesley.

Bertino, E. & Kim, W. (1989). Indexing techniques for queries on nested objects. *IEEE Transactions on Knowledge and Data Engineering*, 1(2), 196-214.

Bloom, B. H. (1970). Space/time trade-offs in hash coding with allowable errors. *Communications of the ACM*, 13(7), 422-426.

Chan, C. Y. & Ioannidis, Y. E. (1998). Bitmap index design and evaluation. In L. M. Haas & A. Tiwary (Eds.), *Proceedings of the 1998 ACM SIGMOD International Conference on Management of Data*, Seattle, Washington (pp. 355-366). New York: ACM Press.

Chen, M. S., Park, J. S., & Yu, P. S. (1998). Efficient data mining for path traversal patterns. *IEEE Transactions on Knowledge and Data Engineering*, 10(2), 209-221.

Comer, D. (1979). The ubiquitous B-tree. *ACM Computing Surveys*, 11(2), 121-137.

Cooley, R., Mobasher, B., & Srivastava, J. (1999). Data preparation for mining world wide web browsing patterns. *Knowledge and Information Systems*, 1(1), 5-32.

Deppisch, U. (1986). S-tree: A dynamic balanced signature index for office retrieval. In *Proceedings of the 9th Annual International ACM SIGIR Conference on Research and Development in Information Retrieval*, Pisa, Italy (pp.77-87). New York: ACM Press.

Faloutsos, C. & Christodoulakis, S. (1984). Signature files: An access method for documents and its analytical performance evaluation. *ACM Transactions on Office Information Systems*, 2(4), 267-288.

Graefe, G. & Cole, R. L. (1995). Fast algorithms for universal quantification in large databases. *ACM Transactions on Database Systems*, 20(2), 187-236.

Guttman, A. (1984). R-trees: A dynamic index structure for spatial searching. In B. Yormark (Ed.), *SIGMOD'84, Proceedings of Annual Meeting*, Boston, Massachusetts (pp. 47-57). New York: ACM Press.

Hellerstein, J. M. & Pfeffer, A. (1994). *The RD-tree: An index structure for sets.* Madison, WI: University of Wisconsin at Madison. (Technical Report 1252)

Helmer, S. (1997). *Index structures for databases containing data items with set-valued attributes.* Mannheim, Germany: Universität Mannheim. (Technical Report 2/97)

Helmer, S. & Moerkotte, G. (1997). Evaluation of main memory join algorithms for joins with set comparison join predicates. In M. Jarke, M. J. Carey, K. R. Dittrich, Fr. H. Lochovsky, P. Loucopoulos, & M. A. Jeusfeld (Eds.), *Proceedings of the 23rd International Conference on*

Very Large Data Bases (VLDB'97), Athens, Greece (pp. 386-395). San Francisco, CA: Morgan Kaufmann.

Helmer, S. & Moerkotte, G. (1999). *A study of four index structures for set-valued attributes of low cardinality.* Mannheim, Germany: Universität Mannheim. (Technical Report 2/99)

Ishikawa, Y., Kitagawa, H., & Ohbo, N. (1993). Evaluation of signature files as set access facilities in OOdbs. In P. Buneman & S. Jajodia (Eds.), *Proceedings of the 1993 ACM SIGMOD International Conference on Management of Data, Washington, DC* (pp. 247-256). New York: ACM Press.

Lou, W., Liu, G., Lu, H., & Yang, Q. (2002). Cut-and-pick transactions for proxy log mining. In C. S. Jensen et al. (Eds.), *Advances in Database Technology (EDBT 2002), 8th International Conference on Extending Database Technology,* Prague, Czech Republic, March 25-27, 2002(pp. 88-105). Berlin: Springer-Verlag.

Morzy, T. & Zakrzewicz, M. (1998). Group bitmap index: A structure for association rules retrieval. In R. Agrawal, P. E. Stolorz, & G. Piatetsky-Shapiro (Eds.), *Proceedings of the 4th ACM SIGKDD International Conference on Knowledge Discovery and Data Mining* (pp. 284-288). New York: ACM Press.

Morzy, T., Wojciechowski, M., & Zakrzewicz, M. (2001). Optimizing pattern queries for web access logs. In A. Caplinskas & J. Eder (Eds.), *Advances in Databases and Information Systems, 5th East European Conference* (ADBIS 2001), Vilnius, Lithuania, September 25-28, 2001 (pp. 141-154). Berlin: Springer-Verlag.

Nanopoulos, A. & Manolopoulos, Y. (2002). Efficient similarity search for market basket data. *The VLDB Journal,* 11(2), 138-152.

Nanopoulos, A., Katsaros, D., & Manolopoulos, Y. (2003). A data mining algorithm for generalized web prefetching. *IEEE Transactions on Knowledge and Data Engineering,* (forthcoming).

Nanopoulos, A., Zakrzewicz, M., Morzy, T., & Manolopoulos, Y. (2002). Indexing web access-logs for pattern queries. In *4th ACM CIKM International Workshop on Web Information and Data Management,* McLean, Virginia (pp. 63-68). New York: ACM Press.

Nanopoulos, A., Zakrzewicz, M., Morzy, T., & Manolopoulos, Y. (2003). Efficient storage and querying of sequential patterns in database systems. *Information and Software Technology,* 45(1), 23-34.

Nørvåg, K. (1999). Efficient use of signatures in object-oriented database systems. In J. Eder, I. Rozman, & T. Welzer (Eds.), *Advances in Databases and Information Systems, Proceedings of the 3rd East European Conference (ADBIS'99),* Maribor, Slovenia, September 13-16, 1999 (pp. 367-381). Berlin: Springer-Verlag.

Pei, J., Han, J., Mortazavi-Asl, B., & Zhu, H. (2000). Mining access patterns efficiently from web logs. In T. Terano, H. Liu, & A. L. P. Chen (Eds.), *Knowledge Discovery and Data Mining, Current Issues and New Applications, Proceedings of the 4th Pacific-Asia Conference (PAKDD 2000),* Kyoto, Japan, April 18-20, 2000 (pp. 396-407). Berlin: Springer-Verlag.

Spiliopoulou, M., & Faulstich, L. (1998). WUM - A tool for WWW ulitization analysis. In P. Atzeni, A. O. Mendelzon, & G. Mecca (Eds.), *The World Wide Web and Databases, International Workshop (WebDB'98),* Valencia, Spain, March 27-28, 1998, selected papers (pp. 184-203). Berlin: Springer-Verlag.

Tousidou, E., Nanopoulos, A., & Manolopoulos, Y. (2000). Improved methods for signature tree construction. *The Computer Journal,* 43(4), 301-314.

Zakrzewicz, M. (2001). Sequential index structure for content-based retrieval. In D. W.-L. Cheung, G. J. Williams, & Q. Li (Eds.), *Knowledge Discovery and Data Mining - PAKDD 2001, Proceedings of the 5th Pacific-Asia Conference,* Hong Kong, China, April 16-18, 2001 (pp. 306-311). Berlin: Springer-Verlag.

ENDNOTES

[1]   This does not apply to SEQ(P) because it represents each equivalent set with several signatures.

[2]   Clearly, after checking the equivalent sets, we have to examine the original sequences, so as to discard the false drops that are due to the use of equivalent sets. However, this step does not relate to the use of the S-tree, and is similar to the corresponding step in the SEQ methods.

[3]   Available at the Internet Traffic Archive: http://ita.ee.lbl.gov/html/traces.html.

[4]   We have measured the performance of TREE(A) for these synthetic data and, as expected, we found that it outperforms SEQ(A) because of its reduced index-scan cost, which, however, is due to the tree index and independent from the approximation technique.

Chapter X

Traversal Pattern Mining in Web Usage Data

Yongqiao Xiao, Georgia College & State University, USA

Jenq-Foung (J.F.) Yao, Georgia College & State University, USA

ABSTRACT

Web usage mining is to discover useful patterns in the web usage data, and the patterns provide useful information about the user's browsing behavior. This chapter examines different types of web usage traversal patterns and the related techniques used to uncover them, including Association Rules, Sequential Patterns, Frequent Episodes, Maximal Frequent Forward Sequences, and Maximal Frequent Sequences. As a necessary step for pattern discovery, the preprocessing of the web logs is described. Some important issues, such as privacy, sessionization, are raised, and the possible solutions are also discussed.

INTRODUCTION

Web usage mining is to discover useful patterns in the web usage data, i.e., web logs. The web logs record the user's browsing of a web site, and the patterns provide useful information about the user's browsing behavior. Such patterns can be used for web design, improving web server performance, personalization, etc.

Several different types of traversal patterns have been proposed in the literature, namely, Association Rules, Sequential Patterns, Frequent Episodes, Maximal Frequent Forward Sequences, and Maximal Frequent Sequences. These patterns differ in how the patterns are defined, and they can be used for different purposes. This chapter examines these patterns and the related techniques used to uncover them.

One important issue about mining traversal patterns, or about web usage mining in general, is the preprocessing of the web logs. Since the web logs are usually not in a format for web usage mining, preprocessing is needed. Such preprocessing becomes complicated or problematic by the current use of the Web. The details about the problems and possible solutions are discussed in this chapter.

The rest of the chapter is organized as follows: The second section, *Web Usage Data*, gives the background to web usage mining. The third section, *Preprocessing*, describes the web log preprocessing. The different types of traversal patterns are described in the fourth section, *Pattern Discovery*. The fifth section, *Pattern Analysis and Applications*, describes the analyses and applications of these patterns. The sixth section, *Conclusion*, concludes the chapter.

Web Usage Data

To characterize the web usage data, the terms defined by the W3C Web Characterization Activity (WCA) (http://www.w3c.org/WCA) are adopted. A *user* is defined as an individual who is accessing the Web through a browser. A *user* session is a delimited set of user clicks across one or more web servers. A click corresponds to a page on the web server, which is uniquely identified by a URI (Universal Resource Identifier). A *server session* is a collection of user clicks to a single web server during a user session.

The web usage data can be collected from different sources, e.g., the *server* side, the *client* side (Catledge & Pitkow, 1995) and the *proxy* side (Cohen et al., 1998). The server usage data correspond to the logs that are collected at a web server. They provide an aggregate view of the usage of a web site by all users. Such web server log data may not be entirely reliable due to the presence of various levels of caching (e.g., client caching by the browser, proxy caching by the proxy server) within the Web environment. The client usage data can be collected by using a remote agent, e.g., Java Applets, or by asking the user to use a specialized browser. The client side data can potentially capture every click of the user, but it requires the user's cooperation to collect.

The proxy usage data are collected at a proxy server, which acts as an intermediate level of caching between the client browsers and web servers. Such data may capture the browsing behavior of a group of anonymous users sharing a common proxy server.

The focus of this chapter is on the usage data at a web server, since all the traversal patterns target such web server logs. The information that a typical log on a web server contains is shown in Table 1.

The IP address is the address of the client machine from which the request is made. The user ID is relevant only when the user logs in to the web server. The time field shows when the page is accessed. The method/URI/protocol records which page (identified by a URI) is accessed, and the method and protocol used for the access. The status field and the size field show the access status (e.g., 200 for success) and the size of the page. The referrer field is from the referrer log, which indicates the page the user was on when he or she clicked to come to the accessed page. If the referrer is not empty (i.e., it is not '-' in the log), it usually means there is a hyperlink from the referrer page to the accessed page. This is useful for preprocessing, as indicated below. The user agent field shows whatever software the user used to access the web server, which is typically a web browser.

PREPROCESSING

The tasks of preprocessing for web usage mining include extraction, cleansing, transformation, sessionization, etc. Extraction is for selecting the related fields from the web logs. Traversal patterns typically require three fields: IP address, access time, and the page accessed. Other fields, such as referrer and user agent, can be used in cleansing and sessionization. Transformation converts the fields to the format required by specific pattern discovery

Table 1: Sample Logs

IP	User	Time	Method/URI/Protocol	Status	Size	Referrer	User Agent
2.2.2.2	-	[29/Feb/2000:02:05:00]	``GET A.htm HTTP/1.1"	200	3043	-	Mozilla/4.05
2.2.2.2	-	[29/Feb/2000:02:05:00]	"GET X.jpg HTTP/1.1"	200	1540	-	Mozilla/4.05
2.2.2.2	-	[29/Feb/2000:02:05:01]	``GET B.htm HTTP/1.1"	200	2012	A.htm	Mozilla/4.05
2.2.2.2	-	[29/Feb/2000:02:05:01]	``GET A.htm HTTP/1.1"	200	3043	-	Mozilla/3.04
3.3.3.3	-	[29/Feb/2000:02:05:01]	``GET A.htm HTTP/1.1"	200	3043	-	SearchEngine

algorithm. The other two important tasks, cleansing and sessionization, are described.

Cleansing

Cleansing filters the irrelevant entries in the web log, such as graphics files. The HTTP protocol is stateless, which requires a separate connection for each file requested from the web server. Therefore, several log entries may result from a request to view a single page, since the files for the graphics embedded in the page are automatically downloaded from the web server. Such filtering can be done by checking the suffixes of the URI name, such as jpg, gif, etc. For the sample logs in Table 1, the second row is such an entry and is, thus, filtered.

Another important issue about cleansing is how to filter the sessions of web robots (Kohavi, 2001). A web robot is a software program that automatically traverses the hyperlink structure of the Web. For example, Internet search engines retrieve the web documents for their index databases. It was shown in Tan and Kumar (2002) that web robot sessions could account for as much as 85% of the total number of HTML pages requested, and take up about 5% of the total sessions on a web server. This could dramatically distort the web usage mining, which is supposed to analyze human users' browsing behavior.

One way to detect web robots is by checking the IP address and the user agent in the log. If they match the well-known robots, such as some popular search engines, such entries are removed from the log. For the sample logs in Table 1, the fifth row is such an entry, which records some search engine's access of the web server, given that the IP address and the user agent of the search engine are well known. The drawback of this approach is that it may fail to detect the new robots (IP unknown yet) and the unconventional ones (identities could be disguised). An alternative solution of building classification models was proposed in Tan and Kumar (2002). It is assumed that the traversal patterns of web robots are inherently different from those of human users. Such patterns can be characterized in terms of the types of pages being requested, the length of the session, the interval between successive HTML requests, and the coverage of the web site. It was shown in Tan and Kumar (2002) that the classification models have high accuracy in detecting web robots. Notice that such a solution itself is a web usage mining problem, which requires the following sessionization for preprocessing. So, the simple method of checking the IP address and the user agent may be used instead.

Sessionization

Identifying the sessions (server sessions) from the web logs, called sessionization, is not a trivial task. It has two subtasks: user identification and session identification. A common way is to use the IP address to identify the user, i.e., all entries with the same IP address belong to the same user. However, this is problematic because: (1) several users may have the same IP address if they use the same proxy server to access the web server, which is not uncommon for the Internet Service Providers (ISPs) for performance and other purposes; and (2) a single user may have multiple IP addresses, since some ISPs or privacy tools randomly assign each request from a user to one of the IP addresses in the pool.

An improved method is to check the user agent and the referrer fields, in addition to the IP address (Cooley & Mobasher et al., 1999). The following heuristics are used: (1) If two entries in the log have the same IP address, but have different user agents, they should belong to two different users. For the sample logs in Table 1, after cleansing, there are three entries left: rows 1, 3 and 4. All three entries have the same IP address, but row 4 has a different user agent than rows 1 and 3. Using this heuristic, there are two sessions instead of one, i.e., row 4 belongs to an independent session. (2) If two entries have the same IP address and the same user agent, and if the referrer field is empty but there is no direct hyperlink connecting the two pages, they should belong to two different users. One more heuristic was suggested in Tan and Kumar (2002): (3) If two entries have different IP addresses, but have the same user agent and share a common domain name (can be obtained from the IP address by a reverse DNS lookup) or the same IP prefix (the same IP address group), they should belong to the same user. No example entries are shown for the last two heuristics in the sample logs in Table 1, since they require extra effort, such as analyzing the hyperlink structure of the web server, and reverse DNS lookup for the second and the third heuristics respectively.

It is important to note that these are just heuristics for user identification, e.g., two users with the same IP address (typical on a multi-user workstation) who use the same browser to browse the same set of pages can be easily confused as a single user, and two requests from different machines but with the same domain name could be assigned to the same user even though they belong to different users.

Besides the heuristics, we can also use other session tracking mechanisms, such as cookies and embedded session tracking. A cookie is a piece of information that is stored at the client machine but sent to the server with each request to track the user connection. Cookies have raised growing privacy concerns, since they rely on implicit user cooperation. Embedded session tracking dynamically modifies the URL of each request to include a unique session identifier, which is done by the web server and does not require storing any information on the client machine.

After the users are identified for the entries in the log, the next step is to identify the sessions. A standard way is to use a timeout. The heuristic is that if the time between two requests from a user exceeds a certain limit, a new session is assumed to have started. Many commercial products use 30 minutes as the default timeout. The session identification can also get complicated due to client caching and proxy caching. Most browsers cache the pages that have been requested to improve performance. As a result, when the user hits the "back" button, the cached page is displayed and the web server is not aware of such backtracking, i.e., no entry for such backtracking is recorded in the log. Proxy servers provide an intermediate level of caching for better performance. Due to proxy caching, multiple users throughout an extended period of time could actually view a single request from the proxy.

Such missing page references due to caching may be inferred by using some heuristic (Cooley & Mobasher et al., 1999): If a page request X is made that is not directly linked from the last page the user requested (let it be Y, and there is no direct hyperlink from Y to X), and if the referrer field is not empty (let it be Z), and if the referrer page occurs in the same session (it is like ..., Z, ..., Y, X, ...), then it is assumed that the user backtracked with the "back" button from page Y to page Z and clicked the hyperlink to go to page X. Therefore, the intermediate pages (i.e., the pages from Z to Y in the above session) are added to the log. Again, this is just a heuristic. It could be a mistake to do this if the user changed the URL directly to page X.

A Web Log Data Set

After all sessions are identified, a session file can be created for pattern discovery. The fields for the session file are transformed to the format that is required by the specific algorithm. Unless otherwise specified explicitly, the following example will be used for the pattern discovery, with the assumption that preprocessing is done appropriately.

Example 1. Table 2 shows an artificial data set for the web server log. The user is identified for each page (in total, three unique users), and the sessions are identified for each user with a timeout 30 time units (in total, five sessions shown in Table 3). For convenience of discussion, the access time is shown as relative time units. All other information is not relevant for the following pattern discovery discussion, and, thus, is not shown.

Table 2: Web Server Log Example   *Table 3: Web Server Log Sorted and Sessionized*

#	User	Time	Page
1	u1	0	A
2	u1	2	B
3	u1	3	A
4	u2	5	A
5	u1	6	C
6	u2	7	B
7	u2	8	A
8	u3	10	A
9	u2	11	C
10	u2	12	D
11	u1	40	A
12	u2	42	A
13	u1	43	E
14	u2	44	E
15	u2	45	F

Session	User	Time	Page
1	u1	0	A
	u1	2	B
	u1	3	A
	u1	6	C
2	u1	40	A
	u1	43	E
3	u2	5	A
	u2	7	B
	u2	8	A
	u2	11	C
	u2	12	D
4	u2	42	A
	u2	44	E
	u2	45	F
5	u3	10	A

PATTERN DISCOVERY

Pattern discovery applies methods and algorithms from different fields, such as statistics, data mining, machine learning, etc., to the prepared data. By applying the statistical techniques to the web usage data, some useful statistics about the users' browsing behavior can be obtained, e.g., the average view time of a page, the most frequently accessed pages, etc. By applying clustering (a.k.a. unsupervised learning) to the usage data, the groups of users that exhibit similar browsing behavior can be found. Such knowledge is useful for market segmentation and personalization.

The focus of this chapter is on discovering traversal patterns from the web usage data. A traversal pattern is a list of pages visited by a user in one session. Several different traversal patterns, and the corresponding methods of discovering them, have been proposed in the literature, namely, Association Rules, Sequential Patterns, Frequent Episodes, Maximal Frequent Forward Sequences, and Maximal Frequent Sequences. The details about each type of traversal pattern are described in each of the following subsections respectively.

Association Rules

Association rules were originally proposed for market basket data (see Agrawal et al., 1993; Agrawal & Srikant, 1994). Association rules describe the associations among items bought by customers in the same transaction, e.g., 80% of customers who bought diapers also bought beer in some store.

Association rules have been applied to web logs (Lan et al., 1999; Cooley et al., 1999; Cooley & Mobasher et al., 1999). A page is regarded as an item, and a session is regarded as a transaction[1]. Since a transaction consists of unique items, the duplicate pages in a session need to be removed, and the order of the pages is ignored. For Example 1, there are five sessions and, thus, five transactions: {A, B, C}, {A, E}, {A, B, C, D}, {A, E, F} and {A} (for short, ABC, AE, ABCD, AEF and A), which are shown in Table 4.

To mine association rules from the transactions, there are two steps: finding the frequent item sets, and then generating association rules from the frequent item sets. Since the second step is straightforward compared to the first one, the research focus is on the first step. An item set (or itemset, for short) is frequent if the support for the itemset is not less than some predefined threshold. The support for an itemset in a database of transactions is defined as the percentage of the transactions that contain the itemset. The support for an association rule $X \rightarrow Y$ is the support for the itemset $X \cup Y$. The confidence for an association rule $X \rightarrow Y$ is the ratio of the support for to the support for itemset $X \cup Y$. For Example 1, suppose the confidence threshold is 90%, and the support threshold is 40%, i.e., an itemset needs to appear in at least two of five transactions to be frequent. All frequent itemsets and association rules are

Table 4: Association Rule Example

Sessions	u1: <A, B, A, C> u1: <A, E> u2: <A, B, A, C, D> u2: <A, E, F> u3: <A>
Transactions	ABC ABCD AE AEF A
Frequent Itemsets	A(100%), B(40%), C(40%), E(40%) AB(40%), AC(40%), BC(40%), AE(40%) ABC(40%)
Association Rules	E → A (40%, 100%) B → A (40%, 100%), B → C (40%, 100%) C → A (40%, 100%), C → B (40%, 100%) AB → C (40%, 100%), C → AB (40%, 100%) AC → B (40%, 100%), B → AC (40%, 100%) BC → A (40%, 100%)

shown in Table 4. The numbers in the parentheses are the support and the confidence for an association rule respectively. For the frequent item A with 100% support, A can be said to be the homepage of a certain site, and then it can be interpreted as every visitor visits the homepage A (100%). For association rule AB→C, with support 40% and confidence 100%, AB can be said to be two pages linked from A to B, and the rule can be interpreted as 40% of users visited pages A, B and C, and 100% of those who visited pages A and B also visited page C.

Mining association rules have attracted a lot of research attention. Improvements and extensions have been made from various perspectives: reducing database passes (Savasere et al., 1995; Toivonenn, 1996); parallelization and distribution (Agrawal & Shafer, 1996); generalization (Srikant & Agrawal, 1995); item constraints (Srikant et al., 1997); integration with database systems (Sunita et al., 1998); long patterns (Han et al., 2000), just to name a few.

For the data given in Table 4, the process for finding the frequent itemsets is shown in Table 5.

Algorithm 1

Input:
> D : database of sessions.
> S_{min} : minimum support threshold.
> C_{min} : minimum confidence threshold.

Output:
> all association rules with support and confidence $\geq S_{min}$ and confidence $\geq C_{min}$.

Method:

(1) L_1 = {frequent items};
(2) C_2 = candidate_gen_apriori(L_1); //candidate itemsets for thesecond pass
(3) **for** (k = 2; $C_k \neq \phi$; k++) **do**
(4)   **foreach** session in D **do**
(5)   count C_k;
(6)   **endforeach**
(7) L_k = {the frequent itemsets in C_k};
(8) C_{k+1} = candidate_gen_apriori(L_k); //candidate itemsets for thenext pass
(9) **endfor**
(10) generate association rules using C_{min} from the frequent itemsets L =$L_1 \cup L_2 \cup ... \cup L_k$;

The most well known algorithm for mining association rules is Apriori (Agrawal & Srikant, 1994), which is shown in Algorithm 1. It makes multiple passes of the database. In the first pass, it counts the support of all the individual

Table 5: Apriori Example

Database Pass	Candidate Itemsets	Frequent Itemsets
1	A, B, C, D, E, F	A, B, C, E
2	AB, AC, AE, BC, BE, CE	AB, AC, AE, BC
3	ABC	ABC

items and determines the frequent items. In each subsequent pass, it starts with a seed set of itemsets found to be frequent in the previous pass. This seed set is used to generate a set of candidate itemsets (the potentially frequent itemsets), the actual support of which is counted during the pass over the data. At the end of the pass, the set of frequent itemsets among the candidate itemsets is determined, and it becomes the seed for the next pass. This process continues until no candidate itemsets are generated. In generating the set of candidate itemsets, Apriori uses the property of the frequent itemsets. This property says that all subsets of a frequent itemset must be frequent. By using the property, the set of candidate itemsets for the next pass can be generated from the set of frequent itemsets found in the current pass, i.e., those itemsets that have one infrequent subset need not be considered in the next pass.

Sequential Patterns

Sequential patterns (Srikant & Agrawal, 1995) were also originally proposed for market basket data. For example, customers buy a digital camera, then a photo printer, and then photo paper. Such sequential patterns capture the purchasing behavior of customers over time.

Sequential patterns have also been applied to Web logs (see Buchner et al., 1999; Spiliopoulou, 2000; Pei et al., 2000). The sessions are ordered by the user ID and the access time. As for association rules, the duplicate pages are discarded. Then, for each user, there is a user sequence, which consists of all sessions of the user. Notice that a sequence is an ordered list of itemsets (page sets) and is shown by the notation of <>, while the items (pages) in the itemsets are not ordered and are shown by the notation of (). The user sequences are shown in Table 6. A sequential pattern is a maximal sequence of itemsets whose support is not less than some predefined threshold. A sequence is maximal if it is not contained in any other sequence. The support of a sequence is the percentage of user sequences that contain the sequence. A sequence $X = <(s_1)(s_2) \ldots (s_n)>$ contains another sequence $Y = <(t_1)(t_2) \ldots (t_m)>$, where $s_i (1 \leq i \leq n)$ and $t_j (1 \leq j \leq m)$ are itemsets, and $m \leq n$, if there exists integers $i_1 < i_2 < \ldots < i_m$, such that $t_j \subseteq s_{ij} (1 \leq j \leq m)$.

For Example 1, let the support threshold be 66%, i.e., a sequential pattern has to appear in at least two user sequences. Table 6 shows two sequential patterns that are maximal. Notice that we assume that no duplicate items are allowed in a sequential pattern.

Algorithm AprioriAll was proposed in Srikant and Agrawal (1995) for finding all sequential patterns given some support threshold. First, the set of frequent itemsets is found from the user sequences using the Apriori algorithm. Notice that the support for an itemset is the ratio of the frequency to the number of users. These frequent itemsets are regarded as sequences of length 1 (1-sequences), and are given in Table 6. Such 1-sequences are then used as the seed set to generate candidate 2-sequences (potentially frequent sequences of length 2) using the downward closure property, which also holds for sequential patterns. In each subsequent pass over the database, the set of candidate sequences is counted, and the frequent sequences are determined and then used as the seed set to generate the candidate sequences for the next pass. This process continues until there are no candidate sequences generated. At last, the frequent sequences that are not maximal are removed. Shown in Table 6 are the frequent itemsets (1-sequences) and the resulting sequential patterns.

AprioriAll was then improved by Generalized Sequential Patterns (GSP) (Srikant & Agrawal, 1996), which is shown in Algorithm 2. Traversal patterns were generalized to allow time constraints, sliding time windows, and user-defined taxonomy. GSP also makes several passes over the database. A k-sequence is defined as a sequence with k items, e.g., sequences <(AB)(C)> and <(A)(B)(C)> are both 3-sequences. Note that a k-sequence here is different from that in AprioriAll. In the first pass over the database, it determines the frequent 1-sequences. Each subsequent pass starts with a seed set, which consists of the frequent sequences found in the previous pass. The seed set is used to generate new candidate sequences, each of which has one more item than the seed sequence. The support for the candidate sequences is then found

Table 6: Sequential Pattern Example

User Sequences	u1: <(ABC)(AE)> u2: <(ABCD)(AEF)> u3: <(A)>
Frequent Itemsets	A(100%), B(66%), C(66%), E(66%) AB(66%), AC(66%), BC(66%), AE(66%) ABC(66%)
Sequential Patterns	<(ABC)(E)> (66%) <(BC)(AE)> (66%)

Algorithm 2

Input:
   D : database D of user sequences.
   S_{min} : minimum support threshold.

Output:
   all sequential patterns with support $\geq S_{min}$.
Method:
(1) L_1 = {the frequent 1-sequences};
(2) C_2 = candidate_gen_gsp(L_1); //candidate 2-sequences for the second pass
(3)   **for** (k = 2; $C_k \neq \phi$; k++) **do**
(4)   **foreach** user sequence in D **do**
(5)   count C_k;
(6)   **endforeach**
(7) L_k = {the frequent k-sequences in C_k};
(8) C_{k+1} = candidate_gen_gsp(L_k); //candidate (k+1)-sequences for the next pass
(9)   **endfor**
(10) return the maximal sequences in $L = L_1 \cup L_2 \cup \ldots \cup L_k$;

---

during the pass over the database. At the end of the pass, it determines the set of frequent sequences, which become the seed for the next pass.

GSP differs from AprioriAll in how the candidate sequences are generated. The candidate sequences for a pass are generated by self-joining the set of frequent sequences from the previous pass. A sequence s_1 joins with s_2 if the subsequence obtained by dropping the first item of s_1 is the same as the subsequence obtained by dropping the last item of s_2. The candidate sequence which results from joining s_1 and s_2 is the sequence extended with the last item in s_2. The added item becomes an individual element if it was an individual element in s_2, and a member of the last element of s_1 otherwise. Some of the candidate sequences are then pruned by using the property of downward closure. Shown in Table 7 are the candidate sequences and the frequent sequences for each pass. The resulting traversal patterns are the same as those generated by AprioriAll.

Frequent Episodes

Frequent episodes were originally proposed for telecommunication alarm analysis (see Mannila et al., 1995; Mannila et al., 1997). Episodes are collections of events which occur together within some time window. In general, they are partially ordered sets of events. There are two special types of episodes: parallel episodes and serial episodes. They differ in whether the

Table 7: GSP Example

Pass	Candidate Sequences	Frequent Sequences
1	<(A)>, <(B)>, <(C)>, <(D)>, <(E)>, <(F)>	<(A)>, <(B)>, <(C)>, <(E)>
2	<(AB)>, <(AC)>, <(AE)>, <(BC)> <(BE)>, <(CE)>,<(A)(B)>, <(A)(C)> <(A)(E)>, <(B)(C)>, <(B)(E)>, <(C)(E)> <(B)(A)>, <(C)(A)><(C)(B)>,<(E)(A)> <(E)(B)>, <(E)(C)>	<(AB)>, <(AC)>, <(A)(B)> <(AE)>, <(BC)>, <(A)(E)> <(B)(E)>, <(C)(E)> <(B)(A)> <(C)(A)>
3	<(ABC)>, <(AB)(E)> <(AC)(E)>, <(BC)(E)> <(B)(AE)>, <(C)(AE)>, <(BC)(A)>	<(ABC)>, <(AB)(E)> <(AC)(E)>, <(BC)(E)> <(B)(AE)>, <(C)(AE)>, <(BC)(A)>
4	<(ABC)(E)> <(BC)(AE)>	<(ABC)(E)> <(BC)(AE)>

events in the episodes are ordered. In parallel episodes, the events are not ordered, while in serial episodes, the events are ordered sequentially. An episode is frequent if it occurs in the event sequence not less than some predefined threshold.

Frequent episodes were also applied to web logs (Mannila et al., 1997). The clicks (pages) correspond to events. They are ordered by the access time, and usually the users need not be identified, i.e., there are no sessions. For Example 1, the entire page sequence is shown in Table 8.

The events (pages) in an episode must occur close enough in time. The user defines how close is close enough by giving the width of the time window within which the episode must occur. These time windows are overlapping. For Example 1, given time window width five, there are 50 time windows. In general, the number of time windows for a time period $[s, t]^2$, given window width w, is t-s+w. Notice that the first and last windows extend outside the sequence so that the first window contains only the first event, and the last window contains only the last event. With this definition, each event is observed

Table 8: Frequent Episode Example

Page sequence	<A BA ACBA ACD						A AEEF>	
	0	5	10	15	20	25	35	40	45
Serial Episodes	<A, B> (12%) <A, C> (14%)							
Parallel Episodes	<A, B> (20%) <A, C> (16%) <B, C> (12%) <A, B, C> (12%)							

in an equal number of windows. In addition to the width of the window, the user also specifies some threshold to define the frequent episodes. Given a threshold 10% in Example 1, a frequent episode has to occur in at least five time windows. An episode occurs in a time window if all events appear in the time window, with the partial order of the episode being respected (for parallel episodes, the order is ignored).

The frequent serial episodes and parallel episodes for Example 1 are shown in Table 8. Only episodes with two or more events are listed. The support for each frequent episode is shown in the parentheses. It can be seen that the set of frequent parallel episodes is a superset of that of frequent serial episodes, since the parallel episodes ignore the order of the events. Notice that, from the frequent episodes, episode rules can also be generated, and the support and the confidence for an episode rule are defined similarly to association rules.

The algorithms (see Mannila et al., 1995; Mannila et al., 1997) are also level-wise (similar to breadth-first search), which is shown in Algorithm 3. They perform multiple passes over the database of sequences. In the first pass, the set of frequent events is identified. In each subsequent pass, a set of candidate episodes is generated by using the frequent episodes found in the previous pass and the downward closure property. The set of candidate episodes is counted during the pass over the database, and the frequent episodes are then determined. The candidate episode generation is similar to that for association rules. The counting of the candidate episodes is done incrementally by taking advantage of overlapping time windows. The details can be seen in Mannila et al. (1997).

Maximal Frequent Forward Sequences

Maximal Frequent Forward Sequences (MFFS, for short) were proposed in Chen et al. (1998). Notice that MFFS was referred to as large reference sequence in Chen et al. (1998). An MFFS describes the path traversal behavior of the user in a distributed information-providing environment such as the World Wide Web. There are two steps involved in mining MFFSs from the sessions. First, each session is transformed into maximal forward sequences (i.e., the backward traversals are removed). The MFFSs are then mined using level-wise algorithms (Park et al., 1995) from the maximal forward sequences.

In the raw sessions, there are often backward traversals made by the user. A backward traversal means revisiting a previously visited page in the same user session. It is assumed that such backward traversals happen only because of the structure of the web pages, and not because the user wants to do this.

Algorithm 3

Input:
    D : sequence D of user clicks.
    S_{min} : minimum support threshold.
    t : time window.
Output:
    all frequent episodes with support $\geq S_{min}$.
Method:
(1) L_1 = {the frequent 1-episode with one event};
(2) C_2 = candidate_gen_episode(L_1); // candidate 2-episodes(with two events)
                         // for the second pass
(3)   **for** (k = 2; $C_k \neq \phi$; k++) **do**
(4)   **foreach** time window of width t in D **do**
(5)   count C_k;
(6)   **endforeach**
(7) L_k = {the frequent k-episodes (with events) in C_k};
(8) C_{k+1} = candidate_gen_episode(L_k); // candidate (k+1)-episodes (with k+1 events)
                         // for the next pass
(9)   **endfor**
(10) return the frequent episodes in $L = L_1 \cup L_2 \cup \ldots \cup L_k$;

When a backward traversal occurs, a forward traversal path terminates. This resulting forward traversal path is called maximal forward sequence. It then backtracks to the starting point of the next forward traversal and resumes another forward traversal path. For example, for the session <A,B,C,B,D,B,A,E>, the resulting maximal forward sequences are <A,B,C>, <A,B,D> and <A,E>. The resulting maximal forward sequences for the sessions in Example 1 are shown in Table 9.

An MFFS is a traversal sequence (consecutive subsequence of a maximal forward sequence) that appears not less than some predefined threshold in the set of maximal forward sequences. The pages in an MFFS are required to be consecutive in the maximal forward sequences; and an MFFS is also maximal, which means that it is not a subsequence of any other frequent traversal sequence. Given a threshold 20% for Example 1, an MFFS has to appear in at least two maximal forward sequences. The resulting MFFSs are shown in Table 9.

Two level-wise algorithms, Full Scan (FS) and Selective Scan (SS), were proposed in Chen et al. (1998). FS utilizes the ideas in DHP (Park et al., 1997) for mining association rules. Similar to Apriori, FS performs multiple passes over the data. In the first pass, FS counts the support for each page (sequence of length 1). At the same time, it also maintains a hash table for the support of the sequences of length 2. A bucket in the hash table may contain the support

Table 9: Maximal Frequent Forward Sequence Example

Sessions	u1: <A, B, A, C> u1: <A, E> u2: <A, B, A, C, D> u2: <A, E, F> u3: <A>
Maximal Forward Sequences	<A, B> <A, C> <A, B> <A, C, D> <A> <A, E> <A, E, F>
Maximal Frequent Forward Sequences	<A, B> (29%) <A, C> (29%) <A, E> (29%)

of multiple sequences. At the end of the first pass, using the same downward closure property generates the set of candidates for the next pass. Unlike Apriori for association rules, however, the set of candidates can be further pruned by using the hash table. If the bucket for a candidate in the hash table has less than the predefined support threshold, the candidate need not be considered in the next pass, since it will not be frequent anyway. In the subsequent passes, in addition to the candidate pruning idea using a hash table, keeping only the frequent pages in the sequences, since the infrequent pages in the sequences have no effect on the support for the MFFSs, also reduces the database of maximal forward sequences. It was shown that the hash table can effectively prunes candidates of length 2. FS is shown below in Algorithm 4.

Algorithm SS further reduces the number of passes required by FS. It tries to generate the candidates aggressively by using the candidates of the previous pass instead of the frequent sequences, so that it counts candidates of different sizes in one pass. However, when the minimum support is relatively small, or when the frequent sequences are long, this aggressive method could generate too many candidates to fit in main memory.

Maximal Frequent Sequences

Maximal Frequent Sequences (MFS) were proposed in Xiao and Dunham (2001). In contrast to maximal frequent forward sequences, MFSs do not remove backward traversals from the sessions. It was argued in Xiao and

Algorithm 4

Input:
  D : database D of sessions.
  S_{min} : minimum support threshold.
Output:
  all maximal frequent forward sequences with support $\geq S_{min}$.
Method:
(1) D_1 = {maximal forward sequences in D};
(2) L_1 = {frequent 1 - sequences (of length 1)};
(3) H_2 = the hash table for 2-sequences (of length 2)};
(4) C_2 = candidate_gen_fs(L_1, H_2); // candidate 2 - sequences (of length 2) for
                                                    // the second pass
(5) D_2 = {sequences in D_1 with only frequent pages left};
(6) **for** (k = 2; $C_k \neq \phi$; k++) **do**
(7)   **foreach** sequence in D_k **do**
(8)   count C_k;
(9)   update hash table H_{k+1} for (k+1) - sequences;
(10)   **endforeach**
(11) L_k= {the frequent k - sequences in C_k};
(12) C_{k+1} = candidate_gen_fs(L_k, H_{k+1});   //candidate (k+1) - sequences
                                                           // for the next pass
(13) D_{k+1} = {sequences in D_k with only frequent k - sequences left};
(14) **endfor**
(15) return the maximal sequences in L = $L_1 \cup L_2 \cup ... \cup L_k$;

Dunham (2001) that such backward traversals are useful for discovering the structures of the web pages. For example, if a pattern <A,B,A,C> is found to be frequent, it may suggest that a direct link from page B to page C is needed, while the resulting maximal forward sequences, <A,B> and <A,C>, lose such information.

An MFS is a traversal sequence (consecutive subsequence of a session) that appears not less than some predefined threshold. Since the backward traversals are kept in the sessions, a traversal sequence may occur in a session more than once. In order to measure the actual number of occurrences of a traversal sequence, the support of an MFS is defined as the ratio of the actual number of occurrences to the total length of all sessions. The length of a session is the number of clicks in the session. The pages in an MFS are required to be consecutive in the sessions. An MFS is also maximal, which means that it is not a subsequence of any other frequent traversal sequence. For Example 1, which has 15 clicks in five sessions, given a support threshold 10 percent, an MFS has to appear twice in the sessions, but not necessarily in different sessions, based on the definition. The resulting two MFSs are shown in Table 10.

Table 10: Maximal Frequent Sequence Example

Sessions	u1: <A, B, A, C> u1: <A, E> u2: <A, B, A, C, D> u2: <A, E, F> u3: <A>
Maximal Frequent Sequences	<A, B, A, C> (13%) <A, E> (13%)

Algorithm Online Adaptive Traversal (OAT) was proposed in Xiao and Dunham (2001). By using the algorithm, the patterns can be mined directly from the sessions. Being online, it incrementally updates the current MFSs once a new session is added. Such an online feature is achieved by using the online suffix tree construction and online pattern extraction. To scale to large data, two

Algorithm 5

Input:
  $S_1, S_2, ..., S_n$: sessions.
  S_{min} : minimum support threshold.
  M : main memory size.
Output:
  all maximal frequent sequences with support $\geq S_{min}$
Method:
(1) ST = an empty suffix tree;
    //first scan
(2)   **for** i from 1 to n **do**
      // if insufficient main memory with inclusion of , compress
      // the suffix tree using frequent sequences.
(3)   **if** (mem(ST $\cup$ S$_i$) > M) **then**
(4)   ST = OAT_compress(ST);
(5)   **endif**
        //update the suffix tree with inclusion of S$_i$
(6)   ST = update(ST, S$_i$);
(7)   **if** (interrupted by the user) **then**
            //do a depth-first traversal of ST and output theMFSs.
(8)   MFS_output_depth_first(ST.root);
(9)   **endif**
(10) **endfor**
     //second scan
(11) **if** (there are sequences not completely counted) **then**
(12)   count them in an additional scan.
(13) **endif**
(14) output the MFSs in the suffix tree.

pruning techniques (local pruning and cumulative pruning) and suffix tree compression were introduced. The idea is to reduce the main memory requirement for the suffix tree. The algorithm is shown in Algorithm 5.

Summary

Table 11 compares the different types of traversal patterns by the following features:

- Ordering. The pages in a traversal pattern can be ordered or not.
- Duplicates, which indicate whether backward traversals are allowed in the traversal pattern.
- Contiguity. The page references in a traversal pattern may be contiguous or not.
- Maximality. A frequent pattern is maximal if it is not contained in any other frequent pattern. A pattern could be maximal or not.

Notice that for frequent episodes, parallel episodes are not ordered, while serial episodes are ordered and the general episodes are partially ordered. Due to the different features of the traversal patterns, the support for each type of pattern is defined quite differently, which is also shown in Table 11.

These features, when used by different patterns, can be used for different purposes. Backward traversals capture the structure information of the Web and, therefore, can be used to improve the design of web pages by adding new links to shorten future traversals. The maximality feature can reduce the number of meaningful patterns discovered. The contiguity and ordering features could be used to predict future references and, thus, for prefetching and caching purposes.

These traversal patterns uncover the associations or sequences among the web pages browsed by the user. They can be used together with other data mining techniques, such as classification and clustering, to further facilitate web usage mining, as shown in Tan and Kumar (2002). In that paper, the authors

Table 11: A Comparison of Traversal Patterns

	Ordering	Duplicates	Contiguity	Maximality	Support
Association Rules	N	N	N	N	freq(X) / # sessions
Sequential Patterns	Y	N	N	Y	freq(X) / # users
Frequent Episodes	Y	N	N	N	freq(X) / # time windows
MFFS	Y	N	Y	Y	freq(X) / # maximal forward sequences
MFS	Y	Y	Y	Y	freq(X) / # clicks

used traversal patterns and classification to distinguish human sessions from robot sessions. However, due to the length and the focus (on traversal pattern mining) of this chapter, for the details about using other data mining techniques for web usage mining, interested readers should consult references such as Tan and Kumar (2002), Zaiane et al. (1998), Perkowitz and Etzioni (1999), etc.

PATTERN ANALYSIS AND APPLICATIONS

Pattern analysis is to analyze the patterns to the needs of the application. It includes filtering uninteresting patterns, visualization, etc. The Web Utilization Miner (WUM) system (Spiliopoulou & Faulstich, 1998) provides a mining language, which allows an analyst to specify characteristics of the patterns that are interesting.

Web usage mining has been applied to many applications (Srivastava et al., 2000), e.g., personalization, system improvement, web design, business intelligence, etc. Specifically, the traversal patterns have been used for site evaluation (Spiliopoulou, 2000), prefetching (Lan et al., 1999; Pandey et al., 2001), network intrusion detection (Lee & Stolfo, 1998; Dokas et al., 2002), fraud detection (Colet, 2002), etc. Interesting results might be obtained through a comparison study of these different patterns.

While web usage mining can discover useful patterns about a user's browsing behavior, it has raised growing privacy concerns (Spiekermann et al., 2002). For example, using cookies to track sessions relies on the user's implicit acceptance of the cookies. Most users want to maintain anonymity on the Web, and do not like their activities on the Web to be monitored or analyzed without their explicit permission. An initiative called Platform for Privacy Preferences (P3P) has been proposed by World Wide Web Consortium (W3C) (http://www.w3c.org/P3P). P3P provides a protocol for allowing the administrator of a web site to publish the privacy policies it follows. When the user visits the site for the first time, the browser reads the privacy policies followed by the site and then compares it to the security setting configured by the user. If the privacy policies are satisfactory, the browser continues requesting pages from the site. Otherwise, a negotiation protocol is used to arrive at a setting which is acceptable to the user.

An interesting technique that incorporates privacy concerns was proposed in Evfimievski et al. (2002). By randomizing the pages in a session (transaction) using a uniform distribution, the web log does not record the exact pages the user visited, and yet useful patterns (e.g., association rules) can still be found from the randomized sessions. Another idea was proposed in Vaidya and Clifton (2002), which vertically partitions the pages for a session across two sources, i.e., for a session, some pages are in one source and the rest in the other source. By partitioning the pages, a web log file does not have a complete view of all pages for a session, and web usage mining is done with the two separate sources.

CONCLUSION

This chapter describes five different types of traversal patterns that can be mined in the web usage data, namely: Association Rules, Sequential Patterns, Frequent Episodes, Maximal Frequent Forward Sequences, and Maximal Frequent Sequences. These patterns are compared and contrasted in four aspects, i.e., ordering, duplicates, contiguity and maximal. They can be used for different purposes. As a necessary step for pattern discovery, the preprocessing of the web logs is also described. Some important issues, such as privacy and sessionization, are raised, and the possible solutions are also discussed.

REFERENCES

Agrawal, R. & Shafer, J. C. (1996). Parallel mining of association rules. *IEEE Transactions on Knowledge and Data Engineering*, 8(6), 962-969.

Agrawal, R. & Srikant, R. (1994). Fast algorithms for mining association rules in large databases. In *Proceedings of the 20th International Conference on Very Large Databases,* Santiago, Chile (pp. 487-499).

Agrawal, R., Imielinski, T., & Swami, A. N. (1993, May). Mining association rules between sets of items in large databases. In *Proceedings of the 1993 ACM SIGMOD international conference on management of data, Washington, DC* (pp. 207-216).

Buchner, A. G., Baumgarten, M., Anand, S. S., Mulvenna, M. D., & Hughes, J. G. (1999, August). Navigation pattern discovery from Internet data. In *Workshop on Web Usage Analysis and User Profiling (WEBKDD-99)*.

Catledge, L. D. & Pitkow, J. E. (1995). Characterizing browsing strategies in the world wide web. *Computer Networks and ISDN Systems*, 27(6), 1065-1073.

Chen, M.-S., Park, J. S., & Yu, P. S. Efficient data mining for path traversal patterns. (1998). *IEEE Transactions on Knowledge and Data Engineering*, 10(2), 209-221.

Cohen, E., Krishnamurthy, B., & Rexford, J. (1998). Improving end-to-end performance of the web using server volumes and proxy filters. In *SIGCOMM* (pp. 241-253).

Colet, E. (2002). Using data mining to detect fraud in auctions. *DSStar*.

Cooley, R., Mobasher, B., & Srivastava, J. (1999). Data preparation for mining world wide web browsing patterns. *Knowledge and Information Systems*, 1(1), 5-32.

Cooley, R., Tan, P.-N., & Srivastava, J. (1999, Aug.). WebSIFT: The web site information filter system. In *Workshop on Web Usage Analysis and User Profiling (WEBKDD-99)*.

Dokas, P., Ertoz, L., Kumar, V., Lazarevic, A., & Srivastava, J. (2002, November). Data mining for network intrusion detection. In *Proceedings of the National Science Foundation Next Generation Data Mining Workshop,* Baltimore, Maryland.

Evfimievski, A., Srikant, R., Agrawal, R., & Gehrke, J. (2002, July). Privacy preserving mining of association rules. In *Proceedings of the 8th ACM SIGKDD International Conference on Knowledge Discovery and Data Mining,* Edmonton, Canada.

Han, J., Pei, J., & Yin, Y. (2000). Mining frequent patterns without candidate generation. In *Proceedings of the ACM SIGMOD Conference.*

Hjelm, J. (2001, June). Web characterization activity. *Retrieved May 20, 2003, from: http://www.w3c.org/WCA.*

Kohavi, R. (2001). Mining e-commerce data: The good, the bad, the ugly. In *Proceedings of the 2001 ACM SIGMOD International Conference on Management of Data,* San Francisco, California.

Lan, B., Bressan, S., & Ooi, B. C. (1999, Aug.). Making web servers pushier. In *Workshop on Web Usage Analysis and User Profiling (WEBKDD-99).*

Lee, W. & Stolfo, S. (1998). Data mining approaches for intrusion detection. In *Proceedings of the 7th USENIX Security Symposium.*

Mannila, H., Toivonen, H., & Verkamo, A. I. (1995). Discovering frequent episodes in sequences. In *Proceedings of the 1st International Conference on Knowledge Discovery and Data Mining (KDD-95)* (pp. 210-215).

Mannila, H., Toivonen, H., & Verkamo, A. I. (1997). *Discovering frequent episodes in event sequences.* Helsinki, Finland: University of Helsinki, Department of Computer Science. (Technical Report C-1997-15).

Pandey, A., Srivastava, J. & Shekhar, S. (2001). A web intelligent prefetcher for dynamic pages using association rules - a summary of results. In *Proceedings of the SIAM Workshop on Web Mining.*

Park, J. S., Chen, M.-S., & Yu, P. S. (1995, May). An effective hash-based algorithm for mining association rules. In M. J. Carey & D. A. Schneider (Eds.), *Proceedings of the 1995 ACM SIGMOD International Conference on Management of Data,* San Jose, California (pp. 175-186).

Park, J. S., Chen, M.-S., & Yu, P. S. (1997). Using a hash-based method with transaction trimming for mining association rules. *IEEE Transactions on Knowledge and Data Engineering,* 9(5), 813-825.

Pei, J., Han, J., Mortazavi-Asl, B., & Zhu, H. (2000, April). Mining access patterns efficiently from web logs. In *Proceedings of the 2000 Pacific-Asia Conference on Knowledge Discovery and Data Mining (PAKDD-00),* Kyoto, Japan (p. 592).

Perkowitz, M. & Etzioni, O. (1999). Adaptive web sites: Conceptual cluster mining. In *Proceedings of the 16th International Joint Conference on Artificial Intelligence.*

Platform for Privacy Project (n.d.). Retrieved May 20, 2003, from: http://www.w3c.org/P3P.

Savasere, A., Omiecinski, E., & Navathe, S. B. (1995). An efficient algorithm for mining association rules in large databases. In *Proceedings of the 21st International Conference on Very Large Databases,* Zurich, Switzerland (pp. 432-444).

Spiekermann, S., Grossklags, J., & Berendt, B. (2002). E-privacy in second generation e-commerce: Privacy preferences versus actual behavior. In *Proceedings of the ACM Conference on Electronic Commerce,* Tampa, Florida.

Spiliopoulou, M. (2000). Web usage mining for web site evaluation. *Communications of the ACM,* 43(8), 127-134.

Spiliopoulou, M. & Faulstich, L. (1998). WUM: A web utilization miner. In *Proceedings of the EDBT Workshop WebDB98.* Valencia, Spain: Springer-Verlag.

Srikant, R. & Agrawal, R. (1995). Mining generalized association rules. In *Proceedings of the 21st International Conference on Very Large Databases,* Zurich, Switzerland (pp. 407-419).

Srikant, R. & Agrawal, R. (1996, March). Mining sequential patterns: Generalizations and performance improvements. In *Proceedings of the 5th International Conference on Extending Database Technology,* Avignon, France.

Srikant, R., Vu, Q., & Agrawal, R. (1997). Mining association rules with item constraints. In *Proceedings of the American Association for Artificial Intelligence*.

Srivastava, J., Cooley, R., Deshpande, M., & Tan, P.-N. (2000). Web usage mining: Discovery and applications of usage patterns from web data. *SIGKDD Explorations*, 1(2), 12-23.

Sunita, S., Shiby, T., & Agrawal, R. (1998). Integrating mining with relational database systems: Alternatives and implications. In *Proceedings of the ACM SIGMOD International Conference on Management of Data (SIGMOD-98)*, Seattle, Washington, June 1998.

Tan, P. & Kumar, V. (2002). Discovery of web robot sessions based on their navigational patterns. *Data Mining and Knowledge Discovery*, 6(1), 9-35.

Toivonen, H. (1996). Sampling large databases for association rules. In *Proceedings of the 22nd International Conference on Very Large Databases*, Mumbai, India (pp. 134-145).

Vaidya, J. & Clifton, C. W. (2002). Privacy preserving association rule mining in vertically partitioned data. In *Proceedings of the 8th ACM SIGKDD International Conference on Knowledge Discovery and Data Mining*, Edmonton, Canada, July 2002.

Xiao, Y. & Dunham, M. H. (2001). Efficient mining of traversal patterns. *Data and Knowledge Engineering*, 39, 191-214.

Zaiane, O. R., Xin, M., & Han, J. (1998). Discovering web access patterns and trends by applying OLAP and data mining techniques. *Advances in Digital Libraries* (pp. 19-29).

ENDNOTES

[1] Sessions are further divided into smaller transactions in Cooley & Mobasher et al. (1999).

[2] s stands for start time, and t stands for terminal time.

About the Authors

David Taniar received his PhD in Computer Science from Victoria University, Melbourne, Australia, in 1997. He is currently a senior lecturer at the School of Business Systems, Monash University, Melbourne, Australia. His research interest is in the area of databases, with particular attention to high performance databases and Internet databases. He is a fellow of the Institute for Management of Information Systems (FIMIS).

Johanna Wenny Rahayu received a PhD in Computer Science from La Trobe University, Melbourne, Australia in 2000. Her thesis was in the area of object-relational database design and transformation methodology. This thesis has been awarded the 2001 Computer Science Association Australia Best PhD Thesis Award. Dr. Rahayu is currently a senior lecturer at La Trobe University.

* * *

Nick Bassiliades received a BSc in Physics (1991) from the Aristotle University of Thessaloniki (AUTH), Greece; an MSc in Artificial Intelligence (AI) (1992) from the University of Aberdeen, Scotland; and a PhD in Parallel Knowledge Base Systems (1998) from AUTH, where he is currently a part-time lecturer in the Department of Informatics. He has published more than 25 papers for journals and conferences, contributed volumes in the area of knowledge base systems, co-authored a book on parallel, object-oriented, and active knowledge base systems, and a book on AI. He is a member of the Greek Computer and AI Societies, and a member of the IEEE and the ACM.

Elizabeth Chang is a professor in IT, has a unique combination of industry/commercial and academic knowledge, and has a strong research record and supervision skills. These are evidenced by her completion of one authored book and more than 70 scientific papers in the areas of software engineering, project management, usability evaluation, e-commerce, etc. As chief investigator, she has received several large federal government grants and industry cash for more than $1.5 million for the years 1997-2003.

Tharam Dillon is dean of Information Technology, University of Technology, Sydney, a position he assumed in July 2003, prior to which he was chair professor of the Department of Computer Science and Computer Engineering and also head of the School of Engineering at La Trobe University, Melbourne — a position he assumed at the beginning of 1986. In December 1998, he took up the position of professor of computing at Hong Kong Polytechnic University and acting head of the Department of Computing until July 2000. He is a fellow of the Institution of Electrical and Electronic Engineers (USA), fellow of the Institution of Engineers (Australia), fellow of the Safety and Reliability Society (UK), and a fellow of the Australian Computer Society. Professor Dillon completed his Bachelor of Engineering (Honors) at Monash in 1967 and was awarded his PhD at Monash in 1974. He held the position of senior lecturer/lecturer at Monash University in the Department of Electrical and Computer Systems Engineering from 1971 until 1985. He has published more than 400 papers in international and national journals and refereed conference proceedings, has written five books and edited five books, and has published 17 chapters in edited books.

Richard Hall is a lecturer in the Department of Computer Science and Computer Engineering at La Trobe University (Australia), taking classes in software engineering, expert systems, microprocessors and information systems. He has a broad range of research interests including artificial intelligence, story modeling, computational linguistics, data mining, medical decision support, medical image processing, computer graphics, advanced visualization, computer networking, and parallel processing. His prior industry experience as lead software designer in the development of computer-aided electronic publishing software for medical guidelines contributed substantially to the development of ideas in this chapter.

Roland Kaschek studied mathematics at the University of Oldenburg, Germany. He received an MSc (1986) from the University of Oldenburg and a PhD in 1990. He then worked at the University of Klagenfurt, Austria, until 1999; was guest lecturer at the Technical University of Kharkov, Ukraine; and a guest professor at the Federal University at Campina Grande in Brazil. From 1999 to 2001, he worked at UBS AG in Zurich (Switzerland) as a software architect and business analyst. Since 2001, he has been the associate professor in Massey University's Department of Information Systems at Palmerston North, New Zealand. His main research interests concern mathematical and philosophical foundations of applied informatics; in particular, conceptual modeling for information systems development.

Zhao Li received his MS in computer technique application from Southeast University, Nanjing, China (2001). In 2002, he was admitted into Nanyang Technological University, Singapore, where he is a PhD student in the School of Computer Engineering. In 2001 and 2002, he was working at Huawei Technologies, Beijing, as a research engineer. His research interests include web data mining, web data extraction, and machine learning.

Zehua Liu is a PhD candidate with the School of Computer Engineering at the Nanyang Technological University, Singapore, where he obtained his BSc in 2001. His research interests include information extraction, digital libraries, and databases. He has published in international conferences including ER, JCDL, etc.

Yannis Manolopoulos received a BEng (1981) in Electrical Engineering and a PhD (1986) in Computer Engineering, both from the Aristotle University of Thessaloniki, Greece. Currently, he is professor at the Department of Informatics of the latter university. He has published more than 130 papers in refereed scientific journals and conference proceedings. He is co-author of a book on *Advanced Database Indexing* and *Advanced Signature Indexing for Multimedia and Web Applications* by Kluwer. He served/serves as PC co-chair of the Eighth Pan-Hellenic Conference in Informatics (2001), the Sixth ADBIS Conference (2002), the Fifth WDAS Workshop (2003), the Eighth SSTD Symposium (2003), and the First Balkan Conference in Informatics (2003). Currently, he is vice-chairman of the Greek Computer Society. His research interests include access methods and query processing for databases, data mining, and performance evaluation of storage subsystems.

Claire Matthews is a senior lecturer in the Department of Finance, Banking and Property, and the acting director of the Centre for Banking Studies, at

Massey University's Turitea campus in Palmerston North (New Zealand). She teaches the theory, principles and practice of banking at both the undergraduate and post-graduate levels. Her research interests include the interaction between banks and customers, bank distribution channels, and internet banking.

Robert Meersman was awarded a PhD in Mathematics at the Free University of Brussels (VUB) (Belgium) in 1976. He was appointed full professor at VUB in 1995. Earlier positions include the University of Antwerp (UIA, 1975-1978) and Control Data Corp. (Data Management Lab, Brussels, Belgium, 1978-1983). There, he worked on the definition of the NIAM (now ORM) method, as well as on languages (RIDL) and the first tools for this methodology. He has held chairs and founded the InfoLabs at University of Limburg (Belgium, 1983-1986) and at the University of Tilburg (The Netherlands, 1986-1995). Professor Meersman was a member and past chairman (1983-1992) of the IFIP WG2.6 on Database, past chairman of the IFIP TC 12 (Artificial Intelligence, 1987-1992), co-founder and current president of the International Foundation for Cooperative Information Systems (IFCIS, since 1994) and of the Distributed Objects Applications Institute (DOA, since 2000). He founded the Systems Technology and Applications Research Laboratory (STAR Lab) at VUB in 1995, and has been the director of STARLab since. His current scientific interests include ontologies, database semantics, domain and database modeling, interoperability and use of databases in applications such as enterprise knowledge management and the semantic web.

Mikolaj Morzy is a research assistant at the Institute of Computing Science at Poznan University of Technology, Poland. He received his MSc in Computing Science in 1998. Currently, he is working on a PhD concerning the integration of data mining techniques with database systems. His research interests include database systems, data warehouses and data mining.

Tadeusz Morzy received his MSc, PhD, and Polish Habilitation from Poznan University of Technology, Poland. He is professor of Computer Science at the Institute of Computing Science, Poznan University of Technology. He has held visiting positions at Loyola University, New Orleans, USA; Klagenfurt University, Austria; University La Sapienza, Italy; and the Polish-Japanese Institute of Information Technology, Warsaw, Poland. He has authored and co-authored more than 70 papers on databases, data mining, and data warehousing. He is co-author of a book on *Concurrency Control in Distributed Database*

Systems (North-Holland), and editor and co-author of the *Handbook on Data Management* (Springer). He served as general chair of the Second ADBIS Conference (1998), and has served/serves on numerous program committees of international conferences and workshops. His research interests include data mining, data warehousing, transaction processing in database and data warehouse systems, access methods and query processing for databases, database optimization, and performance evaluation.

Alexandros Nanopoulos graduated from the Department of Informatics, Aristotle University of Thessaloniki, Greece (November 1996), and obtained a PhD from the same institute in February 2003. He is co-author of 20 articles in international journals and conferences, and co-author of the monograph "Advanced Signature Techniques for Multimedia and Web Applications." His research interests include spatial and web mining, integration of data mining with DBMSs, and spatial database indexing.

Wee Keong Ng is an associate professor at the School of Computer Engineering at the Nanyang Technological University, Singapore. He obtained his MSc and PhD from the University of Michigan, Ann Arbor (1994; 1996 respectively). He works and publishes widely in the areas of web warehousing, information extraction, electronic commerce, and data mining. He has organized and chaired international workshops, including tutorials, and has actively served on the program committees of numerous international conferences. He is a member of the ACM and the IEEE Computer Society. In his spare time, he also arranges music and practices meditation.

George Pallis graduated from the Department of Informatics of Aristotle University of Thessaloniki, Greece (2001). Since November 2001, he is with the Department of Informatics at the University of Thessaloniki, studying toward his PhD. His current research interests include web data caching and storage topologies, and data mining and its applications, mainly to web data.

Ee Lim Peng is an associate professor with the School of Computer Engineering, Nanyang Technological University, Singapore. He obtained his PhD from the University of Minnesota, Minneapolis (1994). Upon graduation, he started his academic career at the Nanyang Technological University. In 1997, he established the Centre for Advanced Information Systems and was appointed the Centre director. His research interests include web warehousing, digital libraries, and database integration. He is currently an associate editor of the

ACM Transactions on Information Systems (TOIS). He is also a member of the editorial review board of the *Journal of Database Management* (JDM), program co-chair of the Fifth ACM Workshop on Web Information and Data Management (WIDM 2003), program co-chair of the Sixth International Conference on Asian Digital Libraries (ICADL 2003), and workshop co-chair of the International Workshop on Data Mining for Actionable Knowledge (DMAK 2003).

Klaus-Dieter Schewe studied mathematics and computer science at the University of Bonn, from which he received an MSc (1982) and a PhD (1985). After five years in the industry, he returned to the University of Hamburg, then worked at the Technical University of Cottbus, from which he received a DSc (1995). He then worked at the Technical University of Clausthal, and joined Massey University (New Zealand) in 2000 as the chair for Information Systems. His major research interests are database theory and systems; design and development of large-scale information systems, including data-intensive web information systems; and foundations of information and knowledge systems. Since 2002, he has been the director of the Information Science Research Centre at Massey University.

Konstantina Stoupa graduated from the Department of Informatics of Aristotle University of Thessaloniki, Greece (2000), and after that, obtained her MBA from the University of Macedonia (Greece) in November 2002. Since February 2001, she has been with the Department of Informatics of Aristotle University of Thessaloniki, studying toward her PhD, which is funded by the State Scholarship's Foundation of Greece. Her current research interests include network security, access control models, and employment of clustering algorithms and XML in access control.

Bernhard Thalheim, born 1952 in Germany. Master's in Mathematics, Dresden University of Technology (1975); PhD in Mathematics, Lomonossov University in Moscow (1979); Advanced PhD (habilitation) in Computer Science, Dresden University of Technology (1985). Since 1986, he has been a professor of Computer Science in Dresden, Kuwait, Rostock, and Cottbus. Currently, he is chair of Database and Information Systems at Brandenburg University of Technology at Cottbus, Germany. His main interests include database and information systems modeling, database theory, DBMS technology, logics, and, recently, web information systems. He has been involved in projects in the area of information systems, e.g., heading more than 30 development projects aiming in the development of information-intensive large or huge websites (e-business, e-learning, information and community sites).

Grigorios Tsoumakas received his BSc in Informatics from the Department of Informatics of the Aristotle University of Thessaloniki, Greece (1999). He received his MSc in Artificial Intelligence from the Division of Informatics of the University of Edinburgh (2000). He is currently a PhD student in the Department of Informatics at the Aristotle University of Thessaloniki. His research interests include machine learning, data mining, and distributed computing. He is a member of the Hellenic Artificial Intelligence Society and the Special Interest Group on Knowledge Discovery and Data Mining of the Association for Computing Machinery.

Athena Vakali received a BSc in Mathematics from the Aristotle University of Thessaloniki, Greece; an MSc in Computer Science from Purdue University, USA (with a Fulbright scholarship); and a PhD in Computer Science from the Department of Informatics at the Aristotle University of Thessaloniki. Since 1997, she has been a faculty member of the Department of Informatics, Aristotle University of Thessaloniki (currently, she is an assistant professor). Her research interests include design, performance and analysis of storage subsystems, and data placement schemes for multimedia and web-based information. She is working on web data management, and she has focused on XML data storage issues. She has published several papers in international journals and conferences. Her research interests include storage subsystem's performance, XML and multimedia data, management and data placement schemes.

Ioannis Vlahavas is a full professor in the Department of Informatics at the Aristotle University of Thessaloniki, Greece. He received his PhD in Logic Programming Systems from the same university in 1988. During the first half of 1997, he was a visiting scholar in the Department of CS at Purdue University. He specializes in logic programming, knowledge-based and AI systems, and he has published more than 100 papers, five book chapters, and co-authored three books in these areas. He teaches logic programming, AI, expert systems, and DSS. He has been involved in more than 15 research projects, leading most of them. He was the chairman of the Second Hellenic Conference on AI. He is leading the Logic Programming and Intelligent Systems Group (LPIS Group, lpis.csd.auth.gr).

Catherine Wallace is a senior lecturer in the Department of Communication and Journalism on Massey University's Turitea campus in Palmerston North (New Zealand). She teaches the Management of Communication Technology, Professional and E-business Writing, and E-business Strategy and Models at the undergraduate level. She is also a teaching fellow on the MBA and DBA program with the Graduate School of Business. Her research interests center around e-business, technology management, uptake and adoption and communication barriers.

Nathalia Devina Widjaya was born in Jakarta, Indonesia. She went to the University of Melbourne, Australia, where she studied Information Systems and obtained her degrees with honors in 2001. Her thesis was about website accessibility. The aim of that research was how to make good accessible websites and why it is important. She works as a sessional tutor and IT support at Melbourne University. Currently, she is doing a Master by Research degree at Monash University in Australia. Her research is about the transformation of XML schemas to object-relational database. She is also a member of the Australian Computer Society.

Marek Wojciechowski is an assistant professor at the Institute of Computing Science, Poznan University of Technology, Poland. He received his PhD in Computer Science from Poznan University of Technology in 2001. His research interests include data mining, web mining, and Internet technologies.

Carlo Wouters is a PhD candidate in the Department of Computer Science and Computer Engineering at La Trobe University, Melbourne (Australia). Research interests include ontologies (extraction of materialized ontology views in particular). He has obtained a BSc in Audio-Visual Sciences (RITS, Belgium), GradDipSc in Computer Science (La Trobe, Australia) and an MSc in Information Technology (La Trobe, Australia).

Yongqiao Xiao received his PhD in Computer Science from Southern Methodist University; an MS in Computer Science from Zhongshan University; and a BS in Accounting and Information Systems from Renmin University of China in 2000, 1995, and 1992, respectively. He is an assistant professor of Computer Science in the Department of Math and Computer Science at Georgia College and State University in Milledgeville, Georgia (USA). Before joining the department, he had worked for two years on predictive modeling in industry. He has been a reviewer for many journals and conferences of ACM and IEEE. His interested research areas are data mining, database, and machine learning.

Jenq-Foung (J.F.) Yao received a PhD in Computer Science from Southern Methodist University; an MS in Computer Science from the University of Wyoming; and a BS in Marine Biology from the National Taiwan Ocean University. He is an associate professor of Computer Science in the Department of Math and Computer Science at Georgia College and State University in Milledgeville, Georgia (USA). Before joining the department, he had worked for several years as a computer consultant, and spent three years as a system programmer at the University of Wyoming. He has authored and reviewed various journals and conferences of ACM, IEEE, and CCSC. His research interests are mobile DBMS, data mining, web application, and data caching.

Maciej Zakrzewicz is an assistant professor at the Institute of Computing Science, Poznan University of Technology. His research interests include data mining, database/data warehouse systems, and Internet technologies. He is currently delivering courses on information systems design and implementation for companies and universities in Poland, Germany, the UK, and the US. He is an author and reviewer of numerous tutorials and publications on frequent itemset discovery, data mining query processing, adaptive websites, database indexing techniques, database tuning, and Java standards for databases and for multitier applications. He received his PhD in Computer Science from Poznan University of Technology (Poland) (1998). Since 1999, he has been the president of the Polish Oracle User Group.

Index

X

Z

NEW from Idea Group Publishing

- **The Enterprise Resource Planning Decade: Lessons Learned and Issues for the Future**, Frederic Adam and David Sammon/ ISBN:1-59140-188-7; eISBN 1-59140-189-5, © 2004
- **Electronic Commerce in Small to Medium-Sized Enterprises**, Nabeel A. Y. Al-Qirim/ ISBN: 1-59140-146-1; eISBN 1-59140-147-X, © 2004
- **e-Business, e-Government & Small and Medium-Size Enterprises: Opportunities & Challenges**, Brian J. Corbitt & Nabeel A. Y. Al-Qirim/ ISBN: 1-59140-202-6; eISBN 1-59140-203-4, © 2004
- **Multimedia Systems and Content-Based Image Retrieval**, Sagarmay Deb ISBN: 1-59140-156-9; eISBN 1-59140-157-7, © 2004
- **Computer Graphics and Multimedia: Applications, Problems and Solutions**, John DiMarco/ ISBN: 1-59140-196-86; eISBN 1-59140-197-6, © 2004
- **Social and Economic Transformation in the Digital Era**, Georgios Doukidis, Nikolaos Mylonopoulos & Nancy Pouloudi/ ISBN: 1-59140-158-5; eISBN 1-59140-159-3, © 2004
- **Information Security Policies and Actions in Modern Integrated Systems**, Mariagrazia Fugini & Carlo Bellettini/ ISBN: 1-59140-186-0; eISBN 1-59140-187-9, © 2004
- **Digital Government: Principles and Best Practices**, Alexei Pavlichev & G. David Garson/ISBN: 1-59140-122-4; eISBN 1-59140-123-2, © 2004
- **Virtual and Collaborative Teams: Process, Technologies and Practice**, Susan H. Godar & Sharmila Pixy Ferris/ ISBN: 1-59140-204-2; eISBN 1-59140-205-0, © 2004
- **Intelligent Enterprises of the 21st Century**, Jatinder Gupta & Sushil Sharma/ ISBN: 1-59140-160-7; eISBN 1-59140-161-5, © 2004
- **Creating Knowledge Based Organizations**, Jatinder Gupta & Sushil Sharma/ ISBN: 1-59140-162-3; eISBN 1-59140-163-1, © 2004
- **Knowledge Networks: Innovation through Communities of Practice**, Paul Hildreth & Chris Kimble/ISBN: 1-59140-200-X; eISBN 1-59140-201-8, © 2004
- **Going Virtual: Distributed Communities of Practice**, Paul Hildreth/ISBN: 1-59140-164-X; eISBN 1-59140-165-8, © 2004
- **Trust in Knowledge Management and Systems in Organizations**, Maija-Leena Huotari & Mirja Iivonen/ ISBN: 1-59140-126-7; eISBN 1-59140-127-5, © 2004
- **Strategies for Managing IS/IT Personnel**, Magid Igbaria & Conrad Shayo/ISBN: 1-59140-128-3; eISBN 1-59140-129-1, © 2004
- **Beyond Knowledge Management**, Brian Lehaney, Steve Clarke, Elayne Coakes & Gillian Jack/ ISBN: 1-59140-180-1; eISBN 1-59140-181-X, © 2004
- **eTransformation in Governance: New Directions in Government and Politics**, Matti Mälkiä, Ari Veikko Anttiroiko & Reijo Savolainen/ISBN: 1-59140-130-5; eISBN 1-59140-131-3, © 2004
- **Intelligent Agents for Data Mining and Information Retrieval**, Masoud Mohammadian/ISBN: 1-59140-194-1; eISBN 1-59140-195-X, © 2004
- **Using Community Informatics to Transform Regions**, Stewart Marshall, Wal Taylor & Xinghuo Yu/ISBN: 1-59140-132-1; eISBN 1-59140-133-X, © 2004
- **Wireless Communications and Mobile Commerce**, Nan Si Shi/ ISBN: 1-59140-184-4; eISBN 1-59140-185-2, © 2004
- **Organizational Data Mining: Leveraging Enterprise Data Resources for Optimal Performance**, Hamid R. Nemati & Christopher D. Barko/ ISBN: 1-59140-134-8; eISBN 1-59140-135-6, © 2004
- **Virtual Teams: Projects, Protocols and Processes**, David J. Pauleen/ISBN: 1-59140-166-6; eISBN 1-59140-167-4, © 2004
- **Business Intelligence in the Digital Economy: Opportunities, Limitations and Risks**, Mahesh Raisinghani/ ISBN: 1-59140-206-9; eISBN 1-59140-207-7, © 2004
- **E-Business Innovation and Change Management**, Mohini Singh & Di Waddell/ISBN: 1-59140-138-0; eISBN 1-59140-139-9, © 2004
- **Responsible Management of Information Systems**, Bernd Stahl/ISBN: 1-59140-172-0; eISBN 1-59140-173-9, © 2004
- **Web Information Systems**, David Taniar/ISBN: 1-59140-208-5; eISBN 1-59140-209-3, © 2004
- **Strategies for Information Technology Governance**, Wim van Grembergen/ISBN: 1-59140-140-2; eISBN 1-59140-141-0, © 2004
- **Information and Communication Technology for Competitive Intelligence**, Dirk Vriens/ISBN: 1-59140-142-9; eISBN 1-59140-143-7, © 2004
- **The Handbook of Information Systems Research**, Michael E. Whitman & Amy B. Woszczynski/ISBN: 1-59140-144-5; eISBN 1-59140-145-3, © 2004
- **Neural Networks in Business Forecasting**, G. Peter Zhang/ISBN: 1-59140-176-3; eISBN 1-59140-177-1, © 2004

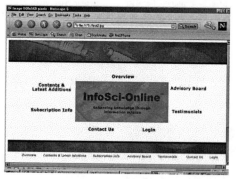